The Ouachita Mountains

The Ouachita Mountains
A Guide for Fishermen, Hunters, and Travelers

by Milton D. Rafferty
and John C. Catau

UNIVERSITY OF OKLAHOMA PRESS : NORMAN AND LONDON

By Milton D. Rafferty

The Ozarks: Land and Life (Norman, 1980)
Historical Atlas of Missouri (Norman, 1982)
The Ozarks Outdoors: A Guide for Fishermen, Hunters, and Tourists (Norman, 1985)
The Ouachita Mountains: A Guide for Fishermen, Hunters, and Travelers (Norman, 1991)

Library of Congress Cataloging-in-Publication Data

Rafferty, Milton D., 1932–
    The Ouachita Mountains : a guide for fishermen, hunters, and travelers / by Milton D. Rafferty and John C. Catau. — 1st ed.
        p.   cm.
    Includes bibliographical references and index.
    ISBN 0-8061-1722-2 (cloth)
    1. Ouachita Mountains (Ark. and Okla.)—Description and travel—Guide-books. 2. Hunting—Ouachita Mountains (Ark. and Okla.)—Guide-books. 3. Fishing—Ouachita Mountains (Ark. and Okla.)—Guide-books.   I. Catau, John C.   II. Title.
    F702.09R34   1991
    917.66'60453—dc20   90-50695
    ISBN 0-8061-2360-5 (pbk.)

The paper in this book meets the guidelines for permanence and durability of the Committee on Production Guidelines for Book Longevity of the Council on Library Resources, Inc. ∞

Contents

Preface   *page* xiii
Chapter
  1. Geography and Climate   3
  2. History and Economy   17
  3. Ouachita Mountain Hunting   36
  4. Floating and Fishing Ouachita Streams   52
  5. Lakes of the Ouachita Province   64
  6. Hiking, Backpacking, and Camping   122
  7. Geology and Rock Hounding   151
  8. North-South Highway Tours   160
  9. East-West Highway Tours   196
10. Fort Smith   222
11. Hot Springs National Park   237
12. Little Rock   254
13. Major Events in the Ouachita Mountains   268
14. Vacation Information   285
Notes   291
Selected References   297
Index   303

Illustrations

Photographs

View of Lake Dardanelle and the Arkansas River Valley with the
  Ouachita Mountains in the background *page* 3
Panoramic view of the Kiamichi Mountains in eastern Oklahoma 4
View of the Petit Jean River Valley from Mount Magazine,
  Arkansas's highest summit 5
Overview of the Ouachita Mountains from Mount Nebo State Park 7
Little River near Hanobia, Oklahoma 8
Hang gliding near Heavener, Oklahoma, with the Ouachita
  Mountains in the background 9
Early morning fog in the Oklahoma Ouachitas 14
Mixed hardwood and pine forest 15
Bluegrass music festival in the Ouachita Mountains of Oklahoma 17
Great Raft in the Red River 20
Loading pulp timber at Heavener, Oklahoma 25
The Ouachita National Forest embraces more than 1.5 million
  acres of mountains, ridges, lakes, and streams 30
Tightwad Coal Mine 31
Ouachita Mountain landscape near Heavener, Oklahoma 33
Partners 39
Wild turkey 41
Mallard ducks 42
Duck hunting 42
Deer herd 43
Bow hunting 44
Squirrel 45
Raccoon 46
Coon hunting 47
Bluegill 53
Rainbow trout 54
Fishing on the Mountain Fork River at Beaver's Bend State Park 60
Canoeing on the Mountain Fork River in southeastern Oklahoma 61
Day's end 67
Night fishing 70
Blue Mountain Lake, near Booneville, in western Arkansas 75
Broken Bow Dam and Lake on the Mountain Fork River in
  southeastern Oklahoma 77
Fishing at Broken Bow Lake 78
Lake Catherine State Park near Hot Springs 79
Water skiing on Lake Catherine 81
Dardanelle Lock and Dam on the Arkansas River 84
Swimming at Greers Ferry Lake 85

Camping in the Ouachitas at Nimrod Lake near Danville, Arkansas   85
Aerial view of De Gray Lake   87
De Gray Lake Resort State Park on a forested island in 13,400-
  acre De Gray Lake   88
Dierks Dam and Lake on the Saline River in west-central Arkansas   91
A family gathering at a Dierks Lake camping area   92
Eufaula Dam and Lake on the Canadian River in east-central
  Oklahoma   94
Boating on Eufaula Lake   95
Gillham Dam and Lake on the Cossatot River near Gillham,
  Arkansas   97
Lake Hamilton near Hot Springs   99
Seaplane for aerial sightseeing at Lake Hamilton near Hot Springs   100
Hugo Dam and Lake on the Kiamichi River near Hugo, Oklahoma   102
Water sports on Hugo Lake in southeastern Oklahoma   102
Robert S. Kerr Lake on the Arkansas River in eastern Oklahoma   104
Swimming at Nimrod Lake near Danville, Arkansas   108
Lake Ouachita near Hot Springs   110
Lake Ouachita on the Ouachita River near Hot Springs   110
Sailing on Lake Ouachita   111
Ozark Lock and Dam on the Arkansas River   113
Pine Creek Lake by moonlight   115
Wister Dam and Lake on the Poteau River in eastern Oklahoma   119
Fishing at Wister Lake in eastern Oklahoma   120
Ouachita Mountain hiking trail   123
Mount Magazine overlook   125
Hiking in the Jack Creek Recreation Area   127
Talimena Skyline Drive in the Ouachita National Forest in eastern
  Oklahoma   130
Swimming at Lake Ouachita   131
Natural bridge at Petit Jean State Park   132
Queen Wilhelmina State Park and Lodge on Rich Mountain near
  Mena, Arkansas   133
Trail ride in southeastern Oklahoma   134
Bird hunting on the Arkansas River near Lake Dardanelle   135
Boat dock at Hochatown State Park at Broken Bow Lake in
  southeastern Oklahoma   137
Scenic view at Flat Rock Park on Lake Dardanelle near
  Russellville, Arkansas   138
Camp-A-Float campsite with RV on Lake Ouachita   146
Camping at one of Lake Ouachita's 538 campsites   147
Water skiing on Pine Creek Lake in southeastern Oklahoma   149
Recreational vehicle campsite at Lake Wister State Park   149
Steeply tilted rock strata in the severely folded and faulted
  Ouachita Mountains on Arkansas Highway 7 near De Gray Lake   153
W. W. Johnson of Amarillo, Texas, displaying the largest diamond
  (sixteen carat, thirty-seven point) ever found at Crater of
  Diamonds State Park by a tourist   155
Sailing on Eufaula Lake in eastern Oklahoma   163

James J. McAlester   164
Robbers Cave State Park near Wilburton, Oklahoma, in the Sans
    Bois Mountains   167
Rock City near Clayton, Oklahoma   169
Spiro Indian Mounds near Spiro, Oklahoma   171
Robert S. Kerr Museum, Poteau, Oklahoma   173
Indian Nations trail ride in the Kiamichi Mountains   175
Runic markings in the Heavener Runestone State Park   177
Talimena Skyline Drive near Talihina, Oklahoma   183
Petting zoo at Queen Wilhelmina State Park on Rich Mountain   184
Historical marker for the Fort Smith-Fort Towson Military Road in
    eastern Oklahoma   185
An early picture of Dardanelle Rock   187
Hot Springs Village   189
Home of world renowned Mountain Valley spring water   190
Five passenger Climber automobile in the Museum of Automobiles
    on Petit Jean Mountain   197
Coal mining near Clarksville, Arkansas, *circa* 1925   200
Wiederkehr Winery near Altus, Arkansas   201
Wiederkehr Winery vineyards   201
Lumbering in the Ouachita Mountains, *circa* 1940   205
Cattle graze peacefully upon the hills of the Ouachita Mountains in
    Arkansas   208
Post office at Pine Ridge, Arkansas   213
Russian Orthodox Church, Hartshorne, Oklahoma   216
Grape stomping at Italian festival, McAlester, Oklahoma   217
Ouachita Mountain lumbering, *circa* 1935   219
Bluegrass music festival in the Ouachita Mountains of Oklahoma   220
Lighthouse Inn on the Arkansas River at Fort Smith   223
Aerial view of downtown Fort Smith   226
Historic Bonneville house in Fort Smith   229
Chimney of General Zachary Taylor's home   230
Judge Parker's courtroom   231
Reconstruction of the standing gallows at Fort Smith   232
Historic Knoble Brewery   233
Fort Smith Municipal Auditorium   234
The Vaughn-Schaap house built in 1879 displays Second Empire
    Victorian styling   235
Natural thermal springs along Bathhouse Row   238
Downtown Hot Springs   239
World-famous Bathhouse Row   239
Visitor to world-famous Hot Springs National Park in therapeutic
    hot mineral water   240
Hot Springs, Arkansas   242
Arlington Hotel, Hot Springs, Arkansas   244
The Promenade, Hot Springs National Park   245
Bathhouse Row   245
Gulpha Gorge campground and nature area in Hot Springs
    National Park   246

Hot Springs National Park Visitor Center   247
Josephine Tussaud Wax Museum   248
Magic Springs Recreational Park, Hot Springs, Arkansas   249
Mid-America Museum, Hot Springs, Arkansas   250
Oaklawn Race Track, Hot Springs, Arkansas   251
Horses leaving the starting gate at Oaklawn, Hot Springs,
    Arkansas   252
View of downtown Little Rock   255
Aerial view of Little Rock and North Little Rock   258
The Henry Moore sculpture in Little Rock's Metrocentre Mall   259
The Arkansas Arts Center in McArthur Park   262
The first State Capitol   263
Arkansas State Capitol   263
Arkansas Territorial Restoration in downtown Little Rock   264
Museum of Natural History and Antiquities in McArthur Park   265
Prison rodeo, McAlester, Oklahoma   283

Figures

Wind Chill Table   12
Recognizing Venomous Snakes   50
Why Fish Don't Bite   66
Popular Artificial Lures   68
Topographic Development on Folded Rocks   153

Table

Climatic Data for Little Rock, Arkansas   10

Maps

1. The Ouachita Province   *page* 6
2. Early Roads and Trails   18
3. Indian Population   22
4. Railroads–1914   24
5. Black Population   26
6. Broiler Chicken Production   28
7. Population Change, 1970–1980   32
8. Total Travel Expenditures–1984   34
9. National Forests and Public Hunting Areas   38
10. Float Fishing and Canoeing Streams   56
11. Blue Mountain Lake   74
12. Broken Bow Lake   76
13. Lakes Catherine and Hamilton   80
14. Lakes Conway, Maumelle, and Winona   82
15. Dardanelle Lake   83
16. De Gray Lake   86
17. De Queen Lake   89
18. Dierks Lake   90
19. Eufaula Lake   93
20. Gillham Lake   96
21. Greeson Lake   98
22. Hugo Lake   101
23. Robert S. Kerr Lake   103
24. McGee Creek Reservoir   106
25. Nimrod Lake   107
26. Ouachita Lake   109
27. Ozark Lake   112
28. Pine Creek Lake   114
29. Sardis Lake   116
30. Wister Lake   118
31. Geology of the Ouachita Province   152
32. North–South Highway Tours   162
33. East–West Highway Tours   198
34. Attractions in Fort Smith   228
35. Attractions in Hot Springs   243
36. Attractions in Little Rock   260
37. State Parks   270

Preface

The Ouachita Mountains is the product of eight years of research and travel in the region. Much of it is drawn from material prepared for field courses the authors have taught at Southwest Missouri State University on the physical and cultural geography of the Ouachita Mountains and from research on the historical geography and economy of the region. Personal interviews and direct field observations, including visits to most of the places discussed, stemmed from a desire to see and know the region.

The Ouachita Mountains is designed to introduce people to the rugged Ouachita Mountains and the more open, but mountainous, Arkansas Valley region to the north. It directs the reader to major attractions and provides background information and interpretation for each of these points of interest. We have relied on maps as a means of presenting geographic information concisely and accurately. The rationale for the guidebook is simple: leisure time is important and valuable time that can be enhanced by a thorough understanding of the available recreational opportunities.

The guidebook is intended primarily for the hunters, fishermen, campers, and others who wish to take advantage of the multitude of outdoor activities in the region. Even so, the armchair traveler also will find the book a pleasant way to vicariously visit new territories or revisit old, familiar places. The organization is both topical and regional. Chapters 1 and 2 provide an overview of the Ouachita Mountains' boundaries, weather and climate, identifying physical and cultural traits, and history. Chapter 3 provides for the hunter a description of the major species of game animals and birds, their habits and likely habitats. A map showing public hunting areas and national forests is included.

Canoeists and fishermen will find that chapter 4 describes major game fish and their habits and habitats. Twelve popular float streams are highlighted, including access points, camping facilities, and scenery. These descriptions are keyed to a map of float fishing and canoeing opportunities. Lake fishermen will find maps and descriptions of twenty-three major Ouachita lakes and reservoirs in chapter 5. The discussion of each lake includes historical background; data on capacity, area, and lake levels; boating and fishing regulations; and a description of fishing possibilities, including access points, services, and suggestions regarding the best places to fish for various species. A map of each lake provides directions to access points and roads. Also included in chapter 5 is a discussion of baits and lures, as well as the major species of fish, their habits and habitats.

Chapter 6 is designed for hikers, backpackers, and camping enthusiasts. It includes a discussion of equipment, suggestions for maximum safety, and an alphabetical listing of the region's camping areas.

Chapter 7 is devoted to geologists and rockhounds, particularly those intrigued by collecting various rocks and minerals. It includes directions to some of the better collecting sites and describes the types of materials to be found at each location.

Chapters 8 and 9 describe a selection of the attractions in small towns and the countryside including spectacular scenery, historical sites, major resorts, theme parks, and other well-developed tourism-recreation service areas. For the reader's convenience, the attractions are arranged in several highway tours that crisscross the region east to west and north to south.

Chapters 10, 11, and 12 deal with the historical geography and major attractions of the region's three largest urban centers—Fort Smith, Hot Springs, and Little Rock.

Chapter 13 is a listing of major events in the Ouachita region and chapter 14 provides names and addresses of sources of vacation information.

Many people have assisted in the preparation of this book. Most of the sources of information are listed in the references, but we would like to especially acknowledge the assistance given to us by the United States Army Corps of Engineers, the National Forest Service, the National Park Service, and several state agencies in Arkansas and Oklahoma. These agencies, which provided data, factual information, and photographs, include the Arkansas Department of Parks and Tourism, the Arkansas Game and Fish Commission, the Oklahoma Tourism and Recreation Department, and the Oklahoma Department of Wildlife Conservation. The Arkansas History Commission kindly provided photographs.

Elias Johnson, a colleague in the Department of Geosciences at Southwest Missouri State University, provided valuable advice and assistance in preparing the maps. Debbie Burns Dohne, Robin Powell, Deana Gibson, and Kathi Snead, coworkers in the Department of Geosciences, provided cheerful and competent assistance throughout the project. Special acknowledgment is also extended to Rick Grefsrud and Patricia Senf for their assistance with the research and preparation of the maps. Finally a heartfelt debt of gratitude is extended to Keith Sutton, *Arkansas Game and Fish* editor, for his review and commentary on the chapters on hunting and fishing.

Milton D. Rafferty
John C. Catau
Springfield, Missouri

The Ouachita Mountains

Geography and Climate

The Ouachita Mountain Region, or simply "the Ouachitas" as it is known locally, is similar in many respects to the Ozark region to the north. Remote and isolated for much of its history, this rustic region is characterized by the persistence of traditional life-styles and technologies. The Ouachitas provide some of the most spectacular mountain scenery in the nation's midsection. With areas of misty hollows and valleys situated between craggy ridges, they are equally inspiring in any season. In particular, the Ouachitas are famous for their panoramic vistas of oak and pine forests shimmering under a blue-gray haze. Within these forests are found waterfalls and clear mountain streams, where nu-

merous bass and catfish lurk, and a marvelous variety of shrubs and flowering plants.

The entire province is a roughly lens-shaped area, 225 miles long and 100 miles wide, lying south of the Boston Mountains section of the Ozark Upland (map 1). The eastern and southern boundaries are located where the Cretaceous and younger aged sedimentary rocks of the Gulf Coastal Plain overlap the Paleozoic rocks of the Ouachita province; the western and northern boundaries are not as distinct. Each of the boundaries, however, can be fairly well established on a map by relying upon a combination of both physical and cultural features. The northern boundary, for instance, runs

View of Lake Dardanelle and the Arkansas River Valley with the Ouachita Mountains in the background. Courtesy of Arkansas Department of Parks and Tourism.

Panoramic view of the Kiamichi Mountains in eastern Oklahoma. Photo by Fred W. Marvel. Courtesy of Oklahoma Tourism and Recreation Department.

roughly parallel to the Arkansas River from Muskogee, Oklahoma, to near Searcy, Arkansas. The eastern boundary follows U.S. Highway 67 southeast from Searcy to Little Rock and then continues along Interstate 30 to near Arkadelphia. The southern boundary extends roughly parallel to the Red River from Arkadelphia to Atoka, Oklahoma, and the western boundary follows U.S. Highway 69 from Atoka, through McAlester, to Muskogee. Altogether the region consists of approximately 20,865 square miles, including all or part of twenty-six counties in Arkansas and ten counties in Oklahoma. The 1980 population of the area was approximately 1.7 million.

LANDFORMS

Landform experts commonly divide the Ouachita province into three subregions: (1) a northern lowland known as the Ar-kansas Valley; (2) a rugged central zone known as the Ouachita Mountains; and (3) a hilly belt in the south known as the Athens Piedmont Plateau.

The Arkansas Valley subregion occupies a twenty-five to thirty-five mile wide band. Although it is composed primarily of the flood plains and river terraces of the Arkansas, Fourche LaFave, Petit Jean, and Poteau rivers and their tributaries, several ridges rise conspicuously above the prevailing lowlands. Magazine Mountain (2,753 feet), which is the highest point in Arkansas, stands in splendid isolation 2,000 feet above the valley and is a major landmark in western Arkansas. Nearly all of the ridges in this subregion are formed from east-west trending, folded rock strata with sandstones of the Jackfork group comprising the most common ridge maker.[1]

View of the Petit Jean River Valley from Mount Magazine, Arkansas's highest summit. Courtesy of Arkansas Department of Parks and Tourism.

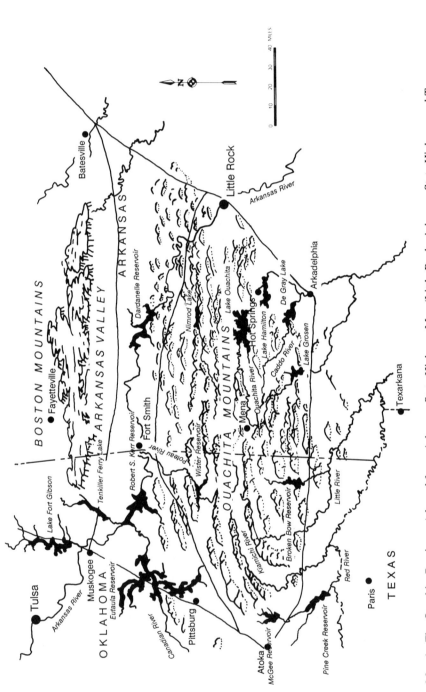

Map 1. The Ouachita Province. *Adapted from:* Arkansas State Highway and Trans-
portation Department, 1985); Oklahoma State Transportation Map (Oklahoma City: Oklahoma Department of Transportation,
1985); Vicksburg Topographic Sheet, 1 : 1,000,000 Series (Washington, D.C.: U.S. Geological Survey, 1978).

The Ouachita Mountain subregion consists of many tightly packed east-west trending ridges and valleys (map 1). It is similar in structure and topography to the Ridge and Valley province within the Appalachian Mountains. The narrow ridges have steep slopes and sharp, uniform crests. The relief between valley floors and ridge tops is as great as 1,500 feet. Several mountain groups are locally recognized including the Caddo, Crystal, Cossatot, Trap, Zig Zag, and Cross Mountains. The highest elevations (1,500–2,000 feet) are found near the Arkansas-Oklahoma border. Several intermontane basins are situated within the mountains. These are wide areas with upland surfaces ranging from about 500 to 1,200 feet that are channeled by many narrow valleys. The southern part of the city of Hot Springs, Arkansas, is built in one of these basins that includes a large portion of the eastern Ouachitas.

The southern extremity of the Ouachita region consists of a hilly belt, roughly fifteen to twenty-five miles wide, that abuts the Gulf Coastal Plain. With elevations ranging between 400 and 1,000 feet, the Athens Piedmont Plateau is dissected by narrow, crooked valleys of southward-flowing trunk streams, and by many tributary valleys that flow at right angles to the trunk streams in a trellis pattern. In many respects, this subregion resembles the Piedmont Plateau of the Appalachian Mountains.

The northern flank of the Ouachita region is drained by the Arkansas River and its tributaries, which include the Poteau, Petit Jean, and Fourche LaFave rivers. The southern portion of the province is drained by the Red River and its tributaries. In addition to the Little River and the Little Missouri River, other important Red River tributaries are the Ouachita River that flows southeastward across the Hot Springs basin and the Kiamichi River that flows southwesterly

Overview of the Ouachita Mountains from Mount Nebo State Park. Courtesy of Arkansas Department of Parks and Tourism.

from its headwaters in the wild country near the Arkansas-Oklahoma boundary. The waters of all these rivers eventually flow into the Gulf of Mexico by way of the Mississippi River.

WEATHER AND CLIMATE

The weather and climatic conditions in the Ouachita Mountains are influenced most heavily by the region's relative position. Its mid-latitude location virtually insures the existence of distinct seasonal fluctuations, and the absence of large nearby water bodies permits continental (or land) influences to prevail. Significantly, the altitude and relief differentials within the region are not sufficient enough to have an appreciable impact on local conditions.

Because the weather conditions are strongly influenced by the capriciousness of contrasting air masses and cy-

Little River near Hanobia, Oklahoma. Photo by Fred W. Marvel. Courtesy of Oklahoma
Tourism and Recreation Department.

Hang gliding near Heavener, Oklahoma, with the Ouachita Mountains in the background. Photo by Fred W. Marvel. Courtesy of Oklahoma Tourism and Recreation Department.

LITTLE ROCK, ARKANSAS   Elevation 257 Feet

Month	Temperatures Average Max	Average Min	Extreme Max	Extreme Min	THI	Wind Chill Factor	Precipitation in inches Total	Snow	Average number of days Not even 0.01" precip.	More than ½" of snow	Clear	Cloudy	Thunderstorms	Fog	90° or higher	32° or lower	% of possible sunshine	Relative Humidity A.M.	P.M.	Wind M.P.H.	Direction
Jan	51	31	78	-4		21	5	3	21	1	14	17	2	3	0	23	45	81	60	9	S
Feb	55	34	83	10		26	4	2	18	0	14	14	2	2	0	17	53	79	56	9	SW
March	63	41	88	17			5	T	21	0	15	16	5	1	0	6	56	77	54	10	WNW
April	74	51	90	30	76		5	T	19	0	17	13	7	1	0	0	59	79	55	10	S
May	82	60	98	40	82		5	0	21	0	19	12	7	1	5	0	65	86	57	8	S
June	90	68	102	49			4	0	22	0	21	9	7	0	17	0	71	87	54	8	SSW
July	93	71	105	56	84		3	0	23	0	22	9	9	1	22	0	69	88	59	7	SW
Aug	93	70	108	52	83		3	0	24	0	23	8	6	1	18	0	71	88	56	7	SW
Sept	86	62	102	38	78		3	0	23	0	21	9	4	1	8	0	66	90	59	7	NE
Oct	76	50	97	31	72		3	0	25	0	22	9	2	2	2	0	70	85	48	7	SW
Nov	61	38	85	17			4	T	22	0	18	12	3	2	0	6	56	83	57	8	SW
Dec	52	32	78	-1		23	4	1	22	0	15	16	1	2	0	17	48	80	61	9	SW
Year	73	51	108	-4			49	6	261	1	221	144	56	16	73	68	62	83	56	8	SW

Notes:
T Indicates "trace"

Average date of first freeze . . . . November 15
      "   "   " last . . . . March 16
      "   freeze-free period . . . . 244 days
10 inches of snow equal approximately one inch of rain.

Table 1. Climatic Data for Little Rock, Arkansas. Source: Local Climatological Data: Little Rock, Arkansas (Asheville, N.C.: National Oceanic and Atmospheric Administration, Environmental Data Service, National Climatic Center, 1981).

clonic storms, variability is the norm.[2] Although the same overall tendencies exist from year to year, considerable variations may occur within the same season in consecutive years.

Most of the region's weather originates to the west. On occasion, the continental winds passing across the nation's midsection will dip down into the Ouachitas bringing unusually cold temperatures in the winter and welcomed cooling trends in the summer. When the more common southern and southwesterly winds prevail, winter warming trends and summer heat waves can result. The mixing together of these different air masses triggers cyclonic storms which, in turn, generate large portions of the area's total annual precipitation. On occasion, when the colliding air masses are especially well developed and the differences in their temperatures are considerable, tornados may evolve. The likelihood of such an occurrence is very slight for any one locality, however; since most of these dangerous storm systems invade the Ouachitas from western Oklahoma and Texas, the western areas are most susceptible to their effects.

The seasonal fluctuations of the Ouachita region produce considerable variations in the average monthly temperatures. For example, Little Rock's average minimum temperature in January is 28°F while the average maximum temperature in July is 92°F (table 1).

Winter usually sets in during the latter part of December and continues through January and February with occasional cold outbursts in early March. Each of the winter months experiences fifteen to twenty days when the minimum temperature falls below freezing. Because the Ouachitas are generally too far south to have their temperatures affected greatly by the strong high pressure cells that traverse the north central states during the winter season, the area's low temperatures rarely fall below zero. When

frigid conditions of this nature do develop, they usually last only two or three days at a time. On occasion, however, the jet stream will dip far enough to the south to usher in a weather system that is marked by prolonged, bitterly cold temperatures. Such was the case during the winter of 1979, when an unusually severe set of conditions caused the region's temperatures to fall as low as −5°F to −10°F for extended periods.

Because of a phenomenon known as wind chill,[3] the relatively moderate air temperatures that characterize the Ouachita winter may appear to be considerably colder when a brisk wind is blowing. On these occasions, the thermometer registers one temperature, but our bodies actually "feel" another. The magnitude of this perceived discrepancy increases with wind velocities (fig. 1). As an example, our bodies lose more heat, and thus feel colder, when the air temperature is 20°F and the wind is blowing at ten miles per hour than when the air temperature is zero and the air is still. Wind chills around 0°F can occur fairly frequently in the Ouachitas; only rarely will they fall as low as −20°F.

Summers in the Ouachita Mountains are warm and humid. Temperatures over 90°F are likely to occur an average of five days in late May, fifteen to twenty days during each of the months of June, July, and August, and for eight days in September. On occasion, extreme temperatures in excess of 100°F will also prevail. The highest temperature ever recorded at Fort Smith, Arkansas, for example, was 113°F, and the record in Little Rock, Arkansas, is 108°F (see table 1).

Just as wind velocity plays a major role in influencing winter comfort, so does the level of humidity influence the summer situation. For this reason, the Temperature Humidity Index (THI) is an excellent indicator of summer comfort.[4] As an expression of the relation-

WIND CHILL TABLE

°F Dry bulb temperatures

MPH	35	30	25	20	15	10	5	0	-5	-10	-15	-20	-25	-30	-35	-40	-45
Calm:	35	30	25	20	15	10	5	0	-5	-10	-15	-20	-25	-30	-35	-40	-45
5	33	27	21	16	12	7	1	-6	-11	-15	-20	-26	-31	-35	-41	-47	-54
10	21	16	9	2	-2	-9	-15	-22	-27	-31	-38	-45	-52	-58	-64	-70	-77
15	16	11	1	-6	-11	-18	-25	-33	-40	-45	-51	-60	-65	-70	-78	-85	-90
20	12	3	-4	-9	-17	-24	-32	-40	-46	-52	-60	-68	-76	-81	-88	-96	-103
25	7	0	-7	-15	-22	-29	-37	-45	-52	-58	-67	-75	-83	-89	-96	-104	-112
30	5	-2	-11	-18	-26	-33	-41	-49	-56	-63	-70	-78	-87	-94	-101	-109	-117
35	3	-4	-13	-20	-27	-35	-43	-52	-60	-67	-72	-83	-90	-98	-105	-113	-123
40	1	-4	-15	-22	-29	-36	-45	-54	-62	-69	-76	-87	-94	-101	-107	-116	-128
45	1	-6	-17	-24	-31	-38	-46	-54	-63	-70	-78	-87	-94	-101	-108	-118	-128
50	0	-7	-17	-24	-31	-38	-47	-56	-63	-70	-79	-88	-96	-103	-110	-120	-128

Wind Chill Index (Equivalent temperature) Equivalent in cooling power on exposed flesh under calm conditions. Wind speeds greater than 40 MPH have little additional chilling effect.

Figure 1. Wind Chill Table. Source: "How Cold Is It?" (pamphlet). (Kansas City, Mo.: National Ocean and Atmospheric Administration, National Weather Service Central Region, 1975); original data, Paul A. Siple and Charles F. Passel, "Measurements of Dry Atmospheric Cooling on Subfreezing Temperatures," *Proceedings of the American Philosophical Society* 89 (1945): 177–99.

ship of humidity and temperature, the THI reveals that a hot, dry, and clear day can be much more comfortable than a "cooler" day (temperature-wise) with oppressively high humidity. The THI is calculated by adding together the dry bulb and wet bulb temperatures, multiplying the sum by a factor of 0.4, and then adding this result to a base of 15°. Most observers agree that 72° is a key THI benchmark since at that level or below, most people "feel" comfortable. When the index reaches 75°, approximately half of the population feels uncomfortably warm (i.e., "sticky"), and when indices of 80° or higher are reached, virtually everyone agrees that the conditions are uncomfortable without air-conditioning. Little Rock's normal THIs for the summer months are 76° in May, 82° in June, 84° in July, 83° in August, 78° in September, and 72° in October.

As the transition from summer to fall occurs in the Ouachitas, an "Indian Summer" frequently develops. This phenomenon, which may last as long as two or three weeks, is characterized by occasional temperatures in the upper eighties and lower nineties, very little wind, and a sky that takes on a hazy, often purplish color in the late afternoon. When combined with the often spectacular change in leaf colors, this is one of the most pleasant periods in the Ouachita year.

The temperatures that characterize any specific location within the Ouachitas are strongly influenced by the presence or absence of water, the nature of the local surface materials, the degree of relief, and the orientation of the slope. Since the south- and west-facing slopes receive the greatest amounts of sunlight, they experience warmer temperatures and higher evaporation rates. Variations of this nature often affect the vegetation. Most mosses, wild flowers, and ferns are found on north-facing slopes along with mixed varieties of trees. South-facing slopes are marked by less undergrowth and the purest stands of oaks and hickories.

Many of the most readily observed temperature variations during the summer months are caused by the nighttime drainage of cool air down the numerous mountain slopes. Beginning an hour or two before sunset, this air flow results in a refreshingly cool breeze for those in the valley areas. Oftentimes it also produces an early morning fog that dissipates by midmorning as valley temperatures climb. The heaviest fogs tend to develop over large water bodies such as Lake Ouachita and Lake Hamilton; however, these fogs also break up and disappear as the sun and temperatures rise.

The mean annual precipitation in the Ouachita region ranges from forty inches on the western border to more than fifty-six inches in the Kiamichi Mountains along the Arkansas-Oklahoma boundary.[5] Representative stations include Little Rock, Arkansas, which receives forty-nine inches in a normal year, and Fort Smith, Arkansas, and McAlester, Oklahoma, which both average forty-two inches a year.

Nearly all of this precipitation comes in the form of rain. Although snowfalls are possible, the average accumulation is minimal. Little Rock, for instance, averages just six inches a year. This constitutes just 2 percent of the total precipitation and is less than half the amount received by Springfield, Missouri, which is only about two hundred miles to the northwest. Many winters pass with only an inch or two of snowfall, and it is not at all unusual for that to melt almost as soon as it hits the ground. Evidence that inordinately heavy snowfalls are possible, however, came late in the winter of 1979 when the Hot Springs area was hit with a thirteen-inch accumulation. As a result of this unusual storm, traffic was snarled for days and some moun-

Early morning fog in the Oklahoma Ouachitas. Photo by Fred W. Marvel. Courtesy of Oklahoma Tourism and Recreation Department.

tain communities were forced to cancel school for more than two weeks.

Although the area's rainfall is fairly evenly distributed throughout the year, a dry season sets in around the latter part of June or the first part of July, and lasts for forty to sixty days. During this period, when most of the rainfall comes from isolated thunderstorms, widespread rains of more than one inch are uncom-

mon. On those occasions when the dry season intensifies and becomes extended, drought conditions can develop that, in turn, can inflict serious damage to the area's farm-related economy.

Heavy downpours in the Ouachitas usually are associated with the passage of squall lines, fronts, and thunderstorms. Because of the area's steep slopes, the runoff is rapid and short-lived "flash

Mixed hardwood and pine forest. Courtesy of Arkansas Department of Parks and Tourism.

floods" are common. Destruction of farmland and personal property can result; however, the damage created by droughts is usually more severe.

The Ouachitas' climate is moderate, pleasant, and healthful; in times of rising energy costs, it should be especially attractive to those seeking a post-retirement home. The relatively mild winters and less humid summers, compared to those of the deep South, are directly reflected in lower utility bills.

SUGGESTIONS FOR CLOTHING

Clothing for the winter months should be layered and relatively heavy. Those who plan to spend lengthy periods outdoors on deer stands, in duck blinds, or simply hiking and exploring are advised to wear a heavy coat, a warm cap or hat, insulated boots, and heavy wool socks. Thermal underwear should be brought along although it may not be needed. By layering one's clothing, it will be possible to shed certain items as the nighttime and early morning chill moderates with the rising sun.

Because the weather during the fall and spring is so unpredictable and erratic, the outdoors person and traveler should be prepared for a variety of conditions. During the late fall and early spring, a full complement of winter clothing is recommended. Thermal underwear usually will not be needed unless one plans to camp out. Campers are also advised to pack an extra blanket that can be thrown over the sleeping bag on those unusually cold nights. Since fall and spring can be quite warm, a lightweight jacket or windbreaker, and several sets of lighter weight clothing are also desirable. The comparatively high precipitation probabilities during both of these seasons make rain gear an absolute necessity.

Summer clothing should be light and loose-fitting. Short-sleeve shirts, light blouses, or T-shirts along with walking shorts, cut-offs, jeans, light dress trousers, or casual slacks are usually preferred.

History and Economy

THE OUACHITAS' HISTORY

There have been three phases in the settlement of the Ouachita Mountains: the Mountain Frontier phase, the "New South" phase, and the Modern phase. The first of these periods was marked by the arrival of white settlers from the southern hill country east of the Mississippi River and the movement of the Choctaw Nation from the Alabama-Mississippi area to Indian Territory (Oklahoma). The original Indian inhabitants—the Quapaw and Caddo tribes—were moved westward to make room for the new immigrants from the East. The

second settlement phase, a part of the post–Civil War period of national development, was characterized by continued rapid immigration, the building of towns and railroad lines, and the emergence and growth of the various commercial activities that followed the introduction of rail transportation. The third settlement phase was stimulated by a post–World War I increase in the availability of automobiles and electricity. The scenic attractions of the Ouachita Mountains became more widely recognized as the years passed, and in conjunction with the construction of several large reservoirs, this led to accelerated

Bluegrass music festival in the Ouachita Mountains of Oklahoma. Photo by Fred W. Marvel. Courtesy of Oklahoma Tourism and Recreation Department.

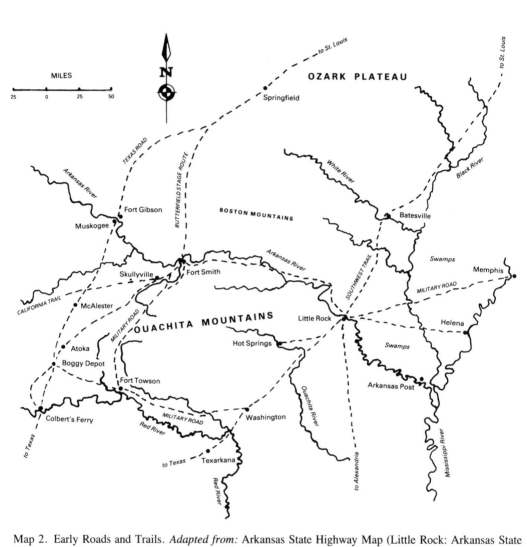

Map 2. Early Roads and Trails. *Adapted from:* Arkansas State Highway Map (Little Rock: Arkansas State Highway and Transportation Department, 1985); Oklahoma State Transportation Map (Oklahoma City: Oklahoma Department of Transportation, 1985); Charles D. Paullin, *Atlas of the Historical Geography of the United States;* Dallas T. Herndon, *Centennial History of Arkansas;* John W. Morris, Charles R. Goins, and Edwin C. McReynolds, *Historical Atlas of Oklahoma,* 2d ed.

population growth and an increase in the significance of the Ouachitas as a tourism and recreation region.

The Mountain Frontier Phase

The first white men to set foot in the Ouachitas were probably Spaniards led by De Soto in 1541, yet it was not until approximately two and a half centuries later that accurate descriptions and accounts of the area became available to the rest of the world.[1] The earliest explorers traveled primarily by canoe along the region's streams. The initial settlements were also tied to the principal watercourses so the pioneers could take full advantage of water travel and communication.

The earliest overland routes tended to follow old Indian trails, most of which were mere paths at the time; wagon passage was generally impossible. Small exploration and trading parties traveled by foot and horseback; however, usage increased and as time passed many of these trails became very important avenues for settlement.

One of the oldest routes leading into Arkansas was known as the "Southwest Trail" (map 2) and was used as early as 1765 by the Chouteaus, Laclede, and other Indian traders. This very important trail began in Saint Louis and ran parallel to the Mississippi River until it reached Cape Girardeau, Missouri. Since the trail passed through Sainte Genevieve, which was the western terminus of one of the earliest ferries across the Mississippi River, many westward settlers were funneled directly on to that route. From Cape Girardeau, the trail left the river and followed a southwesterly course along the edge of the Ozark Upland into the Ouachita Mountains. It crossed the White River eight miles below Batesville, and the Little Red River at Britton's Ferry, a point almost due north of the current location of Searcy. Then it ran in a nearly direct line to Little Rock, from which it continued southwesterly through the present-day sites of Benton, Malvern (once Rockport), Washington, and Fulton. The latter site was located on the Red River, which initially formed the boundary between the United States and Mexico. During the 1830s, the Southwest Trail was improved and designated as the "National Road" or "Military Road" by the federal government.[2] At the same time, a second military road was established from Memphis to Fort Smith, via Little Rock. Today Interstate 30 follows nearly the same general route as the original Southwest Trail.

An alternate route to the western Ouachitas was an extension of the "Ridge Road," the great transportation corridor that cut across the Ozarks region.[3] Following the water divide between the Missouri and Arkansas rivers for much of the way from Saint Louis to Springfield, the trail then divided into two branches. One branch continued in a southwesterly direction toward Joplin and the Tri-State Mining District. From there it became known as the "Texas Trail" as it led to Fort Gibson, the Three Forks settlement (Muskogee), and on to Boggy Depot. The second branch took a more southerly route out of Springfield passing through Fayetteville and Fort Smith. Used by the Butterfield Stage Line, this latter route also continued on to Texas by way of Atoka, Boggy Depot, and Fort Washita.[4]

A second route from Fort Smith to Texas followed the military road marked by Robert Bean and Jesse Chisholm in 1832. This pathway paralleled the Kiamichi River along part of the way.[5] Later, in 1855, the Butterfield Stage Line passed through Indian Territory from Fort Smith to Colbert's Ferry with twelve stage stops in between.[6] Limited access from the Southeast was made possible by a trace linking Natchitoches, Louisiana, on the Red River, with Hot Springs, and ultimately, Little Rock.[7]

Just prior to the Civil War, these were the main land routes penetrating into the Ouachita Mountains. With railroad construction having advanced only to the vicinity of Memphis, Tennessee, the Ouachita region was still relatively isolated and remote. As a matter of fact, the Confederate Army found refuge on the southern side of the wild and trackless Ouachitas, at Washington in Hempstead County, right after the fall of Little Rock. From the same remote staging area, General Sterling Price led his Missouri Militia on a daring, but ill-fated, raid into the Missouri Valley in 1864.

River transportation on the borders of the Ouachita region improved with the development of steamboats. Soon after this new technology was introduced to Mississippi River travel, steamboats be-gan appearing on the Arkansas, Ouachita, and Red Rivers. In 1822 the *Robert Thompson* was the first steamboat to reach Fort Smith, and regular packet service had been established by 1830.[8] The original steamboat on the Ouachita was a small side-wheeler named *The Dime* owned by Jacob Barkman. It began making regular trips between Blakeleytown and New Orleans during the late 1830s.

Navigation of the upper portion of the Red River was blocked for several years by a huge log jam known as the "Great Raft,"[9] and it was not until 1838, when a passageway was created under the supervision of Captain Henry Miller Shreve, that profitable steamboat traffic became possible. Even though the passageway was sufficient to permit regular traffic to travel as high as the mouth of the Kiamichi, the entire log jam was not removed until after the Civil War.

Great Raft in the Red River. Courtesy of Arkansas History Commission.

Even with the problems caused by the Great Raft, the Red River system was an important route into the southern Ouachitas.

Many of the region's early immigrants relied upon the river systems for their initial entrance into the Ouachitas. Rather than attempting to cross the Mississippi alluvial plain, which was swampy and subject to periodic flooding, many folks from Tennessee and Kentucky elected to use the Ohio, Mississippi, and Arkansas river connections. After traveling to Little Rock or Fort Smith by river, many then completed their journey into the Ouachitas by land.

With immigrants arriving from Missouri and the areas to the east where Scotch-Irish influences had been dominant, a similar cultural heritage was established in the Ouachita Province. These settlers were, out of necessity, a hardy lot who relied heavily on forest products and farming for their subsistence.

Another major group of immigrants during the initial settlement phase were Indians from the southeast, mainly Choctaws. Southeastern Oklahoma, including much of the Ouachita Mountains, was once designated as the land of the Choctaw Nation (map 3). When the land they had acquired in western Arkansas in 1818 was ceded to the United States in 1825, most of the Choctaw settlers moved westward into Indian Territory.

Before their removal from the areas east of the Mississippi River during the first half of the nineteenth century, the Choctaws were as advanced in their economic life as any of the Five Civilized Tribes. Most of their food was derived from agricultural activities and included beans, melons, pumpkins, squash, and especially corn. Like the other Indians of the southeastern United States, they also obtained a part of their living through fishing and hunting. In many respects their economy was similar to that of the white frontiersmen. As time progressed, many of the Choctaws adopted various aspects of the white man's commercial agriculture.

The primary impetus for the removal of the Indian nations from their original home was increased pressure for cotton land. A party of prominent Choctaws and Chickasaws surveyed the Ouachitas in 1828 with the intent of finding a suitable tribal home. This early exploration predated the Treaty of Dancing Rabbit Creek, ratified on February 24, 1831, which stipulated that the Choctaws would be moved west of the Mississippi River. Prior to their removal, there were an estimated 19,554 Choctaws. After the completion of the removal, 12,500 had migrated, 2,500 had died, and another 5,000 to 6,000 had decided to remain in Mississippi.[10] Most of the Choctaws who immigrated to the Ouachitas between 1831 and 1855 settled in three general areas: (1) along the Poteau and Arkansas rivers in the northeast; (2) along the Little River, its tributaries, and the Red River in the southeast; and (3) along the Kiamichi and Red rivers in the west. Established during this era were the towns of Boggy Depot, Skullyville, Eagletown, Perryville, and Doaksville.[11]

The Choctaws utilized various routes to the Ouachitas. Large numbers gathered at Vicksburg, Mississippi, and traveled by steamboat up the Mississippi River to the Arkansas River; after continuing on the Arkansas to Little Rock, the migrants switched to land-based modes for the remainder of the journey. The most popular route out of Little Rock was along the National Road that led directly to the southeastern section of the Choctaw Nation. Other steamboats loaded at Vicksburg and traveled down the Mississippi River to the mouth of the Red River; from there they moved up the Red River to the Ouachita River and then on to Encore a Fabri where they disembarked. At this point, the Indians

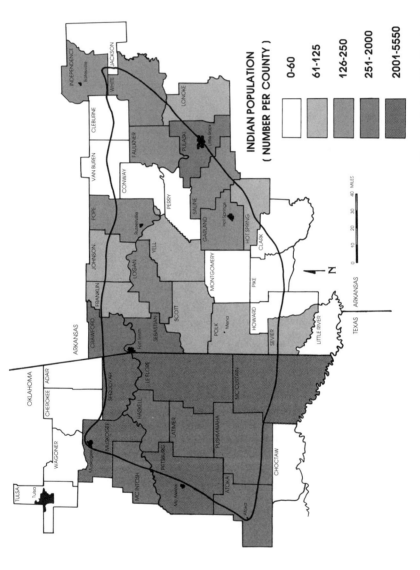

Map 3. Indian Population. *Compiled from:* 1980 Census of Population, Vol. 1, Characteristics of the Population, Chapter B, General Population Characteristics, Part 5, Arkansas, and Part 38, Oklahoma (Washington, D.C.: U.S. Department of Commerce, Bureau of the Census, 1982).

faced a 160-mile overland trek before reaching Fort Towson near the mouth of the Kiamichi River. (A more direct route would have been to remain on the Red River until reaching the mouth of the Kiamichi; however, the Great Raft prevented steamboat navigation on a 60-mile section of the Red River.)

Fort Towson was established in 1824 by Colonel Matthew Arbuckle to keep order among the new settlers in the region. At first the post consisted of a number of log barracks and stockades for defense against Indian attacks, but it was later rebuilt in stone. Robert Bean and Jesse Chisholm blazed a trail from Fort Smith to the new settlement in 1832.

Upon reaching their new homeland, the Choctaws established an agricultural system that produced many of the same food crops they had grown in Alabama and Mississippi. They introduced cotton production into what is now Oklahoma. By 1840 there were twelve gins in the Choctaw Nation producing more than 1,000 bales per year; before long, cotton was the Nation's main agricultural export. By 1867, a Choctaw census revealed an annual production of 211,595 bales.[12]

The cotton-producing Choctaws also initiated the use of slave labor in the Ouachitas. Slaves could be found throughout the Nation; however, a large majority were concentrated within the major cotton-growing areas, most notably the Red River Valley. One wealthy Choctaw, R. M. Jones, in 1860 used his 227 slaves to operate five plantations, business interests in Doaksville, and a small fleet of steamboats.[13] Very few slave owners operated at such a large scale; the average number of slaves per owner was about six.[14] In fact, in 1860, 385 owners controlled 2,297 slaves.[15] With under 400 owners, it is clear that most Choctaws were *not* involved in the use of slaves. This was especially true among those who settled in the more mountainous areas; the smaller farms that characterized the higher elevations did not require supplemental labor.

The New South Phase

Following the Civil War, many of the southern areas of the United States, including the more accessible parts of the Ouachitas, experienced a period of economic development. In the Ouachitas, especially in the larger towns in the Arkansas and Red river valleys, this phase was marked by renewed immigration and considerable economic growth. Railroads were constructed, numerous mining operations were initiated, and several large lumber mills were established. Many of the new immigrant entrepreneurs were attracted by the region's virtually untapped economic potential.

Prior to the War, very few railroads had penetrated into the Ouachita province; most of the lines that were extended across the region after the war originated in either Saint Louis, Kansas City, or Memphis (map 4), but in 1868 the Cairo and Fulton Railroad, which possessed large land grants in Arkansas, consolidated with the Saint Louis, Iron Mountain, and Southern Railroad. Before long, work began on the "Arkansas Extension" of this Saint Louis line; by the fall of 1872 the railroad was in operation as far south as Arkadelphia. In January, 1874, trains began running between Saint Louis and Texarkana. Branch lines were constructed in the Ouachita Mountains from Benton to Hot Springs, and westward from Little Rock, via Conway, Morrillton, Russellville, and Van Buren to Fort Smith. This roadway now forms a part of the Missouri Pacific system. The main line, which parallels the Southwest Trail, runs southwest from Saint Louis through Arkansas and Oklahoma, via Corning, Walnut Ridge, Hoxie, Newport, Bald Knob,

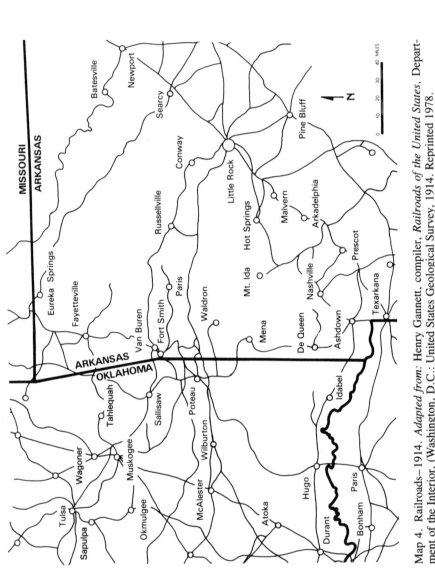

Map 4. Railroads–1914. *Adapted from:* Henry Gannett, compiler, *Railroads of the United States*, Department of the Interior, (Washington, D.C.: United States Geological Survey, 1914. Reprinted 1978.

Little Rock, Benton, Malvern, Arkadelphia, Prescott, Hope, and Texarkana to Galveston, Texas.

In 1872 the Missouri-Kansas-Texas Railroad built a trunk line down the route of the old Texas Trail linking Muskogee, McAlester, and Durant and tapping the coal deposits of Pittsburg County.[16] Later, the Kansas City Southern constructed a line that passed through many Missouri, Kansas, Oklahoma, and Arkansas coalfields; this route passed from Missouri, through the western part of Benton County, Arkansas, and into Oklahoma and re-entered Arkansas near the southwest corner of Scott County then ran south through Mena, DeQueen, Horatio, and Ashdown to Texarkana. A branch of the same system, the Choctaw and Gulf Railroad, extended westward from Waldron into Oklahoma.[17]

Once the main-line railroads provided connections to outside markets, the area's virgin timberlands attracted railroad builders who were also lumbermen. From 1880 to about 1910, rapid railroad expansion prevailed as rails were laid into timber tracts. Newly founded mill towns were connected with their markets.

Railroad development reached a frantic pace as even more entrepreneurs entered the region to exploit the natural resources.[18] In 1897 the Arkansas Central Railroad was extended into the extensive coal deposits of the Arkansas River Valley between Dardanelle and Fort Smith; the Fort Smith and Western Railroad was chartered in 1899 to serve the emerging Oklahoma coal fields. In 1906 the Neimeyer Lumber Company built the Little Rock, Maumelle, and Western Railroad through eight thousand acres of forested land in Pulaski, Perry, and Saline counties; that same year, the Dardanelle, Ola, and Southern Railroad was

Loading pulp timber at Heavener, Oklahoma. Photo by Fred W. Marvel. Courtesy of Oklahoma Tourism and Recreation Department.

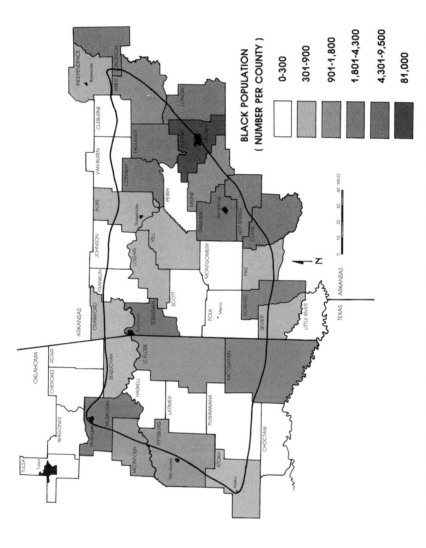

Map 5. Black Population. *Compiled from:* 1980 Census of Population, Vol. 1, Characteristics of the Population, Chapter B, General Population Characteristics, Part 5, Arkansas, and Part 38, Oklahoma (Washington, D.C.: U.S. Department of Commerce, Bureau of the Census, 1982).

chartered to construct track southward from Dardanelle, on the Arkansas River, into the rugged Ouachita Mountain timber tracts. The DeQueen and Eastern Railroad was established primarily to serve the lumber mills within the Dierks brothers' domain; the Texas, Oklahoma, and Eastern was built from DeQueen to Valliant, Oklahoma, with the same purpose in mind. The Memphis, Paris, and Gulf Railroad was initiated by the Brown-Henderson Improvement and Timber Company in 1906 to service their timber operations in the southern Ouachitas; the Prescott and Northwestern rail line was established to carry the output of the Bemis and Whitaker lumber mill in Prescott, Arkansas.

The Hot Springs Railroad evolved under the leadership of a Chicago capitalist named "Diamond Jo" Reynolds. When he visited Hot Springs in 1874 to receive treatment for his arthritis and rheumatism, Reynolds suffered a jolting stagecoach ride from the Saint Louis, Iron Mountain, and Southern depot in Malvern to the springs. Consequently, he vowed that when he returned it would be as a passenger on his own railroad.[19] True to his word, a narrow-gage line, familiarly known as the "Diamond Jo Line," was completed in 1875 and the stage line terminated its service to Hot Springs.

Even though the railroad boom in central Arkansas had subsided by 1900, stock was sold and a charter granted for another line, the Little Rock and Hot Springs Western Railroad, designed to link the two cities within its corporate title. The new company, known as the "Hot Western," competed directly with the "Diamond Jo" line but was beset with labor problems and a series of fires that burned many trestles and roundhouses. The line became a part of the Saint Louis, Iron Mountain, and Southern system in 1910.

The railroads greatly stimulated population growth within the Ouachitas. More and more people arrived from the northern states. Arkansas' population increased by more than 400,000 between 1880 and 1900; population growth in the Oklahoma Ouachitas was also rapid. Most of these new immigrants settled in the sections well-suited for agriculture.

From 1870 to 1920 the northern and western borders of the Ouachita Province were affected by the influx of many immigrants from southern and eastern Europe who settled in the coalfields that developed from Russellville, Arkansas, to McAlester, Oklahoma.[20] By 1889 the mining population in Indian Territory (Oklahoma) was estimated at about two thousand. Most of these settlers were of recent European origins: Czechs, Slovaks, Slovenes, Hungarians, Belgians, Germans, Frenchmen, Englishmen, and Italians. Within five years, the number of immigrant coal miners had doubled; white American miners had also arrived from the eastern coalfields, and several hundred black miners had migrated from Texas (map 5).

The Modern Phase

The third period of occupancy, the Modern Phase, began with World War I and has continued to the present. The Ouachita Province has made the difficult transition from a frontier landscape to the contemporary scene. Many factors influenced this metamorphosis including war-stimulated industries, exploitation of the area's minerals and forests, rising agricultural prices, and especially, various federally sponsored programs. The "poverty" of America's mountain districts was discovered, and the stereotype of the "hillbilly" was born during the Great Depression; through several New Deal agencies, the federal government became an increasingly important influence. The Works Progress Administration (WPA), the Civilian Conservation Corps (CCC), and a host of social agen-

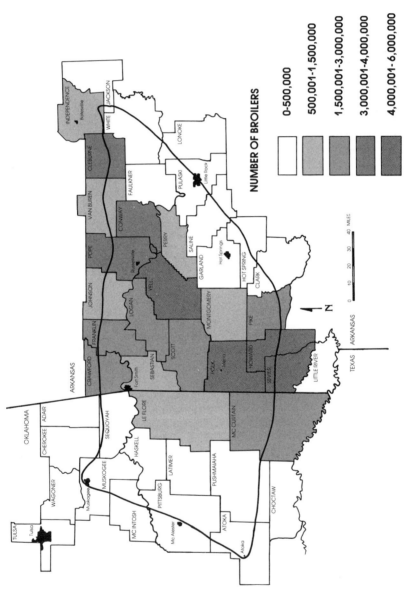

NUMBER OF BROILERS

0-500,000

500,001-1,500,000

1,500,001-3,000,000

3,000,001-4,000,000

4,000,001-6,000,000

Map 6. Broiler Chicken Production. *Compiled from:* 1982 Census of Agriculture, Vol. 1, Geographic Area Series, Part 4, Arkansas, and Part 38, Oklahoma, State and County Data (Washington, D.C.: U.S. Department of Commerce, Bureau of the Census, 1984).

cies provided training, education, employment, and sustenance. The establishment of the Ouachita and Ozark National Forests began the process of restoration and management of the region's cut-over lands. After World War II, the Corps of Engineers sponsored several major dam construction projects that, in turn, led to numerous multipurpose reservoirs that supplemented existing, privately financed Lakes Catherine and Hamilton. Tourism, second-home developments, escalating land prices, and burgeoning population growth have highlighted the recent development of the region's character and economy.

THE OUACHITAS' ECONOMY

Until fairly recently, the Ouachitas' economy was dominated by resource-based industries originally established by the first wave of settlers to the region; these included farming, forestry, and mining.

The emergence of a productive agricultural system was triggered by necessity; with few outside connections, the early settlers were forced to rely upon locally produced food. For this reason, they were attracted to the Arkansas Valley and the alluvial floodplains of larger rivers such as the Fourche LaFave, the Petit Jean, the Poteau, the Ouachita, the Arkansas, and the Kiamichi. These relatively flat areas, with the better soils in the area, offered the best agricultural opportunities.

Corn was the first important cash crop; however, the self-sufficient pioneer families also grew wheat, tobacco, flax, hemp, and cotton. Most of them also raised cattle, hogs, and poultry while supplementing their diets by hunting, fishing, and gathering honey, nuts, fruits, and berries from the nearby countryside.

As transportation improved in the region, more and more farmers shifted from a varied, subsistence-based operation to cash crops. Cotton quickly emerged as one of the most important export crops. Introduced to Arkansas by the original white immigrants, and to Oklahoma by the Five Civilized Tribes, cotton remained the chief cash crop of the Arkansas Valley until it was recently replaced by soybeans in all but Conway County, Arkansas. Cotton continues to be the predominant export crop throughout the Red River Valley.

The more mountainous districts have very little land still under cultivation. Former cotton and corn lands have been diverted to pasture and hay. Small beef-cattle ranches and poultry farms, many operated on a part-time basis, are the main features of modern Ouachita Mountain agriculture (map 6).

When the original white settlers arrived in the Ouachitas, the landscape was heavily forested. With approximately 85 percent of the land covered by trees, the evolution of a commercial timber industry was logical and fruitful. Through the years, this industry comprised a major component of the Ouachita's economy. Commercial forest land is now down to about two-thirds of the total area; however, this still translates to over 5 million acres of forested land. Forest coverage ranges from 90 percent in many of the more mountainous counties to only the ridges and hills in the agriculturally oriented Arkansas Valley.

Among the foremost commercial species of trees within the Ouachitas are the native shortleaf and commercially planted loblolly pines and hardwoods including walnut, hickory, tupelo, gum, and several varieties of oak. Probably the most important of these is the shortleaf pine, whose timber is used extensively for building and manufacturing as well as pulpwood. The loblolly pine, also known as hard pine, produces stronger, firmer, and more durable lumber and is commonly used for heavy beams and trusses. Much of the hardwood output,

The Ouachita National Forest embraces more than 1.5 million acres of mountains, ridges, lakes, and streams. Courtesy of Arkansas Department of Parks and Tourism.

mainly oak, is utilized for cooperage, flooring, and furniture; walnut is prized as a veneer wood.

International Paper and Weyerhaeuser, two of the biggest forest-related corporations in the United States, own extensive forest tracts and large milling operations in the Ouachitas. International Paper has factories in Benton, Delight, Gurdon, and Russellville, Arkansas; Weyerhaeuser has plants both in Arkansas, at Mountain Pine, DeQueen, Dierks, and Brier (Nashville), and in Oklahoma, at Broken Bow, Valliant, and Wright City. Approximately one-fourth of all the manufacturing within the Ouachita Province is timber-related.

The production of geological resources is a third, long-standing component of the resource-based economy of the Oua-

chitas. The most important of these resources have been fuels, especially coal, and bauxite. While the production of these minerals has declined markedly, their significance in the historical development of many communities was paramount.

The major coalfields of Arkansas and Oklahoma lie within the Arkansas Valley and extend westward from Russellville, Arkansas, to the vicinity of McAlester, Oklahoma. The western part of the state produces mainly high-sulphur bituminous coal; air pollution regulations limit its market. Nevertheless, in 1985 nearly fifty thousand short tons of bituminous coal was produced from seven mines in Franklin, Johnson, and Sebastian counties in Arkansas. In 1987 production increased as a result of the Sugarloaf Mining Company's production of coal for export to Spain. The eastern portion of this district, i.e., the areas around Clarksville and Russellville, yield high-grade, semianthracite coal, which has a much lower ash content than the coal from the western fields; unfortunately, there is little demand for this coal in today's energy market.

Coal was burned experimentally as early as 1841 in Little Rock. At first, the mining occurred at places where the coal outcropped along stream channels. The first shaft operation began in 1870 at Spadra (Johnson County), Arkansas; however, coal did not assume commercial importance until after the railroads were extended into the fields in 1883.[21] Almost immediately thereafter, mining in western Arkansas and eastern Okla-

homa experienced rapid development and expansion. By 1920 the Arkansas Commissioner of Mines reported the following inventory of coal operators: sixty-nine in Sebastian County, nineteen in Franklin County, twenty-three in Johnson County, four in Pope County, and thirteen in Logan County.[22] The Oklahoma coalfields, which centered on Colgate, McAlester, and Le Flore counties, were opened between 1873 and 1902 as the railroads penetrated the southeastern part of that state.[23]

Natural-gas production was also centered in the Arkansas Valley area. The first gas well in Arkansas was drilled on the Massard Prairie, south of Fort Smith, in 1901.[24] During the next twenty years, numerous new wells were drilled as the field extended southwestward near Po-

Tightwad Coal Mine. Courtesy of Arkansas History Commission.

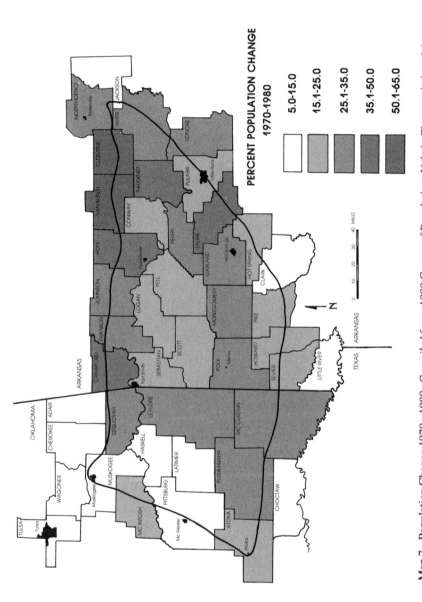

Map 7. Population Change 1970–1980. *Compiled from:* 1980 Census of Population, Vol. 1, Characteristics of the Population, Chapter B, General Characteristics, Part 5, Arkansas, and Part 38, Oklahoma (Washington, D.C.: U.S. Department of Commerce, Bureau of the Census, 1982)

teau and Wilburton, Oklahoma. Many of these wells struck gas at depths ranging from 750 to 3,200 feet. The availability of gas permitted the emergence of zinc smelters in Fort Smith and Van Buren that processed ores from Arkansas and the Tri-State District (Kansas-Missouri-Oklahoma) until about 1960 when the gas field was depleted.

Bauxite was discovered south of Little Rock in June, 1887, by Dr. John C. Branner, a state geologist.[25] The first shipment of ore occurred in 1899. Today, the greater part of the ore is extracted from the Bryant field near Bauxite, Arkansas, by Reynolds Mining Corporation, Alcoa, and American Cyanamid Company. Smelters at Jones Mill (Hot Springs County) and Gum Springs (Clark County) convert the bauxite to aluminum metal.

Primary (resource-based) industries have declined or disappeared altogether in many Ouachita communities, as the region's overall economy has shown clear signs of diversification; the major growth sectors now include manufacturing, tourism, and recreation services.

The Ouachitas have benefited from the national decentralization of manufacturing and population. This trend, which the popular press has referred to as a flow from the Snowbelt to the Sunbelt, has produced a significant reversal of the long-standing concentration of people and activities in the northeastern quadrant of the country. The net outmigration from the northeast has favored the less densely populated areas of the nation, especially scenic regions like the Ouachita Mountains where growth in tourism and recreation and the establishment of small manufacturing plants can support the population (map 7).

Many of the forces that triggered the national dispersion of manufacturing are

Ouachita Mountain landscape near Heavener, Oklahoma. Photo by Vick Pakis. Courtesy of Oklahoma Tourism and Recreation Department.

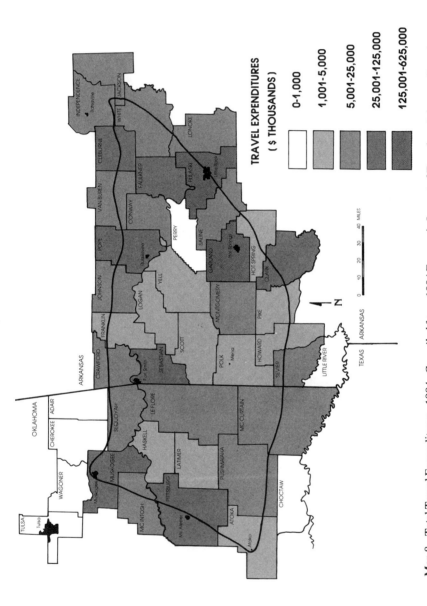

Map 8. Total Travel Expenditures–1984. *Compiled from:* 1984 Economic Impact of Travel on Arkansas Counties, prepared by the U.S. Travel Data Center (Little Rock: Arkansas Department of Parks and Tourism, 1984); and 1984 Economic Impact of Travel on Oklahoma Counties, prepared by the U.S. Travel Data Center (Oklahoma City: Oklahoma Tourism and Recreation Department, 1984).

the consequences of industrial maturity. The new plants in the Ouachitas have tended to be nonunion, highly automated, and frequently branch plants of a national company.[26] Many manufacturers can reduce the cost of production by locating in smaller cities and rural areas where construction costs, wages, utilities, and taxes are lower. Of particular importance to the Ouachita economy, many poultry processing plants have sprung up in association with the rapidly growing broiler-chicken and turkey industries of western Arkansas.

With tourists spending over $750 million dollars in the region annually, the tourism and recreation industry has emerged as another major component of the Ouachita Mountain economy.[27] The combination of heavily forested mountains, cascading creeks and rivers, more than a dozen large reservoirs, and a reputation for a bucolic, "down home," low-cost vacation has made the Ouachitas an increasingly popular tourist destination (map 8). The region's strategic location in the south-central agricultural heartland of the United States makes its many natural and man-made attractions accessible to large numbers of people.

Although the greatest growth in the travel and tourism industry is fairly recent, some of the region's outside reputation predated the Civil War. In particular, the "nation's spa" in Hot Springs, Arkansas, has a long history of attracting visitors from all over the nation.

Business and governmental leaders in the Ouachitas must recognize the significance of the area's position in revenue-generating activities; rational economic and developmental policies that will permit the region to benefit from its many attractions while avoiding the exploitive precedents from the past are needed. Earlier efforts to take advantage of the agricultural, mineral, and forest resources often left the landscape scarred; a repeat of the past could harm the very resources upon which the travel and tourism industry so heavily depends. Uncontrolled development, especially in the heavily used areas near the larger lakes, could cause a deterioration of the scenic and aesthetic values, traffic congestion, water pollution, problems of solid-waste disposal, and the loss of traditional cultural values. Both the newcomer and the longtime mountain resident must embrace a philosophy of conservation and preservation to ensure the wise and continued use of the area's many natural resources.

Ouachita Mountain Hunting

The Ouachita Mountain Region with its clear streams and dense forests was a hunting and fishing paradise for its original Indian inhabitants. The primitive hunting technologies employed by these early residents helped to prevent the widespread decimation of the wildlife; even after the immigrant Choctaws introduced firearms into the area, wanton game kills were carefully avoided.[1] As a result of Indian abilities and attitudes, the first white settlers encountered an environment that still possessed abundant supplies and varieties of animals.

These bountiful conditions soon began to change, however, as the white settlers laid out farms, modified the wildlife habitats, and hunted the game, both for food and sport. During the early settlement until approximately 1860, many of the larger animal species were almost entirely killed or driven out of the area. While wild game was a major part of the mountain pioneers' diet, there is ample written record that these early settlers also hunted bear, bison, and deer for sport.[2] By the end of the initial settlement period, most of the area's bison herds had been completely and permanently eliminated. The bear population, once so abundant, had dwindled to extremely small numbers.[3]

The period from 1860 to about 1900 was characterized by a growing human population and an expanding agricultural base. The emphasis then, as now, was on cultivated plants and domesticated animals; little consideration was given to maintaining wildlife as a supply of game and fur.[4] Forests were destroyed by fire and ax; prairies were plowed into farms; and bottomland marshes were drained at an ever-increasing rate. With undisturbed cover diminishing in size, some of the native wildlife species were driven to other, less fully developed areas. To some extent, the decline in the larger species was offset by an increase in farm game such as quail, rabbits, skunks, and doves.

The hunting activities of this second phase were largely a carry-over from the preceding period: both commercial shooting and sport hunting occurred in a very casual manner; turkeys and passenger pigeons were slaughtered at roost; quail were hunted and sold for a few cents a dozen; and deer and elk were killed in numbers far beyond the actual needs of the settlers.

As the twentieth century began, the population and agricultural growth continued; however, for the first time, the concept of game management began to emerge. The Arkansas legislature passed several game laws, and once a territorial government was established in Oklahoma, a similar set of laws was adopted there.[5] Although specific features of the laws were not identical, they covered the same general topics: (1) open and closed seasons were established for deer, turkey, prairie chicken, and quail; (2) restrictions were placed on the manner in which game could be taken or killed; and (3) enforcement procedures were set so that violators could be prosecuted. Even after these new policies were adopted, however, traditional attitudes toward game and family food requirements prevailed and poaching and out-of-season hunting continued.

Modern game and fish management in the Ouachitas began with the establishment of state agencies designed to oversee management activities. In Oklahoma, the Game and Fish Protective Association successfully lobbied for a 1909 law that led to the formation of a Game and Fish Department and the appointment of a state game warden.[6] A similar agency, the Arkansas Game and Fish Department, was established in 1915.[7] The staff of these agencies has traditionally been charged with numerous responsibilities: (1) enforcement of game and fish laws; (2) restoration and management of appropriate wildlife habitats; (3) development of varied fish and animal propagation techniques; (4) construction and monitoring of artificial lakes; and (5) the establishment and maintenance of public hunting areas. The methods used to accomplish these goals have steadily improved as new research discoveries have been made.

These state-sponsored activities have received significant support from the federal government. For example, the Pittman-Robertson Act of 1938 resulted in federal aid being made available to individual states for the purpose of wildlife restoration. Later, the Dingell-Johnson Act (1950) produced the same kind of aid for state fisheries.[8] The money for these programs is derived from excise taxes on sporting arms and ammunition, fishing rods and reels, and certain other fishing equipment. Funds are apportioned to states on the basis of their hunting and fishing license sales.

Thanks in part to the state Game and Fish Departments, the present wildlife inventory in the Ouachitas is substantial. Thousands of migrant waterfowl flocks pass through the province each autumn and spring; the sloughs and lakes of the Arkansas and Red river bottoms afford these birds nocturnal resting places. The Arkansas Valley grain fields attract large numbers of migrating birds and quail; quail also are found in brush patches all over Arkansas and Oklahoma. Frogs and fish are plentiful; rabbits, squirrels, and opossums are very common; and beavers, otters, raccoons, skunks, and minks are plentiful enough to support a modest rebirth of commercial fur trapping.

The chief species of songbirds include cardinals, mockingbirds, whippoorwills, phoebes, goldfinches, robins, brown thrashers, blue jays, and several varieties of warblers. English sparrows, starlings, and crows are also quite numerous.

It is not difficult to find a Ouachita hunting place. In addition to two national forests, there are more than a dozen public hunting areas owned and managed by either the Arkansas Game and Fish Commission or the Oklahoma Department of Wildlife Conservation (map 9). In Oklahoma, even the state forests are open to hunting. Individual maps of each state's hunting areas and maps of individual districts in the national forests may be obtained by writing to the following state agencies.

Forest Supervisor
Ouachita National Forest
P.O. Box 1270
Hot Springs, Arkansas 71901
Telephone (501) 321-5202

Forest Supervisor
Ozark National Forest
P.O. Box 1008
Russellville, Arkansas 72801
Telephone (501) 968-2354

Arkansas Game and Fish
  Commission
2 Natural Resources Drive
Little Rock, Arkansas 72205
Telephone (501) 223-6300

Oklahoma Department of Wildlife
  Conservation
1801 Lincoln Boulevard
Oklahoma City, Oklahoma 73105
Telephone (405) 521-3851

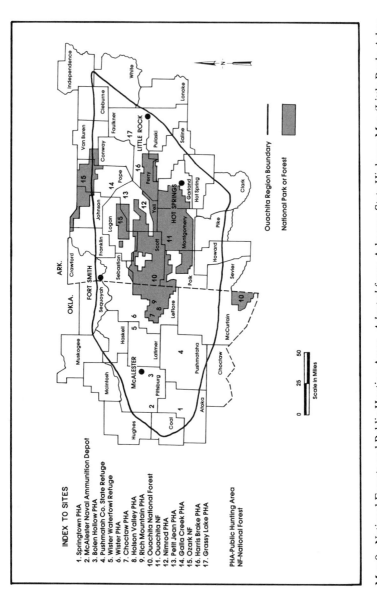

Map 9. National Forests and Public Hunting Areas. *Adapted from:* Arkansas State Highway Map (Little Rock: Arkansas State Highway and Transportation Department, 1985); Oklahoma Official State Transportation Map (Oklahoma City: Oklahoma Department of Transportation, 1985); information leaflets (Little Rock: Arkansas Game and Fish Commission, 1985 and Oklahoma City: Oklahoma Department of Wildlife Conservation, 1985).

The Ouachita National Forest contains 1,276,973 acres spanning eight districts. The Ozark National Forest lies mainly in the northwestern Arkansas Ozarks, but one large block is situated south of the Arkansas River. Since each National Forest district includes considerable private land, frequently from 30 to 50 percent, it is crucial that hunters exercise extreme caution when entering unfamiliar properties. In both Arkansas and Oklahoma, the state Wildlife agencies maintain several public hunting areas (map 9) that are managed to encourage optimum wildlife populations; they are open to public hunting only during the appropriate season.

Arms and ammunition requirements for game hunting are not stringent in the Ouachita Mountains. Shotguns and .22 caliber rifles are standard weapons when hunting most feathered game. Duck hunters usually use no. 4 shot; turkey hunters rely either on no. 4 or no. 6 shot; and those after quail and doves utilize standard shotgun loads of no. 7.5 or no. 8. Deer hunters can employ any standard deer caliber, or a shotgun load; the latter is safer in the heavy Ouachita cover.

Many of the fur-bearing animals, particularly foxes, raccoons, opossums, and coyotes are popular prey for hound enthusiasts; the South has always been noted for excellent hunting dogs. Each year hunters, with the help of their dogs, take several thousand pelts.

Accommodations for hunters are ex-

Partners. Courtesy of Oklahoma Game and Fish Department.

cellent, varied, and well distributed throughout the region; there are motels and restaurants with a wide range of prices, and camping facilities are generally good. Additional information may be obtained from:

Arkansas Department of Parks and
Tourism
1 Capitol Mall
Little Rock, Arkansas 72201
Telephone (501) 682-7777

Oklahoma State Board of Tourism
P.O. Box 60000
505 Will Rogers Building
Oklahoma City, Oklahoma 73146
Telephone (405) 521-2406 or (800)
652-6552

In the following discussion, common game species in the Ouachita Mountains are described along with their habitat preferences. Prime hunting areas and tips for hunters are included in some cases. Refer to the map of National Forests and Public Hunting Areas for orientation.

MOURNING DOVES

The mourning dove is a pigeon-like game bird favored by sportsmen across the nation. The twelve-inch-long bird is generally gray with a bluish cast on its wings, a whitish breast, and a pointed tail. While doves range throughout the Ouachitas, and there is fair dove shooting in some national forests and public hunting areas, the best hunting opportunities are found on private land. The best Arkansas dove hunting is found in the east where grain crops are grown; the premier locations are where milo is available. In the Ouachitas, this translates into the Arkansas, Red, and Ouachita river valleys, as well as a few of the valleys of larger tributary streams. Experienced dove hunters prefer to hunt just after sunrise and just before dusk when doves are most likely to move to water and feeding grounds.

WILD TURKEY

The wild turkey is the most prized game bird in the Ouachita Mountains. Similar to the domestic turkey, but not as large, the average wild turkey gobbler (male) weighs eighteen pounds.

Turkeys were abundant during the pioneer days in Arkansas and eastern Oklahoma; however, because of heavy hunting, the cutting of timber, and the growth of farming, by 1900 the Ouachita turkey population had declined to a few hundred birds found only in the more remote sections. After experimenting briefly with stocking farm-raised turkeys, the Arkansas and Oklahoma wildlife agencies turned to releasing birds trapped in the wild as breeding stock in favorable habitats.

Each year since World War II, the wild turkey range has grown so that now many Ouachita Mountain counties utilize an open season.[10] The Ouachita and Ozark national forests are excellent turkey hunting areas; several state forests and public hunting areas also provide good hunting opportunities, most notably the Petit Jean and Nimrod public hunting areas in Arkansas, and the Choctaw, Rich Mountain, and Holson Valley areas in Oklahoma.

BOBWHITE QUAIL

The bobwhite quail, known for its delicious flavor, is a favored game bird across the South. A typical quail is eight to ten inches long, weighs from five to seven ounces, and is generally dark brown. While the male (cock) exhibits a conspicuous white throat and white eye stripes, the female (hen) is buff colored.

Bobwhite quail are among the leading game birds bagged in the Ouachita Mountains. They are well adapted to life on the farmland margins where, between agricultural wastes and natural forage, they can find abundant food. Brushy fence rows provide both protection from predators and access to forage areas. Although the best quality quail hunting occurs on privately owned land in the Arkansas and Red river valleys where grain is grown, quail enthusiasts can also assume that most of the mountain public hunting areas, the state forests, and the national forests will provide fairly good hunting opportunities.[11]

When hunting in heavy cover, most quail hunters use a bird dog.

WATERFOWL

While the heavily forested Ouachita Mountains are not a prime waterfowl habitat, thousands of ducks and geese funnel down the bordering rivers including the Red and Arkansas. Among these

Wild turkey. Courtesy of Oklahoma Game and Fish Department.

Mallard ducks. Courtesy of Oklahoma Game and Fish Department.

Duck hunting. Courtesy of Oklahoma Game and Fish Department.

feathered migrants, mallards are more prevalent, but pintails, teal, and wood ducks are also quite common.[12] Snow geese and white-fronted geese are bagged in modest numbers.

The best waterfowl hunting occurs near border rivers and large reservoirs; backwater swamps and oxbow lakes bordering the Arkansas and Red rivers offer especially good hunting opportunities.

DEER

The white-tailed deer is the most popular large game animal in the Ouachitas. While bucks (males) can weigh 75 to 300 pounds and the smaller does (females) can weigh from 50 to 200 pounds, most of the deer killed in the Ouachita Mountains typically weigh between 120 and 160 pounds.[13] Deer can live in woodlands, swamps, and farmlands though they prefer second growth woods where they can feed primarily on twigs and shrubs. When available, acorns are their favorite food. Found in every county in the Ouachita region, the total deer population probably exceeds 250,000.

Deer were abundant when the region was first settled; however, the cutting and burning of forests, commercial hunting, and poaching activities severely decimated the population. By the 1920s the white-tail population had become so small that hunting seasons were closed in many areas. Through breeding-stock transplants and habitat management, the deer population has once again become large enough to permit hunting.

Although most deer hunting occurs on private land, the national forests, state forests, and public hunting areas also provide quality opportunites. The Caney Creek and Fort Chaffee Wildlife Management areas are especially noted for large quantities of deer and high yields of trophy animals.[14] In all these areas, the better hunting environments are found in remote interior districts.

COTTONTAIL RABBITS

The cottontail rabbit is usually about thirteen to sixteen inches long with two-and-a-half- to three-inch ears. It is typically brown or gray with white feet and tail. Most of the cottontails in the Ouachitas weigh from two to four pounds.[15]

Deer herd. Courtesy of Arkansas Fish and Game Commission.

Bow hunting. Courtesy of Oklahoma Game and Fish Department.

Generally found in briar patches, brush piles, and well-developed fence rows, the cottontail is most productive in the border districts of the Ouachitas, particularly the northwest, where farmlands provide a mixture of woodlots and covers. Because the national and state forests are more heavily forested, they provide rather poor rabbit hunting opportunities.

SQUIRRELS

Three kinds of squirrels are found in Arkansas and Oklahoma: the gray squirrel, the fox squirrel, and the flying squirrel.[16] The gray squirrel is normally six- teen to twenty inches long including the tail, and has a white underbelly. The fox squirrel, which is the largest of the three varieties, ranges from nineteen to thirty inches long including the tail and is usually a yellowish-rust color, with orange shading on the underbelly. Occasionally a solid black variety may be encountered. The small gray or brown flying squirrel, which is only ten inches including its flattened tail and has large eyes, is not a game species.

Squirrels are found in large numbers along the northern and western borders, but gray squirrels are also found in the heavily forested interior districts. Some

Squirrel. Courtesy of Arkansas Fish and Game Commission.

of the very best hunting lands are in the national and state forests and the public hunting areas. Autumn and spring hunting seasons are allowed in Arkansas and Oklahoma.

COYOTE

The coyote has become increasingly common in the western Ouachitas in recent years. The typical coyote weighs twenty to fifty pounds and is reddish gray to gray with rusty legs, feet, and ears. Although similar to a dog, the coyote has a bushier tail and a more pointed nose. As the number of coyotes has grown, they have become popular for pelts and provide considerable sport for hunters, especially those with trailing hounds.

OPOSSUMS

The opossum, or 'possum, is the only North America mammal with a pouch for its young, much like that of the kangaroo. It is best known for its ability to "play possum," or play dead, when hurt or cornered.

Opossums range from twenty-four to forty inches long, including a nine to twenty-inch tail, and weigh nine to thirteen pounds. They are about the size of a house cat, but have heavier bodies, shorter legs, and a more pointed nose. The opossum's face is white with black, paper-thin ears. The body is whitish-gray to black, and the tail is rat-like. The opossum is numerous and widely distributed throughout the Ouachitas. It is trapped primarily for its pelt.

RACCOONS

The raccoon, ringtail, or just "coon," is probably the most common furbearer in the region. It provides considerable recreation for those who like to use their dogs to chase them. Coon hunters' asso-

Raccoon. Courtesy of Arkansas Fish and Game Commission.

Coon hunting. Courtesy of Arkansas Fish and Game Commission.

ciations are numerous throughout the region and coon dogs are traded and sold at prices that often seem unbelievable to the uninitiated.

Raccoons are medium-sized animals, ranging from twenty-six to forty inches long, including an eight to twelve inch tail, and weighing twelve to thirty-five pounds. With a salt-and-pepper-colored body, their distinctive features are a black mask over the eyes and alternating rings of yellowish-white and black on the tail.

Raccoons are found almost everywhere within the Ouachitas including both the hills and the bottomland woods. They are trapped and hunted for their pelts as well as for sport.

SKUNKS

There are two skunk species found in the Ouachita region, the striped skunk and the spotted skunk, which is also known as the civet cat.

The striped skunk averages about twenty to thirty inches long, including the tail, and weighs from six to fourteen pounds. It is black with a narrow white stripe up the middle of its forehead and a wide white area on the back of the neck which usually divides into a V at the shoulder and continues as two stripes down the back. The tail may or may not be white-tipped. The spotted skunk, on the other hand, is smaller; it ranges from thirteen to twenty-three inches long including the tail, and weighs just one to two pounds. It is black with a white spot on the forehead, one under each ear, and four broken white stripes along the neck, back, and sides. The tail has a white tip. The color patterns of both these skunks may vary considerably, with different proportions of black and white.

Both species are more numerous in the border areas than in heavy forests. They are trapped primarily for their pelts.

MINKS

The mink is one of the most valuable furbearers native to the Ouachitas. It is seventeen to twenty-six inches long including a bushy tail about five to nine inches long and weighs one to three pounds. Males tend to be larger than females. Minks live throughout the region; however, they are seldom seen because of their nocturnal habits. Minks are taken primarily by trappers who sell their pelts.

BEAVERS

The beaver is the master engineer of the animal world. Its dams, lodges, canals, and tunnels are expertly built for its own benefit. Ranging from thirty-four to forty inches long, including the tail, most beavers weigh from thirty-six to sixty pounds. They are rich brown with a naked, scaly, paddle-shaped tail.

The beaver is found region-wide, though it is probably most numerous in the eastern and southern Ouachitas where it often causes considerable damage to property by building dams and flooding water-adjacent lands and destroying valuable timber along lakes and streams. Beavers are taken primarily by trappers.

FOXES

There are two fox species found in the Ouachitas, the gray fox and the red fox. The gray fox is thirty-two to forty-five inches long including the tail, and weighs seven to thirteen pounds. It is salt-and-pepper gray above with rust-colored-sides, feet, and legs. The gray fox's tail is bushy with a black tip. In contrast, the red fox is thirty-six to forty-one inches long and weighs ten to fifteen pounds. It is reddish yellow on its back with a white belly, and black legs and feet. Its bushy tail is white tipped. Both varieties are found throughout the mountains, although the gray fox seems more numerous. They are taken primarily by trappers and hunters who chase them with dogs.

BOBCAT

The bobcat, bay lynx, or wildcat is probably the best known, wild member of the cat family. It averages thirty to thirty-five inches long including a five-inch tail, and weighs fifteen to thirty-five pounds. Its coloration ranges from pale to reddish brown with black streaks and spots. It has a black-tipped tail, and one white spot on each black ear. Bobcats are found throughout the region and are probably more common than most people realize.

VENOMOUS SNAKES

Many people have an unreasonable fear of snakes; they often think every snake is dangerous. The majority of North American snakes are not only harmless, but also beneficial. Of the several dozen species of snakes inhabiting the Ouachitas, only five are venomous: the copperhead, the western cottonmouth, the western pygmy rattlesnake, the timber rattlesnake, and the coral snake. Both species of rattlesnakes are most numerous in Oklahoma; the cottonmouth is confined mostly to Arkansas, and the copperhead is found throughout the region. All of the Ouachita Mountains' venomous snakes are most active at night, and none are usually aggressive.

Most snake bites occur when people try either to kill or to handle snakes. Each year about 8,000 people are bitten by venomous snakes in the United States. Perhaps 12 die, which amounts to a fraction of 1 percent. By comparison, approximately 120 people die of beestings, and 150 die after being struck by lightning.

The likelihood of being bitten by a snake can be greatly reduced by following a few simple rules:

1. Stay away from areas where there may be a concentration of venomous snakes, such as swamps, marshes, and cliffs.

2. Wear protective footgear in areas where venomous snakes may be encountered. Thick leather or rubber boots or high-top hiking shoes can help protect feet, ankles, and lower legs.

3. Never reach under rocks or logs. Rather than stepping directly *over* rocks or logs, step *on* them first, before continuing.

4. Step lively when hiking. Carefully inspect the ground, particularly around large rocks or logs, when you stop and especially before sitting down.

5. Wear rubber boots when fishing in streams that harbor cottonmouths. If a cottonmouth should fall into the canoe or boat, don't panic—get to shore and flip the snake out with a paddle. Efforts to kill the snake in the boat may cause boaters to be bitten or to fall into the water.[17]

6. Avoid any snake not easily identified as nonvenomous.

Except for the coral snake, the venomous snakes in Arkansas and Oklahoma are pit vipers; they have an opening, or sensory pit, on each side of the head (see fig. 2) and enlarged, hollow teeth called fangs. While pit vipers have elliptical pupils, harmless snakes have round pupils.

The victim of a venomous snakebite will normally show two puncture wounds at the site of the bite; sometimes, however, only one fang mark may be present (harmless snakes leave small toothmarks in the shape of a v). In the event of a venomous snakebite, seek medical attention immediately.

Anyone planning to spend time outdoors should learn the color and mark-

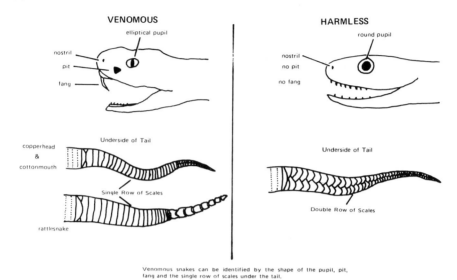

Figure 2. Recognizing Venomous Snakes. *Adapted from:* Roger Conant, *A Field Guide to Reptiles and Amphibians of Eastern and Central North America,* 2d ed. (Boston: Houghton Mifflin, 1975), plate 34 and Tom R. Johnson, "Missouri's Venomous Snakes," *The Missouri Conservationist,* June, 1979, 5.

ings of the venomous snakes to be able to identify and avoid them.

Copperhead (*Agkistrodon contortrix*)

The copperhead, which is perhaps the region's most common venomous snake, will reach twenty-four to twenty-six inches long. They usually make their homes on rocky hillsides and along the edge of forests; in the latter case, they can be found among the trees and heavy brush. Copperheads also may be found in the vicinity of abandoned farm buildings. Their diet consists of mice, lizards, small snakes, and frogs.

Western Cottonmouth (*Agkistrodon piscivorus leucostoma*)

The cottonmouth is a heavy-bodied, dark-colored, semiaquatic snake, thirty to forty-two inches long. The precise coloration may be black with little or no pattern, or dark brown with some even darker crossbands on the back. The mouth lining is white, which has led to the common name, "cottonmouth."

The cottonmouth, or "water moccasin," a dangerously venomous snake that can deliver a fatal bite, is known to exist in two quite different habitats. In eastern Arkansas, they live in wetland habitats, including swamps, oxbow lakes, ponds, ditches, sloughs, and bayous. In the Ouachitas, they occur in rocky streams and river sloughs. Many of the region's harmless water snakes are often mistaken for cottonmouths and are needlessly killed. Cottonmouths are primarily fish eaters, but also eat frogs, other snakes, lizards, and rodents.

Western Pygmy Rattlesnake (*Sistrurus miliarius streckeri*)

At just fifteen to twenty inches in length, the pygmy is the smallest North American rattlesnake. It has a skinny tail with very small rattles, is generally light grayish to brown, and has a row of small, dark brown spots down the back and similar spotting on each side. Most specimens also have a rust-colored stripe down the back. In the Ouachitas, this small snake prefers to live under rocks in brushy areas. It is so secretive, few people ever encounter one. Pygmy rattlesnakes prey on small lizards, snakes, frogs, and mice. Although their bite is seldom fatal, a victim should still seek immediate medical attention.

Timber Rattlesnake
(*Crotalus horridus*)

The Ouachita Mountains' largest venomous snake, the timber rattler reaches lengths averaging three to five feet. Its coloration generally is tan or yellowish-tan, and the markings along the back are dark brown. There is often a rusty-brown to yellow stripe down the back.

This rattlesnake prefers to live in rocky, hilly, and forested regions. It eats rodents, rabbits, squirrels, and other small mammals. Although timber rattlesnakes are dangerously venomous, there are usually very few cases of rattlesnake bites in the region in any one year.

ARKANSAS AND OKLAHOMA HUNTING REGULATIONS

Regulations vary somewhat in Arkansas and Oklahoma regarding legal equipment, bag limits, possession limits, and special fees for each game animal. Likewise, open seasons vary from state to state and from year to year. Hunters should request the most recent hunting regulations from the wildlife agencies at the addresses listed below:

Arkansas Game and Fish
  Commission
2 Natural Resources Drive
Little Rock, Arkansas 72205
Telephone (501) 223-6300

Oklahoma Department of Wildlife
  Conservation
1801 North Lincoln Boulevard
Oklahoma City, Oklahoma 73105
Telephone (405) 521-3851

License regulations for hunting on national forest lands are the same as those for the respective states. Information pertaining to any special hunting regulations on national forest lands may be obtained by contacting the Forest Service district offices or the central offices listed previously.

Floating and Fishing Ouachita Streams

The Ouachitas are blessed with magnificent water resources. Two great rivers—the Arkansas and the Red—flow along the northern and southern boundaries of the region. Other, largely spring-fed Ouachita rivers and streams flow outward from the interior of the region into these two major systems. Among the most important streams draining northward to the Arkansas River are the Poteau, Fourche LaFave, and Petit Jean. The rivers flowing southward as part of the Red River system include: the Ouachita, Saline, Little Missouri, Little River, Glover, Mountain Fork, and Kiamichi. There are also twenty public reservoirs with a combined shoreline of over three thousand miles, and several private lakes that offer fishing for a fee.

Because of the variety, the Ouachita Mountains' angler has a wide choice of fishing opportunities. From wilderness streams to popular lakes, from wading and casting to trolling from boats, from fishing the bank of a quiet cove to fishing from the air-conditioned docks provided on some lakes, nearly everyone's personal preferences can be satisfied.

Opportunities for headwaters fishing, which is among the most exciting kinds, are plentiful in the Ouachita Mountains. When it rains, the water that does not seep into the ground runs off in little rivulets; to this is added water from the area's many springs; as they join together, they form a headwater stream, which is by far the clearest, coolest, and most beautiful of running waters.

Since mountain headwaters are "young," they possess few of the soil nutrients usually leached from the watershed; as a consequence, they support relatively few insects and plants that, in turn, serve as fish food. With limited food, the number of fish surviving in the headwaters is relatively small, but they are hardy, swift, and cunning—an attractive combination for many sport fishermen.

Some of the finest angling opportunities in the midsection of the United States are found in the Ouachita streams. Smallmouth bass, longear sunfish, and rock bass are most abundant in the cold, fast water where the mountain streams have their greatest gradient. As the current slackens downstream and long quiet pools replace the riffles, largemouth bass, bluegill, and green sunfish become predominant; even farther downstream, in the deeper, slower and more turbid waters, is the habitat of the crappie, carp, buffalo, and shad as well as eel and flathead catfish.

Altogether, the Ouachitas have an extremely rich fish inventory consisting of over 150 species and subspecies. This great diversity is explained partially by the area's great waterways, especially the Arkansas, Red and the Ouachita rivers, having served as highways for fish distribution throughout the ages. Man has supplemented the natural variety by introducing such species as carp and rainbow trout.

GAME FISH

Even with scores of different species of fish in the Ouachita Mountain waters, the prized game fish number only about a dozen; without a doubt, the most desired species are bass, in several varieties. The largemouth black bass, also known locally as "big-mouth" or "green" bass, inhabits all the region's lakes and streams. It has a cannibalistic

Bluegill. Courtesy of Arkansas Fish and Game Commission.

nature and possesses excellent game and food qualities when caught. The small-mouth black bass, also known locally as "bronze" or "brown" bass, is found primarily in the swift-running, clear, and cold streams. It is a high quality, highly valued game fish that readily responds to both artificial and live bait.

The spotted black bass closely resembles the largemouth with its mottled lateral line, but it derives its name from the dark spots that form definite rows below the lateral line. It can offer a thrilling fight when hooked since it tends to seek the bottom. The rock bass, locally known as "red-eye" or "goggle-eye," also offers a courageous battle when taken in fast water on light tackle. The white bass, which is a native to the larger streams and deep lakes in the region, is also referred to as the "striped" or "bar" bass. They spawn in deep water and travel in schools as adults, feeding near the surface and readily taking minnows or artificial bait.[1]

Another popular game fish is the crappie; two species, black and white, are caught in quiet, warm, and shallow embayments, particularly where there is considerable brush or driftwood. Crappie take artificial and live baits readily and can provide spirited fishing action when an angler is lucky enough to encounter a school.

The green sunfish, locally known as the "black perch" or "sun perch," will respond to minnows or flies, but most are caught with worms. They are commonly found in the shallow arms of lakes and in small streams. Bluegills, another popular prey, favor streams, shallow lake water, and ponds.

The walleyed pike, also known as "jack salmon" or "jack fish," is taken in the clearer streams and deeper lakes. With an elongated and yellowish body, the walleye may exceed eight pounds. An active fish, it will rise to both artificial and live bait and offers a good fight when hooked.

Two species of channel catfish—spotted and blue—are found in all of the Ouachitas' major streams and lakes. Highly prized as food, most of the channel catfish are caught by game fishermen. Some, however, are the target of commercial fishing operations.

Although rainbow and brown trout

Rainbow trout. Courtesy of Arkansas Fish and Game Commission.

are not native to the Ouachitas, they have adapted to suitable environments wherever they have been introduced. The tailwaters below Lake Ouachita, Lake Hamilton, and Lake Greeson are the best trout fishing locales.[2] Both species, which can grow to more than ten pounds, are great battlers and excellent table fare.

FLOAT FISHING

Float fishing, always popular with local residents, gained outside enthusiasts after the railroads were constructed and increasing numbers of visitors were introduced to the Ouachita Mountains' scenic attractions. Prior to World War II, most float trips were semiwilderness outings in which those who were fortunate enough to participate, used wooden, flat-bottomed johnboats and were led by paid fishing guides. Following the war, and particularly since the mid-1960s, Ouachita Mountain river floats have become self-led, family and group sporting activities that may or may not involve fishing.

These changes in the nature of floating excursions have been stimulated by several related developments. The availability and increased use of automobiles have greatly increased the accessibility of the floatable Ouachita region streams. Any location open to the public has become a potential spot for starting ("putting-in") and ending ("taking-out") one's trip. Wooden johnboats have been largely replaced by first fiberglass, and then aluminum varieties that are lighter, more maneuverable, and more easily transported. Although the aluminum johnboat is now considered the best selection for float fishing, aluminum canoes are more popular among those who float for recreation and sport. The flat-bottomed johnboat is the best choice for novice floaters. Many local families own their own canoes; however, as a service for those who do not, particularly for those from large cities like Little Rock, Fort Smith, Tulsa, Oklahoma City, Memphis, Dallas, Texarkana, and Shreveport, numerous canoe rental businesses have sprung up along the more popular Ouachita streams.

The popularity of canoeing and float fishing in the Ouachita Mountains does not rival that of the spring-fed Ozark upland streams to the north. It is becoming more commonplace, however, to see as many as a dozen canoes embarking from the many popular put-in spots. The Ouachita streams are especially attractive to families since they are so low in summer that families with small children can travel by canoe with little fear. The few places that present difficulty for the novice occur at shallow riffles where the concerned paddler can usually step out and lead the canoe around the trouble spot. There is an abundance of natural but primitive camping sites on the streams' many gravel bars.

The sporting aspects of canoeing consist of successfully running the intermittent rapids.[3] Where waters cut into a particularly resistant layer of rock, a series of rapids or a shoal is usually formed. Most of the Ouachita streams consist of a series of relatively calm pools broken by an occasional rapid where the streams cut through one of the many resistant ridges. Excitement and anticipation can run high when one is within

earshot of the rushing waters as they plunge down a boulder-strewn rapid. The most challenging rapids are found in the water gaps, or miniature canyons, that develop where streams cut through long ridges.

The scenery along Ouachita riverways is truly spectacular. Those content to float along at a leisurely pace are able to comprehend fully the breathtaking landscape: limpid pools are so clear that the lunker fish may be seen at depths of eight to ten feet; gnarled oaks mottled with lichens cling to craggy bluffs and hover over dilapidated farmhouses and abandoned fields; towering pines cast their shadows across quiet cerulean waters.

Floating can be both a pleasurable and exciting experience for the angler or canoeing enthusiast, if a few simple safety rules are obeyed.

1. Since the unexpected can happen on a free-flowing river, it is always advisable to wear a life jacket.

2. The chances of serious problems can be reduced by avoiding a river during its flood stages. Watch for sudden rises in the water when on the river. Also select campsites with the possibility of sudden changes in river conditions in mind; in particular, camp at least four feet above water level.

3. It is always best to canoe with others; groups of three or four canoes are desirable.

4. Be aware of, and stay within, the canoer's ability. Do not overreach. When uncertain, walk the canoe through or around the rapid.

5. Always scout a large rapid before attempting to run it.

6. Know first aid and carry a well-stocked first-aid kit.

7. Dress appropriate to the season. Be certain shoes will not hinder

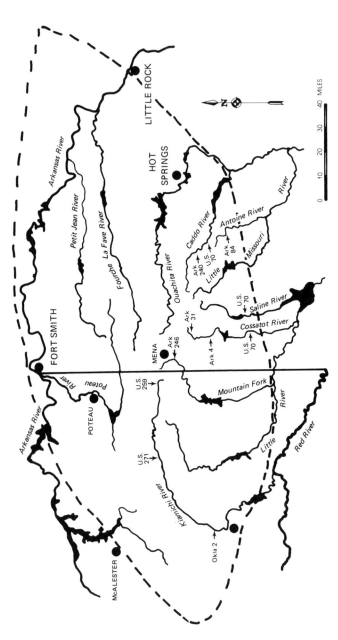

Map 10. Float Fishing and Canoeing Streams. *Adapted from:* Arkansas State Highway Map (Little Rock: Arkansas State Highway and Transportation Department, 1985); Arkansas County Highway Maps, Scale 1:126,720 (Ouachita Mountain counties) (Little Rock: Arkansas State Highway and Transportation Department, 1978); Oklahoma Official State Transportation Map (Oklahoma City: Oklahoma Department of Transportation, 1985); Oklahoma County Highway Maps, Scale 1:126,720 (Ouachita Mountain counties) (Oklahoma City: Oklahoma Department of Transportation, 1978); information leaflets, (Little Rock: Arkansas Department of Parks and Tourism, 1985 and Oklahoma City: Oklahoma Tourism and Recreation Department, 1985).

swimming; tennis shoes are the ideal choice.

8. In case the craft capsizes, hold onto it since it has excellent floatation. If the water is extremely cold, or worse rapids are ahead, one may wish to swim to shore. When holding on to a canoe, get on the upstream side to avoid being trapped against downstream obstacles.

9. Never stand up or abruptly change positions while in the craft.

10. Get familiar with the stream, and check the water conditions before embarking. Be aware of all the potential trouble spots and plan exactly where to take-out.

11. Keep all gear stored as low as possible in the center of the craft.

12. All valuables should be placed in waterproof, airtight containers. Store a change of dry clothing in a waterproof container such as a plastic garbage bag. Wallets and important papers, including fishing licenses, can be carried in plastic sandwich bags.

13. Always carry spare paddles. One extra paddle per canoe is a good rule; however, more may be needed on an especially long trip.

14. Carry out whatever is carried in. Do not bury litter; bag it and carry it out.

15. Improperly controlled fires can be a tremendous hazard. Be certain that any fire is out before leaving. Drown the coals and scatter the ashes.

16. Since much of the land along Ouachita streams is in private ownership, respect the property rights of others. Always obtain permission before entering private property; trespassing can have serious consequences.

17. For the novice or family, the flat-bottomed johnboat may be the best selection. It is more stable, one can stand or change seats with minimum risk, and it has more capacity for gear and people.

Float streams are among the great treasures of the Ouachita Mountains; they differ from the streams of most other regions by more vicissitudes in flow than those that are fed by large springs, such as those in the Ozarks. Ouachita streams are alternately "haystack-filled" torrents and gentle, quiet, meandering waterways that are ideal for inexperienced canoeists and safe family outings.

The region's tightly folded geologic strata exert strong influences on stream courses and gradients. Where streams originate high in the Ouachitas, they fall rapidly as they flow through narrow gorges cut into resistant rock ridges. In their middle courses, the streams wind slowly across erosional valleys, cutting from time to time through intervening ridges in rock-walled gorges. As the mountains give way to flatlands, the identity of the streams changes as the current slows and gravel and sandbars become more common.

Many of the Ouachita Mountains' most popular canoeing and fishing streams, the location of the rivers, and their major access roads are depicted in map 10. Detailed county road maps, showing gravel roads and highways, are available from the Arkansas State Highway and Transportation Department, 10324 Interstate 30, Little Rock, Arkansas 72209, telephone: (501) 569-2000, and the Oklahoma Department of Transportation, 200 N.E. 21st Street, Oklahoma City, Oklahoma 73105, telephone: (405) 521-2554. Detailed U.S. Geological Survey topographic maps are available from the Arkansas Geological Commission, 3815 W. Roosevelt Road, Little Rock, Arkansas 72204, telephone: (501) 371-1488 or 663-9714, and the Oklahoma Geological Survey, 830 Van Vleet Oval, Norman, Oklahoma 73019, telephone: (405) 325-3031. Names of the appropriate maps are provided with the following descriptions of each river.

Antoine River

The Antoine River rises in the southern foothills of the Ouachita Mountains about midway between Lake Greeson and the DeGray Reservoir. It follows a southerly course until joining the Little Missouri River on the Gulf Coastal Plain, just southeast of Murfreesboro. The terrain it passes through varies from rolling to level and is densely wooded. The stream bed ranges from gravelly to sandy.

The Antoine can be floated best during high-water periods in the spring and fall. Access points include: a bridge on a farm-to-market road east of Shawmut, a gravel road leading north from Arkansas 26 about a mile west of Antoine, and the Highway 29 bridge to the east of Antoine. The county highway maps for Clark and Pike counties (Arkansas) are the best sources of information on the available access roads.

Caddo River

The Caddo River rises in the mountains of western Arkansas, flows eastward to the north of Missouri Mountain, turns to a southerly course at Norman, and cuts through Nelson Mountain in a rockbound water gap south of the town of Caddo Gap. It then flows southeasterly past Glenwood and DeGray Lake. The Caddo is swift and clear as it flows through this beautifully wooded mountain terrain.

The Caddo River can be floated from Norman to Glenwood in the spring, and from Glenwood to DeGray Lake at most other times. Popular access points are found at the highway bridges at Norman and Caddo Gap, on Arkansas 240 to the south of Caddo Gap, from U.S. 70 at Glenwood, at Arkansas 923 to the north of Amity, and on Arkansas 84 northeast of Amity. The county highway maps for Montgomery, Clarke, and Pike counties (Arkansas) have detailed information on access roads.

Cossatot River

The Cossatot River rises in west-central Arkansas, seven miles southeast of Mena, and flows southward to a point where it merges with the Little River, fourteen miles southeast of DeQueen. Along the way it is temporarily checked by Gillham Dam, located six miles northeast of Gillham.

The Cossatot flows through especially picturesque country in its upper reaches; scenic mountain vistas overlook a sea of mixed pine and hardwood forests. The Cossatot plunges rapidly as it cuts through several narrow gorges with ragged rock pinnacles jutting out in midstream. The water gaps create cascading falls and lengthy rapids. Below Gillham Dam, the river gradually loses its mountain stream identity as it courses peacefully across the southwest Arkansas flatlands.

The whitewater conditions that prevail in the upper Cossatot make canoeing very hazardous; even experienced canoers should approach this stretch with extreme caution and proper equipment. Late summer dry spells often make the river above Gillham Lake difficult, if not impossible, to float. The river bed in this section is rock floored; gravel bars are common in the lower reaches of the river.

Southeast of Mena, the Cossatot River borders the western extreme of the Caney Creek Wilderness, a 14,433 acre area set aside by the Eastern Wilderness Areas Act of 1975. Motorized vehicles are not allowed within the Wilderness, but a nine-mile trail, designed for hikers and backpackers, runs east to west following Caney Creek through the heart of the area and connects forest roads 38 and 31.

Canoes can be launched from public

land on the upper Cossatot near several highway bridges. Arkansas 31, which follows the Cossatot River gorge through the margin of the Caney Creek Wilderness Area, also offers several places where canoes can be put in. Other access points on the upper Cossatot include bridges on Arkansas 176 west of Hartley, on Arkansas 4 east of Wickes, and on a gravel road east of Duckett. Below Gillham Dam, canoes can be launched at several other bridges: from Arkansas 380 east of Gillham, on a timber access road northeast of DeQueen, off U.S. 70–71 east of DeQueen, and from Arkansas 24 west of Lockesburg. Highway maps for the Arkansas counties of Polk, Howard, and Sevier provide details for each of these access roads.

Fourche LaFave River

The Fourche LaFave River rises on the north flank of Fourche Mountain in western Arkansas and flows eastward until it joins the Arkansas River. It occupies the valley south of Dutch Creek River. The stretch from U.S. 71 to Nimrod Lake usually can be floated only in the spring and fall when the water level is high. This upper portion of the river can be reached most easily from several bridges and short access roads off Arkansas 28.

Downstream from Nimrod Lake, the Fourche LaFave meanders sluggishly past the Harris Brake Game Management Area. River accesses include the Nimrod Lake Project Use Area, several short roads leading off Arkansas 60, and bridges on Highways 9, 216, and 113. The best sources of detailed information on access roads in this area are the general highway maps for Conway, Scott, and Yell counties (Arkansas).

Glover River

The Glover River rises in the mountains of northwestern McCurtain County (Oklahoma), and flows due south until it joins the Little River. It is the only float stream in the Oklahoma Ouachitas that is unobstructed by a dam. The water levels are sufficiently high for exciting canoeing in spring and fall; however, during July and August, the rapids and shoals are usually too shallow for trouble-free floating. The river can be reached from gravel roads near Battiest, from private timber access roads leading north from Oklahoma 3, and from the bridge on Arkansas 3 near Glover. The highway map for McCurtain County, Oklahoma, shows the location of several timber access roads and farm-to-market roads leading to the river.

Kiamichi River

The Kiamichi is the most popular float stream in the Oklahoma Ouachitas. It originates on the south slope of Rich Mountain, northwest of Mena, Arkansas, only a stone's throw from the headwaters of the Ouachita River. The Kiamichi flows to the west before turning south to join the Red River. The scenery on the upper reaches—including memorable Rich Mountain and Talimena Drive—is unequaled in the entire Ouachita Mountain Province.

Even though the Kiamichi is one of the largest streams in the region, it is subject to low water during the summer months. The best floating opportunities occur in the spring and fall when the water levels tend to be higher. During these times, the upper Kiamichi is challenged by experienced canoeists who are treated to several thrilling whitewater hazards; for this reason, it is not recommended for the inexperienced floater.

Access points on the Kiamichi include: the highway bridges on Oklahoma 259 at Big Cedar and Oklahoma 271 at Clayton; numerous points along the section of Oklahoma 2 that parallels the river; the bridges on Oklahoma 271 north of Antlers; on Oklahoma 7 east of Antlers; and on U.S. 70 east of Hugo. Highway maps for LeFlore, Pushmataha, and Choctaw counties (Oklahoma) show the location of several timber access roads and farm-to-market roads that also lead to the Kiamichi.

Little Missouri River

The Little Missouri River rises in the Missouri Mountains in western Montgomery County, Arkansas. The headwaters area is notable for its spectacular pine-forested ridges and valleys. The river cascades through a series of whitewater gorges, including the extraordinary Little Missouri Falls in its upper stretches, before leveling off for a more leisurely journey across the southern Piedmont to Lake Greeson. Because the upper portion has several treacherous

spots, it is best left to experienced canoeists and kayakers.

The Little Missouri can be reached conveniently from several points on Arkansas 43, which follows the Little Missouri gorge, and from bridges on Arkansas 84 west of Langley, and a timber access road about two miles downstream from Arkansas 70 east of New Hope. Highway maps for Montgomery and Pike counties (Arkansas) furnish details on these river access roads.

Mountain Fork River

The Mountain Fork River rises in the mountains west of Mena, Arkansas, and flows southwest into Oklahoma, before turning south to Broken Bow Lake. The stretch from the bridge on Arkansas 246 to Broken Bow Lake is floatable when high-water periods occur in spring and fall. During these times, the river offers

Fishing on the Mountain Fork River at Beavers Bend State Park. Photo by Fred W. Marvel. Courtesy of Oklahoma Tourism and Recreation Department.

Canoeing on the Mountain Fork River in southeastern Oklahoma. Photo by Fred W. Marvel. Courtesy of Oklahoma Tourism and Recreation Department.

a fast and challenging float not recommended for novice canoeists. Canoes can be put in at the Arkansas 246 bridge and taken out either at Smithville or downstream at a gravel road that crosses the north end of the lake. The river, below Broken Bow Lake from Beaver Bend State Park to U.S. 70, is floatable year round. Highway maps for Polk County (Arkansas) and McCurtain County (Oklahoma) show the location of several timber access roads that offer approaches to the river.

Petit Jean River

The Petit Jean River originates north of Poteau Mountain in western Arkansas and flows eastward until it joins the Arkansas River. It drains the broad valley between Magazine Mountain and Dutch Creek Mountain, which helps to account for the Petit Jean River's sluggish flow.

The river normally can be floated from Blue Mountain Lake to its mouth. Access points include the Blue Mountain Lake outlet use area, a bridge on a gravel road two miles southeast of Belleville, and several bridges on Arkansas 27, 7, and 154. The general highway map of Yell County (Arkansas) provides detailed information on the location of access roads.

Poteau River

The Poteau River rises in the valley between Dutch Creek Mountain and Poteau Mountain in western Arkansas, flows westward into Oklahoma, and then heads north to join the Arkansas River at Fort Smith. The upper river, from Waldron, Arkansas, to Wister Lake, can be floated only during fall and spring when the water is sufficiently high. Access to this stretch is fairly easy from several short roads that intersect with Arkansas 28.

The lower portion of the river, from

Wister Lake to Fort Smith, is sluggish, yet it attracts a steady clientele of fishermen from Poteau and Fort Smith. This section of the river is accessible from several bridges in the vicinity of Poteau and Fort Smith and from short access roads leading off U.S. 59 and Oklahoma 9. The best sources of detailed information on access roads are the county highway maps for Scott County, Arkansas, and LeFlore County, Oklahoma.

Ouachita River

The Ouachita River begins as a mountain stream in the Acorn Basin, northwest of Mena, Arkansas, and meanders eastward through the heart of the Ouachita National Forest to a point just west of Hot Springs, where its flow is checked by three man-made dams. The river then flows southward into Louisiana, with inputs along the way from the Caddo, Little Missouri, and Saline rivers. The Ouachita is the largest and longest river within the Ouachita Mountain region.

While the upper waters are confined by a number of small gorges cut in the ridges, between the ridges quiet pools prevail. Farther downstream the channel widens and its pools deepen. Once again, fall and spring are the best seasons to float since the flow of the river is restricted during the dry summer months; only the stretch immediately above Lake Ouachita is usually floatable year-round.

A unique, educational float is the sixteen-mile Ouachita Geo-Float Trail from the Lake Ouachita Spillway Recreation Area to Beady Mountains Recreation Area (see chapter 5).[4] A guidebook can be obtained at the Lake Ouachita Visitors Center which describes the many unique geologic features encountered on this excursion.

Above Lake Ouachita, direction signs clearly identify put-in sites and access roads; convenient mileage signs have been placed by the U.S. Forest Service

to inform canoeists of distances to downstream landings and public use areas—nine camping areas and landing points allow travelers to select float trips of varying distance and challenge; the upper river can be reached from gravel roads leading north from Arkansas 8 at Board Camp, and south from Arkansas 88 at Cherry Hill, Pine Ridge, and Ogden. Highway maps for Montgomery and Polk counties include details on river access roads; maps of access areas that are maintained by the National Forest Service are available from the Ouachita National Forest, P.O. Box 1270, Hot Springs, Arkansas 71901, telephone: (501) 321-5202.

Saline River

The Saline River originates in the eastern Ouachita Mountains in central Arkansas and flows southward where it converges with the Ouachita River, east of El Dorado. The Saline is the only completely free-flowing stream, unobstructed by dams, in the entire Ouachita River Basin. From its source to its mouth, the Saline covers some 204 miles.

The upper mountainous reaches of the Saline River consist of a series of fast-running shoals interspersed with small pools; the most rockbound and hazardous shoals are found in the mountain canyons. As the Saline flows southward and the mountains give way to flatlands, the river gradually changes. While gravel and boulders cover the Saline's bottom in the mountainous sections, the channel consists of sand and mud in the flatlands.

The upper reaches provide an excellent habitat for smallmouth bass; the downstream species include largemouth bass, crappie, bluegill, and channel catfish. Between Benton and Jenkins Ferry State Park is especially popular among float fishermen.

Services and supplies are readily

available in the many surrounding towns; access to the river is fairly easy from road and highway bridges. Below the Arkansas 84 bridge west of Athens is a fairly easy section to float; it can be reached from four or five all-weather gravel roads located between the Arkansas 84 bridge and the bridge on Arkansas 4, north of Dierks. Below Dierks Lake, the river can be reached most easily from the Horseshoe Bend Use Area and from bridges on Arkansas 24 west of Nashville, and Arkansas 27 west of Mineral Springs. The general highway map of Howard County, Arkansas, is the best guide to the roads and access points on the Saline River.

Lakes of the Ouachita Province

At the turn of the century, there were only about one hundred large (over 500 acres) reservoirs in the United States. By 1968, however, the total was twelve hundred, combining for about 9.4 million acres at conservation levels.[1] Seven years of active construction later (1975), there were more than 12 million acres of water in man-made reservoirs throughout the United States.

These lakes were built for a variety of reasons including flood control and hydroelectric power generation. While many have remained virtually undeveloped, others have created an environment which has stimulated recreation and tourist-related opportunities. Often the attraction of swimmers, boaters, and anglers has created the need for support services such as restaurants, motels, campgrounds, shopping outlets, and entertainment facilities.

In the Ouachitas, the many narrow gorges cutting through the mountain ridges have made reservoir construction nearly ideal. There are now twenty-three major lakes in the Ouachitas; although most are small- to medium-sized, they cover more than two hundred thousand acres with a shoreline in excess of three thousand miles.[2] True to the national experience, several of these lakes have become popular for tourists and sportsmen; others remain pristine and relatively isolated.

Almost without exception, the Ouachita lakes, like their Ozark neighbors to the north, offer very good fishing possibilities. With devoted anglers in mind, a brief discussion of basic information—the habits and habitats of the most common fish in Ouachita lakes, an inventory of the area's twenty-three major reservoirs including (1) historical information and statistical data, (2) the overall geography of each lake, (3) the location of public access points, and (4) a discussion of the general fishing conditions— and specific information pertaining to camping and recreational facilities near each of these lakes is included.

The productivity of lakes varies considerably; although the average fish harvest from lakes in the United States falls between fifteen and twenty pounds an acre, the range runs from less than a pound to over one hundred pounds an acre.[3] This variability holds true in the Ouachitas where some lakes resemble sluggish rivers and others are more like natural lakes. Because the man-made reservoirs are fed by rivers and streams, they tend to have higher rates of water exchange (flow through). With forested watersheds, which cut back on the amount of silt and organic matter that is washed into a reservoir, most of the mountain lakes do not age as fast as those whose watersheds consist of cultivated areas.

To enhance fishing prospects in the Ouachitas, biologists have searched for a better understanding of the fluctuations of fish populations; horsepower limits and prudent boating restrictions have decreased areas where high speeds are permitted, thus enabling anglers to pursue their sport relatively undisturbed throughout the year.

WHY FISH DO NOT ALWAYS BITE

Most avid fishermen are aware that lake productivity tends to decline through the summer season, due in part to changes in food supplies and dissolved oxygen. In the spring or fall when the water is cool and the dissolved oxygen is adequate at all depths, fish feed normally, and they generally show an interest in live bait and artificial lures (see figure 3).

During the summer, most of the fish are crowded into the upper strata of the reservoir because the dissolved oxygen has been depleted by the bacterial decay of plant and animal remains. Because the surface waters are warmer, many species become less active and thus harder to catch, though some fish, like crappie and striped bass, stay as deep as possible even in the summer.

FISHING RULES

Since fish tend to follow predictable patterns, the knowledgeable angler can almost always locate a good fishing spot. Henry ("Hank") Small, a renowned fishing consultant and professional bass tournament participant, offers the following suggestions for those who wish to increase their chances of success:

1. Try fishing after a warm rain, especially in runoff areas.

2. Go home during a cold rain because fishing will generally be poor.

3. The best fishing occurs when the barometer is rising, especially between 29.90 and 30.10.

4. When the barometer is steady or falling, fish as close to cover as possible.

5. Fishing directly after the passage of a cold front will seldom produce good results.

6. Use red baits in the spring and white baits in the fall.

7. Fish deep water from 11:00 A.M. to 3:00 P.M.

8. Start fishing at the points first. If the results are unsatisfactory, work back into the coves.

9. Fishing is best during a full or new moon. It is also very good during the first and last quarters.

10. Match the catch. Use baits that have a similar appearance to fry fish.

11. Throw spinner baits when the water level is rising.

12. Throw crank baits when the water level is steady.

13. Use jig and frogs, worms, spoons, and other such baits when the water level is falling.

14. Cloudy days are better for fishing than sunny days.

15. When fish are surfacing, throw top-water or buzzing baits.

16. Always vary retrieves.

17. Fish bottom baits in a "lift and drop" manner.

18. "Bump the stump" or bump the lure into as many objects as possible to attract fish. This is especially true in the summer months.

19. Fish in the direction that the wind is coming from.

BAITS AND LURES

Live baits are most popular with Ouachita Mountain anglers. Minnows, crayfish, and worms, which constitute the bulk of the diet for most game fish, are especially good bait; grubs taken from rotten logs are also excellent bait. Those in pursuit of bass, channel catfish, and sunfish will find that grasshoppers are very effective.

Mussels (fresh water pearls), found in many gravel bars and riffles, are attractive for redhorse and sucker fishing. Around the turn of the century, mussels from Arkansas rivers were removed from the shells and the shells were used in downstream button factories; this practice almost destroyed the mussel population. Today, the mussel is used only as bait and the shells are discarded.

Experienced Ouachita fishermen usually have their favorite places to collect bait. Minnows and crayfish can be seined

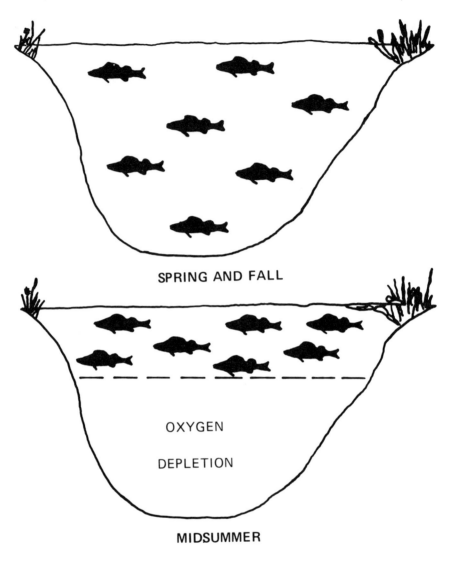

SPRING AND FALL

OXYGEN

DEPLETION

MIDSUMMER

(Above) Reservoir conditions in spring and fall. An abundant supply of dissolved oxygen and cool water permit fish distribution at all depths. These conditions usually furnish better fishing.

(Below) Reservoir conditions in midsummer. Dissolved oxygen has been depleted in the deeper water through bacterial decomposition. Most fishes are now confined to the warm surface strata where there is a renewed supply of dissolved oxygen. Under these conditions deep-trolling is a waste of the fisherman's time. Too-warm surface waters may cause the fishes to cease feeding.

Figure 3. Why Fish Don't Bite. *Adapted from:* Noel P. Gist, ed. *Missouri: Its Resources, People, and Institutions* (Columbia: Curators of the University of Missouri, 1950), 146.

Day's end. Courtesy of Oklahoma Game and Fish Department.

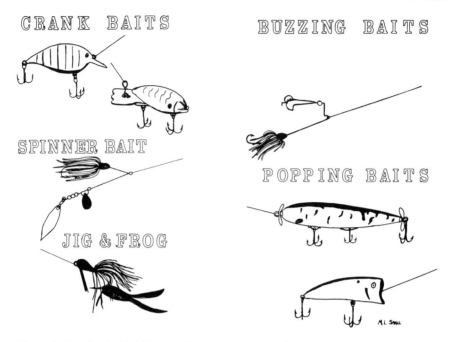

Figure 4. Popular Artificial Lures. Drawn by M. L. Small.

in shallow waters of small tributary streams; shallow pools of less than two feet with rocky bottoms are especially productive since many prey animals hide there.

Earthworms come from humus-rich soils. Often "fishing fever" develops among those who uncover earthworms while gardening in March and April. Since small worms can frequently be dug out of leaf litter in log jams, one may replenish the supply of live bait while on a long float trip.

The baits used to attract and hook catfish are varied; beef and chicken livers, chicken entrails, stink baits, and dough baits are most popular. Experienced anglers know that flathead cats prefer live bream or minnows, while most blue cats are hooked on cut shad.

The most popular artificial lures are crank baits, buzz baits, spinner baits, popping baits, rubber worms, and jig and frog baits (see figure 4). The colors, materials, and exact forms of these lures are extremely varied, as each angler seems to have a favorite "sure thing."

THE HABITS AND HABITATS OF OUACHITA LAKE FISH

White Bass

The white bass is one of the sportiest fish in Ouachita lakes. When other fish are not to be found, the white bass will often save the day by providing a good fight and delicious fillets.

During the early spring, white bass congregate under bridges, along rock causeways, and in deep pools at the mouths of rivers and creeks running into the lakes; when the water temperature reaches 60°F, they begin to spawn, releasing and fertilizing their eggs in the open water. The white bass is most vulnerable to fishermen's hooks just before and during its spawning run.

Crappie

Crappie fishing is best in March and April when spawning takes place in brushy coves. The black crappie (calico bass) prefers reasonably clear water; the more abundant white crappie is more tolerant of turbid water. Both species seldom stray far from brush piles, flooded timber, and weeds.

Since crappie are easily spooked by heavy line, oversized hooks, and impatient techniques, many crappie anglers resort to ultralight spinning gear; this permits the sportsman to handle the two to six pound line and light lures. Eight-and-a-half feet fly rods provide better reach when working in the brushy areas, and six pound line is strong enough to straighten the hook when it gets snagged. Inexperienced anglers should consult an operator of a boat dock or bait and tackle shop before stocking up with gear designed to catch two- to three-pound crappie.

Minnows are deadly bait for crappie; simply hook the minnow through the back and set one or two feet beneath the surface on small bobbers during spawning season. Jigs are also highly effective, but are customarily used when fishing among brush and timber; however, they can be hung under a bobber and then worked in open water. Since crappie bite with a light touch and have a "paper mouth" which is easily torn, successful anglers must develop a *feel* for the correct hit.

Walleye

The walleye or jack salmon is one of the finest tasting fresh water fishes, and therefore one of the most eagerly sought species. The best time to fish for walleye is during the March and April spawning season when this normally individualistic fish tends to congregate together. Like their salmon cousins, the walleye "run" up creeks and rivers to the most shallow spots during the spring; during this migration, their activity sometimes becomes intense enough to turn the water white.

Under normal circumstances the walleye travels in small and loose aggregations; they are wide-ranging and decidedly nocturnal fish that move to shoal areas to feed during the late evening and night hours before returning to deeper waters for the daylight period. For this reason, both bank and boat fishermen can have success by night fishing, which requires a few special precautions. The following tips, taken from *Outdoor Oklahoma,* are advice for the inexperienced night fisherman:

1. Always follow the area's boat and water rules and laws.
2. Check boat lights (or lantern) and fuel levels before launching. Take along at least one powerful flashlight.
3. Be sure everyone aboard wears an approved personal floatation device at all times.
4. Be prepared for rain and cooler temperatures. Take appropriate clothing.
5. Don't fish an unfamiliar lake or river for the first time after dark. Choose small areas where the fish-holding structure is well enough known to fish it "blind." When moving to another spot, go slowly.
6. Use a depth finder if possible. Most action will occur in or near shallow water, where boat hazards are most likely.
7. Take along a compass.
8. Let someone know the intended fishing location and time of return.
9. When severe weather is likely, don't go fishing. Summer thunder-

Night fishing. Courtesy of Oklahoma Game and Fish Department.

storms can move in very quickly and lightning and high winds can pose a threat to those on the water.[4]

Black Bass

The black bass is the unquestioned king of the Ouachita aquatic community. A supreme predator, it offers both tremendous fishing enjoyment and excellent eating. As a tribute to its popularity, there are numerous bass fishing clubs throughout the United States, and expert anglers compete in professional bass fishing tournaments for thousands of dollars worth of prizes. Recreational or competitive, black bass fishing in the Ouachitas offers an interesting and very challenging sport.

Three species of black bass are found in the Ouachita region: the largemouth bass (*Micropterus salmoides*), the smallmouth bass (*Micropterus dolomieui*), and the spotted (Kentucky) bass (*Micropterus puntulatus*). While all three are native to Ouachita waters, their habitat preferences vary. The largemouth bass, the most abundant of the black bass, favors lakes, reservoirs, and larger rivers. Prime largemouth habitats exist in swampy oxbow lakes and reservoirs.[5] Smallmouth and spotted bass, on the other hand, live well in impounded water but prefer fast-moving streams with rocky bottoms. When encountered in reservoirs and lakes, these two species are found almost exclusively in rocky areas.

The best time to fish for black bass is late spring. Although there are times when bass will strike anything that moves, the most productive artificial lures are jigs and spinner baits of any size and color; purple, black, or blue plastic worms; and dark colored crank baits. Minnows are usually the most successful natural bait.

Most bass fishermen favor six to eight pound test line on a spinning, spin cast, or bait casting reel. A limber but sensitive rod and small lures also are popular.

Catfish

Catfish are another target of Ouachita sport fishermen. All four of the area's main species (channel, blue, bullhead, and flathead) spend most of their time near the bottom of the lakes scavenging for aquatic insects, crayfish, dead fish, and almost anything edible. As catfish grow to two or more pounds, they also begin preying on live fish.

Catfish favor extreme upper ends of coves and reservoirs, where water coming from rivers and streams carries significant quantities of food and where temperature and oxygen concentrations are favorable. Another popular catfish habitat is the shallow mud flats where the primary attraction is the presence of large quantities of aquatic insects and crustaceans; catfish also like to concentrate along rock lines (riprap) of dam embankments.[6]

The most productive fishing occurs from April through November when the water temperature ranges from 60° to 80°F. At other temperatures activity de-creases among all the catfish varieties, and though some may be caught, the challenge is certainly greater.

Because of the catfish's varied diet, a wide variety of baits are effective. Live baits include earthworms, minnows, crayfish (crawdads), and frogs. Though attractive year round, they are most productive during the spring fast-fishing season when water levels are rising. Stink baits, on the other hand, are more effective when the fish must be coaxed into biting, i.e., when the water is either very cool or very warm. There are dozens of stink-bait recipes, and each has its supporters and detractors. Several different stink baits are sold at boat docks and bait stores.

The best tackle to use for catfish is a matter of personal preference. The rod should be fairly stiff with a sensitive tip; the stiffness is necessary when one is lucky enough to hook a particularly large fish. Channel catfish may be as large as twenty-five pounds, while flatheads and blues can exceed forty-five pounds. For this reason, a fairly heavy line—eight-to-twelve-pound test monofilament line is preferred by many catfish anglers—and stout hook should be used. Free-to-slide egg or swivel sinkers allow the fish to take the bait and move off without feeling the weight of the sinker; the weights should only be large enough for an adequate cast and holding the bait in place.

For beginning fishermen, a closed-faced spinning reel is inexpensive and easy to use, yet dependable, and durable. Because live bait is so effective in catfish fishing, many experienced anglers prefer bait casting reels; open-faced spinning reels are not well adapted to bait fishing.

Setlines are a popular alternative to rod-and-reel fishing; several varieties are utilized including trotlines, limblines, throwlines, and banklines. The hook or hooks are baited and the line thrown out into the water; one or both ends of the line are anchored to floats, stakes, or limbs. Since the fish hook themselves when they take the bait, this form of fishing can be very productive at night when catfish are more active.

In both Arkansas and Oklahoma, all setlines must carry the owner's identification. They must be checked at least once every twenty-four hours, and it is unlawful to use them within 150 yards of any dam. Good sportsmanship requires that all lines be removed once the fishing is concluded. The remnants of markers and old lines detract from the aesthetic value of the surroundings, and hooks left in the water can be extremely hazardous to swimmers and boaters.

Trout

The tailwater portion of the Little Missouri River, just below Greeson Dam, is periodically stocked with rainbow trout. Brown trout have been released in the Albert Pike Recreation area in hope that a continuing population can be established. Trout are also found a few miles below the dams at Lakes Ouachita, Hamilton, and Catherine, and three other dams on the Ouachita River, near Hot Springs, also support trout fishing.

The best trout fishing usually occurs in the winter, but many boat docks and marinas located near dam sites offer night fishing trips during the summer.

The most common nongame fish in the Ouachitas are: gar, carp, buffalo, drum, and suckers; these fish may be taken by setlines, gigs or spears, snagging, bow and arrow, and noodling (i.e., by using one's hands), in addition to rod-and-reel techniques.

Game fish may be caught *only* by hook and line attached to a pole or rod, or by using a setline; regulations regarding use of gigs, spears, and spearguns are different in the two states. For specific details of the fishing regulations, contact the respective game management agencies:

Arkansas Game and Fish
 Commission
2 Natural Resources Drive
Little Rock, Arkansas 72205
Telephone (501) 223-6300

Oklahoma Department of Wildlife
 Conservation
1801 North Lincoln
Oklahoma City, Oklahoma 73105
Telephone (405) 521-3851

The license regulations for fishing on national forest lands are identical to those of the respective states. Any specific questions regarding fishing on these federally controlled lands can be obtained from the Forest Service district offices and from the central offices:

Ouachita National Forest
P.O. Box 1270
Hot Springs, Arkansas 71901
Telephone (501) 321-5202

Ozark National Forest
P.O. Box 1008
Russellville, Arkansas 72801
Telephone (501) 968-2345

State and federal game and fish laws are applicable to the U.S. Army Corps of Engineers' lakes. Boats on any of these lakes for more than three days must obtain a permit from the resident engineer. Information regarding the use of these and other man-made reservoirs can be obtained from:

Blue Mountain Lake (See Nimrod-
 Blue Mountain Lakes Project)

Broken Bow Lake Project Manager
United States Army Corps of
 Engineers
P.O. Box 730
Broken Bow, Oklahoma 74728
Telephone (405) 494-6374

Lake Catherine
Arkansas Power and Light Company
Public Affairs Office
P.O. Box 551
Little Rock, Arkansas 72203
Telephone (501) 371-4082 or
372-3900

Conway Lake
Arkansas Game and Fish
Commission
2 Natural Resources Drive
Little Rock, Arkansas 72204
Telephone (501) 223-6300

Dardanelle Lake Project Manager
United States Army Corps of
Engineers
P.O. Box 1087
Russellville, Arkansas 72801
Telephone (501) 968-5008

De Gray Lake Project Manager
United States Army Corps of
Engineers
30 IP Circle
Arkadelphia, Arkansas 71923
Telephone (501) 246-5501

De Queen Lake (see Milwood Tri-
Lakes)

Dierks Lake (see Milwood Tri-
Lakes)

Eufaula Lake Project Manager
United States Army Corps of
Engineers
Route 4, P.O. Box 5500
Stigler, Oklahoma 74462
Telephone (918) 799-5843

Greeson Lake Project Manager
United States Army Corps of
Engineers
Route 1
Murfreesboro, Arkansas 71958
Telephone (501) 285-2151

Lake Hamilton (See Lake Catherine)

Hugo Lake Project Manager
United States Army Corps of
Engineers
P.O. Box 99
Sawyer, Oklahoma 74756
Telephone (405) 326-3345

Robert S. Kerr Lake Project
Manager
United States Army Corps of
Engineers
HC-61, Box 419
Sallisaw, Oklahoma 74955-9445
Telephone (918) 775-4475

Maumelle Lake
Little Rock Municipal Water Works
P.O. Box 1789
Little Rock, Arkansas 72203
Telephone (501) 372-5161

McGee Creek Lake Project Manager
Bureau of Reclamation
McGee Creek Lake
P.O. Box 71
Farris, Oklahoma 74542
Telephone (405) 889-7307

Milwood Tri-Lakes Resident Office
De Queen Project Office
Route 1, Box 37A
Ashdown, Arkansas 71822
Telephone (501) 584-4161

Nimrod-Blue Mountain Lakes
Project Manager
United States Army Corps of
Engineers
Plainview, Arkansas 72857
Telephone (501) 272-4324

Ouachita Lake Project Manager
United States Army Corps of
Engineers
P.O. Box 4
Mountain Pine, Arkansas 71956
Telephone (501) 767-2101

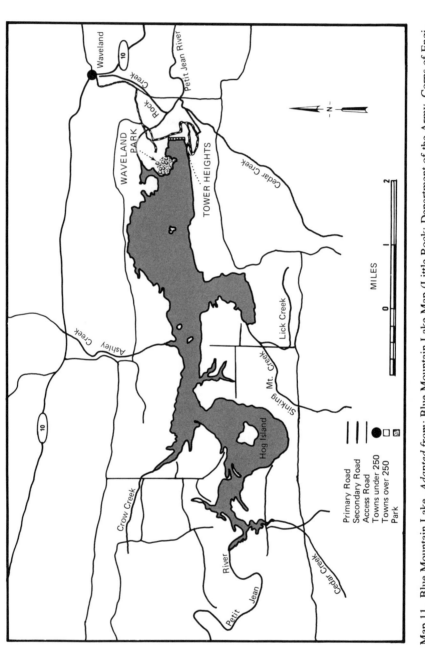

Map 11. Blue Mountain Lake. *Adapted from:* Blue Mountain Lake Map (Little Rock: Department of the Army, Corps of Engineers, Little Rock District, 1974).

Ozark Lake Project Manager
United States Army Corps of
Engineers
Route 1, Box 267R
Ozark, Arkansas 72949
Telephone (501) 667-2129

Pine Creek Lake Project Manager
United States Army Corps of
Engineers
Route 1, Box 400
Valliant, Oklahoma 74764
Telephone (405) 933-4239

Sardis Lake Project Manager
United States Army Corps of
Engineers
P.O. Box 129
Clayton, Oklahoma 74536-0129
Telephone (918) 569-4131

Winona Lake (See Maumelle Lake)

Wister Lake Project Manager
United States Army Corps of
Engineers
Route 2, Box 7B
Wister, Oklahoma 74966-9501
Telephone (918) 655-7206

FISHING GEOGRAPHY OF THE OUACHITA MOUNTAIN LAKES

For easy reference, the major lakes in the Ouachita region are presented in alphabetical order. Provided for each lake are: (1) historical and statistical information, (2) overall geography of the lake, (3) location of public access points, and (4) fishing conditions.

Blue Mountain Lake (see map 11)

Blue Mountain Dam is located at river mile 74.4 on the Petit Jean River, one and a half miles southwest of Waveland, Arkansas. Within the shadow of famous Mount Magazine, the surrounding coun-

Blue Mountain Lake, near Booneville, in western Arkansas. Courtesy of U.S. Army Corps of Engineers, Little Rock District.

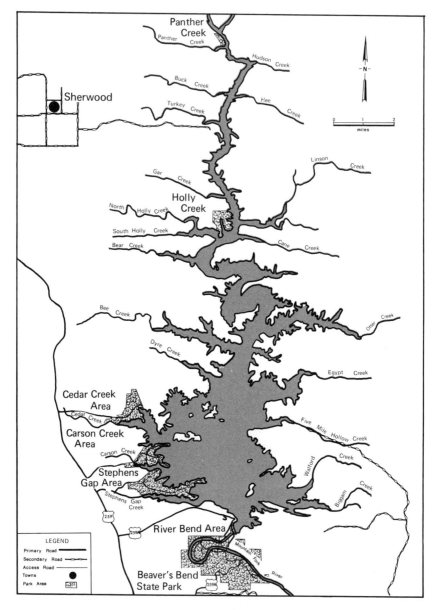

Map 12. Broken Bow Lake. *Adapted from:* Broken Bow Lake Map (Tulsa: Department
of the Army, Corps of Engineers, Tulsa District, n.d.).

tryside is so beautiful visitors are often
inspired to take leisurely hikes. The
more adventurous even search for colorful rocks and minerals.

The construction of Blue Mountain

Dam was initiated in 1940, and completed seven years later at an approximate cost of $4,770,000. The earth-fill
dam is 2,800 feet long and stands 115
feet above the stream bed. The lake,

which impounds the runoff from a 488-square-mile drainage area, stands 387 feet above mean sea level. It rises to 419 feet at flood-control pool. The normal conservation pool covers 2,910 acres (4.5 square miles) and has a 50-mile shoreline.[7]

Ever since 1947, fishermen from all parts of the nation have come to Blue Mountain Lake; they have hooked largemouth, spotted, and white bass; bream; and crappie. Since trotline fishing for catfish is usually very productive and there is no closed season, fishermen are found at the lake the year round.

Water skiing, swimming, scuba diving, and boating are also popular pastimes. Those less enthusiastic about the water enjoy basking in the sun and resting in the abundant shade of the pine and hardwood trees that surround the lake's four parks (see chapter 6 for a more detailed discussion of the area's facilities).

Broken Bow Lake (see map 12)

Broken Bow Dam is in McCurtain County, Oklahoma, approximately ten miles northeast of Broken Bow and one mile northwest of Beaver's Bend State Park. It was built between 1961 and 1969 by the U.S. Army Corps of Engineers as a multipurpose project. The lake was designed to impound the flow of the Mountain Fork River, for flood control, recreation, hydroelectric power,

Broken Bow Dam and Lake on the Mountain Fork River in southeastern Oklahoma. Courtesy of U.S. Army Corps of Engineers, Tulsa District.

water-supply supplements, and fish and wildlife habitat.

The earth embankment dam, which is 3,650 feet long and 225 feet above the stream bed, impounds a lake that is 14,200 acres (22.2 square miles). At power-pool elevation (599.5 feet above mean sea level), the lake has 180 miles of shoreline and stretches 22 miles into the Ouachita Mountain country where the unusual scenic beauty beckons to all nature enthusiasts.[8] The mountainous terrain is densely forested with a variety of pines and hardwoods, with under-cover of holly groves, beauty bushes, and a succession of flowering perennials.

Outdoor sportsmen are attracted to the area; anglers rate the fishing on the crystal-clear, island-dotted lake as among the best in the state for large-mouth bass, smallmouth bass, spotted bass, white bass, black and white crap-pie, channel and flathead catfish, and various species of sunfish.

Approximately fifty-four hundred acres of project land made available to the Oklahoma Department of Wildlife Conservation as a wildlife management area provide excellent hunting oppor-tunities. With the exception of devel-oped recreation areas, state parks, land near the dam and project structures, and lands within the McCurtain County State Game Preserve, all the project lands are open to hunters year round.

Two nature trails are available for hikers: Big Oak nature trail and Beaver Lodge nature trail. Since many species

Fishing at Broken Bow Lake. Courtesy of U.S. Army Corps of Engineers, Tulsa District.

Lake Catherine State Park near Hot Springs. Courtesy of Arkansas Department of Parks and Tourism.

of birds are native to the project lands, birdwatchers experience many interesting sightings; however, local residents often avoid the woods during the summer since ticks are also plentiful.

The Corps of Engineers and the State of Oklahoma operate ten public use areas. Beaver's Bend State Park, Carson Creek Area, Stephens Gap Area, and River's Bend Area are the most completely developed. See chapter 6 for available facilities.

Lake Catherine (see map 13)

Lake Catherine is the oldest of the Ouachita Mountain lakes. Remmel Dam, which impounds the Ouachita River to form the lake, was completed in 1924 by the Arkansas Power and Light Company[9] at a cost of $1.5 million. The lake's close proximity to Hot Springs, which already had a well-established national reputation as a recreational spa, greatly contributed to its popularity and use.

Compared to the lakes that subsequently have been created by the U.S. Army Corps of Engineers, Lake Catherine, eleven miles long with eighty miles of shoreline, is small. Because the lake is privately owned, lakefront lots have been sold for resort and second-home developments. Lake Catherine is well-known for its many fine youth camps as well as its fishing, which for more than a half century has brought success to anglers who fish for crappie, bream, largemouth bass, and channel catfish.

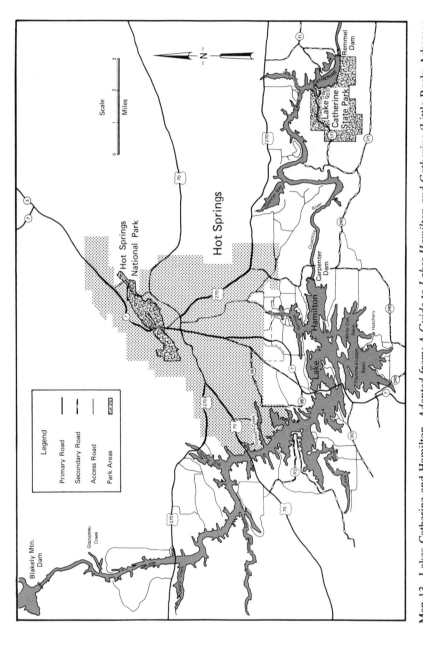

Map 13. Lakes Catherine and Hamilton. *Adapted from: A Guide to Lakes Hamilton and Catherine* (Little Rock: Arkansas Power and Light Company, Public Affairs Department, n.d.).

Water skiing on Lake Catherine. Courtesy of Arkansas Department of Parks and Tourism.

Lake Conway (see map 14)

Lake Conway is between Conway and Little Rock, in Faulkner County, Arkansas. Built in 1948 by the Arkansas Game and Fish Commission, the dam is on Palarm Creek in an area which was mostly wooded creek bottoms. Arkansas sportsmen contributed $36,000 toward the land acquisition; however, the total cost of the land and lake development was $160,047. The 6,700-acre lake is the largest ever constructed by a state wildlife agency.[10]

Lake Conway is best known for its fishing; anglers from all over the nation are drawn to its excellent bass and bream fishing. The stump- and brush-laden waters also provide excellent habitat for bluegill, catfish, and crappie. The high productivity of catfish and crappie is also partly explained by an eighty-acre nursery pond on the east side of the lake.

Lake Conway is served by fifteen commercial boat docks that handle tackle, bait, and ice, in addition to boat and motor rentals; some also have picnic and/or camping areas. Private fishing boats may be launched free at dock sites not posted to the contrary. Brannon's and Gold Creek are along Interstate 40 on the Stone Dam Creek arm of the lake; Bream's Nest, Sevier's, Lawrence's, Martin's, and Northshore are on the west shore and can be reached from access roads off U.S. 65; Paradise dock is on Stermer's pond, a western inlet; and Highway dock is off U.S. 89 near the dam. Two other docks, Adam's Lake and Palarm Creek, are situated on the eastern shore.

Dardanelle Lake (see map 15)

The Dardanelle Lock and Dam is a major part of the McClellan-Kerr Arkansas River Navigation System, which

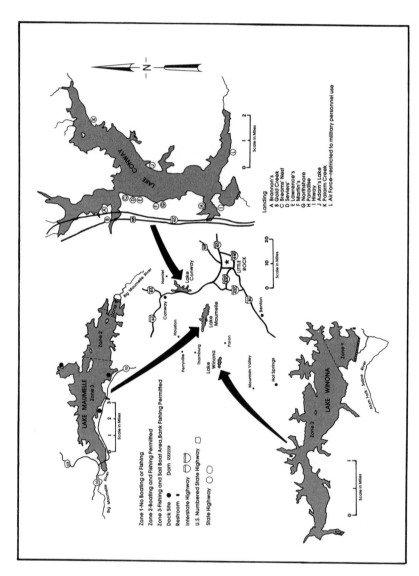

Map 14. Lakes Conway, Maumelle, and Winona. *Adapted from:* Conway Lake Map, Maumelle Lake Map. (Little Rock: Little Rock Department of Public Utilities, 1985).

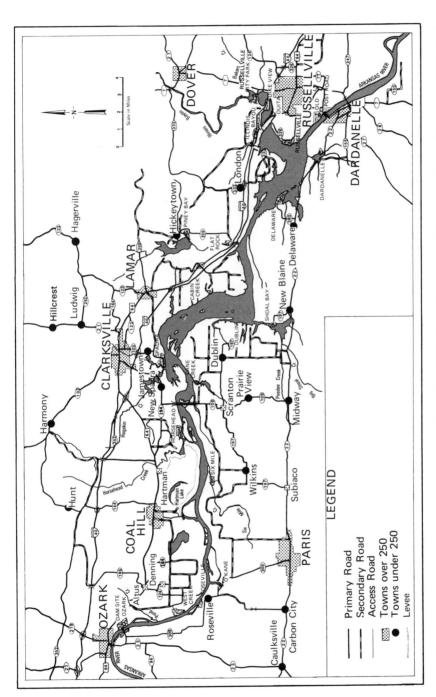

Map 15. Dardanelle Lake. *Adapted from:* Dardanelle Lake Map (Little Rock: Department of the Army, Corps of Engineers, Little Rock District, 1979).

Dardanelle Lock and Dam on the Arkansas River. Courtesy of U.S. Army Corps of Engineers, Little Rock District.

includes several multi-purpose lakes and a canalized navigation route from Catoosa, Oklahoma (fifteen miles east of Tulsa), to the Mississippi River.

The lock and dam, built between June, 1957, and November, 1969, are 338 feet above sea level, and the lake they have created covers 34,300 acres (53.5 square miles) at conservation pool.[11] On the extreme northern boundary of the Ouachita Province, Lake Dardanelle extends westward into Pope, Yell, Logan, Johnson, and Franklin counties. Two miles at its maximum width and 50 miles long, it reaches upstream to the Ozark-Jets Taylor Lock and Dam. The 315 miles of shoreline afford ample opportunities for fishing, camping, and just plain relaxing.

There is no closed season at Dardanelle. This, and the region's relatively mild winters, leads to excellent fishing opportunities the year around. White bass move into the tributary arms to spawn during the spring, normally April and May. These same backwaters are also prime catfish areas; the mudflats and standing timber in these larger arms and coves provide ideal catfish habitats. Crappie fishing is strong in Illinois Bayou, Piney Creek, Little Spadra Creek, Horsehead Creek, Six Mile Creek, Cane Creek, Shoal Creek, Delaware Creek, and Hayes Creek.

The lake's picturesque shoreline is ideal for nature and camera enthusiasts. There is an abundance of wildlife in nearby Ozark and Ouachita national forests where hunting for deer, turkey, and other game is popular.

Swimming at Greers Ferry Lake. Courtesy of U.S. Army Corps of Engineers, Little Rock District.

Camping in the Ouachitas at Nimrod Lake near Danville, Arkansas. Courtesy of U.S. Army Corps of Engineers, Little Rock District.

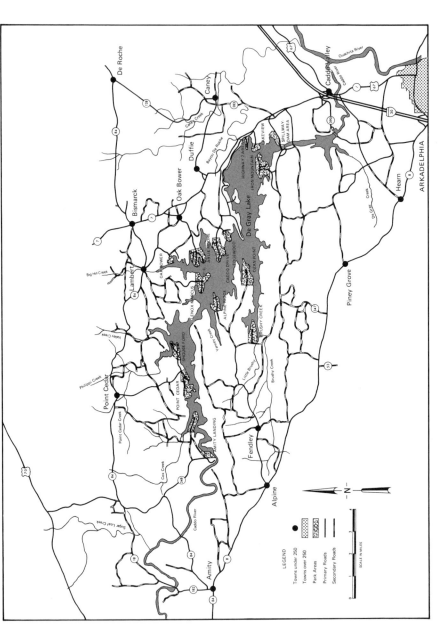

Map 16. De Gray Lake. *Adapted from:* De Gray Lake Map (Vicksburg, Miss.: Department of the Army, Corps of Engineers, Vicksburg District, 1980).

Half a dozen towns of modest size are within a mile or two of the lake and provide ample services and supplies for fishermen. Russellville, Clarksville, Ozark, and Paris are large enough to provide a range of accommodations. Detailed information on overnight lodging, restaurants, and recreational opportunities may be obtained by writing the Chambers of Commerce of these towns (see chapter 14).

Boat ramps are available at the lake's many access areas; some also have picnic tables, camping sites, and other recreational facilities. On the south shore are public access areas such as Dardanelle, Delaware, Shoal Bay, Dublin, Cane Creek, Six Mile, O'Kane, Roseville, and South Ozark. Those on the north shore include Russellville, Quita, Dikeville, Russellville City Park, Illinois, Bayou, Flat Rock, Piney Bay,

Cabin Creek, Spadra, Horsehead, West Creek, and the Ozark Dam site. See chapter 6 for information pertaining to camping and recreation facilities.

De Gray Lake (see map 16)

De Gray Dam was built between 1963 and 1972 at a cost of $63,800,000. The earth-fill dam near Arkadelphia, Arkansas, impounds the Caddo River, thus forming a lake more than 15 miles long. When filled to conservation level (i.e., the normal water level) De Gray Lake covers 13,400 acres (20.9 square miles) and provides 207 miles of shoreline.[12]

De Gray has a reputation as a lake where anglers can expect to hook largemouth bass, smallmouth bass, spotted bass, black and white crappie, channel and flathead catfish, and several varieties of sunfish. Two fairly large arms and several smaller inlets provide excel-

Aerial view of De Gray Lake. Courtesy of U.S. Army Corps of Engineers, Vicksburg District.

De Gray Lake Resort State Park on a forested island in 13,400-acre De Gray Lake. Courtesy of Arkansas Department of Parks and Tourism.

lent crappie and bass fishing. The inlets and smaller coves are excellent for channel catfish, particularly after the creeks have carried a fresh supply of food into the lake. Areas of special note are the Brushy Creek Arm on the south side of the lake, Hill Creek, Benton Creek, Point Cedar Creek, and Cox Creek.

Paved access is provided at Iron Mountain, Shouse Ford, Arlie Moore, Highway 7, the spillway area, Amity Landing, Caddo Drive, and De Gray State Park. These areas provide seventeen paved ramps and seventy-nine lanes. The Iron Mountain, Caddo Drive, Arlie Moore, and Shouse Ford public-use areas are fully developed with boat ramps, camping facilities, electricity, showers, drinking water, restrooms,

picnic areas, and sanitary dump stations. See chapter 6 for details for each site.

De Queen Lake (see map 17)

De Queen Lake is on the Rolling Fork River, in Sevier County, about four miles northwest of De Queen, Arkansas. It was built by the U.S. Army Corps of Engineers between 1966 and 1977. The earthfill embankment is 2,360 feet long and rises 160 feet above the stream bed. At conservation pool, the lake stands 437 feet above mean sea level, covers 1,680 acres (2.6 square miles), and offers 32 miles of shoreline.[13]

The crystal clear lake and its picturesque surroundings invite visitors year round to enjoy fishing, boating, skiing,

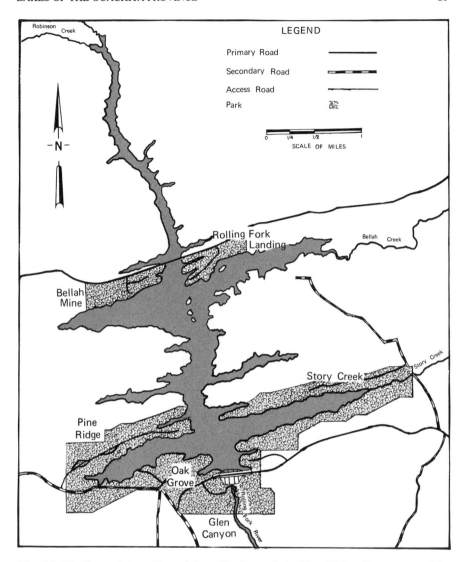

Map 17. De Queen Lake. *Adapted from:* De Queen Lake Map (Tulsa: Department of the Army, Corps of Engineers, Tulsa District, 1978).

scuba diving, picnicking, camping, hiking, and hunting. All of the shoreline is publicly owned, so boaters may go ashore wherever they wish.

The predominant fish species in De Queen lake include largemouth, smallmouth, and spotted bass; black and white crappie; channel and flathead catfish; and many varieties of sunfish. The Arkansas Fish and Wildlife Department also stocks the lake with walleye.

The unusual geography of the lake is created by the Rolling Fork River, which cuts across alternating east–west valleys

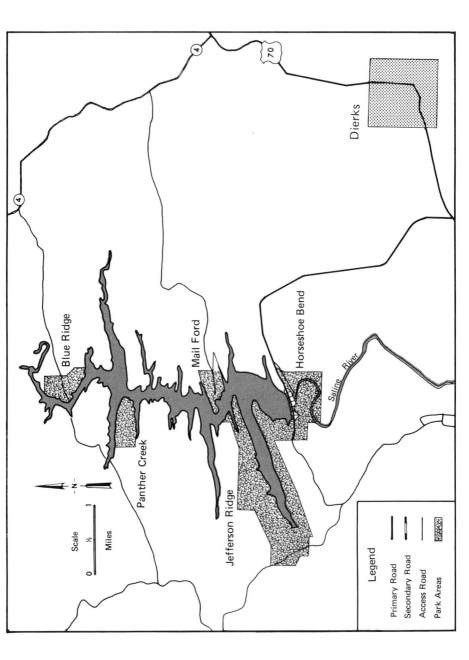

Map 18. Dierks Lake. *Adapted from:* Dierks Lake Map (Tulsa: Department of the Army, Corps of Engineers, Tulsa District, 1980).

and ridges. The flooded valleys form six symmetrical lake arms, three on each side. The Belle Creek and Story Creek arms and the upper lake on the Rolling Fork arm are excellent crappie areas during the spring.

There are seven public-use areas; Oak Grove public-use area is fully developed with boat ramps, drinking water, a picnic area, restrooms, showers, campsites, and electricity; boat ramps are available at Pine Ridge, Rolling Fork Landing, Story Creek, and Bellah Mine; Glen Canyon and Overlook areas have only drinking water and restrooms. See chapter 6 for details on facilities.

Dierks Lake (see map 18)

Dierks Lake is one of seven lakes in the Little River basin. The dam and appur-

tenant works—located on the Saline River about five miles northwest of Dierks, Arkansas, near the border between Sevier and Howard counties— were constructed between 1968 and 1976 at an estimated cost of $15.8 million. The earth-fill dam is 2,760 feet long and rises 153 feet above the river bed; the lake covers 1,360 acres (2.16 square miles) at conservation pool and has 41.5 miles of shoreline.[14]

With an attractive, heavily forested shoreline and deep, clear water, Dierks Lake and the surrounding land are appealing for outdoor recreation. The sport-fish population includes largemouth and spotted bass, crappie, and channel catfish. The downstream fishing is also excellent.

The geography of Dierks Lake is

Dierks Dam and Lake on the Saline River in west-central Arkansas. Courtesy of U.S. Army Corps of Engineers, Tulsa District.

A family gathering at a Dierks Lake camping area. Courtesy of U.S. Army Corps of Engineers, Tulsa District.

heavily influenced by the geologic structure and physiography of the Ouachita Mountains. The north-south trending main channel expands into ragged inlets that penetrate the east–west valleys which are bounded by craggy hogback ridges. Public-use areas at Blue Ridge on the east shore, Jefferson Ridge on the west shore just above the dam, and Horseshoe Bend just below the dam provide boat ramps, picnic tables, fireplaces, refuse containers, sanitation facilities, camp sites, and drinking water. See chapter 6 for details on the camping facilities.

Eufaula Lake (see map 19)

Eufaula Lake is in Oklahoma on the northwest border of the Ouachita Moun-tains. The Eufaula Dam, which impounds the Canadian River about 27 miles upstream from its confluence with the Arkansas River, is about 12 miles east of Eufaula and 31 miles south of Muskogee. The U.S. Army Corps of Engineers' project was designed for flood control, hydroelectric power, water supply, recreation, and wildlife conservation purposes. The total project, completed in 1964, cost $121,735,000. The earth embankment dam is 3,200 feet long and 114 feet above the stream bed. It impounds a 102,200 acre (159.6 square miles) lake with 600 miles of shoreline at power-pool level.[15]

The fish and wildlife resources within the Eufaula Lake district provide a variety of recreational opportunities.

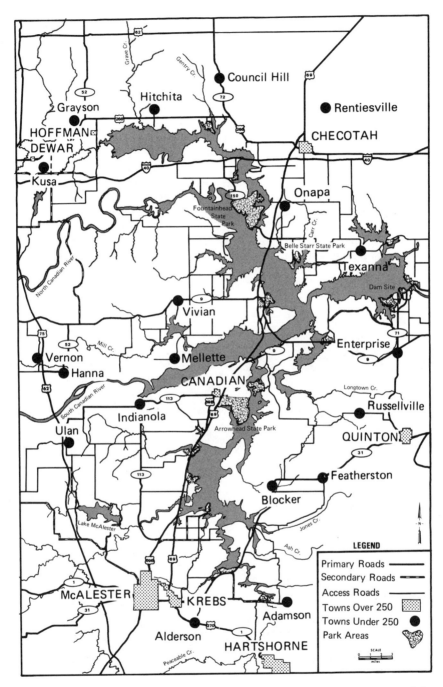

Map 19. Eufaula Lake. *Adapted from:* Eufaula Lake Map (Tulsa: Department of the Army, Corps of Engineers, Tulsa District, 1977).

Anglers can pursue striped, largemouth, and white bass; crappie; catfish; walleye; and numerous kinds of sunfishes.

By land or water, the region's natural beauty may be seen in nearly every nook and cranny of the lake; boaters may see the changing shoreline scenery of meandering chains of bays and channels set in rolling prairie backed by lofty forested hills; three picturesque nature trails are available for those who prefer to experience the many treasures by land—Belle Starr, Crowder Point, and the Terrapin Trail; and powerhouse tours are also available.

The geography of Eufaula Lake is complicated by four major arms formed by relatively large streams—North Canadian River, Deep Fork River, Canadian River, and Peaceable Creek—and smaller inlets including Duchess Creek, Mill Creek, House Creek, Coal Creek, and Ash Creek. Tree stumps and standing timber are commonplace in the main lake, about two miles above the dam, and in the upper parts of the major arms of the lake where crappie and largemouth-bass fishing are especially fruitful. Numerous bays and coves provide good feeding grounds for white bass.

Twenty-one park areas have been developed by the Corps of Engineers; the State of Oklahoma maintains two park areas that offer lodges with guest rooms, deluxe cottages, convention facilities, fishing docks, golf courses, picnic areas,

Eufaula Dam and Lake on the Canadian River in east-central Oklahoma. Courtesy of U.S. Army Corps of Engineers, Tulsa District.

Boating on Eufaula Lake. Courtesy of U.S. Army Corps of Engineers, Tulsa District.

and campgrounds. See chapter 6 for details on facilities in these parks.

Gillham Lake (see map 20)

Gillham Lake is on the Cossatot River, about six miles northeast of Gillham, Arkansas. The earth-fill dam was built as a U.S. Army Corps of Engineers' project between 1963 and 1976. It is 1,750 feet long, and stands 160 feet above the stream bed. The lake has a normal pool 502 feet above sea level that covers 1,370 acres (2.1 square miles) and a ragged, heavily forested thirty-six-mile shoreline.[16]

The irregular outline of Gillham Lake is typical of the Ouachitas; branching arms flood the lowlands between craggy ridges. The main inlets are French and White Oak creeks on the east shore and Little Coon and Opossum creeks on the west shore.

The most common sport fish are spotted bass, largemouth bass, crappie, and channel catfish. Four public-use areas—French Creek, Cossatot Point, Coon Creek, and Little Coon Creek—offer facilities and access to the lake. The Cossatot Reefs public-use area, located just below the dam, provides access to the lower Cossatot River. See chapter 6 for more details on the camping and recreational facilities at these public-use areas.

Greeson Lake (see map 21)

Another U.S. Army Corps of Engineers' project, Greeson Lake was built at an estimated cost of $12.5 million.

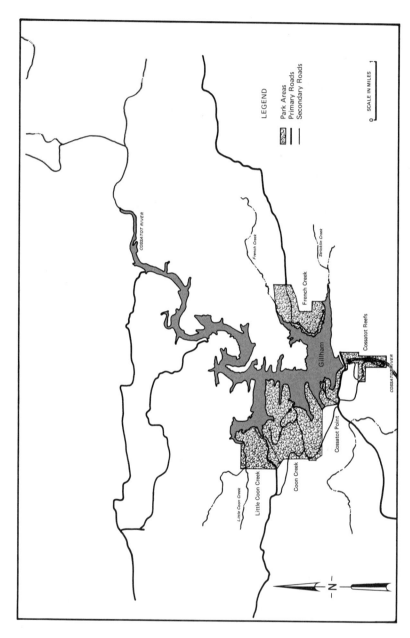

Map 20. Gillham Lake. *Adapted from:* Gillham Lake Map (Tulsa: Department of the Army, Corps of Engineers, Tulsa District, 1980).

Gillham Dam and Lake on the Cossatot River near Gillham, Arkansas. Courtesy of U.S. Army Corps of Engineers, Tulsa District.

Located in Pike County, Arkansas, near Murfreesboro, it developed when the Narrows Dam impounded the Little Missouri River.

Greeson Lake extends up the river's valley about 11 miles and has a surface area of approximately 2,500 acres (3.9 square miles) at minimum power pool (conservation pool). The shoreline is approximately 70 miles. The elevation of the lake at conservation pool is 504 feet above mean sea level.[17] As is the case with most of the Ouachita lakes, Greeson Lake is operated for flood control, hydroelectric power, conservation, and recreational purposes.

The configuration of Greeson Lake is determined by the ridge and valley topography of the immediate region.

Branching off from the main north-south channel, several long arms are formed in the east-west trending tributary valleys; land formed by resistant rock ridges separates these lake arms. The larger tributary arms, named for the creeks that enter their upper reaches, on the east shore are Cowhide Creek, Shelton Creek, Laurel Creek, Bear Creek, Self Creek, and West Fork, and on the west shore are Rock Creek, Little Creek, Hog Creek, and Parker Creek.

Greeson Lake largemouth and small-mouth bass, crappie, white bass, bluegill, and channel and flathead catfish fishing is excellent. The upper portions of the tributary arms are especially good for bass and crappie, particularly during spring spawning runs. Wide-

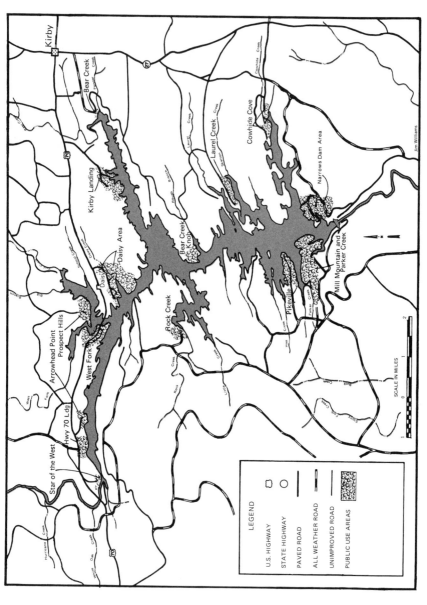

Map 21. Greeson Lake. *Adapted from:* Greeson Lake Map (Vicksburg, Miss.: Department of the Army, Corps of Engineers, Vicksburg District, 1977).

LEGEND

U.S. HIGHWAY

STATE HIGHWAY

PAVED ROAD

ALL WEATHER ROAD

UNIMPROVED ROAD

PUBLIC USE AREAS

SCALE IN MILES

Kirby

Bear Creek

Kirby Landing

Daisy Area

Daisy

Arrowhead Point

Prospect Hills

West Fork

Hwy 70 Ldg

Star of the West

Rock Creek

Bear Creek Knob

Laurel Creek

Cowhide Cove

Pikeville

Mill Mountain and
Parker Creek

Narrows Dam Area

Jim Williams

spread standing timber and rocky bottoms provide excellent shelter. Following heavy rains, the upper arms and coves provide excellent channel catfish angling. Since the west shore of the lake consists of the Greeson Lake Public Hunting Area, many visitors are drawn to the excellent hunting prospects.

Sixteen public use areas serve Greeson Lake; fourteen of these have boat ramps. The Prospect Hills area serves the Ouachita Council of the Boy Scouts of America. See chapter 6 for additional information on camping and recreational facilities.

Hamilton Lake (see map 13)

Hamilton Lake is the second of the two hydroelectric power projects built by the Arkansas Power and Light Company.

Completed in 1931, Carpenter Dam, named for a well-known Ouachita riverboat captain, is 115 feet high, 1,165.6 feet long, and cost over $7 million to construct. Hamilton Lake is 24 miles long, covers 9,000 acres (14 square miles) and possesses 240 miles of shoreline.[18]

The shores of Hamilton Lake are privately owned and developed with resorts, boat docks, estates, and second homes. The irregular outline of Hamilton Lake results in dozens of expansive arms and embayments. There are several wooded islands in the lake; the largest of these are Big Goat Island, Little Goat Island, and Long Island.

Many sheltered coves and rocky points provide varied fish habitats: crappie, largemouth bass, bream, and channel

Lake Hamilton near Hot Springs. Courtesy of Arkansas Department of Parks and Tourism.

Seaplane for aerial sightseeing at Lake Hamilton near Hot Springs. Courtesy of Arkansas Department of Parks and Tourism.

catfish are the longtime favorites of Hamilton Lake anglers. More recently, walleye have been introduced. Trout are stocked in the upper part of the lake where cool water is released from Lake Ouachita and the Arkansas Game and Fish Department maintains a trout hatchery just below the dam. (These trout, released in the tail waters of Hamilton Lake, also provide good fishing downstream in Lake Catherine.)

In addition to fishing, the lake offers boating, swimming, skiing, and sailing. Party barges and ski-boat rentals are available; several marinas are joined by a seaplane base during the summer; amphibian "ducks" offer tours of both the lake and the surrounding mountains.

Because Hamilton Lake is privately owned and older than the U.S. Army Corps of Engineers' lakes, it is lined with hundreds of private homes, some luxuriant showplaces, others modest to rustic; condominiums; mobile home parks; commercial campgrounds; restaurants; and other tourist attractions.

Hugo Lake (see map 22)

Hugo Lake is a part of the U.S. Army Corps of Engineers' flood-control system for the Red River. The dam and appurtenant works were completed in 1974 at a cost of approximately $37 million. The 10,200 foot dam impounds a lake that covers 13,250 acres (20.7 square miles) at conservation (normal) pool, with a shoreline that is 110 miles long.[19]

The geography of Hugo Lake is rather simple; the main channel is aligned north-south with numerous small coves and rocky points. Salt Creek and Long Creek are the two large arms on the western shore. Because nearly half of the lake's area (or about 5,000 acres) is uncleared, fishermen are provided a refuge from skiers. Boating lanes have been cut through the uncleared upper half of the lake and designated by an identification code; the east-west lanes utilize a system of numbers while the north-south lanes use letters; the old river channel is marked "RC."

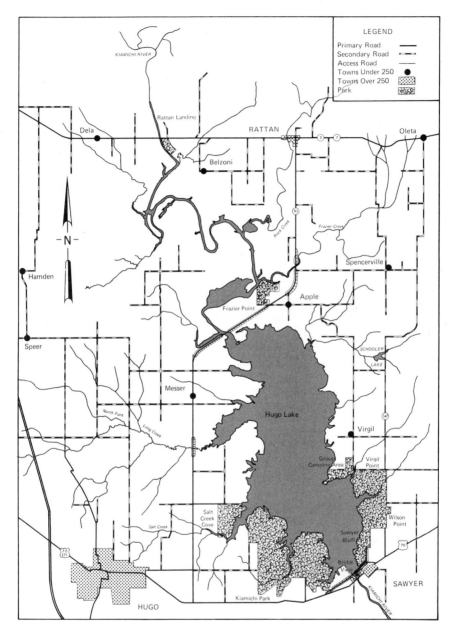

Map 22. Hugo Lake. *Adapted from:* Hugo Lake Map (Tulsa: Department of the Army, Corps of Engineers, Tulsa District, 1978).

Hugo Dam and Lake on the Kiamichi River near Hugo, Oklahoma. Courtesy of U.S. Army Corps of Engineers, Tulsa District.

Water sports on Hugo Lake in southeastern Oklahoma. Photo by Fred W. Marvel. Courtesy of Oklahoma Tourism and Recreation Department.

Hugo Lake has earned a good reputation among sportsmen; nearly all of the main fish species native to the Ouachita region can be caught there, including largemouth bass, spotted bass, crappie, white bass, channel and flathead catfish, bluegill, sunfish, buffalo, carp, and drum. The upper lake is surrounded by an 18,196-acre wildlife management area administered by the Oklahoma Department of Wildlife Conservation. Maps of the public hunting areas are available from the Hugo Resident Office and the Tulsa District Office of the Corps of Engineers.

There are nine public-use areas serving Hugo Lake. See chapter 6 for a discussion of these areas.

Robert S. Kerr Lake (see map 23)

The Robert S. Kerr Lock and Dam complex is a major component of the U.S. Army Corps of Engineers' multipurpose project designed to improve navigation of the Arkansas River and its tributaries in Arkansas and Oklahoma. Built between 1964 and 1970, the lock and dam are located on the Arkansas River, approximately 8 miles south of Sallisaw, Oklahoma. The resultant lake is 460 feet above mean sea level and covers 42,000 acres (65.6 square miles). It inundates

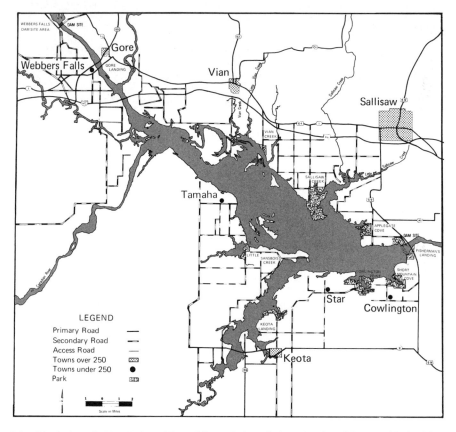

Map 23. Robert S. Kerr Lake. *Adapted from:* Robert S. Kerr Lock and Dam and Lake Map (Tulsa: Department of the Army, Corps of Engineers, Tulsa District, 1978.

Robert S. Kerr Lake on the Arkansas River in eastern Oklahoma. Courtesy of U.S. Army
Corps of Engineers, Tulsa District.

portions of Muskogee, Le Flore, Sequoyah, and Haskell counties, and is
about 330 miles above the confluence of
the White (Arkansas Navigation Channel) and Mississippi rivers.[20] Approximately 20,800 acres of the project lands
have been made available for the Sequoyah National Wildlife Refuge.

In the picturesque, mesalike hill country on the extreme northwestern corner
of the Ouachita province, Kerr Lake occurs where the rocks are less folded and
the dominant landforms are the long
cuestas that range *en echelon* across the
Central Lowlands. The lake has some
250 miles of rugged, irregular shoreline
and many tributary arms. It is especially
beautiful in early spring, when flowering shrubs and leaf buds on the hickory
and blackjack oaks lend a soft glow to
the landscape, and again, in the fall

when the changing leaves create a beauty
that is hard to match.

Kerr Lake is noted for its bass, crappie, catfish, and walleye fishing at the
very productive tributary arms and three
shallow areas in the main lake where the
original timber has not been cleared.
The subsurface structure and food conditions of these sites create excellent fish
habitats. The three major arms of the
lower lake (Little Sallisaw Creek, Little
Sansbois Creek, and Sansbois Navigation Channel) are fished primarily for
crappie and black bass. The Little Sallisaw Creek arm is an especially "hot"
crappie area in March, April, and May.

The upper reaches of the lake also
offer many good fishing sites; crappie
and black bass angling is good in the
Vian Creek access area where Vian
Creek, Little Vian Creek, and an oxbow

arm, all heavily timbered and brushy, provide exceptional habitats. Bluegill are also attracted to these bushy inlets where the water is generally less than twenty feet deep. The arms of the Canadian, Illinois, and Arkansas rivers are fished heavily for all species but are particularly well-known first-rate channel catfish waters.

The north shore access areas with public boat ramps include the Dam Site, Sallisaw Creek, Vian Creek, and Gore Landing; south shore access areas are located at Short Mountain Cove, Cowlington Point, Deota Landing, Little Sansbois Creek, and Webbers Falls. See chapter 6 for specific information regarding camping and recreation facilities available at these sites.

Lake Maumelle (see map 14)

Lake Maumelle is about 15 miles northwest of Little Rock, Arkansas, on the Big Maumelle River. It was built at a cost of $9 million to provide Little Rock with an adequate and wholesome water supply. The dam, completed in 1958 for the Little Rock Municipal Water Works, is 2,550 feet long and 67 feet high. The lake has an area of 13.9 square miles and a shoreline of 70 miles.[21]

Boating and fishing are permitted and camping is available at nearby Maumelle Park. The lake is divided into three zones by markers and buoys. Fishing and boating are prohibited in zone one near the dam. Zone two is reserved primarily for pleasure and speed boats; however, fishing is permitted. The last zone is a fishing zone where bass, crappie, bream, catfish, and other fish common to Arkansas lakes are found.

Three boat docks offer tackle, bait, and ice, as well as boat and motor rentals. Docks one and three are on the south shore alongside Arkansas 10; dock two is on the north shore and can be reached by a lake access road.

McGee Creek Reservoir (see map 24)

McGee Creek Reservoir, originally proposed as a U.S. Army Corps of Engineers' project, was constructed by the U.S. Bureau of Reclamation in southeastern Oklahoma on McGee Creek, a tributary of Muddy Boggy Creek, which in turn is a major tributary of the Red River. The McGee Creek Dam, about 2,300 feet long and 155 feet high, impounds a lake that extends approximately fourteen miles up McGee Creek and about twelve miles up Potapo Creek at conservation level.

An unusually wide variety of recreational opportunities are available; most of the facilities are in the lower portion of the reservoir including fifty-seven campsites, eighteen individual picnic sites, six group picnic shelters, eight boat-launching lanes, a swimming beach, and eight built-in campsites, as well as hiking and equestrian trails.

Nimrod Lake (see map 25)

Nimrod Lake is nine miles southeast of Plainview, Arkansas, on the Fourche La Fave River. Built by the U.S. Army Corps of Engineers between 1940 and 1942 at a cost of $3,773,000, Nimrod Dam stands 97 feet above the stream bed and is 1,012 feet long. The lake is 345 feet above sea level and covers 3,550 acres (5.5 square miles) at conservation pool. It has 77 miles of shoreline.[22]

The lake's idyllic setting in the Fourche La Fave River valley is impressive; the north shore, raggedly indented by more than a half-dozen small creeks, is dominated by the summits of Danville and Ola mountains; the straighter south shore hugs a series of hogbacks and offers a spectacular view of Fourche Mountain. The surrounding, heavily forested land lies within the Ouachita National Forest.

There are many recreational oppor-

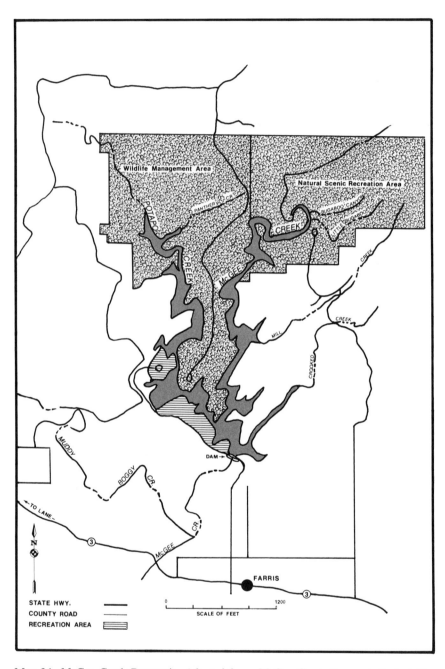

Map 24. McGee Creek Reservoir. *Adapted from:* McGee Creek Reservoir Project Map (Washington, D.C.: Department of the Interior, Bureau of Reclamation, 1984).

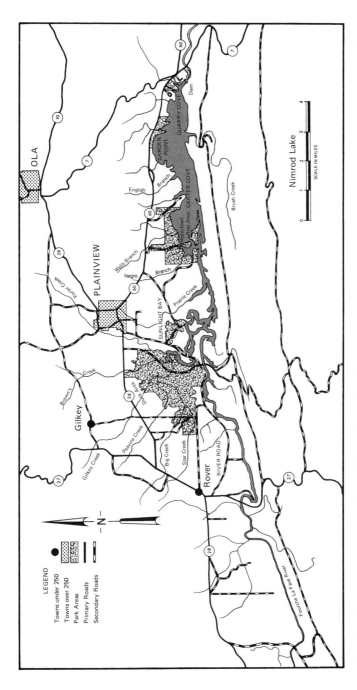

Map 25. Nimrod Lake. *Adapted from:* Nimrod Lake Map (Little Rock: Department of the Army, Corps of Engineers, Little Rock District, 1973).

Swimming at Nimrod Lake near Danville, Arkansas. Courtesy of U.S. Army Corps of Engineers, Little Rock District.

tunities in the Nimrod Lake area for outdoor sports enthusiasts. In addition to lake fishing—which centers on largemouth bass, white bass, channel cat, crappie, and bream—a large (2,400 acres) public hunting area is managed by the Arkansas Game and Fish Commission. The Commission also oversees a wildlife refuge and a 1,200-acre goose sanctuary on the lake.

The access points and recreation areas at Nimrod Lake are well-developed; boats, motors, and bait are available at Sunlight Bay, about two miles south of Plainview; public launching ramps have been built at Garden Point, Carter Cove, Quarry Cove, River Road, and Sunlight Bay. See chapter 6 for a more detailed discussion of the camping and recreational facilities.

Ouachita Lake (see map 26)

Ouachita Lake is the largest lake in Arkansas. Situated in the Ouachita River Valley to the west of Hot Springs, it was created when the U.S. Army Corps of

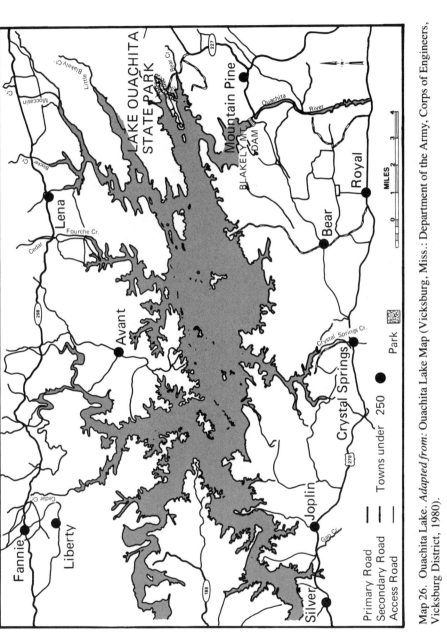

Map 26. Ouachita Lake. *Adapted from:* Ouachita Lake Map (Vicksburg, Miss.: Department of the Army, Corps of Engineers, Vicksburg District, 1980).

Lake Ouachita near Hot Springs. Courtesy of Arkansas Department of Parks and Tourism.

Lake Ouachita on the Ouachita River near Hot Springs. Courtesy of Arkansas Department of Parks and Tourism.

Engineers constructed Blakely Mountain Dam in 1955. The $30 million project was designed for flood control, hydroelectric power, and recreation.

When at power pool the lake extends a distance of about 20 miles and covers an area of approximately twenty thousand acres (31.25 square miles).[23] Because the lake flooded an area of folded ridge and valley topography, it has a rather arresting geography. The main channel lies in the east-west trending Ouachita Valley. Mountain ridges arise in nearly all directions: Hickory Nut, Bear, and Brady mountains crowd the southern shore; Blakely Mountain is near the dam site; and Mill Creek Mountain rises on the east. Streams originating in the mountains create several tributary arms that cause the lake's ragged border and good habitat for fish.

Three tributary arms on the south shore (Crystal Springs, Caney, and Walnut creeks) form a major inlet considered especially good for crappie and largemouth bass fishing. The South Fork arm has several smaller tributary arms and dozens of bays and rocky points that provide excellent habitats for crappie and largemouth bass. This arm is also a very productive area during the spring and fall for both white bass and catfish. The upper part of the lake (the Ouachita River arm) has a reputation for excellent catfish and white bass fishing.

The popularity of Ouachita Lake is at least partly attributed to the surrounding beautiful and heavily forested, mountainous terrain, and its accessibility from Hot Springs and surrounding towns. Lake access roads intersect with highways 270, 27, 298, and 5.

Access points to the lake are plentiful. On the north shore, near the Montgomery and Garland county line, a complex branching arm is formed by Cedar, Redbank, Muse, North Fork, and Daley creeks, which is accessible from both the Irons Fork and Avant access areas.

Sailing on Lake Ouachita. Courtesy of Arkansas Department of Parks and Tourism.

The Cedar Fourche Creek arm has direct access from the Cedar Fourche access area. Lena Landing, on the Fisher Creek arm, offers access to the northeast trending parallel arms on Big Blakely Creek and Little Blakely Creek. Boat ramps from Lake Ouachita State Park lead to the Mill Creek and Bear Creek portions of the lake. See chapter 6 for information on the area's camping and recreational facilities.

Ozark Lake (see map 27)

On the Arkansas River in west-central Arkansas between Ozark and Fort Smith and a part of the McClelland-Kerr Arkansas River Navigation System, Ozark Lake was formed when the Ozark-Jeta Taylor Lock and Dam was completed in 1964. It stretches 36 miles from this lock and dam to Lock and Dam no. 13

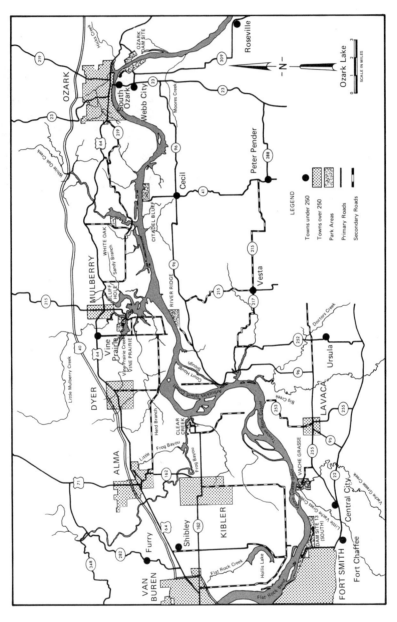

Map 27. Ozark Lake. *Adapted from:* Ozark Lake Map (Little Rock: Department of the Army, Corps of Engineers, Little Rock District, 1976).

Ozark Lock and Dam on the Arkansas River. Courtesy of U.S. Army Corps of Engineers,
Little Rock District.

near Fort Smith. At normal navigational
pool, the lake covers about 10,600 acres
(16.5 square miles) with 173 miles of
shoreline.[24]

The McClellan-Kerr Arkansas River
Navigation System is a U.S. Army
Corps of Engineers' project designed to
permit navigation from a point on the
Verdigris River, a tributary of the Arkansas, near Tulsa, Oklahoma, to the
main channel of the Mississippi River.
Navigational charts of the portion from
the Mississippi through Lock and Dam
no. 13, including Ozark Lake, may be
purchased from the District Engineer's
office in Little Rock (District Engineer,
U.S. Army Corps of Engineers, P.O.
Box 867, Little Rock, Arkansas 72203,
telephone (501) 378-5551). Charts of
the portion further upstream to the port

of Catoosa, near Tulsa, may be purchased from the District Engineer's
office in Tulsa (District Engineer, U.S.
Army Corps of Engineers, 224 South
Boulder, Tulsa, Oklahoma 74103, telephone (918) 581-7307).

The countryside surrounding Ozark
Lake is prosperous and varied with a
view of cultivated fields, vineyards,
and pastures hemmed in by the rugged
Boston Mountains on the north and the
craggy Ouachitas on the south.

Most native Arkansas game fish may
be caught during the year-round season
on Ozark Lake. Popular with anglers are
crappie, largemouth bass, bream, and
channel catfish; and the Arkansas Game
and Fish Commission stocks the lake
with striped bass and walleye.

As a convenience to lake visitors,

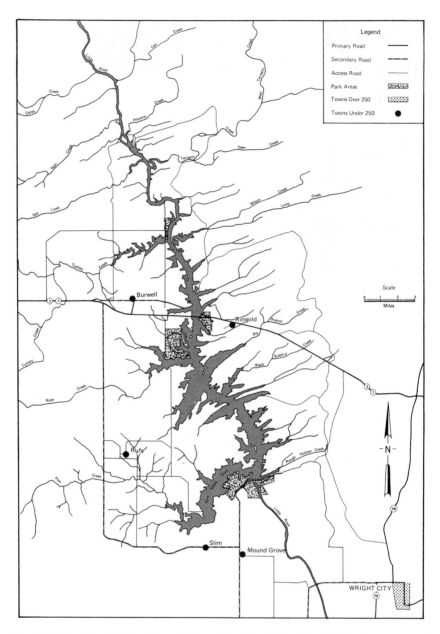

Map 28. Pine Creek Lake. *Adapted from:* Pine Creek Lake Map (Tulsa: Department of the Army, Corps of Engineers, Tulsa District, 1976).

Pine Creek Lake by moonlight. Courtesy of U.S. Army Corps of Engineers, Tulsa District.

nine parks have been constructed along the shoreline. North-shore public-use areas include: Clear Creek, Vine Prairie (near Mulberry), Bluff Hole (also near Mulberry), White Oak, and the Ozark Dam Site. The south-shore areas include: Citadel Bluff, River Ridge, Vache Grasse, and the Lock and Dam no. 13 Site. Chapter 6 includes a more detailed discussion of the available facilities.

Pine Creek Lake (see map 28)

Pine Creek Dam is located on the Little River, approximately 8 miles north of Valliant in McCurtain County, Okla-

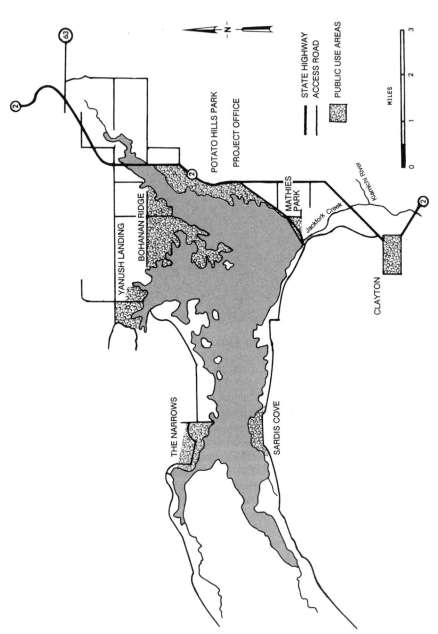

Map 29. Sardis Lake. *Adapted from*: Sardis Lake Map (Little Rock: Department of the Army, Corps of Engineers, Little Rock District, 1978).

homa. Built as a U.S. Army Corps of Engineers' project between 1963 and 1969, this earth-fill embankment is 7,510 feet long and stands 124 feet above the Little River's stream bed. Pine Creek Lake is 438 feet above mean sea level at conservation pool. It covers 3,800 acres (5.9 square miles) and has 74 miles of shoreline.[25] Pine Creek Lake is one of seven lakes authorized and built in an effort to control and develop the water resources in the Little River basin while also aiding flood control on the Red River.

The geography of Pine Creek Lake is typical of lakes in areas with folded rock strata. The main channel is aligned north-south and cuts across several east-west trending ridges and valleys; the flooded valleys form arms that intersect the main channel at right angles. The largest arms on the west shore are Pine Creek Cove, Rock Creek, and Turkey Creek. The east arms include Black Sulphur Creek, Big Branch Creek, and Long Creek.

Fishing prospects on Pine Creek Lake are excellent. Several tributary arms have standing timber, which makes excellent fish habitat. The productivity of the lake is so great that it is often the site for bass derbies. Other popular targets among anglers are crappie, bream, and channel catfish.

Of the six public-use areas, the most fully developed are Pine Creek Cove and Little River Park. Boat launching facilities have been installed at Little River Park, Lost Rapids Park, and Pine Creek Cove. See chapter 6 for a more complete inventory of this area's facilities.

Sardis Lake, formerly Clayton Lake
(see map 29)

Sardis Dam is on Jackfork Creek, a tributary of the Kiamichi River, about 3 miles north of Clayton and 5 miles northwest of Tuskahoma in Pushmataha County, Oklahoma. Sardis Dam and Lake (formerly Clayton Lake) are the result of a U.S. Army Corps of Engineers' project designed for flood control and recreation, which was completed in 1982 at an estimated cost of $52.8 million and is about 14,400 feet long and 65 feet high. It impounds a lake that covers 14,360 acres and has a shoreline of 117 miles at normal pool.[26] Sardis Lake is nearly surrounded by mountains: the Jackfork Mountains to the west; the Winding Stair Mountains to the north; and the Potato Hills to the northeast. The upland areas are covered with oak and pine forests, while the bottomlands show more oaks and hickories.

Fishing on Sardis Lake is good for largemouth and spotted bass, white crappie, channel catfish, and bluegill. Stumps, downed timber, and submerged brush provide an excellent subsurface cover for young fish. The brush islands along the north shore are noted for crappie and bluegill. Because of Sardis Lake's relatively remote location, the fishing pressure is fairly light.

Five areas on the lake were originally planned for recreational facilities; however, funding cuts have limited the development, thus far, to boat ramps. Potato Hills Park is on the east shore; Bohanon Ridge and the Narrows are on the north shore; and Sardis Cove and the Mathies areas are on the south shore.

Lake Winona (see map 14)

Lake Winona was built as a municipal water supply by the city of Little Rock between 1936 and 1938, with assistance from the Progressive Works Administration (PWA). The dam, on the Alum Fork of the Saline River, is 2,800 feet long and 115 feet high. Lake Winona covers 1.9 square miles and has 25 miles of shoreline.[27] Water from the lake is piped to Little Rock with very little pumping.

Because Lake Winona is so close to

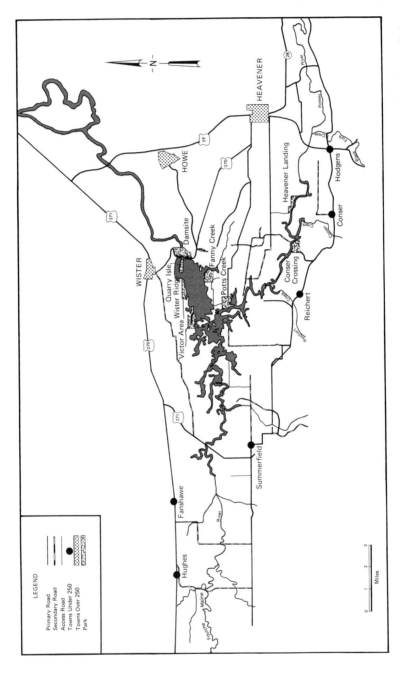

Map 30. Wister Lake. *Adapted from:* Wister Dam and Reservoir Map (Tulsa: Department of the Army, Corps of Engineers, Tulsa District, 1969).

Wister Dam and Lake on the Poteau River in eastern Oklahoma. Courtesy of U.S. Army Corps of Engineers, Tulsa District.

Little Rock, fishing and other recreational uses are extremely heavy. This pressure has caused the city to use buoys and markers to divide the lake into zone one, near the dam and off limits to boaters and anglers, and zone two, the remainder of the lake, which is open to boating and fishing; camping is strictly prohibited. Access to the lake is available through a boat ramp on the north shore.

Wister Lake (see map 30)

Wister Dam and Lake are on the Poteau River, about 2 miles south of Wister, Oklahoma. The dam was completed in 1949 by the U.S. Army Corps of Engineers at a cost of $10.5 million. It is a 5,700-foot long earth embankment. At normal pool, the lake is 471.6 feet above sea level. Wister Lake covers 4,000 acres (6.25 square miles) and has 115 miles of shoreline.[28]

The geography of Wister Lake is rather simple compared to other Ouachita Mountain lakes. The main channel branches into two arms in the upper reaches: the Poteau River arm and the Fourche Maline River arm. Scores of inlets with good brush structure and an equal number of rocky points provide excellent cover for several varieties of fish. The surrounding area is relatively open, and there is less pine timber than in the other more rugged sections of the Ouachitas.

Fishing at Wister Lake in eastern Oklahoma. Courtesy of U.S. Army Corps of Engineers, Tulsa District.

An abundance of bluegill, channel catfish, flathead catfish, largemouth bass, and crappie attracts fishermen from considerable distances. The recent stocking of walleye has added even more variety to the fishing. The Oklahoma Department of Wildlife Conservation manages 5,000 acres of the Fourche Maline Arm as a wildlife refuge and another 12,996 acres as a wildlife habitat under a license agreement.

In addition to hunters and fishermen,

the lake attracts water sports enthusiasts, campers, and hikers. Access to the lake is made easy by its eight public-use areas. The lower lake can be reached from six boat ramps: Victor area, Wister Ridge, Quarry Isle, Dam Site, Fanny Creek, and Potts Creek. The upper Poteau River arm is reached most easily from boat ramps at Conser Crossing and Heavener Landing. See chapter 6 for details on the available facilities.

Hiking, Backpacking, and Camping

The Ouachita Mountains provide superb hiking terrain. The region is sparsely settled and heavily forested. The scenery is truly spectacular. With the Ouachita and Ozark national forests and numerous state parks, the region offers ample opportunities where hikers need not be concerned with trespassing on private property.

While specialized books on hiking and backpacking are the best source of information concerning equipment, hiking techniques, and safety, a few simple suggestions are worthy of special emphasis. The best equipment available may not be the best suited for your needs in the Ouachitas; for example, only on very rare occasions during the winter months would a camper need a sleeping bag designed for bitter winter chills. The discussion of climate in chapter 1 can serve as a useful guide in selecting proper boots, clothing, and sleeping bags. Advice regarding tents, backpacks, and frames can be obtained from stores specializing in camping and backpacking gear where employees are usually both experienced and sincerely interested in outdoor activities; their suggestions merit careful consideration.

The essentials for a wilderness backpacker include: a tent, sleeping bag, extra clothes, cookware, mosquito netting, food, candle stubs for starting fires, fifty feet of general purpose nylon cord, a good pocketknife, maps, nylon tape for mending, a shovel or garden trowel, a whistle for signaling, plastic bags for wet clothes, a small towel, soap, a toothbrush, lip protector, insect repellent, menstrual supplies, shaving materials, a small mirror, glasses, hand cream, sunscreen oil, toilet paper, a flashlight, a canteen, a collapsible water container, and first-aid supplies, including a snakebite kit.

Common ailments among backpackers are overexposure, snake bite, skin irritations from contact with poisonous plants, and sunburn. Dehydration and heat exhaustion should be guarded against during the hot Ouachita summers.

The most common poisonous snakes are the copperhead and rattlesnake (see chapter 3); in the event that someone is bitten, minimize the victim's exertion and seek medical attention at once. When hiking in very isolated areas, inexpensive snake-bite kits are essential equipment; the instructions should be read and learned before the kit is needed.

Poison sumac, oak, and ivy are widespread in the area and can cause considerable discomfort to those susceptible individuals. Ticks, chiggers, and mosquitos can be a considerable irritant during certain times of the year; small seed ticks are especially troublesome in the summer.

Potable water is available at most developed campgrounds and picnic areas. It is not a good idea to drink or use spring water for cooking or cleaning dishes unless the spring is marked as safe. Clear, sparkling spring water can be very deceptive; although it can look cool and refreshing, most stream water is contaminated with disease-causing organisms.

Never camp or hike alone; partners are invaluable in case of accident or emergency. When hiking, periodic rest stops of about ten minutes every hour

Ouachita Mountain hiking trail. Courtesy of Arkansas Department of Parks and Tourism.

are a good idea. Do not panic if lost or disoriented; stop, sit down, and calmly try to reconstruct the route taken, then retrace the path marking the trail along the way. If such a technique should fail, simply walk down hill to a creek or stream. This should eventually lead to a river, which, in turn, should lead to a settlement.

HIKING AREAS IN THE OUACHITA MOUNTAINS

The national forests provide more than two million acres of rugged, forested, wild country. Maps of these forests, complete with the location of campsites, streams, forest roads, hiking trails, and other useful information, can be obtained from the Forest Supervisor Headquarters:

Ouachita National Forest
P.O. Box 1270

Hot Springs, Arkansas 71901
Telephone (501) 321-5202

Ozark National Forest
P.O. Box 1008
Russellville, Arkansas 72801
Telephone (501) 968-2354

Useful for selecting an area for a hiking and/or camping trip, the scale of these maps is too small to use as a guide through the woods. For more detailed information use the U.S. Geological Survey (U.S.G.S.) 7½ minute quadrangle maps, which are essential for wilderness backpacking trips.

U.S.G.S. topographic maps for any area of the country can be ordered by writing to the:

Map Information Office
U.S. Geological Survey
Washington, D.C. 20242

The quadrangles for Arkansas and Oklahoma can also be ordered from the respective state geological surveys:

Arkansas Geological Commission
3815 West Roosevelt Road
Little Rock, Arkansas 72204
Telephone (501) 371-1488 or
    663-9714

Oklahoma Geological Survey
830 Van Vleet Oval
Norman, Oklahoma 73019
Telephone (405) 325-3031

A pamphlet describing topographic maps and their symbols is available free on request, and if you need assistance identifying the specific quadrangles, a free "Index" to the Arkansas and Oklahoma maps is also available.

The National Forest maps show the location of ranger district offices. The rangers and district foresters have an intimate knowledge of the area and can help set courses and give advice on road and trail conditions.

Camping and hiking are permitted anywhere in the national forests without a special permit. Except after long dry spells, fires are allowed; however, users are responsible for all fires they light and any damage caused to public property as a result of such fires.

CAMPING AND HIKING AREAS IN THE OUACHITA AND OZARK NATIONAL FORESTS

While the Ouachita National Forest is almost entirely within the Ouachita Mountain district, only one section of the Ozark National Forest lies south of the Arkansas River. Both of these forests were established largely through the purchase of privately owned land and both still contain significant private holdings. Most of the timber lands were cut-over during the peak lumbering era.

Of the thirty-three camping areas in the Ouachita portions of these two for-

ests, thirty are in the Ouachita National Forest and three are in the Ozark National Forest. Understanding and obeying a few simple rules can assure a pleasant, happy, and safe outdoor experience, while also helping to protect the natural beauty of the mountains. These guidelines include:

1. For most sites, the regular camping season extends from May through September. Use is on a first come, first served basis, and stays are limited to fourteen consecutive days on any one site.

2. Camper use fees are collected at most campgrounds by a self-registration (honor) system.

3. Camp units are limited to a single family, except where signs specifically permit multiple-family use.

4. Firewood and electrical and sewage hookups are not provided.

5. For convenience and security, all recreational and camping sites are visited regularly by Forest Service and local law enforcement personnel.

6. Each campsite has car and trailer parking, a table, a fireplace, and tent areas. Picnic units usually have a table and fireplace with centralized parking.

7. Safe drinking water, sanitary facilities (restrooms), and garbage containers are usually located nearby.

8. Since lifeguards are not provided, children should be supervised at all swimming sites.

9. During periods of heavy rain, especially in the spring, the water levels in rivers and streams can rise rapidly; many become extremely fast and dangerous; use extreme caution.

10. Poisonous plants and snakes are natural residents; treat them with respect.

11. When traveling and recreating in undeveloped areas of the forest, carry out all unburnable trash, avoid

cutting or otherwise killing live plants, bury human wastes, and make certain fires are completely extinguished.

12. Respect the rights of private property owners; public lands are intermingled extensively with private lands.

Camping areas in the national forests are listed alphabetically in the following inventory, which begins with those in the Ozark National Forest and continues with those in the Ouachita National Forest. Additional information about the camping areas and use of the national forests can be obtained by contacting the supervisors' headquarters mentioned earlier, and by contacting the ranger district office for each campground.

Mount Magazine overlook. Courtesy of Arkansas Department of Parks and Tourism.

CAMPING AREAS AND ACCOMMODATIONS IN THE OZARK NATIONAL FOREST

Cove Lake—Magazine Ranger District—29 Campsites

Cove Lake is a 160-acre lake near Magazine Mountain, the highest point in Arkansas. The campsites can be reached by following Arkansas 109 south from Paris and then turning southeast (left) on Arkansas 309 for nine miles. These roads are negotiable by camping trailer rigs. The available facilities include twenty-nine family camping units, twenty-four family picknicking units, central restrooms, drinking water, a swimming area, a bathhouse, fishing, and a boat rental operation. Outboard motors are limited to 10 h.p. during weekends and holidays. Camping trailers are permitted, but no special trailer utilities are available.

Mount Magazine Recreation Area— Magazine Ranger District— 16 Campsites

The Mount Magazine Recreation Area offers rugged mountain scenery atop Ar-

kansas' highest summit. The bluffs are spectacular and the panoramic view of the Arkansas Valley, Boston Mountains, and Ouachita Mountains is unequalled.

Access is gained by following Arkansas 109 south from Paris for one mile, and then turning southeast (left) on Arkansas 309 for seventeen miles. These roads are negotiable by camping trailers. The facilities include sixteen camping units, chemical toilets, drinking water, and picnic tables.

Spring Lake—Magazine Ranger District—13 Campsites

Spring Lake is an eighty-two-acre impoundment in a beautiful mountain setting. Follow Arkansas 27 southwest from Dardanelle for nine miles, then turn west (right) on Arkansas 307 for three miles to the Forest Development Road no. 1602; continue four miles to Spring Lake. All the roads are negotiable by camping trailer rigs.

The available facilities include thirteen camping units, picnic tables, restrooms, drinking water, a swimming area, showers, and boat ramps. Outboard motors are limited to 10 h.p. Seasonal hunting is allowed nearby. Although camping trailers are permitted, no special trailer facilities are available.

CAMPING AREAS AND ACCOMMODATIONS IN THE OUACHITA NATIONAL FOREST IN ARKANSAS

Albert Pike—Caddo Ranger District—39 Campsites

The chief attractions are a natural pool in the Little Missouri River and a scenic drive over a Forest Service road. Follow Forest Service Road 73 (a gravel road) north from Langley, Arkansas, for six miles.

The available facilities and attractions include camping units, a swimming area, sanitary facilities, drinking water, showers, hiking, and fishing.

Bald Springs—Caddo Ranger District—17 Campsites

The chief attraction of the Bald Springs site is a small scenic stream. Access by following Forest Service Road 38 (a gravel road) northwest from Athens, Arkansas, for nine miles and then turning east (right) on Forest Service Road 106 (also gravel) for a half mile.

The site's facilities and attractions include seventeen camping units, a picnic area, swimming, sanitary facilities, drinking water, a bathhouse, and hiking trails.

Fourche Mountain—Fourche Ranger District—5 Campsites

The Fourche Mountain camping area offers a scenic view from a mountain top. It is on Arkansas 27, four miles south of Rover, Arkansas. The facilities and attractions include five camping units, a picnic area, nearby hunting, sanitary facilities, and drinking water.

Fulton Branch Float Camp— Womble Ranger District— 5 Campsites

Fulton Branch is a float camp on the Ouachita River. Take U.S. 270 northwest from Mount Ida, Arkansas, for half a mile; turn north (right) on Arkansas 27 for one mile; and then northwest (left) on a county road for five miles.

The facilities and attractions include camping units, a picnic area, sanitary facilities, drinking water, float fishing, canoeing, and hiking.

Gap Creek—Womble Ranger District—No Campsites

The Gap Creek picnic area is situated on a scenic mountain stream twenty-four miles west of Hot Springs, Arkansas, on U.S. 270.

The facilities include five picnic units, sanitary facilities, and drinking water.

Hickory Nut Mountain—Womble Ranger District—8 Campsites

This site's picnic area offers a beautiful vista of Lake Ouachita and the surrounding area from atop Hickory Nut Mountain. To reach the site, travel on U.S. 270 west from Hot Springs, Arkansas, for twenty-three miles, then turn north (right) at a sign on Forest Service Road 47 and continue for three and a half miles.

The facilities include eight camping units, a picnic area, sanitary facilities, and drinking water.

Iron Springs—Jessieville Ranger District—13 Campsites

This camping area is in a wooded roadside setting on a stream near a spring. It is approximately four and a half miles north of Jessieville, on Arkansas 7. The facilities and attractions include campsites, picnic units, sanitary facilities, drinking water, a shelter, and a wading area.

Hiking in the Jack Creek Recreation Area. Courtesy of Arkansas Department of Parks and Tourism.

Jack Creek—Cold Springs Ranger District—5 Campsites

The chief attractions of this area are a natural pool in Jack Creek, a scenic overlook, and rugged rock bluffs. Travel on Arkansas 23 south from Booneville, Arkansas, for three miles, turn east (left) on Arkansas 116 for one mile, and then turn south at a sign on Forest Service Road 19 for five miles, before turning east (left) on Forest Service Road 141 for one mile. The last three miles of road are graveled.

The facilities include five camping units, swimming, sanitary facilities, drinking water, and a shelter.

Knoppers Ford—Cold Springs Ranger District—6 Campsites

This ford is located at a natural pool in Sugar Creek. Access it by taking Arkansas 23 south from Booneville for three miles, turning east (left) on Arkansas 116 for one mile, and then turning south at a sign for seven miles on Forest Service Road 19. The last four miles of road are graveled.

The facilities and attractions include six camping units, sanitary facilities, drinking water, a shelter, fishing, and swimming.

Lake Sylvia—Winona Ranger District—19 Campsites

This campground is located on a beautiful ten-acre lake in the mountains southwest of Perryville, Arkansas. Take Arkansas 9 south from Perryville for nine miles before turning west (right) at a sign for four miles of graveled road.

The facilities and attractions include nineteen camping units, swimming, sanitary facilities, drinking water, a bath-house, fishing, and hiking trails. No boat motors are allowed on the lake.

Little Missouri Falls—Caddo Ranger District—No Campsites

The chief attraction of this forested pic-nic area is a trail leading to the water-falls overlook. Access can be gained by traveling east for six miles on Arkansas 8 from Big Fork, and turning south (right) on a graveled Forest Service road for one mile.

The facilities and attractions include five picnic units, sanitary facilities, drinking water, hiking trails, and fishing opportunities.

Little Pines—Poteau Ranger District—21 Campsites

The Little Pines area is in secluded backwoods beside one-hundred-acre Hinkle Lake, which is managed by the Arkansas Game and Fish Commission. Travel on Arkansas 248 west from Wal-dron for twelve miles. The last seven miles are on a graveled rural road.

The facilities and attractions include twenty-one camping units, a picnic area, restrooms, drinking water, a bathhouse, a shelter, a boat ramp, swimming, and fishing. No skiing is allowed on the lake.

Mill Creek—Poteau Ranger District—27 Campsites

This campsite is located at a natural pool in a scenic portion of Mill Creek. It is five miles east of Y City, Arkansas, on U.S. 270. The facilities and attractions include twenty-seven camping units, sanitary facilities, drinking water, swimming, a bathhouse, fishing, and a hiking trail.

Rich Mountain Picnic Area—Mena Ranger District—No Campsites

The Rich Mountain picnic area and lookout tower offer a breathtaking view from the highest point in the Ouachita

National Forest. It is off Arkansas 88, nine miles west of Mena, Arkansas, on Talimena Scenic Drive. There are five picnic units.

River Bluff Float Camp—Womble Ranger District—7 Campsites

The River Bluff float camp is situated on the Ouachita River. It is accessible by traveling on U.S. 270 northwest from Mount Ida, Arkansas, for half a mile; turning north (right) on Arkansas 27 for one mile, and then turning left on a county road for four miles.

The facilities and attractions include seven camping units, a picnic area, sani-tary facilities, drinking water, float fish-ing, canoeing, and hiking.

Rocky Shoals Float Camp—Womble Ranger District—7 Campsites

The Rocky Shoals float camp is also on the Ouachita River. It can be reached by traveling six miles northwest from Mount Ida, Arkansas, on U.S. 270, and then continuing north (right) on a short spur just before crossing the Ouachita River bridge.

The facilities and attractions include camping units, a picnic area, restrooms, drinking water, float fishing, canoeing, and hiking opportunities.

Shady Lake—Mena Ranger District—97 Campsites

This campsite is on a scenic twenty-five-acre lake in a remote mountain set-ting. Travel on Arkansas 84 west from Langley for ten miles before turning north (right) and traveling for five miles on Forest Service Road 38.

The facilities and attractions include ninety-seven camping units, sanitary fa-cilities, drinking water, shelters, boat-ing, swimming, bathhouses, showers, fishing, and hiking. No boat motors are allowed on the lake.

South Fourche—Jessieville Ranger District—7 Campsites

South Fourche is a convenient roadside campground situated on an attractive stream. The campsite is one mile south of Hollis, Arkansas, on Arkansas 7, one of the area's most popular routes for viewing the autumn foliage. The facilities and attractions include seven camping units, a picnic area, restrooms, drinking water, and fishing.

CAMPING AREAS AND ACCOMMODATIONS IN THE OUACHITA MOUNTAINS OF OKLAHOMA

Billy Creek—Kiamichi Ranger District—11 Campsites

Billy Creek camping area is located near a natural pool in a stream. Visitors should take Oklahoma 63 west from Big Cedar for six miles before turning north (right) at a sign on Forest Service Road 22 for three miles.

The facilities and attractions include eleven camping units, a picnic area, and fishing.

Horsethief Spring—Kiamichi Ranger District—No Campsites

This historic spring and picnic area is located on Talimena Scenic Drive. It can be reached by following Oklahoma 1 west from the junction with U.S. 259 for six miles. The facilities include four picnic units and sanitary facilities.

Kulli—Tiak Ranger District— No Campsites

The chief attraction at this area is a seven-acre lake. Visitors will need to travel on Oklahoma 87 and U.S. 259 south from Idabel for three miles before turning east at a sign on Forest Service Road 212 for six miles, and then south at a sign on Forest Service Road 77 for one mile.

The facilities and attractions include eleven picnic units, a bathhouse, restrooms, drinking water, swimming, fishing, and hiking.

Mazarn—Caddo Ranger District— 7 Campsites

This camping area is in a forested setting near a natural pool along Mazarn Creek. It can be reached by traveling on U.S. 70 northeast from Glenwood, Arkansas, for 19 miles, and turning northwest (left) on a paved road for 2.2 miles at Pearcy, Arkansas.

The facilities and attractions include seven camping units, sanitary facilities, drinking water, fishing, hiking, and swimming.

Old Military Road—Kiamichi Ranger District—No Campsites

This picnic area is on a historic old road on Talimena Scenic Drive. It is one mile east from the junction of Oklahoma 1 and U.S. 271. A National Historic Site, its facilities include four picnic units and sanitary facilities.

Pipe Spring—Kiamichi Ranger District—No Campsites

The Pipe Spring picnic area is on U.S. 259 approximately one and a half miles south of the junction with Oklahoma 1. The available facilities include five picnic units and sanitary facilities.

Winding Stair—Kiamichi Ranger District—26 Campsites

This mountaintop camping area is adjacent to Talimena Scenic Drive. To gain access, take U.S. 259 north from Big Cedar, Oklahoma, for five miles, and turn west (left) on Oklahoma 1 (Talimena Scenic Drive) for three miles.

The facilities include twenty-six camping units, a picnic area, restrooms, and drinking water.

Talimena Skyline Drive in the Ouachita National Forest in eastern Oklahoma. Photo by Fred W. Marvel. Courtesy of Oklahoma Tourism and Recreation Department.

CAMPING AND ACCOMMODATIONS IN ARKANSAS STATE PARKS

Daisy State Park—118 Campsites

The major attractions of this site are the forested hill country and the fishing opportunities on Lake Greeson.

Daisy State Park, located off U.S. 70 west of Kirby, Arkansas, offers campsites, showers, restrooms, trailer dump stations, picnic areas, and boat ramps. For information and reservations call or write: Daisy State Park, Daisy Route, Box 66, Kirby, Arkansas 71950, telephone (501) 398-4487.

De Gray State Park—113 Campsites

De Gray State Park, on De Gray Lake north of Arkadelphia, Arkansas, is accessible from Interstate 30 and Arkansas 7. The park offers 113 campsites, showers, restrooms, trailer dumping stations, a park store, a coin laundry, boat ramps, and fishing on De Gray Lake.

The De Gray State Park Lodge has ninety-six guest rooms each with two double beds. Open year-round, the lodge has complete dining and convention facilities. For information and reservations, call or write: De Gray State Park Lodge, Box 375, Arkadelphia, Arkansas 71923, telephone (501) 865-4591.

Lake Catherine State Park— 70 Campsites

This park is on Lake Catherine just beyond the southern edge of Hot Springs, Arkansas. Its facilities and attractions include seventy campsites, showers, restrooms, trailer dump stations, a park store, a coin laundry, boat ramps and fishing.

Housekeeping cabins also are available. They include five rustic cabins with heat, air conditioning, and stone fireplaces; eight duplex units with electric heat and air conditioning; and four deluxe units. While the deluxe units and the rustics are open year-round, the duplex units are open only from April through October. For information and reservations, call or write: Lake Catherine State Park, Route 19, Box 360, Hot Springs, Arkansas 71901, telephone (501) 844-4176.

Lake Dardanelle State Park—
97 Campsites

This state park on the shores of Lake Dardanelle is accessible from Arkansas 326. The park is divided into three areas on opposite sides of the lake and on Illinois Bayou. It offers ninety-seven campsites, showers, restrooms, trailer dump stations, and boat ramps. Water sports and fishing are popular activities. For information and reservations, call or write: Lake Dardanelle State Park, Route 5, Box 527, Russellville, Arkansas 72801, telephone (501) 967-5516.

Lake Ouachita State Park—
102 Campsites

This state park is on the east shore of Lake Ouachita. It can be reached from Hot Springs by way of U.S. 270 and Arkansas 227. The campsites have showers, restrooms, picnic areas, trailer dump stations, a park store, and a coin laundry. Boat ramps are available for water sport and fishing activities on the lake.

Housekeeping cabins are available year-round. For reservations and rates, call or write: Lake Ouachita State Park, Star Route 1, Box 160 A, Mountain Pine, Arkansas 71956, telephone (501) 767-9366.

Mount Nebo State Park—
25 Campsites

Located east of Dardanelle, Mount Nebo State Park is accessible from Arkan-

Swimming at Lake Ouachita. Courtesy of U.S. Army Corps of Engineers, Vicksburg District.

Natural bridge at Petit Jean State Park. Courtesy of Arkansas Department of Parks and Tourism.

sas 155. The campsites have showers, restrooms, picnic areas, a park store, miniature golf, an overlook shelter, multipurpose courts, and a nature trail. For information and reservations, call or write: Mount Nebo State Park, Dardanelle, Arkansas 72834, telephone (501) 229-3655.

Petit Jean State Park—127 Campsites

This park, located southwest of Morrilton on Petit Jean Mountain, may be reached from Arkansas 154. Travelers on I-40 should use exit 108 at Morrilton, then travel nine miles south on Arkansas 9, before going twelve miles west on Arkansas 154. The campsites have showers, restrooms, trailer dump stations, and picnic areas.

The Mather Lodge and Restaurant, which has twenty-four guest rooms, is open April through October. Housekeeping cabins are also available year-round including eight rustics with heat, air conditioning, and stone fireplaces; eight duplexes; and twelve overnight cabins with no cooking facilities. For reservations and rates, call or write: Petit Jean State Park, Route 3, Box 34 D, Petit Jean Mountain, Morrilton, Arkansas 72110, telephone (800) 628-7936.

Queen Wilhelmina State Park— 42 Campsites

This park is on top of Rich Mountain on scenic Talimena Trail (Arkansas 88), thirteen miles just west of Mena, Arkansas. Its facilities include forty-two campsites, restrooms, showers, a park store, and a coin laundry.

The Queen Wilhelmina Lodge and Restaurant affords an exquisite view of the wild Ouachita Mountain ridges and valleys. Thirty-eight guest rooms are available. For information and reservations, call or write: Queen Wilhelmina State Park, P.O. Box 470, Mena, Arkansas 71953, telephone (501) 394-2864.

Queen Wilhelmina State Park and Lodge on Rich Mountain near Mena, Arkansas. Courtesy of Arkansas Department of Parks and Tourism.

CAMPING AND ACCOMMODATIONS AT OKLAHOMA STATE PARKS AND RESORTS

Arrowhead State Park and Resort—
92 Campsites

Arrowhead State Park is eighteen miles south of Interstate 40 on U.S. 69. Its facilities include picnic areas, campgrounds, restrooms, showers, a swimming area, and boat ramps.

Built from native stone and timber, Arrowhead Resort, owned by the Choctaw Indian Nation, overlooks Eufaula Lake. There are 106 rooms and 104 cottages. The guest rooms are spacious, comfortable, and inviting. The dining rooms offer excellent food and friendly service. For information and reservations, call or write the resort at Route 1, HC67 Box 57, Canadian, Oklahoma 74425, telephone (918) 339-2204. For camping information and reservations call the park office (918) 339-2204.

Beavers Bend State Park—
179 Campsites

This park can be reached by traveling seven miles north of Broken Bow on Oklahoma 259 and then east about five miles on Oklahoma 259A. It consists of 3,482 acres along the Mountain Fork River below Broken Bow Dam. In addition to rental cabins and campsites, the facilities include recreation vehicle sites, a coin laundry, picnic areas, a park store, restrooms, showers, hiking trails, a swimming beach, and boat ramps. For information and reservations, call or write: Beavers Bend State Park, Box 10, Broken Bow, Oklahoma 74728, telephone (405) 494-6538.

Fountainhead State Park—
84 Campsites

This park is located off Interstate 40, fourteen miles southwest of Checotah, overlooking Eufaula Lake. Facilities include an eighteen-hole golf course, pic-

Trail ride in southeastern Oklahoma. Photo by Fred W. Marvel. Courtesy of Oklahoma Tourism and Recreation Department.

nic areas, water, a marina, enclosed fishing docks, and boat ramps. For information and reservations call or write: Fountainhead State Park, P.O. Box HC60-1340, Checotah, Oklahoma 74426, telephone (918) 689-5311.

Hochatown State Park—
157 Campsites

Twelve miles north of Broken Bow on U.S. 259, and then three miles east, this park occupies 1,713 acres along the shores of Broken Bow Lake. Cabins, campsites, and recreational vehicle sites are available. Other facilities include restrooms, showers, picnic areas, a marina, a boat rental, and a golf course. For information and reservations, call or write: Hochatown State Park, P.O. Box 10, Broken Bow, Oklahoma 74728, telephone (405) 494-6452.

Robbers Cave State Park—
111 Campsites

Five miles north of Wilburton on Oklahoma 2, this park covers 8,435 acres and includes five lakes totaling over 100 acres. The available facilities include picnic shelters, tables, showers, restrooms, a swimming beach and pool, bathhouses, boat rentals, a ball diamond, and a grocery store. Housekeeping cabins and group camps are available.

The Tom Hale Boy Scout Camp is located near the center of the park, adjacent to the Fourche Maline River. Just north of the scout camp is Robbers Cave, which is said to have been used by robbers and highwaymen during the early settlement period. For information and reservations, call or write: Robbers Cave State Park, P.O. Box 9, Wilburton, Oklahoma 74578, telephone (918) 465-2562.

Bird hunting on the Arkansas River near Lake Dardanelle. Courtesy of U.S. Army Corps of Engineers, Little Rock District.

Talimena State Park—24 Campsites

This park is six miles north of Talihina on U.S. 271. It consists of restrooms, showers, picnic tables, electrical hook-ups, and playgrounds. For information and reservations, call or write: Talimena State Park, P.O. Box 318, Talihina, Oklahoma 74571, telephone (918) 567-2052.

Wister Lake State Park—
100 Campsites

Twelve miles southwest of Poteau near Wister on U.S. 270, this park encompasses 3,040 acres on the shores of Wister Lake. Its facilities include campsites, picnic shelters, showers, restrooms, sanitary stations, a swimming beach, boat rentals, boat ramps, a café, a grocery store, and a swimming pool. Housekeeping cabins and group camp-

ing facilities are available. For information and reservations, call or write: Wister Lake State Park, Route 2, Box 6B, Wister, Oklahoma 74966, telephone (918) 655-7756.

CAMPING AREAS AT U.S. ARMY
CORPS OF ENGINEERS
PROJECTS IN THE OUACHITA
MOUNTAINS

BLUE MOUNTAIN LAKE

For more information contact: Project Manager, Plainview, Arkansas 72857, telephone (501) 272-4324.

Ashley Creek—10 Campsites

The Ashley Creek area is approximately two miles south of Blue Mountain. It offers boat and motor rentals, a bait shop, a boat ramp, a picnic area, campgrounds, water, group shelters, and toilets.

Lick Creek—7 Campsites

The Lick Creek area is approximately 2.2 miles south of Waveland and then west for 2.9 miles. The available facilities include a boat ramp, picnic areas, campgrounds, water, group shelters, and toilets.

Hise Hill—9 Campsites

The Hise Hill area, which is approximately two miles east of Sugar Grove, includes a boat ramp, a picnic area, campgrounds, water, group shelters, and trailer parking.

Outlet Area—29 Campsites

The Outlet Area is approximately fourteen miles south of Waveland and includes picnic areas, campgrounds, water, toilets, a scenic overlook, and a dump station.

Waveland Park—51 Campsites

Waveland Park, which is approximately one mile south of Waveland, includes a boat ramp, picnic areas, campgrounds, water, a group shelter, toilets, a bathhouse, a trailer park, and a dump station.

BROKEN BOW LAKE

For more information contact: Project Manager, P.O. Box 730, Broken Bow, Oklahoma 74728, telephone (405) 494-6374.

Beavers Bend State Park—
157 Campsites

Beavers Bend State Park is located just below the dam at Broken Bow Lake. See the state parks listing in this chapter for details on facilities and attractions.

Carson Creek Area—32 Campsites
(*concessionaire*)

The Carson Creek area is accessible by traveling approximately 2.5 miles west of Sherwood, turning south on U.S. 259

for another 15.5 miles, and then heading east for 1.5 miles. Facilities include a boat ramp, a camping area, picnic areas, restrooms, showers, water, a trailer dump station, electric outlets, a concession stand, and a playground.

Hochatown State Park—
157 Campsites

Hochatown State Park is fifteen miles north of Hugo, Oklahoma, on U.S. 259. See the state parks listing in this chapter for details on facilities and attractions.

Holly Creek—72 Campsites

Holly Creek is on the west shore, 7.5 miles east of Sherwood on a lake access road. The facilities include a boat ramp, a camping area, and restrooms.

Panther Creek—12 Campsites

The Panther Creek area is on the western shore of the lake. From Bethel, travel two miles east before turning north on U.S. 259; after six miles, turn back southwest for another two and a quarter miles on an access road. The facilities include a camping area and restrooms.

River Bend Area—12 Campsites
(*concessionaire*)

The River Bend area is on the west shore approximately five miles north of Broken Bow on U.S. 259, and then five miles east on an access road, before heading south for one and a quarter miles. Facilities include a camping area, a picnic area, a swimming area, restrooms, showers, a concession stand, water, a nature trail, a trailer dump station, electric outlets, and a playground.

Stevens Gap Area—72 Campsites
(*concessionaire*)

Stevens Gap area is on the west shore approximately eight miles north of Broken Bow on U.S. 259 and then east on an access road for one and a quarter

Boat dock at Hochatown State Park at Broken Bow Lake in southeastern Oklahoma. Photo by Fred W. Marvel. Courtesy of Oklahoma Tourism and Recreation Department.

miles. The facilities include a boat ramp, a camping area, a picnic area, a swimming area, restrooms, showers, water, a trailer dump station, electrical outlets, a concession stand, and a playground.

DARDANELLE LAKE

For information contact: Project Manager, P.O. Box 1087, Russellville, Arkansas 72801, telephone (501) 968-5008.

Cabin Creek—5 Campsites

The Cabin Creek area is two miles west of Knoxville. Facilities include a camping area, trailer parking, drinking water, restrooms, a picnic area, a group shelter, and a boat ramp.

Cane Creek—8 Campsites

Cane Creek is three miles northwest of Dublin. Facilities include a camping area, trailer parking, drinking water, restrooms, a picnic area, a group shelter, and a boat ramp.

Delaware—15 Campsites

The Delaware area is two and a half miles northeast of Delaware on Arkansas 393. Facilities include a camping area, trailer parking, drinking water, restrooms, a picnic area, a group shelter, an overlook shelter, and a boat ramp.

Flat Rock—15 Campsites

The Flat Rock area is four miles southeast of Knoxville. Facilities include a camping area, trailer parking, drinking water, restrooms, a picnic area, a group shelter, and a boat ramp.

Horsehead—10 Campsites

Access to Horsehead is 4.7 miles southeast of Hartman. Facilities include a camping area, trailer parking, drinking water, restrooms, a picnic area, group shelter, and a boat ramp.

Old Post Road—16 Campsites

Old Post Road access is three and a half miles southwest of Russellville. This well-equipped area includes a camping

Scenic view of Flat Rock
Park on Lake Dardanelle
near Russellville, Arkan-
sas. Courtesy of U.S.
Army Corps of Engineers,
Little Rock District.

area, trailer parking, a dump station,
drinking water, restrooms, a picnic
area, a group shelter, a playground,
multipurpose courts, an overlook shelter, softball-baseball fields, and a boat
ramp. Overnight accommodations and a
café are available nearby.

Piney Bay—39 Campsites

Piney Bay access is two miles south
of Hickeytown on Arkansas 359. Facilities include camping, trailer parking, a
dump station, electrical outlets, drinking water, restrooms, a picnic area, a
group shelter, and a boat ramp.

Riverview Dam Site West—
   22 Campsites

Dam Site West is in north Dardanelle.
Facilities include a camping area, trailer
parking, drinking water, restrooms, a
picnic area, and an overlook shelter.
Overnight accommodations and softball-
baseball fields are available nearby.

Shoal Bay—60 Campsites

Shoal Bay access is 16.6 miles east of
Dardanelle on Arkansas 22. Facilities
include a camping area, trailer parking,
a dump station, electrical outlets, drinking water, restrooms, a picnic area, a

group shelter, boats, motors, bait, a boat ramp, and a marine dumping station.

Spadra—37 Campsites

Spadra access is three miles south of Clarksville on Arkansas 103. Facilities include a camping area, trailer parking, drinking water, restrooms, showers, a picnic area, a group shelter, a café, boats, motors, bait, and a boat ramp. Overnight accommodations are available nearby.

DE GRAY LAKE

For more information contact: Project Manager, 30 IP Circle, Arkadelphia, Arkansas 71923, telephone (501) 246-5501.

Alpine Ridge—49 Campsites

The Alpine Ridge area is accessible by traveling approximately five and a half miles east of Alpine before taking a left fork for another one and a quarter miles. Facilities include a camping area, restrooms, water, a boat ramp, and a picnic area.

Arlie Moore—41 Campsites

Arlie Moore access is approximately one and a half miles southwest of Oak Bower on a lake access road. Facilities include electricity, showers, water, a sanitary dump station, a picnic area, a boat ramp, and restrooms.

Caddo Drive—30 Campsites

The Caddo Drive area is on the north shore. From Duffie (Old De Roche) travel a half mile west on Arkansas 128, then south on Arkansas 7 for .6 mile and then back west for another 3 miles. Facilities include a boat ramp, restrooms, electricity, showers, water, a sanitary dump station, and a picnic area.

De Gray State Park—113 Campsites

This park, which is north of the dam, is approximately eleven miles north of

Arkadelphia on Arkansas 7. See the state parks listing in this chapter for an inventory of the facilities.

Edgewood—34 Campsites

Edgewood access is available a half mile west of Old De Roche on Arkansas 128, then south on Arkansas 7 for .6 mile, and then back west for another 2.5 miles. Facilities include electricity, showers, water, a sanitary dump station, and restrooms.

Iron Mountain—36 Campsites

Iron Mountain access is approximately two miles west of De Gray Dam on a lake access road. From Arkadelphia, travel north on Arkansas 7 for seven miles, then east four miles past the dam on a lake access road. Facilities include electricity, showers, water, a sanitary dump station, a picnic area, a boat ramp, and restrooms.

Oak Brower Group Use Area— (*reservations required*)

Oak Brower, a camping area for organized groups, is approximately 1.75 miles southeast of Lambert on an access road. Facilities include a sleeping shelter and a dining hall.

Shouse Ford—83 Campsites

The Shouse Ford area is approximately three miles south of Point Cedar on a lake access road. Facilities include water, restrooms, a boat ramp, and picnic areas.

DE QUEEN LAKE

For more information contact: Project Office, Milwood Tri-Lakes Project, Route 1, Box 37A, Ashdown, Arkansas 71822, telephone (501) 584-4161.

Bella Mine—20 Campsites

The Bella Mine area is 6.3 miles southwest of Gillham by way of U.S. 71 and a lake access road. Facilities include water, restrooms, a boat ramp, and picnic areas.

Oak Grove—38 Campsites

The Oak Grove area is immediately west of De Queen Dam. It is 10.6 miles southwest of Gillham by way of U.S. 71 and a lake access road. Facilities include camping areas, drinking water, restrooms, a picnic area, showers, a dump station, electrical hookups, and a playground.

Pine Ridge—35 Campsites

Pine Ridge is on the west shore twelve miles southwest of Gillham by way of U.S. 71 and lake access roads. Facilities include water, restrooms, a boat ramp, a picnic area, showers, and a dump station.

Rolling Fork Landing—No Campsites

Rolling Fork Landing is on the east shore on the Bella Creek arm. It is 5.3 miles southwest of Gillham by way of U.S. 71 and a lake access road. Facilities include water, restrooms, a boat ramp, and a picnic area.

Story Creek—No Campsites

The Story Creek area is on the east shore, 6.5 miles southwest of Gillham by way of U.S. 71 and a lake access road. Facilities include water, restrooms, a boat ramp, a picnic area, and a group shelter.

DIERKS LAKE

For more information contact: Project Office, Milwood Tri-Lakes Project, Route 1, Box 37A, Ashdown, Arkansas 71822, telephone (501) 584-4161.

Blue Ridge—21 Campsites

Blue Ridge access is approximately 2.75 miles north of Dierks on U.S. 70 and then left on Arkansas 4 for seven miles. Facilities include a camping area, water, and restrooms.

Horseshoe Bend—11 Campsites

The Horseshoe Bend area is approximately two and a half miles west of Dierks on U.S. 70, then north four miles. Facilities include restrooms and an overlook.

Jefferson Ridge—84 Campsites

Jefferson Ridge access is located approximately 2.5 miles west of Dierks on U.S. 70, then north 5.5 miles. Facilities include a camping area, water, restrooms, and a boat ramp.

EUFAULA LAKE

For more information contact: Project Manager, Route 4, P.O. Box 5500, Stigler, Oklahoma 74462, telephone (918) 799-5843.

Arrowhead State Park— 92 Campsites

Arrowhead State Park is off U.S. 69 at Canadian. See the state parks listing in this chapter for a list of the facilities.

Belle Starr Park—123 Campsites

Belle Starr Park is accessed by traveling eight miles south of Checotah on U.S. 69, then east two miles on Oklahoma 150, and then back south for another one and a half miles. Facilities include boat ramps, a picnic area, a camping area, water, a group shelter, restrooms, showers, swimming, a bathhouse, nature trails, a trailer dump station, a marine dump station, and concession services.

Broken Cove—47 Campsites

The Broken Cove area is approximately three miles north of Enterprise on Oklahoma 71, then one mile west. Facilities include a boat ramp, a picnic area, a camping area, water, group shelters, restrooms, showers, a swimming area, a bathhouse, and a trailer dump station.

Crowder Point East—21 Campsites

Crowder Point East is eight miles north of McAlester on U.S. 69 at the Rock Creek exit. Facilities include boat ramps, picnic areas, restrooms, water, a group shelter, showers, a swimming area, a bathhouse, nature trails, and a trailer dump station.

Dam Site North and South—
  48 Campsites

Dam Site North and South accesses are approximately five miles north of Enterprise on Oklahoma 71. Both areas have boat ramps, picnic areas, and restrooms. The south area also has a camping area, water, a group shelter, showers, a swimming area, a bathhouse, a nature trail, a dump station, and concession services.

Elm Point—13 Campsites

The Elm Point area is approximately four miles south of Blocker on Oklahoma 31. Facilities include a boat ramp, a picnic area, a camping area, water, restrooms, and a swimming area.

Fountainhead State Park—
  84 Campsites

Fountainhead State Park is approximately eight miles south of Checotah on U.S. 69, then west on Oklahoma 150 for another two miles. See the state parks listing in this chapter for a list of the facilities.

Gentry Creek Cove—42 Campsites

The Gentry Creek Cove area is approximately nine miles west of Checotah on Oklahoma 266, and then north for half a mile. Facilities include a boat ramp, a picnic area, a camping area, water, restrooms, and a swimming area.

Hickory Point—7 Campsites

The Hickory Point area is two miles west of Adamson, and then a half mile north on a lake access road. Facilities include a boat ramp, a picnic area, a camping area, water, restrooms, and a swimming area.

Highway 9 Landing—82 Campsites

The Highway 9 Landing is seven miles west of Enterprise on Oklahoma 9. Facilities include a boat ramp, a picnic area, a camping area, water, restrooms, showers, a swimming area, a bathhouse, a trailer dump station, and concession services.

Highway 31 Landing (*group camping by reservation only*)

The Highway 31 Landing is five miles west of Krebs on Oklahoma 31. Facilities include a boat ramp, a picnic area, a camping area, water, a group shelter, and restrooms.

Holiday Cove—15 Campsites

Holiday Cove access is six miles west of Checotah on Interstate 40, and then one and a quarter miles south on a marked road. Facilities include a boat ramp, a picnic area, a camping area, water, a group shelter, and restrooms.

Juniper Point—16 Campsites

The Juniper Point area can be reached by traveling approximately four and a quarter miles north of Krebs on U.S. 69, then east for a mile, and then back north for another three miles. Facilities include a boat ramp, a picnic area, a camping area, water, a group shelter, restrooms, showers, a swimming area, and a bathhouse.

Mill Creek Bay—11 Campsites

The Mill Creek Bay area is a mile east of Vivian on Oklahoma 9, and then north for two miles. Facilities include a boat ramp, a picnic area, a camping area, drinking water, and a group shelter.

Oak Ridge—13 Campsites

The Oak Ridge area is six miles north of Eufaula on U.S. 69. Facilities include a boat ramp, a picnic area, a camping area, water, and restrooms.

Porum Landing—48 Campsites

Porum Landing is three miles south of Texanna. Facilities include a boat ramp, a picnic area, a camping area, water, restrooms, showers, a swimming area, a trailer and marine dump station, and concession services.

GILLHAM LAKE

For more information contact: Project Office, Milwood Tri-Lakes Project, Route 1, Box 37A, Ashdown, Arkansas 71822, telephone (501) 584-4161.

Coon Creek Area—21 Campsites

The Coon Creek area is five and a half miles east of Grannis, Arkansas, on a gravel road, and then right on a short access road. Facilities include a boat ramp, a camping area, water, and restrooms.

Cossatot Reef Area—30 Campsites

The Cossatot Reef area is approximately six miles from Grannis, Arkansas, on a gravel access road. Facilities include a boat ramp, a camping area, water, and restrooms.

LAKE GREESON

For more information contact: Project Manager, Route 1, Murfreesboro, Arkansas 71958, telephone (501) 285-2151.

Arrowhead Point—23 Campsites

The Arrowhead Point area is 3.5 miles east of Newhope on U.S. 70. Facilities include a boat ramp, a picnic area and campground, water, and restrooms.

Bear Creek—19 Campsites

The Bear Creek area is .3 mile south of Kirby on Arkansas 27, then right on an all weather road for 2 miles. Facilities include a boat ramp, a picnic area and campground, water, nature trails, motorbike trails, and restrooms.

Cowhide Cove—54 Campsites

The Cowhide Cove area can be reached by driving 3.5 miles north from Murfreesboro on Arkansas 19, then east on Chaney Trace for approximately 4.5 miles, and then back west for 0.5 mile on an unimproved road. Facilities include a boat ramp, a picnic area and campground, water, nature trails, and restrooms.

Daisy State Park—118 Campsites

The park is a mile west of Daisy on U.S. 70. See the state parks listing in this chapter for a list of the facilities.

Highway 70 Landing—No Camping

The Highway 70 Landing is four miles east of Newhope on U.S. 70. Facilities include a boat rental, tackle and bait concessions, overnight cabins, a commercial trailer park, water, and restrooms.

Kirby Landing—87 Campsites

Kirby Landing is 2.25 miles west of Kirby on U.S. 70, and then south for 1 mile. Facilities include a boat rental, fishing boats, tackle and bait concessions, a boat ramp, a picnic area, a campground, water, nature trails, and restrooms.

Laurel Creek—24 Campsites

Laurel Creek is 5 miles south of the town of Kirby, and then west on a gravel road for 3.75 miles. Facilities include a boat ramp, a picnic area, a campground, water, nature trails, and restrooms.

Mill Mountain and Parker Creek— 60 Campsites

The Mill Mountain and Parker Creek area is accessed by traveling approximately five miles north of Nathan, then one and a half miles east, and then on a left fork for another half mile. Facilities include a boat ramp, a picnic area, a camping area, water, nature and motorbike trails, and restrooms.

Narrows Dam Area—24 Campsites

The Narrows Dam area is four miles north of Murfreesboro on Arkansas 19, and then on the left fork for one mile. Facilities include boat rental, tackle and bait concessions, a boat ramp, a restaurant, overnight cabins, a picnic area and campground, water, nature trails, and restrooms.

Pikeville—12 Campsites

Pikeville can be reached by traveling 5.5 miles north of Nathan on a gravel road, then east for a mile, then south for a mile, and then back east for another mile. Facilities include a boat ramp, a picnic and campground, water, nature trails, and restrooms.

Rock Creek—10 Campsites
(*primitive*)

The Rock Creek area is eight miles north of Nathan, and then left for a half mile. Facilities include a boat ramp, a picnic area and campground, water, nature trails, and restrooms.

Self Creek—72 Campsites

The Self Creek area is a mile west of Daisy on U.S. 70. Facilities include boat rental, tackle and bait concessions, a boat ramp, a restaurant, overnight cabins, a picnic area and campground, water, and restrooms.

Star of the West—21 Campsites

The Star of the West area is two and a half miles east of Newhope on U.S. 70, and then right for a quarter mile. Facilities include a picnic area, a campground, water, and restrooms.

HUGO LAKE

For more information contact: Project Manager, P.O. Box 99, Sawyer, Oklahoma 74756, telephone (405) 326-3345.

Group Camping Area (*group camping by reservation only*)

The Group Camping area is 1.25 miles southwest of Virgil on a lake access road. Facilities include water, restrooms, a camping area, four group shelters, a swimming beach, and a bathhouse.

Kiamichi Park—110 Campsites

Kiamichi Park is four miles east of Hugo on U.S. 70. Facilities include a boat ramp, a picnic area, water, restrooms, a group shelter, showers, a camping area, a swimming beach and bathhouse, nature trails, and a dump station.

Rattan landing—13 Campsites

The Rattan Landing area is four and a half miles west of Rattan on Oklahoma 7. Facilities include a boat ramp, a camping and picnic area, water, and restrooms.

Salt Creek Cove—25 Campsites

Salt Creek Cove area is six miles northeast of Hugo on Oklahoma 93. Facilities include a boat ramp, a camping and picnic area, water, restrooms, showers, and a dump station.

Virgil Point—52 Campsites

Virgil Point is two miles southeast of Virgil on a lake access road. Facilities include a boat ramp, water, restrooms, a camping area, a swimming area, showers, and a dump station.

ROBERT S. KERR LAKE

For more information contact: Project Manager, HC-61, Box 419, Sallisaw, Oklahoma 74955-9445, telephone (918) 775-4475.

Applegate Cove—27 Campsites

The Applegate Cove area is south of Sallisaw on U.S. 59. Facilities include boat ramps, a picnic area, toilets, water, a trailer sanitary station, swimming, and a camping area.

Cowlington Point—28 Campsites

The Cowlington Point area is five miles north of Oklahoma 9 and three miles west of Oklahoma 59. Facilities include water, toilets, a picnic area, a trailer sanitary station, electrical hookups, boat ramps, a camping area, and a swimming area.

Gore Landing—15 Campsites

Gore Landing is one and a half miles east of Gore on U.S. 64. Facilities include boat ramps, a camping area, a swimming area, toilets, picnic areas, electrical hookups, and a trailer sanitary station.

Keota Landing—32 Campsites

The Keota Landing area is three miles north of Keota on a paved county road. Facilities include toilets, a picnic area, water, a boat ramp, a trailer sanitary station, a camping area, and a swimming area.

Sallisaw Creek—11 Campsites

The Sallisaw Creek area, which is accessible from the McKey Road exit on I–40, is southwest of Sallisaw on the north side of the lake. Facilities include a picnic area, boat ramps, toilets, water, a camping area, and a trailer sanitary station.

Short Mountain Cove—58 Campsites

The Short Mountain Cove area is on the south side of the lake, one and a half miles west of Highway 59 over a gravel road. Facilities include water, a picnic area, toilets, boat ramps, trailer sanitary stations, and a camping area.

McGEE CREEK LAKE

For more information contact: Project Manager, Bureau of Reclamation, McGee Creek Lake, P.O. Box 71, Farris, Oklahoma 74542, telephone (405) 889–7307.

The camping facilities and access areas include five recreation and camping areas with boat ramps on the west shore above the dam, on the main channel, and on the Potapo Creek arm. Dedication ceremonies for the project were conducted 22 August 1986; however, the lake was not completely full until February, 1987.

W. D. MAYO LOCK AND DAM AREAS

LeFlore Landing—14 Campsites

LeFlore Landing is near Spiro, just off Oklahoma 9. Facilities include a picnic area, restrooms, showers, water, trailer sanitary stations, a boat ramp, and a camping area.

NIMROD LAKE

For more information contact: Project Manager, Nimrod-Blue Mountain Project, Plainview, Arkansas 72857, telephone (501) 272-4324.

Carden Point—9 Campsites

Carden Point is five miles southeast of Plainview on Arkansas 60. Facilities include a boat ramp, a picnic area, campgrounds, water, restrooms, and trailer parking.

Carter Cove—16 Campsites

Carter Cove is three miles southeast of Plainview on Arkansas 60, and then south for about three-quarters of a mile. Facilities include a boat ramp, a picnic area, a campground, water, a group shelter, restrooms, a swimming area, a bathhouse, and trailer parking.

County Line—20 Campsites

County Line area is approximately a mile northwest of Fourche Junction on Arkansas 7. Facilities include boat and motor rentals, a bait concession, a boat ramp, a picnic area, campgrounds, water, restrooms, a swimming area, a bathhouse, trailer parking, and electricity.

Project Point—6 Campsites

The Project Point area is approximately a quarter mile northwest of Fourche Junction on Arkansas 60. Facilities include a picnic area, campgrounds, water, restrooms, and trailer parking.

Quarry Cove—31 Campsites

Quarry Cove is a half mile northwest of Fourche Junction on Arkansas 60, and then south a mile. Facilities include boat launching, a picnic area, campgrounds, water, a group shelter, restrooms, a swimming area, a bathhouse, and trailer parking.

River Road—15 Campsites

River Road area is a half mile southeast of Fourche Junction on Highway 7 (turn right before crossing the bridge). Facilities include a boat ramp, a picnic area, campgrounds, water, a group shelter, restrooms, and trailer parking.

Sunlight Bay—28 Campsites

Sunlight Bay is two miles south of Plainview on Steve Road, and then left on Sunlight Road. Facilities include boat rental and bait concessions, a boat ramp, a picnic area, a campground, water, a group shelter, restrooms, and trailer parking.

OUACHITA LAKE

For more information contact: Project Manager, P.O. Box 4, Mountain Pine, Arkansas 71956-0004, telephone (501) 767-2101.

Big Fir—17 Campsites

The Big Fir area is sixteen miles northeast of Mount Ida on Arkansas 188. Facilities include a campground and picnic area, water, and restrooms.

Brady Mountain—71 Campsites

The Brady Mountain area is seventeen miles west of Hot Springs on U.S. 270, and then seven miles north on a lake access road. Facilities include boat rental, tackle and bait concessions, a restaurant, overnight and vacation lodging, a trailer park, campgrounds, a picnic area, water, restrooms, a boat ramp, boat storage, and group picnic shelters.

Buckville—5 Campsites

The Buckville area is 3.6 miles south of Avant on a lake access road. Facilities include a campground, a picnic area, and water.

Crystal Springs—62 Campsites

The Crystal Springs area is 2.9 miles northwest of Crystal Springs on a lake access road. Facilities include boat rental, tackle and bait concessions, a restaurant, overnight and vacation lodging, a trailer park, campgrounds, a picnic area, water, restrooms, a boat ramp, and boat storage.

Denby Point Gap Creek—
67 Campsites

Denby Point Gap Creek is two miles northeast of Silver on a lake access road. Facilities include boat rental, tackle and bait concessions, a restaurant, overnight and vacation lodging, a trailer park, a campground and picnic

Camp-A-Float campsite with RV on Lake Ouachita. Courtesy of Arkansas Department of Parks and Tourism.

area, water, restrooms, a boat ramp, and boat storage.

Highway 27—10 Campsites

The Highway 27 area is 2.5 miles south of Washita on Arkansas 27, and then east on a lake access road. Facilities include campgrounds, a picnic area, water, a boat ramp, boat storage, and restrooms.

Irons Fork—5 Campsites

Irons Fork is 4.2 miles east of Fannie on Arkansas 298, and then one mile south on a lake access road. Facilities include a campground, a picnic area, water, and restrooms.

Joplin—65 Campsites

The Joplin area is 2.4 miles north of Joplin on a lake access road. Facilities include boat rental, a bait shop, a restaurant, overnight and vacation lodging, a trailer park, a campground and picnic area, water, a boat ramp, boat storage, and restrooms.

Lake Ouachita State Park— 102 Campsites

Lake Ouachita State Park is on the east shore of the lake. See the state parks listing in this chapter for a list of the facilities.

Lena Landing—10 Campsites

Lena Landing is one mile south of Lena on a lake access road. Facilities include a boat rental and bait shop, a restaurant, overnight and vacation lodging, a trailer park, campgrounds, a picnic area, water, restrooms, and boat storage.

Little Fir—25 Campsites

The Little Fir area is 3 miles east of Rubre on Arkansas 188, then north 2.2 miles on a lake access road. Facilities include a boat rental and bait shop, a restaurant, a trailer park, a campground, a picnic area, water, a boat ramp, boat storage, and restrooms.

Stephens Park—9 Campsites

Stephens Park is one mile west of Mountain Pine on a lake access road. Facilities include a campground, a picnic area, water, a picnic shelter, and restrooms.

Tompkins Bend—75 Campsites

The Tompkins Bend area is 1 mile west of Joplin on U.S. 270, and then north for 2.4 miles on a lake access road. Facilities include a boat rental and bait shop, a restaurant, overnight and vacation lodging, a trailer park, campgrounds, a picnic area, water, a boat ramp, boat storage, and restrooms.

Camping at one of Lake Ouachita's 538 campsites. Courtesy of Arkansas Department of Parks and Tourism.

Twin Creek—15 Campsites

The Twin Creek area is one mile northwest of Silver on a lake access road. Facilities include a campground, a picnic area, water, and restrooms.

OZARK LAKE

For more information contact: Project Manager, Route 1, Box 267R, Ozark, Arkansas 72949, telephone (501) 667-2129.

Citadel Bluff—36 Campsites

The Citadel Bluff area is seven miles east of Mulberry on an access road leading off U.S. 64. Facilities include a picnic area, a nature trail, restrooms, and a playground.

Clear Creek—40 Campsites

The Clear Creek area is eight miles southeast of Alma by way of Arkansas 162 and a lake access road. Facilities include a boat ramp, water, restrooms, and a group shelter.

Dam Site 13 South—24 Campsites

The Dam Site 13 South area is two miles north of Barling. Facilities include boat ramps, water, showers, a dump station, and restrooms.

Lee Creek—14 Campsites

Lee Creek is on the waterfront at Van Buren, Arkansas. Facilities include water, a boat ramp, dump stations, and restrooms.

Ozark Dam Site South—
  41 Campsites

Ozark Dam Site South is one mile south of Ozark on Arkansas 23. Facilities include water, restrooms, and a boat ramp.

River Ridge—24 Campsites

River Ridge is eleven miles west of Cecil on Arkansas 96. Facilities include

a boat ramp, water, showers, restrooms, and a group shelter.

Vache Grasse—30 Campsites

Vache Grasse is 3.5 miles northwest of Lavaca on Arkansas 255. Facilities include a boat ramp, water, restrooms, and a group shelter.

Vine Prairie—6 Campsites

Vine Prairie is two miles south of Mulberry on a lake access road. Facilities include a boat ramp, water, restrooms, a dump station, and a group shelter.

White Oak—8 Campsites

The White Oak area is seven miles east of Mulberry by way of U.S. 64 and a lake access road. Facilities include a boat ramp, water, restrooms, a dump station, and a group shelter.

PINE CREEK LAKE

For more information contact: Project Manager, Route 1, Box 400, Valliant, Oklahoma 74764, telephone (405) 933-4239.

Little River Park—76 Campsites

Little River Park is on the west shore, one mile south of Arkansas 3 near Burwell. Facilities include a boat ramp, a picnic area, a camping area, drinking water, restrooms, a swimming beach, a nature trail, and a trailer dump station. Thirty-seven of the seventy-six campsites have electricity.

Lost Rapids Park—20 Campsites

Lost Rapids Park is on Arkansas 3 one mile west of Ringold. Facilities include a boat ramp, a picnic area, a camping area, drinking water, restrooms, and a trailer dump station. There are no electrical hookups.

Water skiing on Pine Creek Lake in southeastern Oklahoma. Courtesy of Oklahoma Tourism and Recreation Department.

Recreational vehicle campsite at Lake Wister State Park. Photo by Fred W. Marvel. Courtesy of Oklahoma Tourism and Recreation Department.

Pine Creek Cove—30 Campsites

Pine Creek Cove is at Pine Creek Dam spillway eleven miles northwest of Wright City by way of Oklahoma 98 and 3. Facilities include a boat ramp, a picnic area, a camping area, drinking water, restrooms, and a swimming beach.

Turkey Creek Landing—17 Campsites

Turkey Creek Landing is on the west shore three miles north of Oklahoma 3 from a lake access road. Facilities include a boat ramp, a picnic area, a camping area, drinking water, restrooms, and a trailer dump station.

WISTER LAKE

For more information contact: Project Manager, Route 2, Box 7B, Wister, Oklahoma 74966-9501, telephone (918) 655-7206.

Dam Site—8 Campsites

Dam Site is 1.5 miles south of Wister on U.S. 270. Facilities include a picnic area, a campground, restrooms, and water.

Quarry Island—5 Campsites
(*concessionaire*)

Quarry Island is two miles southeast of Wister on U.S. 270. Facilities include a boat ramp, twenty-three picnic areas, water, electricity, a group picnic site with shelter, a grocery store, and five rental cabins.

Victor Area—61 Campsites
(*concessionaire*)

The Victor area is six miles southwest of Wister by way of lake access roads. Facilities include a boat ramp, electricity, water, and a group camping area with sleeping quarters, kitchen, and a basketball court.

Wister Ridge—24 Campsites
(*concessionaire*)

Wister Ridge is four miles south of Wister by way of lake access roads. Facilities include a boat ramp, restrooms, picnic areas, electricity, water, a swimming area, a restaurant, a group picnic area with shelter, and five rental cabins.

Geology and Rock Hounding

GEOLOGIC STRUCTURE AND HISTORY

Most of the rocks within the Ouachita Mountain region are sedimentary. Consisting primarily of shale, sandstone, chert, novaculite, tuff, limestone, and conglomerate, these sedimentary rocks have been affected only slightly by metamorphism. There are instances, however, where shale has been converted into slate, and where beds of sandstone have been cemented into quartzite.[1]

Igneous rocks occur in three small areas: (1) Potash Sulphur Springs in the Hot Springs district; (2) Magnet Cove in northern Hot Springs County; and (3) near Murfreesboro in Pike County, Arkansas. At the first two sites, intrusive masses of nephelite syenite and related rock types were forced upward into the sedimentary strata late in Lower Cretaceous time and early in Upper Cretaceous time (i.e., approximately seventy-five million years ago). At the latter site are several small diamond bearing peridotite "pipes," also of Cretaceous age.

All of the sedimentary beds, which are as much as 37,000 feet thick and range in age from Ordovician (500 million years before the present) to Pennsylvanian (310 million years before the present), have been subjected to intense compression (map 31). Recent theories relating to the plate tectonics of the earth's crust have hypothesized that the deformation of the fold belt was produced by a collision of the North American continent with another continent or island arc.[2] Besides additional uplifting of the entire subsurface materials above the sea, this compression produced numerous east-west folds and a number of thrust fault slices. The intensity of this deformation was greatest in the central Ouachita Mountains and decreased beyond that area. In many cases, the eroded edges of these folds and the upturned edges of the thrust slices are now apparent at the surface (fig. 5).

One of the outstanding geologic features within the Ouachitas is a gigantic upfold (Novaculite anticlinorium) that makes up the core of the mountain range and whose axis extends southwest from a point a few miles southwest of Little Rock to the vicinity of Glover, Oklahoma.[3] The eastern and western ends of this great upfold are concealed by overlapping Central Lowlands deposits.

Many of the smaller folds within the region overlap one another lengthwise. They are often closely compressed and/or overturned so that the beds on both sides of the structural axis dip in the same direction. While some folds are overturned toward the north, others are overturned toward the south. As one approaches the Arkansas Valley in the northern portion of the province in Arkansas, the folds become more open with little, if any, evidence of overturning. However, the northern part of the Ouachitas in Oklahoma consists of a series of fault slices in which the ridges are the upturned layers of resistant rock and the valleys represent the shattered rock associated with each fault zone. Throughout the Ouachitas, many adjacent folds are nearly equal in height. Consequently, the same beds appear at the surface in each fold. Beds tilted at angles of forty degrees or more are very common.

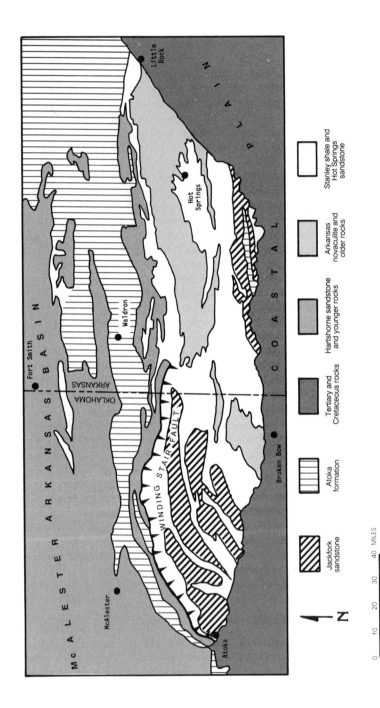

Map 31. Geology of the Ouachita Province. *Adapted from:* H. D. Miser, "The Structure of the Ouachita Mountains of Oklahoma and Arkansas," *Oklahoma Geological Survey Bulletin 50* (1929); L. M. Cline, "Stratigraphy of the Late Paleozoic Rocks of the Ouachita Mountains, Oklahoma," *Oklahoma Geological Survey Bulletin 85* (1960).

Steeply tilted rock strata in the severely folded and faulted Ouachita Mountains on Arkansas Highway 7 near De Gray Lake. Courtesy of Arkansas Department of Parks and Tourism.

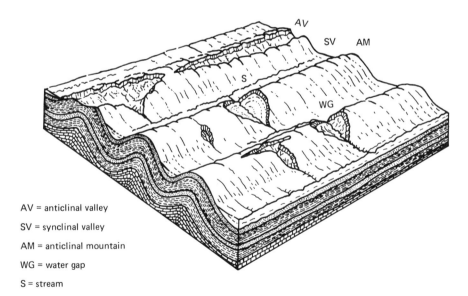

AV = anticlinal valley

SV = synclinal valley

AM = anticlinal mountain

WG = water gap

S = stream

Figure 5. Topographic Development on Folded Rocks. *Adapted from:* O. D. von Engeln, *Geomorphology: Systematic and Regional.* (New York: The Macmillan Company, 1948), 325.

Although faults (or fractures) in the rock layers are numerous, they are not as common as one might expect in an area marked by such intense compression. This is partly because the great thickness of the shale distributed throughout the folded beds permitted them to adjust to the crustal shortening by shearing and crumpling rather than by great thrust faulting. Most of the existing faults were produced by breaking the beds in closely compressed anticlines. The largest fault in the entire region is the great Choctaw fault in southeastern Oklahoma; it measures at least 120 miles long and marks the northern boundary of the Ouachita Mountains.

The severe folding and faulting has profoundly influenced the development of the region's landforms. Many structural synclines (downfolds) and anticlines (upfolds) have become valleys and ridges, respectively, but a larger number have become synclined ridges and anticlinal valleys, respectively, as the result of the tremendous geologic erosion caused by streams. Consequently, the repetitive ridge and valley landscape stems primarily from the erosion of alternating anticlines and synclines.

ROCK HOUNDING

The Ouachita Mountains are perhaps the best territory in America's midsection for the collection of rocks and minerals because the region and its rock units have been subjected to several disturbances including great heat, pressure, fracturing, and folding. Sedimentary rocks predominate; some of the sedimentary deposits, however, have been metamorphosed.

As an aid to those interested in collecting or purchasing geologic specimens, a discussion of the area's major rocks and minerals as well as the most popular collecting sites and rock outcrops is included here. Since rock shops

and crystal quarries come and go, the inventory is restricted to the larger, more permanent businesses. In a similar manner, instead of providing a complete list of all the available collection sites, the roster of these locations is designed to provide information only for the more interesting possibilities. Specific directions to each of the collection sites may be obtained at any of the area's numerous rock shops.

On August 1, 1906, John W. Huddleston picked up two glittering pebbles on his farm, two and a half miles southeast of Murfreesboro, Arkansas; he sent the stones to a Little Rock jeweler, who upon their examination, pronounced that they were genuine diamonds. The stones were subsequently sent to New York City where they were authenticated by several other experts and then cut and polished by the renowned firm of Tiffany and Company.

With the hope that additional diamonds could be found, the Arkansas Diamond Company was formed in 1908. John T. Fuller, a mining engineer who had experience working with the De-Beers Company of South Africa, was employed to examine and comment on the Pike County field. He reported that:

The diamond-bearing rock occurs in South Africa in what is there locally known as a "pipe," which is the neck, or vent, of an old volcano, filled up solid with the diamond-bearing rock. This rock is technically known as peridotite, a rock of bluish-green color, and known in Africa as Kimberlite, or more popularly as blue ground. That the diamond-bearing rock found on your property in Pike County is peridotite is unquestioned. That it occurs on the property in a "pipe" similar to its occurrences in South Africa has been, to my mind, sufficiently demonstrated.[4]

Based upon this information, the company was able to authorize capital stock worth $1 million for the development of the diamond field. A reduction plant was

W. W. Johnson of Amarillo, Texas, displaying largest diamond (sixteen carat, thirty-seven point) ever found at Crater of Diamonds State Park by a tourist. Courtesy of Arkansas Department of Parks and Tourism.

erected and by 1920 over five thousand diamonds had been extracted from the rock. The success of this operation stimulated the emergence of a second company, the Kimberlite Diamond Company, which operated for several years during the 1920s.

Today the diamond field is the focal point of Arkansas' Crater of Diamonds State Park. For a small fee, visitors may search the area of the ancient volcanic intrusion and keep any diamonds they are lucky enough to find. The park is a "must stop" on every rock hound and lapidarist's list of Ouachita collecting sites.

The Arkansas portion of the Ouachitas, in particular, the mountains around Hot Springs, and especially Crystal Mountain, have yielded large quantities of impressive quartz crystals. When first cut and polished, some of the finest specimens of the popular stone closely resemble diamonds; unfortunately, their luster is not as permanent. Still, many of the visitors to this famous resort area purchase "Hot Springs diamonds" as watch charms, scarf pins, and rings.

Novaculite, another Ouachita stone of commercial significance, occurs in great abundance along the high ridges in the northern half of Garland County northeast of Hot Springs. Two varieties are commonly recognized. The "Arkansas Stone" is generally white with a bluish tint; however, depending upon the amount of iron and manganese oxides present, it may also show a red, gray, black, brown, or yellow tint. The "Ouachita Stone" resembles the "Arkansas Stone" in all its chemical and physical properties, but it is more porous and occurs in greater abundance.

Both varieties make excellent whetstones. Archaeological research indicates that prehistoric Indians used the stones for making arrowheads and for cutting tools. As early as 1818 whetstones made from the novaculite in Garland County were floated down the Ouachita and Mississippi Rivers to New Orleans where they were marketed as "Washita Oil Stones." The first large whetstone producing factory was established in 1840.[5]

Today, the market for this remarkable stone continues to benefit from its international reputation as a sharpening stone for tools and instruments. Though marketed in a variety of sizes ranging from a small pocket whetstone to elaborate sets of stones used for very specialized sharpening purposes, most of the "Arkansas Stone" is shipped in five- to fifteen-pound blocks, while the more common Ouachita variety is shipped in blocks as large as fifteen hundred pounds.[6]

Ouachita Rock Shops

Ar-Scenic Spring Gift Shop, 307 Mount Ida Street, Hot Springs, Arkansas 71901, telephone (501) 623-1722, offers a wide variety of jewelry fashioned from locally produced minerals.

The Basket House, 4620 Central Avenue, Hot Springs, Arkansas 71913, telephone (501) 525-2652, sells quartz jewelry and other collectibles.

Burrow's Mining Company, Mount Ida, Arkansas 71957, telephone (501) 867-3664, has a large mineral yard and a sizeable collection of jewelry and gems.

Coleman's Crystal Mines and Rock Shops, Star Route 1, P.O. Box 160, Highway 7N, Jessieville, Arkansas 71949, telephone (501) 984-5328—there are three in the Hot Springs vicinity—is probably the most widely publicized rock shop in the region. Located on Arkansas 7 north of Hot Springs, it offers jewelry made with local stones, many fine lapidary pieces, and various unusual mineral specimens. A large yard contains bulky items such as geodes, quartz crystals, barite roses, and multicolored slag glass. For a small fee, visitors may dig for quartz crystals in the Coleman mine located two miles southwest of Blue Springs.[7]

Coleman's Rocks-R-Gems is at 1700 E. Grand, Hot Springs, Arkansas 71901, telephone (501) 624-7280; and the third, called T.J.'s Gift Shop, is on Highway 7 North, Mountain Valley, Arkansas 71949, telephone (501) 623-9740.

Crater of Diamonds State Park, Murfreesboro, Arkansas 71958, telephone (501) 285-3113, located two miles southwest of Murfreesboro on Arkansas 301, has a gift shop that offers a good selection of lapidary items and souvenirs. Visitors can pay a small fee for the right to search for real diamonds on a "finders keepers" basis.

Crystal Pyramid, 264 Central Avenue, Hot Springs, Arkansas 71901, telephone (501) 623-2620, sells rocks, jewelry, gifts, and souvenirs.

House of Crystals, 376 Whittington Avenue, Hot Springs, Arkansas 71901, telephone (501) 624-7843, stocks a large assortment of lapidary items, crystals, and gifts.

Ocus Stanley and Son Rock Shop, P.O. Box 163, Mount Ida, Arkansas 71957, telephone (501) 867-3556, has one of the largest and most complete mineral and rock yards in the region and is known especially for superb specimens of quartz and fluorite. For three generations, the Stanley family has quarried minerals from the mountains southeast of Mount Ida. Visitors may dig in the crystal quarry for a small fee; serious collectors should ask for specific directions to those areas that have only recently been exposed and tend to be less picked over.

Roca Poca Gem and Lapidary, 5319 West 65, Little Rock, Arkansas 72203, telephone (501) 568-5435, stocks gems, polished stones, and lapidary supplies.

Stoneciphers, 370 Central Avenue, Hot Springs, Arkansas 71901, telephone (501) 623-7481 markets a large selection of cut quartz, other crystals, lapidary pieces, and jewelry.

Wright's Rock Shop, Highway 270 West, Hot Springs, Arkansas 71901, telephone (501) 767-4800, just west of Hot Springs, is one of the area's largest outlets. The shop and the accompanying yard contain over fifty thousand mineral specimens, gems, fossils, jewelry pieces, and collectibles.

NOTABLE COLLECTING SITES AND ROCK EXPOSURES

Collecting Site 1

Magnet Cove, an area of unusual rocks and minerals, derives its name both from the presence of magnetite in the soil and from the basin-like shape of the valley. Located in northern Hot Springs County, about twelve miles east of the city of Hot Springs, Arkansas, the cove is readily accessible since U.S. 270 passes through the center.

The cove, approximately five square miles in area, is an elliptical basin with a northwest-southeast diameter of about three miles. The rim of the basin, broken only where Cove Creek enters and exits the basin, consists of an outer belt of light-colored nepheline syenites and an inner belt of phonolites. A large part of the cove's interior is covered by deep residual and alluvial soils that are presumed to be underlain by ijolite; within this ijolite core are at least two large masses of carbonatite, one of which is exposed at the Kimsey calcite quarry.[8]

Early settlers discovered the unique features of the cove when their compass needles behaved erratically. The presence of the magnetite ore (lodestone) underlying the slope, and on the surface as pebbles, had a strong enough effect to disrupt compass readings; both the cove and the settlement that evolved nearby

were named Magnet. George Featherstonhaugh, a British geologist who visited Colonel James Sevier Conway at the
cove in 1834, was so enthusiastic about
the site he commented that "the pro-
prietor will certainly possess one of the
most enviable estates in America" if it
were not so isolated. Featherstonhaugh
also expressed his belief that the igneous
rocks in this area were the result of volcanic activity.[9]

Several Saint Louis capitalists bought
a ten-acre tract within the cove around
1878 with plans to mine the lodestone
(magnetite) for commercial gain. Before
long, however, they discovered that the
high-grade deposits were very limited,
and the project was abandoned. Subsequent mining efforts have focused primarily on deposits of titanium and barite.
The Magnet Cove Titanium Corporation
operated an open-pit mine in the area
from 1934 through 1944; the Kimsey
Calcite Quarry still operates in the carbonatite deposits northwest of the U.S.
270 bridge over Cove Creek. A second
short-lived attempt to mine magnetite
occurred in 1950–51 when the Kimsey
magnetite pit produced limited quantities of the mineral for shipment to the
steel mills in Birmingham, Alabama.
The now-abandoned Diamond Jo Quarry
once removed nephaline syenite rock
from the cove's rim for use as a building
material.

An inventory of the major igneous intrusive rock types in the cove includes
many varieties unfamiliar even to many
geologists. These include:

Carbonatite, a coarsely crystalline calcite, which occurs as dikes and irregular bodies and, in this area, contains
concentrations of apatite, monticellite,
magnetite, perovskite, and black garnet.
Ijolite, a fine- to coarse-grained rock
composed chiefly of nepheline, diop-
site, and black garnet, contains biotite in
some instances; however, it does not
possess any feldspars.

Phonolite, a fine-grained rock that may
appear gray to greenish to black, is
locally brecciated and banded.
Garnet Pseudoleucite Syenite is a light
gray, medium-grained rock composed
of white pseudoleucite, tabular feldspar,
pyroxene, and black garnet.
Nepheline Syenite is a light gray,
medium- to coarse-grained rock composed of magnetite and pyroxene with
accessory shpene, perovskite, and feldspathoids.
Jacupirangite, a heavy, black, medium-
to coarse-grained rock, is comprised of
magnetite and pyroxene with accessory
shpene, perovskite, and feldspathoids.

There are indications that the igneous
intrusive rocks in Magnet Cove originated from as many as three different
periods of igneous activity.[10]

Collecting Site 2

Talclose shale can be found exposed in
an area in the northeastern part of Saline
County, Arkansas. Situated close to
soapstone deposits, which are also exposed in nearby pits, this site is about
four miles north of the hamlet of Avilla.
Visitors should request specific directions from a local resident.

Collecting Site 3

Nepheline syenite is exposed 0.3 mile
south of Fourche Creek on Arkansas 367
in Pulaski County and at the Dixon exit
off U.S. 65 on the southern outskirts of
Little Rock.

Collecting Site 4

Quartz crystals are exposed in a sandstone bluff on the south side of U.S.
270, approximately 0.3 mile east of the
Garland-Montgomery County line. The
better crystals occur in red clay pockets.
This location should be observed with
extreme caution since it is so close to the
highway and the bluff is noted for its
instability.

Collecting Site 5

Garnet crystals may be found in an open field off U.S. 270 just east of Hot Springs. The "mine," which is located within the Magnet Cove basin, was opened commercially in 1979 after numerous geology groups and clubs had on several occasions visited the site. The mine where, for a small fee, visitors may search the field for red, black, and yellow stones is only open on Sunday afternoons. The higher quality stones found there can make very good ring settings.

Collecting Site 6. Crater of Diamonds State Park

Crater of Diamonds State Park is open to those who wish to pay a small fee in order to prospect for these precious stones. (See earlier discussion of this site in this chapter.)

Collecting Site 7. Caddo Gap

Caddo Gap, which is one mile south of the town of Caddo Gap on Arkansas 8, was formed when the Caddo River cut a spectacular gorge through the mountain of the same name. The exposed rock reveals evidence of at least two directions of folding in severely disturbed beds of novaculite, shale, graywacke, and thin chert-sandstone conglomerates. Although it is an excellent location for photographing tight folds in vertical to recumbent rock strata, it is also a dangerous place to stop since there is little place to park and the passing traffic can be heavy.

North-South Highway Tours

The Ouachita Mountains of Arkansas have been a popular tourist destination for several generations. The Hot Springs area, for instance, had earned a national reputation as an attractive resort before the turn of the century. With two national forests, several swift rivers, more than a dozen lakes, and superb scenery, the long-recognized opportunities for recreation in the Arkansas Ouachitas have contributed greatly to the overall development of the subregion.

The recognition and exploitation of the attractions within the Oklahoma Ouachitas, on the other hand, has been a relatively recent phenomenon; in the past, this rugged and sparsely settled area served almost exclusively as a retreat for hunters, fishermen, and wilderness campers. After the construction of several large dams during the 1960s and 1970s, which led to the formation of several sizeable lakes, the real potential for establishing a tourist-linked economy became evident. Since the 1960s the number of retirement homes, motels, resorts, and lakefront attractions has grown steadily. Even with these developments, the Oklahoma Ouachitas continue to lag behind their Arkansas counterparts. The future of this subregion as a major tourist area, however, is clearly promising.

Those who journey to the Ouachitas will experience some of the most spectacular scenery in the south-central portion of the United States. Along Ouachita highways are ranches, farms, sawmills, factories, tiny hamlets, quiet country villages, and prosperous towns that offer scenic variety and insights into the area's material culture. To serve as a guide to many of these intriguing features, several possible tours that can be taken throughout the region are described; each of the tours follows interstate and federal or state highways that traverse many of the rural sections of the Ouachitas (see map 32).

TOUR A1: MUSKOGEE TO ATOKA BY WAY OF U.S. 69

U.S. 69 follows the old Texas Road that once skirted the western boundary of the Ouachita Mountains province. The route has served both as a conduit for immigrants to Texas and as a drover's trail for herds of cattle driven to northern railheads. Many of the towns along U.S. 69 were founded as railheads when the Missouri-Kansas-Texas Railroad (Katy) was built through the area in the 1870s.

Muskogee

Muskogee (population 42,480),[1] the Indian capital of the Five Civilized Tribes, is a western border town near the junction of the Ozark Plateau and the Ouachita Mountains. It is a port on the Arkansas River Navigation Channel and is served by a large network of roadways, including the Muskogee Turnpike, U.S. 69 and 64, and Oklahoma highways 10, 16, and 51. Its stature as an important transportation hub was assured when the Missouri Pacific Railroad and the Missouri-Kansas-Texas Railroad selected the town for the location of division shops and switching yards. The town's name came from the Creek Indians who, because they spoke the Muskogee language, were sometimes called Muskogees.[2]

In pioneer days, the vicinity around Muskogee was known as Three Forks because of the proximity of the confluences of the Grand (Neosho), Verdigris, and Arkansas rivers. Muskogee became a distribution point for supplies shipped up the Arkansas River to Fort Gibson. Licensed Indian traders, such as Auguste P. Chouteau, relied heavily upon these river connections; Chouteau operated a trading post that used keelboats to send furs and agricultural produce down the Arkansas. The Three Forks area was also the crossing point for the Texas Road, a wagon route leading from Saint Louis to Texas.[3]

During the early settlement, several distinguished Americans visited the region and were struck by its beauty and potential for commerce. Thomas Nuttall, a professor at Harvard College and famed naturalist, spent a month in the area in 1819;[4] Washington Irving, the noted author, visited the area in 1832 and recorded his impressions of his travels in a journal that was later published;[5] and George Catlin, the famous artist, visited the area and painted several Indian portraits.

While steamboat commerce never lived up to the expectations of these early visitors, the railroads permitted the opening of productive agricultural lands as well as the exploitation of extensive coal and oil deposits to the south and west. A mixture of events during the period between 1890 and 1920—land allotments to the Indians, the influx of new settlers, the building and expansion of railroads, the founding of towns, the clearing of land for farms, the discovery and exploitation of coal and oil deposits, and the awarding of statehood to Oklahoma—contributed to a boom in Muskogee's economy and growth.[6] Oil development in the early 1900s triggered the arrival of three new railroads to Muskogee: the Saint Louis and San Francisco (Frisco), the Midland Valley, and the Kansas, Oklahoma and Gulf.[7]

World War II and the establishment of the army's Camp Gruber, a metals processing plant, and a navy fuel plant, brought additional growth to the city. More than a hundred manufacturing plants now operate in Muskogee where access to four railroad systems and excellent highway connections are provided. The manufacturing base is diversified and includes the production of glass products, paper products, clothing, furniture, optical equipment, and fertilizers. More than a dozen additional plants produce food and kindred products.

The Missouri-Kansas-Texas Railroad passes directly through the city, dividing it nearly in half. Okmulgee Avenue, which forms the main business street, runs at right angles to the railroad. While U.S. 64 (business route) is an older commercial development, newer commercial strips have grown up along West Okmulgee Avenue (U.S. 62) and Shawnee Street. Fast food businesses, motels, gas stations, and other typical "strip" businesses are prominent along these streets.

Oktaha

Oktaha (population 376) was founded when the Missouri-Kansas-Texas Railroad extended its tracks south of Muskogee and built a depot at the site. The town was named for Oktahasars Harjo, or Sands, a well-known Creek chief of the Civil War period.[8] Following a now-familiar pattern for small rural towns, Oktaha has experienced a slow decline over the past half century as rural residents bypassed the community to shop in the larger stores in Muskogee. This trend showed signs of reversing during the 1970s as the town's population nearly doubled from 193 to 376. Much of this growth probably can be attributed to the fact that Oktaha has become a bedroom suburb for Muskogee.

Checotah

Checotah (population 3,580) is near the junction of U.S. 69 and Interstate 40

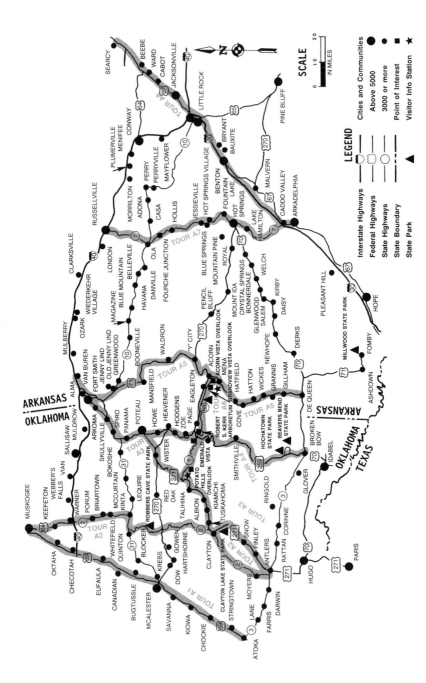

Map 32. North–South Highway Tours. *Adapted from:* Arkansas State Highway and Transportation Department, 1985); Oklahoma State Transportation Map (Oklahoma City: Oklahoma Department of Transportation, 1985).

Sailing on Eufaula Lake in eastern Oklahoma. Photo by Fred W. Marvel. Courtesy of Oklahoma Tourism and Recreation Department.

in north-central McIntosh County. The Missouri-Kansas-Texas Railroad built a depot here in 1872 and named it after Samuel Checote, a Creek chief.[9] A post office was established in 1887. Checotah grew slowly but steadily as a trade center for an agricultural and stock-raising area until about 1960 when the rate of growth increased slightly. A half dozen manufacturing plants provide employment for about 300 workers; the largest of these, White Stag Manufacturing Company, employs approximately 150 in the production of ladies' sportswear.

Eufaula

Eufaula (population 3,600) is situated on a point of land separating two great arms of Eufaula Lake. The arrival of the railroad, in 1872, stimulated the emergence of the town. Its name stems from an old Creek Indian town on the west bank of the Chattahoochee River in Ala-

bama, Yufala, which means "they split up here and went other places."[10]

Once the Record Town for Recording District No. 12, Indian Territory, and currently the county seat of McIntosh County, Eufaula has maintained a modest level of prosperity as a farm marketing and local governmental center. Eufaula Boarding School, the successor to Asbury Mission, was opened in Eufaula in 1892.[11] In recent years the growing tourist and recreation business around Eufaula Lake has helped the town prosper. Boat docks and rentals, boat repair and storage, bait shops, motels, and restaurants have been established to serve visitors. In 1980, Eufaula's half dozen small manufacturing firms employed 155 workers.

Canadian

Canadian (population 279), on the South Canadian Arm of Eufaula Lake, takes its name from the river. Since the mid-1960s, when Eufaula Lake was formed, this small settlement has experienced modest growth as services are provided to the lake's visitors.

Bugtussle

Bugtussle is a hamlet in Pittsburg County, nine miles northeast of McAlester. Its name is a colloquialism meaning "a rustic settlement or backwoods area." [12] Bugtussle gained an unusual level of fame when one of its former residents, Carl Albert, served as Speaker of the United States House of Representatives.

McAlester

McAlester (population 18,820), the seat of Pittsburg County and an important regional shopping town, is situated at the junction of U.S. 69 and 270. Its beginnings can be traced back to 1870 when a tent store was erected at the crossroads of two well-traveled Indian Territory routes, the California Trail and the Texas Road. James J. McAlester, the store's owner, is also credited with opening the first coal mines in Pittsburg County after studying a geologist's memorandum book. [13] Having married a Chickasaw woman, McAlester gained citizen's rights in the Choctaw Nation including mining rights, and the right to collect royalties for the coal mined on Choctaw land. An astute businessman, McAlester accumulated considerable wealth and political power. He later served as Oklahoma's lieutenant governor.

The town that grew up around James McAlester's store is now called North McAlester. Most of present-day McAlester was built after the Rock Island Railroad built a line to a junction with the Missouri-Kansas-Texas (Katy) Railroad. The main business district is located on one of a series of hills that dominate the city's setting. The Pitts-

James J. McAlester. Courtesy of the Oklahoma Historical Society.

burg County courthouse and many of the most important business buildings are strung out along Carl Albert Boulevard, one of the city's oldest principal business thoroughfares. U.S. 69 serves as McAlester's principal string "strip," with numerous motels, gas stations, and fast-food restaurants.

McAlester's economy is well-balanced with government services, retail trade, private sector services, and manufacturing. The larger manufacturing firms include: Champion Rubber Company (inner tubes), Elsing Manufacturing Company (clothing), Hatler Farms, Inc. (poultry feeds), Holsum Baking Company (bakery goods), Seamproof Corporation (clothing), Lockheed California Company (airframes), McAlester Milling Company (feeds), Meeco Marinas, Inc. (boat docks), and Rockwell International Corporation (electronic assemblies). Many McAlester residents are employed at the U.S. Army Ammunition Depot that is located in nearby Savanna.

Savanna

Savanna (population 828), in Pittsburg County ten miles southwest of McAlester, supposedly was named for the private railroad car of Robert Stevens, the general manager of the Missouri-Kansas-Texas Railroad. Once a prosperous coal-mining town in the Choctaw Nation, a mine explosion in 1887 caused Savanna's mines to close,[14] which began a slow decline that continued until the United States Army Ammunition Depot was established during World War II. Since the arrival of this facility Savanna has experienced renewed prosperity.

Kiowa

Kiowa (population 866), in southern Pittsburg County, was founded in 1872 when the Missouri-Kansas-Texas Railroad extended its track south of McAlester; the town was named for Kiowa Hill.[15] The nearby Pine and Jack Fork mountains are known for their good deer hunting.

Chockie

Chockie is the remains of an old Choctaw village located eight miles northeast of Stringtown on U.S. 69. The town was first named Chickiechockie in honor of two daughters of Captain Charles LeFlore of nearby Limestone Gap; the girls had been named for the respective Chickasaw and Choctaw nationalities of their mother and father. When Chickie, who became the wife of Lee Cruce, Oklahoma's second governor, died early in the twentieth century, her name was removed from the depot sign.[16]

The settlement, never very large, is all but gone and the surrounding hill country is sparsely settled. It was along this lonely stretch of tracks that trains were sometimes ambushed in the latter years of the nineteenth century; railroad cuts near Limestone and Stringtown reportedly were favorite points for raids.

Stringtown

Stringtown (population 1,047) stretches out along the Missouri-Kansas-Texas Railroad and U.S. 69. Tilted and disturbed rock strata and long, low ridges hint of the grand mountains that rise farther to the east. First a stagecoach stop on the road from Fort Smith to the Red River, Stringtown later prospered as a lumber mill site after the railroad arrived in 1872. When the original post office opened in July, 1877, it was named Sulphur Springs. The present town name is a modification of its original name, Springtown.[17]

Although the town's name has no connection with its current form, it does stretch north-south in a stringlike manner alongside the railroad tracks and highway. Stringtown serves as a local trade center for the surrounding farms and ranches and for many of the visitors to nearby Atoka Reservoir. Two small manufacturing establishments—Fugate Lumber Mills and Pressure Creosoting, and Stringtown Materials, Inc. (gravel products) employ about twenty workers combined.

Atoka

Atoka (population 3,850), an old Choctaw town at the junction of U.S. 69 and 75 and Oklahoma 3 and 7 at the extreme southwestern tip of the Ouachita Mountains, is the seat of Atoka County. Both of these political entities were named for a subchief of the Choctaw Nation, Captain Atoka.[18]

The town was established in 1867 by the Reverend J. S. Murrow, a Baptist missionary. Shortly afterwards Rev. Murrow founded the Atoka Baptist Academy, which later was absorbed into the Murrow Indian Orphan's Home on the Bacone College campus in Muskogee.[19]

Atoka has long been a trade and service center for the surrounding farms and villages. It has managed to maintain a modest level of prosperity as the county seat and a market center. Two manufacturing firms are especially noteworthy: Debbie Ann, Inc. (clothing) and Ethan Allen, Inc. (furniture). The town's unusual attractions include the Chuckwagon Musical Museum (located downtown on U.S. 69 and 75) and a Confederate cemetery, which commemorates the 1864 Muddy Boggy battle site and lies north of Atoka (east of U.S. 69) on the north bank of Muddy Boggy Creek.

TOUR A2: MUSKOGEE
   TO ANTLERS BY WAY OF
   U.S. 64 AND OKLAHOMA 2

Oklahoma 2 traverses the Ouachita province north-south, providing travelers with an untrammeled view of the rural countryside. One of the least traveled of the north-south highways that cut across the region, the road runs against the grain of the topography and winds up and down steep grades while crossing numerous ridges and valleys.

Muskogee (see tour A1)

Keefeton

Keefeton (population 220), ten miles south of Muskogee on U.S. 64, was named for J. H. Keefe, vice president of the Santa Fe Railroad.

Warner

Warner (population 1,310) is on U.S. 64 in southern Muskogee County near an interchange with Interstate 40. Formerly called Hereford, the town elected to change the name in 1905 to honor William Warner, the United States Senator from Missouri.

The business district, comprised of one- and two-story brick and frame buildings, consists of the usual array of grocery stores, service stations, clothing stores, machine shops, implement dealerships, churches, and schools. In 1908 the Connors State Agricultural College was established in Warner, and the curriculum was later expanded to include more general junior college courses. The *1980 Oklahoma Directory of Manufacturers and Products* lists only one small manufacturer—Warner Furniture Manufacturing—with just twenty employees.

Porum

Porum (population 668), in southwestern Muskogee County, was named for J. Porum Davis, commonly known as Dave Porum, a prominent Indian leader. While Porum's population has remained fairly stable for the past half century, like many other small towns, it has lost most of its businesses and taken on more of an exclusive residential function.

Porum was the home of Tom Starr—half Irish and half Cherokee—who was an ardent supporter of Major Ridge and the Treaty party when the Cherokee Nation was established in present-day Oklahoma. When his father, James Starr, was killed during the bloody reprisals that followed the arrival of the main body of Cherokees, Tom Starr set about killing as many of the nontreaty party as possible. His vendetta was so successful that the Cherokee government, unable to either capture or kill him, finally agreed to award him $100,000 and complete amnesty if he would cease the killings. Starr then moved to Briartown where he pursued a quiet life.[20]

Briartown

Briartown is a tiny hamlet situated north of the Arkansas 2 bridge on the Canadian River.

Robbers Cave State Park near Wilburton, Oklahoma, in the Sans Bois Mountains. Photo by Fred W. Marvel. Courtesy of Oklahoma Tourism and Recreation Department.

Whitefield

Whitefield (population 240), a small hamlet just south of the Arkansas 2 bridge on the Canadian River, was first called Oklahoma. The original post office was established in 1888, and at that time the name was changed to honor a pioneer Methodist minister, Bishop George Whitefield.[21]

Kinta

Kinta (population 303) is in southern Haskell County at the junction of Oklahoma 2 and 31. The name is said to be an Indian word for beaver. Kinta is in the valley of Sans Bois Creek. Tucker Knob, a prominent peak in the Sans Bois Mountains, can be seen about five miles to the southwest; at a similar distance to the northwest, one can see Beaver Mountain.

The town is clustered along a two-block, curbed and guttered stretch of Oklahoma 2 and 31 that serves as the main business district. Many of the buildings are one-story, false-fronted brick structures built around the turn of the century. Approximately half of these are now abandoned. A car wash, quick-shop gasoline and grocery store, and a few other businesses occupy new and remodeled buildings.

Lewisville

Lewisville, three miles west of Kinta, is one of those rural communities that has retained its name long after its function as a rural center has ceased.

Robbers Cave State Park

Robbers Cave State Park is fourteen miles south of the junction of Arkansas 2 and 31 and five miles north of Wilburton. See chapter 6 for a description of the available facilities and attractions.

Wilburton

Wilburton (population 3,260), the seat of Latimer County, was named, according to local reports, either for Will Burton, a contractor who helped bring the Choctaw, Oklahoma, and Gulf Railroad into the Oklahoma coal fields in the 1890s, or for Elisha Wilbur, the president of the Lehigh Valley Railroad. Now that coal mining is no longer important in the area, the chief economic support for the community is derived from recreational and educational activities. Eastern Oklahoma State University, founded in 1909 as a School of Mines and Metallurgy at the west edge of town, is built around a grassy commons that serves as a practice field for the cheerleaders and marching band and as a place to lounge and study. The massive buildings and throngs of young people seem somewhat out of place in such a small community.

Wilburton offers a picturesque setting in a valley situated between the Sans Bois Mountains and Blue Mountain. Bandy Creek, a headwaters stream in the Poteau River basin flows through the southern part of the town. To the west, the Wilburton Basin widens to ten or fifteen miles accommodating extensive hayfields and pastures that support a cattle-ranching industry.

Damon

Damon, a nearly abandoned hamlet six miles south of Wilburton, is situated in an upland basin in the Winding Stair Mountains. Blue Mountain is located a mile to the north and Eight Mile Mountain is about six miles to the south. Damon consists of a half dozen houses and a community church.

Yanush

Yanush (population 180) is a tiny hamlet on the north shore of Sardis Lake. The name, which is a Choctaw word meaning "buffalo," is derived from nearby Buffalo Creek.[22] Yanush consists of an all-faith church, a general store and gasoline station, and a string of houses along the highway. Several new houses and mobile homes have been built along a three-mile stretch of Oklahoma 2 just north of Yanush. Signs advertising lots for sale indicate efforts to stimulate the development of property for retirement homes near Sardis Lake.

South of Yanush the highway crosses the Buffalo Creek arm of Sardis Lake. In spite of its location in a sparsely settled section of Oklahoma, a few commercial camping areas, lodges, and boating supply businesses have appeared along the highway near the lake.

Clayton

Clayton (population 833) is at the junction of U.S. 271 and Arkansas 2 in Pushmataha County. Situated in the Kiamichi River Valley, it is virtually surrounded by mountains: to the northeast, the Potato Hills; to the west, the Jack Fork Mountains; and to the south, the Kiamichi Mountains.

Clayton was founded in 1887 when the Saint Louis and San Francisco Railroad (Frisco) was extended through the Ouachita Mountains. It was named for Clayton, Missouri, a Saint Louis suburb. Clayton serves as the focal point for an increasing number of sportsmen and campers who visit nearby Sardis Lake and the rugged, forested, Kiamichi Mountains. Oklahoma's largest deer and wild turkey populations are found in the Clayton hinterland. In addition, fishing is considered excellent on Sardis Lake. Rock City, an isolated area of giant rock formations, is ten miles to the west of Clayton. Inquire locally for specific directions to the site.

The terrain around Clayton is rugged and heavily timbered. Many of the rural residents wrest their living from the for-

Rock City near Clayton, Oklahoma. Photo by Fred W. Marvel. Courtesy of Oklahoma Tourism and Recreation Department.

ests. Belcher Bridge Supply and Reese Tie Company are two of Clayton's forest-related industries. Recently, a modest growth in recreation services has helped to stimulate the local economy.

Nearly all of Clayton's businesses are built along U.S. 271 and Arkansas 2. A windshield survey would produce the following inventory: a mobile home park, Sardis Store, a Dairy Barn, a car wash, Alene's Odds and Ends Store, K-Country Restaurant, a federally supported low-income housing development, Alexander's Grocery, and the A and A Motel. Also along the highway are several service stations, auto repair shops, and quick-stop gasoline and grocery establishments. A two-block business district with one-story, false-fronted buildings and sidewalks with canopies, houses grocery stores, insurance offices, a farmers' union, and clothing stores.

South of Clayton, Oklahoma 2 has been rebuilt, and as a result, several old railroad towns—Dunbar, Eubanks, Wadena, Kosoma—have been bypassed. These towns were built, four to eight miles apart, to serve as lumber shipping points when the Saint Louis and San Francisco Railroad entered the Kiamichi Valley in 1887. Today, logs are trucked out of the mountains to sawmills in Antlers, Broken Bow, and other larger towns. The roadbed of the abandoned railroad is visible at several points along the highway.

Moyers

Moyers (population 100) was established as a lumber shipping center on the Saint Louis and San Francisco Railroad (now abandoned), six miles north of Antlers. It was named for Roy A. Moyer, a longtime resident.[23]

Moyers is situated in a tributary valley that enters the Kiamichi Valley where it cuts through the mountains. The most imposing structure in town is the two-story school building, though a half

dozen small businesses also are scattered along the route of Oklahoma 2 as it passes through the community.

Antlers

Antlers (population 3,110), on the southern fringe of the Ouachita Mountains, is located at the junction of U.S. 271 and Oklahoma 2, 3, and 7. It is the seat of Pushmataha County and serves as a prosperous trading and service center. Local legend holds that the town was named after an Indian custom of fastening a set of antlers to a tree to mark the site of a spring; a large spring near Antlers was once marked in this way.[24]

During the winter of 1892–1893 Antlers was the scene of a bitter political dispute known locally as the "Locke War." The conflict grew out of a disagreement over the distribution of money from a government land claim to the Choctaw Nation. The leader of the insurrectionists, who barricaded themselves at Antlers, was Victor M. Locke. Federal troops were called in to restore order.

Although lumbering remains the chief industry of this district, ranching has recently increased in importance. Rodeos, livestock shows, and saddle clubs are popular forms of recreation. Two main manufacturing plants—Diaper Jeans, Inc. (girls' dresses) and Ethan Allen, Inc. (furniture) employ about 225 workers.

TOUR A3: FORT SMITH, ARKANSAS, TO ANTLERS BY WAY OF U.S. 271

Fort Smith (see chapter 10)

Scullyville

Scullyville, a nearly abandoned hamlet southwest of Fort Smith, Arkansas, once served as the capital of the northern district of the Choctaw Nation. Founded in 1832, it was an important social and political center for the Choctaws, and as

Spiro Indian Mounds near Spiro, Oklahoma. Photo by Fred W. Marvel. Courtesy of Oklahoma Tourism and Recreation Department.

such, it attracted many notable figures such as frontier artist George Catlin. The name, Scullyville, is derived from the Choctaw word *iskuli,* meaning money. It was here that the U.S. Indian agents paid annuities to the Choctaws.[25]

Spiro

Spiro (population 2,221) was founded in 1895 when the Kansas City Southern Railroad was extended through the region. Located in one of the first areas to be settled in present-day Oklahoma, Scullyville, an old Choctaw settlement, was devastated during the Civil War; when the railroad arrived most of the remaining settlers moved to the new town of Spiro. Like so many other Ouachita Mountain towns, the business district is a museum piece of turn-of-the-century commercial architecture. Spiro is primarily a service and trade center for the surrounding villages, farms, and ranches. Its largest manufacturing estab-

lishment, Sunset Glass, Inc., employs approximately twenty-five workers. The ability to hand "pull" glass is a special skill now developed to a remarkable degree in the local area.

Spiro is perhaps best known for the Indian mounds located just north of town. A highly significant archaeological discovery, the mounds were first studied by professionals in 1936–38. Today, the site is open to visitors, and many artifacts are on display. Other artifacts from the Spiro mounds are available for viewing at the University of Oklahoma in Norman, the Oklahoma Historical Museum in Oklahoma City, and the Philbrook Museum in Tulsa.

Panama

Panama (population 1,425) was established as a coal shipping point when the Kansas City Southern Railway expanded south through the Ouachitas. Situated in a water gap where the Poteau River cuts through Backbone Mountain, it was named after the Panama Canal which was under construction at the same time.[26] After the local coal mines were closed, Panama's population declined; however, the town's economy has recently stabilized as a market and service center for the surrounding farms and ranches. Remnants of the coal-mining era are still evident in the numerous brush-covered strip mines seen along highway 59–271 to the north.

Panama is built along the railroad on the south bank of Coal Creek. Most of the houses date back to the turn-of-the-century coal-mining era when the town prospered.

The business district on Oklahoma 59–271 is a typical collection of one-story frame and brick structures occupied by a bank, a Baptist Church, a Pentacostal Church, a Nazarene Church, several quick-stop service stations, a welding and repair shop, a hardware store, and a half dozen other miscellaneous businesses. Several empty commercial buildings are evidence of the town's reduced fortunes.

South of Panama, Highway 59 crosses several low ridges and intervening swales including the valley of Brazil Creek. Cavanal Mountain stands as a lonely landmark on the south horizon marking the location of the town of Poteau.

Poteau

Poteau (population 7,710), the seat of LeFlore County, is situated in a picturesque valley between massive Cavanal Mountain (2,369 feet elevation) and Sugar Loaf Mountain (2,600 feet elevation). Founded in 1887, it became one of the more important towns in the Choctaw Nation. Its streets depart from the normal grid pattern to accommodate the rugged terrain. Its name, which comes from the French word for "post," was taken from the nearby Poteau River,

one of Oklahoma's few north-flowing streams.[27]

Poteau has passed through several economic stages. Coal mining became important when the railroads arrived. The Saint Louis-San Francisco Railroad (now Burlington Northern) came into the area in 1888 and the Kansas City Southern Railroad arrived just a few years later. When the coal-mining activities declined, lumbering and truck farming received increased emphasis. Today, the area's economy is based heavily on livestock farming; however, Poteau does possess a substantial amount of manufacturing. The largest manufacturers are Graphics Panel Unit (electronics), Humil Manufacturing Company (women's clothing), and Modern Carpet Industries, Inc.

Poteau's business district is a cluster of brick and stone two-story buildings along Dewey Street and the adjacent four to five square blocks. A newer string-street business district, typical of many American towns, has grown up along U.S. 59–271. Near the edge of town are the usual farm implement and automobile dealerships, night clubs, taverns, and a Johnson Controls manufacturing plant. Closer to the old business district is Poteau's "fast-food strip" which is comprised of various restaurants, motels, and gas stations.

Visitors to Poteau find spectacular scenery (the town is surrounded by some of the highest mountains in Oklahoma) and a lively sense of humor among the residents. A popular tourist postcard pictures Mount Cavanal as "the world's highest hill." This observation is based on the fact that while geomorphologists generally classify areas under 2,000 feet relief as hills, Mount Cavanal rises 1,999 feet above Poteau.

The Kerr Museum, a popular visitor attraction, is housed in the plush mountainside mansion of the late Senator Robert S. Kerr, six miles south of Po-

Robert S. Kerr Museum, Poteau, Oklahoma. Photo by Fred W. Marvel. Courtesy of Oklahoma Tourism and Recreation Department.

teau just off U.S. 59. The museum contains a re-creation of Senator Kerr's Washington, D.C., office; numerous mementos of his long political career; runestones from the local area; and materials from the Spiro Indian mounds.

Poteau's interesting city hall is housed in the old Frisco (Saint Louis and San Francisco) Railroad depot and is tastefully refurbished; it is appealing both to railroad buffs and historic preservationists. Still another notable feature is Carl Albert Junior College, which has a student body of more than four hundred.

Wister

Wister (population 982), unlike many other small Ouachita Mountain towns, has experienced modest growth over the past twenty years. Its strategic location

at the junction of U.S. 270 and 271, in the shadows of the most majestic ranges in the Ouachita Mountains, and near Wister Lake, gives it an exceptional advantage as a service center for hunters, fishermen, and tourists. The town began in 1890 as Wister Junction when the Arkansas and Choctaw Railroad came westward into Oklahoma and formed a junction with the Saint Louis and San Francisco Railroad's Texas branch.[28] In addition to the usual assorted small-town commercial establishments, there is the seemingly ubiquitous sawmill—Bennett Sawmill, Inc.—which employs a dozen workers.

Caston

Caston, a nearly abandoned hamlet, is at the junction of U.S. 270 and 271 in

LeFlore County. First named Maxey, its name was changed to Caston in 1887.

Winding Stair Mountains

The Winding Stair Mountains, some of the highest and grandest mountains in the region, rise just south of Caston. U.S. 271 crosses the Fourche Maline River about a mile south of Caston and then begins a long series of loops and switchbacks as it climbs the north slope of the Winding Stair range. The summit presents a spectacular panoramic view of the impressive ridge and valley terrain. The highway descends the steep south slope of the mountains through a second series of tortuous switchbacks and loops.

Talihina

Talihina (population 1,387) is situated near the north edge of a mountain basin which is drained by the headwaters of the Kiamichi River. From a vantage point in Talihina, one can see the surrounding mountains: to the north and east is the Winding Stair Range; to the south, the towering Kiamichi; and to the west, the knobby Potato Hills.

Talihina was a small, unnamed missionary settlement when, in 1888, the Saint Louis and San Francisco Railroad laid tracks through the Winding Stair Mountains. Since the Choctaw word for railroad is talihina, the railroad's arrival had obvious significance.[29] Even after the railroad arrived, Talihina remained fairly isolated until 1919 when a reliable road was cut through the forest by convict labor.

Talihina serves mainly as a shopping and service center for the surrounding farms and ranches. Motels, restaurants, and gas stations cater to the tourists and sportsmen who visit the surrounding forests and streams. Many of the area's residents make their living from the forest; others are employed by Talihina's

two manufacturers, the Reese Tie Company and the Talihina Charcoal Company, both of which process timber and manufacture wood products.

Talihina's commercial businesses are strung out along U.S. 271 as it winds its way through the town. Its isolated location enables Talihina to offer more specialized services than most towns of a similar size. There are the usual grocery-gasoline convenience stores, a mortuary, locally owned fast-food restaurants, grocery stores, and repair shops. A cluster of brick, one-story commercial buildings lines a three-block-long central business district; this "downtown area" houses assorted businesses including a Western Auto store, a movie theater, and a hardware store. Near the south edge of town is the South Park Plaza shopping center, a small off-street shopping area consisting of a half dozen businesses. The south side is also the site of a redimix concrete plant.

Albion

Albion (population 165) was once a fairly prosperous lumber town. Today, wages earned in sawmills and in the timber industry continue to support many of the families in the area. The village's setting, sheltered in the Kiamichi River Valley between the rugged Winding Stair and Kiamichi mountains, offers spectacular scenery. The name Albion is derived from the Roman name for England.

Albion's few existing businesses are scattered along U.S. 271. Abandoned buildings and weed overgrown ruins of former businesses give the town a forlorn and desolate appearance. The businesses that still remain—Grandpa's Store, an antiquated flea market, the Eagle Repair Shop (with a sign advertising custom welding and horseshoeing), and Eleta's Beauty Shop—are all located on the highway. A block to the north on a low ridge is the post office

Indian Nations trail ride in the Kiamichi Mountains. Photo by Fred W. Marvel. Courtesy of Oklahoma Tourism and Recreation Department.

and the remains of red brick Armstrong Grocery Store. The latter's size and hilltop location make it the most imposing structure in town, in spite of its gaping windows and crumbling walls.

Kiamichi

Kiamichi, another of eastern Oklahoma's nearly abandoned street villages, stretches out along the Burlington Northern Railroad which parallels the Kiamichi River. The settlement dates to 1887 when the Saint Louis and San Francisco Railroad was built. The name, pronounced Ki-a-MEESH-i, is patterned after the French word *kamichi,* which means "horned screamer," a species of bird.[30] All that remains of the town is a long-since abandoned and de-crepit store building and a half dozen old dwellings.

Tuskahoma

Tuskahoma (population 200) is another Ouachita Mountain town that dates back to the 1887 construction of the Saint Louis and San Francisco Railroad in Pushmataha County. More than fifty years of Choctaw settlement preceded the railroad's arrival; in fact, Tuskahoma was the Choctaw capital when delegates were assembled to draft a new constitution in 1834. Because of the Treaty of Dancing Rabbit Creek, agreed to in Mississippi in 1830, the Choctaws were to receive enough funds to erect a new council house in the approximate center of the land they were to occupy.

The site selected, now marked only by a pile of rocks from a crumbling chimney, is about 1.5 miles northwest of the present site of Tuskahoma. The new capital was called *Nunih Wayah,* a name copied from an earlier capital in the east.[31] When the post office was established in 1884, the official spelling of the town's name was *Tushka Homma,* or "red warrior," in the Choctaw language.[32] The spelling was revised later to its present form.

Tuskahoma, located approximately a half mile south of U.S. 271, consists of a Church of Christ, a Methodist Church, a nondenominational church named Harmony Hill Tabernacle, White's Grocery and Feed Store, and perhaps two dozen houses.

Approximately one and a half miles north of Tuskahoma are the current Choctaw council grounds and capital. A red brick, two-story capital building, built in 1880, stands at the entrance to a picnic area and several ball fields. A modern council house is located just north of the old capital building.

A historic marker for the old Choctaw capital, Nunih Wayah, and the entrance to a public fishing lake of the same name are located on the highway approximately a mile west of Tuskahoma.

Clayton (see tour A2)

South of Clayton the highway crosses the Kiamichi Mountains and traverses hill country, which gradually flattens to a rolling piedmont in the vicinity of Antlers. Indications of the importance of the lumber industry in this area are the large tracts of clear-cut timber and various sizes of replanted shortleaf pine.

Sardis Lake Recreation Area

The Sardis Lake Recreation Area, eight miles south of Clayton on Peal Creek, includes 410 acres of forested hills surrounding the 75-acre Sardis Lake. The access area on the east shore of the lake is equipped with picnic facilities, swimming area, boat dock, and rental facilities.

Snow

Snow (population 20) is a nearly abandoned hamlet in the valley of Cedar Creek, a tributary of the Kiamichi River. It was named for George Snow, an early resident and merchant. The town consists of a few abandoned business buildings, a decrepit and abandoned Baptist Church, a post office in a mobile home, and about a dozen scattered houses.

Finley

Finley (population 90) is a waning hamlet nestled in Cedar Creek valley. Ranching and lumbering are the principal activities in the area. Finley's business buildings are located along a wide stretch of highway that passes through a scattered array of houses. More of the business buildings are abandoned than occupied; the few occupied structures that remain house a repair shop, an Assembly of God church, a beauty parlor, and a couple of gasoline stations.

Antlers (see tour A2)

TOUR A4: POTEAU TO BROKEN BOW BY WAY OF U.S. 59 AND 259

This tour traverses some of the most scenic landscapes in the Ouachitas. It loops and twists through the Winding Stair and Kiamichi mountains and the Ouachita National Forest, then passes to the west of Broken Bow Lake. It connects with Tour A3 at Poteau.

Poteau (see tour A3)

South of Poteau, Highway 59 passes through a series of low ridges, or hummocks, formed on resistant folded rock strata. The Winding Stair Mountains loom on the south horizon through the customary bluish haze.

Runic markings in the Heavener Runestone State Park. Photo by Fred W. Marvel. Courtesy of Oklahoma Tourism and Recreation Department.

Howe

Howe (population 562) is a LeFlore County village located five miles north of Heavener. It was named for Dr. Herbert M. Howe of Philadelphia, a director of the Kansas City, Pittsburg, and Gulf Railway (now the Kansas City Southern).

The small business district consists of scattered buildings along U.S. 59 and includes a half dozen quick-shop service stations, a couple of restaurants, and two or three other businesses.

Heavener

Heavener (population 2,770) is another of Oklahoma's railroad towns. The original site was surveyed in 1896 alongside the newly laid tracks of the Kansas City, Pittsburg, and Gulf Railway (now the Kansas City Southern Railway). Named for Joseph Heavener, the owner of the

town site, this community is situated in an area that the Choctaws referred to as the "Prairie of the Tall Grass." [33] Poteau Mountain, a massive 1,200-foot-high mesalike mountain that consists of massive beds of sandstones and shales interbedded with coal seams, hovers over the town to the northeast.

Although the railroad yards are still important, employment there is greatly reduced from earlier days. The largest manufacturing firm, Burnett Lumber Company, employs forty-five workers.

Heavener's business district is T-shaped. The older portion is quartered in a cluster of old, red brick and native stone buildings fronting on the railroad tracks and extending in an east-west direction for two or three blocks. A somewhat newer business strip has emerged along U.S. 59, which parallels the railroad tracks as they pass through the town in a north-south direction. The highway business strip consists of the usual collection of convenience stores, gasoline stations, and fast-food restaurants, interspersed with other businesses and abandoned buildings.

Heavener Runestone State Park, two miles east and perched high on the west side of Poteau Mountain, is the site of the discovery of a large slab of Savannah sandstone on which runic letters six to nine inches tall have been carved.[34] While some have suggested that Viking explorers were responsible for these inscriptions, the authenticity of this site is still open to question.

South of Heavener the highway passes through a ridge and valley landscape mantled by a heavy cover of shortleaf pine and oak-hickory forests. The rural homes in this area are of varied architectural styles and materials including older lapboard-sided shed-room cabins, simple T- and L-shaped houses, and contemporary structures.

Hodgen

Hodgen (population 175), in central LeFlore County, is one of a string of timber shipping points established along the Kansas City Southern Railway when it was extended south through the Ouachitas in 1896. It was named for J. W. Hodgens, a timber buyer for the Kansas City Southern Railway. To the south of Hodgen, U.S. 59 follows the Black Fork River into the Kiamichi Mountains.

The town consists of a collection of approximately two dozen residences and a small highway business district made up of a church, a truck stop, a butane dealership, and a quick-shop gas station called the Ouachita Country Store.

Zoe

Zoe, a waning hamlet in LeFlore County, is situated nine miles south of Heavener. It was named for Zoe Thomason, a local resident.

Stapp

Stapp is a nearly abandoned hamlet ten miles south of Heavener. It was established as a timber yard and shipping point on the Kansas City Southern Railway. To the south of Stapp, U.S. 59 swings east into Big Creek Valley as it climbs west through a gap between Winding Stair Mountain (to the west) and Rich Mountain. The highway descends in a tributary valley of the Kiamichi River. To the west of the gap, the mountains reach elevations in excess of 2,000 feet. Several turnout overlooks on U.S. 259 provide spectacular views of the heavily forested ridge and valley terrain.

Big Cedar

Big Cedar is a mountain village at the junction of U.S. 259 and Oklahoma 63. A monument commemorates President John F. Kennedy's visit to Big Cedar on October 29, 1961, to speak at a highway dedication. Visitors of Big Cedar enjoy some of the most spectacular mountain scenery Oklahoma has to offer: to the northeast is towering Rich Mountain; to the northwest are the Winding Stair Mountains; and to the south is the famous Kiamichi range. All of these rugged mountains are mantled with a combination of shortleaf pine and oak-hickory forests.

Now a ghost town, this tiny community probably had its greatest population (about fifty people) in 1910,[35] when it boasted a general store, a blacksmith shop, a gristmill, and a sawmill; three years later only the store and sawmill were still standing. Activity in the town increased briefly during the 1930s when a stave mill was established.

South of Big Cedar, U.S. 259 traverses the Ouachita National Forest and large blocks of land owned by major lumber companies. Sizeable areas have been clear-cut and are in various stages of reforestation; newly cut tracts are ragged and torn and covered with slash; other locations reveal the region's long history of lumbering through their varying tree heights.

Smithville

Smithville (population 133), an old McCurtain County Choctaw settlement on Oklahoma 4 one mile west of the junction with U.S. 259, is in an upland basin drained by the Mountain Fork River. The surrounding mountains are some of the most spectacular in the Ouachita province. South of Smithville, U.S. 259 follows the Mountain Fork River gorge, and in the process serves a number of attractive fishing camps. When founded in 1886, Smithville was named *Hatobi,* which is Choctaw for "warrior man." The name was changed in 1890 in honor of an intermarried Choctaw resident, Joshua N. Smith.

A marker near the junction of Oklahoma 4 and U.S. 259 commemorates Smithville as well as the Folsum Training School for Choctaw Students, Sealy Methodist Chapel, and Big Lick Presbyterian Church.

South of Smithville, U.S. 259 follows the divide beween two southerly flowing tributaries of the Red River: the Glover River to the west and the Mountain Fork River to the east. Large-scale lumbering operations have left expanses of cleared and reforested land interspersed with mature timber in this sparsely settled section. Near the access roads that lead east to Broken Bow Lake a few tourism and recreation businesses have evolved including canoe rentals, quick-shop gasoline and bait stores, and a few recreational vehicle campgrounds.

Since development around Broken Bow Reservoir is in the initial stage, most of the activities are geared toward fishermen and outdoorsmen, and consist primarily of businesses offering gasoline, picnic, boating and camping supplies, recreational vehicle camping, and low-budget lodging.

Hochatown State Park

Hochatown State Park is three miles east of U.S. 259 and some twelve miles north of Broken Bow. The park occupies 1,713 acres on the shores of Broken Bow Lake. Chapter 6 includes a description of the available facilities and attractions.

Beavers Bend State Park

Beavers Bend State Park is situated five miles east of U.S. 259 and approximately seven miles north of Broken Bow. It consists of 3,482 acres along the Mountain Fork River just below Broken Bow Dam. Chapter 6 includes a description of the available facilities and attractions.

Broken Bow

Broken Bow (population 3,880), located at the junction of two federal highways—70 and 259—and Oklahoma 7 in the heart of Oklahoma's three million acres of commercial timberland, is the archetypical lumber town. It was built in 1911 by the Dierks brothers and named for their Nebraska home. The lumbermill, erected in 1912 and expanded over the years, is now operated by the Weyerhaeuser Corporation. In fact, when all of the Dierks operations in Arkansas and Oklahoma were merged with the Weyerhaeuser Corporation in 1966, a new mill facility was constructed. Two other major employers in town are Hally Creek Fryers (poultry processing) and Thomason Lumber Company. Each year a Forest Festival is held in early June in honor of Broken Bow's long-established ties with the forest industry. Broken Bow's Memorial Indian Museum holds many items dating back to the area's first Choctaw settlements in the 1830s.

Because McCurtain County contains nearly a million acres of forestland, Broken Bow is widely known as a service center for thousands of deer hunters and other outdoor enthusiasts; the Glover River, Mountain Fork River, and Little River attract large numbers of canoeists; fishermen by the thousands frequent nearby Broken Bow Lake.

Broken Bow's business district is laid out along the crossroads formed by north-south U.S. 259 and east-west U.S. 70 and Oklahoma 7. The collection of businesses includes: quick-shop gasoline stations, a locally owned telephone company, an assortment of fast-food restaurants, repair shops, a Wal-Mart store, marine stores, car dealerships, motels, grocery stores, and an assortment of locally owned businesses typical of small rural towns. The presence of a city park and curbed and guttered streets is an indication of the town's stature as a regional center of importance.

TOUR A5: FORT SMITH TO DE QUEEN BY WAY OF U.S. 71

U.S. 71 passes through some of the most scenic landscapes in the Ouachita Mountains; south of Fort Smith it crosses Backbone Mountain, passes east of Sugar Loaf Mountain, through the Sebastian County coal fields, past massive Poteau Mountain and Fourche Mountain before turning east up Big Creek Valley to Mena, Arkansas. South of Mena, the highway winds through the broken hill country that borders the Rolling Fork River.

Fort Smith (see chapter 10)

Greenwood

Greenwood (population 3,300), situated on Arkansas 10 two miles east of U.S. 71, is the county seat and leading coal-mining town in Sebastian County, the leading coal-producing county in the state.[36] Many of the residents of the town and the surrounding farming communities are employed in Greenwood's half dozen manufacturing plants; the largest of these are Bobbitt Manufacturing Company (furniture) and Greenwood Industries, Inc. (display equipment).

Mansfield

Mansfield (population 1,000), located in southern Sebastian County at the junction of U.S. 71 and Arkansas 96 and 378, is adjacent to one of western Arkansas' natural gas fields. In earlier days the area around Mansfield was renowned for its productive fruit farms and especially for its giant peaches.

The business district is built along U.S. 71 and the adjoining side streets. Many of the red brick buildings date back to the turn of the century when a large brick manufacturing plant operated in the community. Williams and Son Moulding Company, a fabricator of crating lumber, bed slats, and moulding, employs workers from Mansfield and the surrounding area.

Waldron

Waldron (population 2,780) is built with the two-story red brick Scott County Courthouse as the focal point of its commercial district. The town is in an open basin surrounded by mountains: to the north are East Poteau Mountain and Pilot Knob; to the west is Chaleybeate Mountain; and to the south is Piney Mountain. The Poteau River flows across the basin in a westerly direction.

Waldron is a prosperous trading and service town. Several service stations, motels, and restaurants cater to the passing highway traffic. Machine shops, automobile and farm implement dealers, a livestock sales barn, feedstores, professional offices, and the usual array of retail stores serve both Waldron's residents and the people from the surrounding hinterland. Many of the residents work in manufacturing at Big Pine Lumber Company, Hardwood Products Company, Poteau Valley Industries, Inc. (furniture), Valmac Processing (poultry products), and Waldron Furniture Manufacturing Corporation.

South of Waldron, U.S. 71 cuts through two hogback mountains—Piney Mountain and Ross Mountain—and then winds five miles across a broad upland before descending into the valley of the Fourche LaFave River.

Y City

At Y City, the highway passes through Mill Creek Mountain in a watergap cut by a stream of the same name. The hamlet, at the junction of U.S. 71 and 270, consists of a grocery store-gas station and a half dozen houses. South of Y City, U.S. 71 passes westward up the Johnson Creek Valley; it then traverses Fourche Mountain by means of a series of loops and curves, from which it descends into the Acorn Valley near the headquarters of the Ouachita River.

Mena

Mena (population 5,000), the Polk County seat, is one of the larger towns in western Arkansas. It was founded in 1896 when the Kansas City Southern Railway was extended through the mountains. The name Mena was selected by several Dutchmen who had invested heavily in the railroad as a tribute to the Netherlands' Queen Wilhelmina.[37]

Mena occupies a low divide separating the headwaters of the Ouachita and Mountain Fork rivers; lofty mountains rise to the north and west of the town. Many of the town's businesses are strung out along U.S. 71, which parallels the tracks of the Kansas City Southern Railway, and Arkansas 88, which serves as the town's main street. One of Mena's most famous landmarks is the Norris Goff House. Goff teamed with Chester

Lauck, also a onetime Mena resident, to create a popular radio show during the 1930s and 1940s that focused on the escapades of Lum and Abner as they interacted with various fictitious characters who visited a small-town general store; it is said to have been patterned after the life styles in nearby Pine Ridge.

According to the 1980 *Arkansas Directory of Manufacturers,* ten manufacturing plants in Mena produce lumber and special wood products, electric motors, leather goods, poultry feed, aluminum castings, precut log homes, ready-mix concrete, and men's clothing. Many of the workers in these plants commute more than fifty miles over winding mountain roads.

Hatfield

Hatfield (population 410) was founded in 1896 as a shipping point on the newly extended Kansas City Southern Railway. Today, the main street businesses consist of a bank, a drive-in restaurant, two gasoline stations, a welding shop, a school, two grocery stores, a paint store, and a lumber-supply store. Just to the north of Hatfield, on the west side of the road, is a small building with a large sign boasting, "Christian Motorcyclists Association."

Cove

Cove (population 391) is a tiny town situated along U.S. 71 and the Kansas City Southern railroad tracks. The business area consists of a half dozen abandoned business buildings, a weather-beaten motel, a convenience store, the Hungry Hound Restaurant, a fast-food business, a grocery store, a school, and a Baptist Church. Arkansas 4 offers a western route from Cove to nearby Watson, Oklahoma.

Hatton

Hatton (population 200) consists of a small lumber mill, a church, a quick-shop store, a service station, and a handful of houses scattered along the highway.

Wickes

Wickes (population 464) was founded by the Arkansas Townsite Company when the Kansas City Southern Railway arrived in the area. The town, which stretches along U.S. 71 for nearly a mile, has a business district consisting of one-story, false-front brick and frame buildings. Also located along the highway are a rock shop, a high school, a grocery store, an insurance office, and a church. The town's tallest structure is its water tower.

During the 1920s, Wickes was the site of a cannery and two lumber mills. Later, however, when strawberry and vegetable growing were no longer viable industries and when most of the virgin timber had been cut, these facilities were closed and abandoned.

Grannis

Grannis (population 349) is the home of Lane Processing, Inc., a major packer of fresh and frozen poultry products. Broilers and hens from poultry farms in western Arkansas and eastern Oklahoma are trucked to the processing plant where they are dressed and packaged. The resulting products are shipped by large diesel trucks pulling "reefers" (refrigerated trailers) over U.S. 71 to distant markets. The operation's boilers, cutting rooms, chill rooms, and warehouses occupy a ten-acre tract on the west side of the highway. Across the street one encounters a grocery, a service station, and a handful of other businesses. Just north of Grannis is an impressive five-story modern office building that houses the general offices of Lane Processing. Although the large building and its parking lots would seem more "at home" in Little Rock or Fort Smith, the company

has decided to locate the center of its far-flung Arkansas operations in tiny Grannis.

Gillham

Gillham consists of a grocery store, a fire station, a ceramic shop, a half dozen empty business buildings, and the residences of its 252 inhabitants.

De Queen

De Queen (population 4,500), situated at the junction of U.S. 71 and 70, was incorporated in 1897 and named for a major investor in the Kansas City Southern Railway. Although the investor's name was originally De Geoijen, it was later anglicized to De Queen.[38] The seat of Sevier County since 1905, De Queen was once the connecting point for two railroads built by the Dierks Lumber and Coal Company (now the Weyerhaeuser Corporation): the De Queen and Eastern, and the Texas, Oklahoma, and Eastern.

Around the turn of the century, the extensive forest lands of southwest Arkansas and southeast Oklahoma attracted the Dierks brothers (Henry, Hans, and Peter), a family of lumber barons. Their business, the Dierks Lumber and Coal Company, had experienced remarkable progress since incorporating in 1895; with a large lumber operation in Nebraska, the company required a steady supply of wood. This led to their interest in the Ouachita province. After several large properties in the area were purchased by the Dierks, the rail lines were extended to several of their mills; the De Queen mill thus became part of a large regional network.[39]

As the biggest town in a large, but sparsely populated area, De Queen is an important shopping, service, and entertainment center. The business district includes several specialty stores; hospital-care and various professional ser-

Talimena Skyline Drive near Talihina, Oklahoma. Photo by Fred W. Marvel. Courtesy of Oklahoma Tourism and Recreation Department.

vices also are available; and a golf course is located on the east edge of town along U.S. 70.

Many residents from the area earn their living in De Queen's manufacturing plants. The largest manufacturers are: Baldwin Piano and Organ Company; Frames, Inc. (furniture parts); Montaire Poultry, Inc. (processed poultry); and Poag Lumber and Tie Company (lumber and railroad ties). Inev-itably, the town's newspaper is *The Queen Bee*.

TOUR A6: TALIMENA SCENIC DRIVE

The Talimena Scenic Drive, which extends fifty-four miles along the mountain crests between Mena, Arkansas, and Talihina, Oklahoma, on Arkansas 88 and Oklahoma 1, derives its name from the names of the towns at either

Petting zoo at Queen Wilhelmina State Park on Rich Mountain. Courtesy of Arkansas Department of Parks and Tourism.

terminus; the drive is entirely within the Ouachita National Forest.

Visitor Information Station

A visitor information station is located .2 mile west of Mena on Arkansas 88. Various information brochures and maps of the immediate area are available.

Acorn Vista Overlook

Acorn Vista Overlook, 2.6 miles west of Mena, affords a magnificent view of the Acorn basin and community. The basin, formerly called "Gourd Neck" because of its peculiar shape, is portrayed on engraved maps at the overlook. It is a low pass between Fourche and Rich mountains, which is drained by the Ouachita River. The Kansas City Southern Railway and U.S. highways 59 and 270 pass through the basin.

Grandview Overlook

The Grandview Overlook is 6.1 miles west of Mena. It provides a commanding view of the south slope of Rich Mountain and a large portion of the Mountain Fork River Basin; to the west are the Kiamichi and Winding Stair mountains in Oklahoma. From this point an excellent view of the dwarf forests of the upper slopes of Rich Mountain can be seen. The dwarf trees that comprise the forest are mainly black oak and post oak which range from about three to eight feet tall; these trees have been pruned, shaped, and restrained by ice storms, severe winter temperatures, and poor soils. Many have been strongly "flagged" by the prevailing winds; their short south limbs and long north limbs create the illusion that the trees are leaning to the north.

Queen Wilhelmina State Park

Queen Wilhelmina State Park is on the crest of Rich Mountain, 12.2 miles west of Mena. The park was developed in the 1960s on the site of the Queen Wilhelmina Inn, a resort hotel built in 1896 as a tourist attraction by investors in the Kansas City Southern Railway. Unfortunately, because of its remote location, the old inn was never a great success. It fell into decay as the years passed. Much of the stone in this original structure was used to rebuild the present inn in the same basic style. Chapter 6 includes additional information on the available facilities and attractions.

The area to the west of the Queen Wilhelmina State Park offers additional excellent examples of the dwarf or "elfin" forests on the exposed crest of Rich Mountain. These unusual stunted and flagged trees are created by a combination of freezing rain, fog, wind chill, droughty soils, and exposure.

Emerald Vista

Emerald Vista is 30.4 miles west of Mena, Arkansas. The overlook, which can be reached by traveling .7 mile off Oklahoma 1, provides a commanding view of the Poteau River Valley, Cedar Lake, Wister Lake, and the Winding Stair Mountains.

Robert S. Kerr Aboretum

The Robert S. Kerr Aboretum, 30.7 miles west of Mena, Arkansas, is an interpretive center for the Ouachita Moun-

Historical marker for the Fort Smith-Fort Towson Military Road in eastern Oklahoma. Photo by Fred W. Marvel. Courtesy of Oklahoma Tourism and Recreation Department.

tains. The emphasis is on vegetation and forest ecology.

Potato Hills Overlook

Potato Hills Overlook is 51.3 miles west of Mena, Arkansas, on Oklahoma 1. The southern view, across the Potato Hills, reveals a forested area consisting of a mixture of shortleaf pine and scrub oak. The Potato Hills derive their name from their fancied resemblance to the "hills" or mounds in which potatoes are planted.

Visitor Information Station

A second Visitor Information Station is located at the intersection of Oklahoma 1 and U.S. 271. Mena, Arkansas, is fifty-four miles east; Talihina, Oklahoma, is seven miles southwest; and Poteau, Oklahoma, is thirty miles northeast.

TOUR A7: RUSSELLVILLE TO
   ARKADELPHIA BY WAY OF
   ARKANSAS 7

Russellville

Russellville (population 19,590), the Pope County seat and the largest town between Little Rock and Fort Smith, has received national publicity in recent years as the site of an Arkansas Power and Light Company nuclear power plant.

The town was named for Dr. T. J. Russell, a British-born and British-educated physician, who immigrated there in 1835. Incorporated in 1870, Russellville prospered during the 1880s when a railroad was extended up the Arkansas Valley and the economy of the region began to recover from the widespread stagnation caused by the Civil War.

Russellville was the primary home of Jeff Davis (1862–1913), a U.S. Senator and three-term governor. Davis was especially noted for his colorful and forthright speech. His often-quoted credo was: "I am a Hard Shell Baptist in religion; I believe in foot-washing, saving your seed potatoes, and paying your honest debts."[40]

While Russellville is the home of Arkansas Polytechnic University (Arkansas Tech), its twin city on the south side of the river, Dardanelle, is famous for Indian lore. Two excellent state parks are in the immediate area—Lake Dardanelle State Park and Mount Nebo State Park. Lake Dardanelle, a 34,000-acre fishermen's paradise, is known for its lunker-sized largemouth bass. Since the Ozark National Forest headquarters is in Russellville, those interested in outdoor recreation activities can stop by the office for advice and information.

Russellville has a history of steady population growth. During the 1970s, for instance, the population increased nearly 20 percent, from 11,750 to 14,031. Many of the newcomers have found employment in Russellville's well-developed manufacturing sector. The largest manufacturers include Bibler Brothers, Inc. (pallets), Dow Chemical Company (graphite), International Paper Company (shipping containers), Morton Frozen Foods, Valmac Processing (poultry products), and Rockwell International Corporation (parking meters).

Dardanelle

Dardanelle (population 3,700) may be named for a rocky hogback that juts into the Arkansas River. The craggy sentinel was a landmark for both explorers and settlers as they voyaged up the river on keelboats. The settlement that grew up beside this cliff was one of the first in the Arkansas Valley. In fact, when Thomas Nuttall traveled down the Arkansas in 1819, he found a Mr. Raphael operating a Cherokee trading post near this site.[41] A sizeable settlement grew up around the trading post; however, the town was not officially platted until 1843.

The origin of Dardanelle's name is

An early picture of Dardanelle Rock. Courtesy of Arkansas History Commission.

uncertain. One version suggests that the name was a corrupted form of the family name of Jean Baptiste Dardenne, who owned a sizeable land grant across the river while Arkansas was still under Spanish rule. A more recent explanation suggests that the town's name stems from a fancied resemblance of the landmark rock to the Straits of Dardanelle.

Dardanelle was the site of an important meeting in 1820 between Robert Crittenden, the Secretary of the Arkansas Territory, and the Cherokee tribal chiefs. Despite the eloquent oratory of Chief Black Fox, the Cherokees were persuaded to withdraw from the Arkansas Valley and move into the Ozark Upland to the north.[42] According to legend, this historic meeting took place near the two great Council Oaks on the riverbank behind the current waterworks on North Front Street.

During the Civil War, Dardanelle changed hands several times as both sides fought for control of the Upper Arkansas River.

By 1870, the Little Rock and Fort Smith Railroad was under construction up the Arkansas Valley; the new line reached Russellville in 1873. Unfortunately, this key linkage was across the river and five miles north of Dardanelle, which meant that produce from the south bank of the river had to be hauled by wagon and ferry to the rail siding at Russellville. The situation began to improve on February 13, 1883, when another railroad, the Dardanelle and Russellville Railway, was chartered. From August, 1883, until 1890, when a wood and steel pontoon bridge was completed, it was necessary to ferry the railroad cars across the Arkansas by steamboats. It was not until 1927 that a permanent steel bridge was constructed to carry the railroad across the river. The opening of the coal deposits between Dardanelle and Russellville by the Southern Anthracite Coal Company (later named the Bernice Coal Company) provided the revenue needed to keep the line operating long after passenger business declined.[43] Even after the coal mines closed, the line has continued to operate as a spur connecting the town's industries with the Missouri Pacific Railroad at Russellville.

Dardanelle's Front Street parallels the Arkansas River; the residential section sprawls out to the southwest. The Yell County Courthouse, which serves the northern half of the county, is at the upper end of Front Street near the Arkansas 7 bridge. Most of the town's businesses are strung out to the south along Arkansas 7. The largest manufacturer in town is Valmac Industries, Inc., a producer of poultry feed and processed poultry products. Their rather large plant is on Arkansas 7 near the southeast edge of town. Mount Nebo State Park is situated five miles to the west on Arkansas 155 (see chapter 6 for a list of the available facilities and attractions). South of Dardanelle, Arkansas 7 traverses fertile fields planted primarily in soybeans, cotton, and rice.

Centerville

Centerville (population 300), seven miles south of Dardanelle at the junction of Arkansas 7 and 154, is comprised of a crossroads cluster of buildings including a gasoline station and a small cluster of a dozen or so houses. It serves as the western gateway to both Holla Bend National Wildlife Area and Petit Jean State Park (see chapter 6 for a description of the available facilities and attractions).

Ola

Ola (population 1,121) is situated in the Petit Jean River Valley within the shadow of Ola Mountain at the junction of Arkansas 10, 7, and 28. The community is sustained by forest-related industries and its service function with the nearby farmers and ranchers. Two wood products plants (Deltic Farm and Timber Company and Wilson Wood Lumber Company) provide employment for many of the town's residents. About two blocks of business buildings are strung out along Arkansas 7 and an intersecting business street. Among the businesses is a small motel.

South of Ola, Arkansas 7 climbs to the summit of Ola Mountain and a panoramic southern view across Nimrod Lake and the Fourche LaFave River Valley.

Fourche Junction

Fourche Junction (population 50) is a scattered settlement at the junction of Arkansas 7 and 60. A quick-shop store and a dozen or so houses are the only structures that remain. About a half mile south of Fourche Junction are Nimrod Dam and the Nimrod Lake that formed from the blocking of the Fourche LaFave River. Farther to the south, Arkansas 7 traverses the heavily forested Fourche Mountain through a series of loops and switchbacks; trucks loaded with pine logs creep up the mountain in low gear and sometimes create slow travel on this stretch of the highway.

Hollis

Hollis, in the valley of the South Fourche LaFave River and tucked under a craggy bluff of Fourche Mountain, is eleven miles south of Fourche Junction. It is one of those tiny hamlets that has no precise city limits. The businesses (a gas station-convenience store and a gift shop) are about a half mile north of the river. Houses are scattered along the highway to the north for approximately a mile.

Arkansas 7 negotiates a rugged section of the mountains south of Hollis by following Bear Creek and Trace Creek

Hot Springs Village. Courtesy of Arkansas Department of Parks and Tourism.

deep into the mountains. It then crosses over a low gap in Short Mountain and continues into a headwaters valley of the Middle Fork of the Saline River. The highway, by constantly looping and turning, manages to maintain a fairly easy grade; nevertheless, trucks that are heavily loaded with logs cut from the surrounding mountains must creep up the longer slopes in lower gears.

Jessieville

Jessieville (population 100) is a tiny roadside settlement whose businesses consist of a combination grocery store-gas station and a fast-food drive-in.

Blue Springs

Blue Springs is a scattered settlement comprised of a café, a grocery store-gas station, and a few houses. Coleman's Rock Shop (see chapter 7) is one of the largest and best known in the Ouachitas.

Hot Springs Village

Hot Springs Village (population 2,083), situated twelve miles north of Hot Springs, is the third planned community built in Arkansas by Cooper Communities, Inc. The earlier communities (Cherokee Village and Bella Vista) are in the Ozark region of northern Arkansas.

The Hot Springs Village landscape is dominated by pine forests and man-made lakes. The houses and commercial buildings are designed to take maximum advantage of the attractive setting provided by Cedar Mountain and several small tributaries of the Ouachita and Saline Rivers. Property owners have access to fishing and boating, golf courses, a clubhouse complex for indoor activities, and recreational centers with swimming pools, tennis courts, and other games areas. Land owners in the community have the option of building their own home or contracting with Cooper Communities, Inc. for complete property development. A village leasing agency aids absentee property owners in renting their homes to vacationers.

Since the village is privately owned, it provides its own public utilities, security force, and fire protection. Hot

Home of world renowned Mountain Valley spring water. Courtesy of Arkansas Department of Parks and Tourism.

Springs Village has grown rapidly since the first construction began in the late 1960s; in fact, although the U.S. Census Bureau did not report on Hot Springs Village in 1970, by 1980 its population was determined to be 2,083.

Mountain Valley

Mountain Valley (population 100) is a tiny roadside village about ten miles north of Hot Springs. In addition to the ubiquitous gas station-convenience store and small fast-food drive-ins, a real-estate office that specializes in country "estates" is within easy driving distance of Hot Springs.

About a mile west of the community, on a clearly marked road, is Mountain Valley Spring. Originally known as Lockett Spring, the name was changed in 1871 when a druggist, named Peter Greene, purchased and renamed it. At

one time the spring's reputation extended into several states; a posh hotel was constructed on the adjoining property; and horse-drawn carriages met incoming trains to transport the visitors through the tall pines to the lodge. Unfortunately, the Mountain Valley Hotel was destroyed by a fire in 1934 and was never rebuilt.

Today, several million gallons of Mountain Valley Spring water are bottled annually for shipment throughout the country. A quaint, turn-of-the-century springhouse—complete with Grecian arbors, flower gardens, and a promenade—still exists in a splendid grassy glen, surrounded by tall pines.

Fountain Lake

Fountain Lake (population 250) is linked to Hot Springs by a string of residences and businesses that have developed along Arkansas 7. The village, built along the valley between Blowout Mountain and Indian Mountain, consists of a handful of businesses and about three dozen houses. Several booths for a large flea market occupy part of the east highway frontage. Along the west side of the highway are old motels and tourist courts dating from the early days of automobile touring in the 1920s and 1930s. Many of the motels have been abandoned now that Hot Springs' tourist business has shifted from the central city bathhouses to the racetrack and lakeshores on the south side of the city.

Hot Springs (see chapter 11)

Just south of Hot Springs is a street village that has evolved along Arkansas 7 between the city and Lake Hamilton. The retail outlets in this village include gas stations, grocery stores, bait shops, liquor stores, fast-food drive-ins, and real-estate offices. The latter cater to the many vacationers who visit the area and live in the houses that line the lake's many coves. The Hot Springs Mall, a major regional shopping center, was built in the early 1980s to serve the city of Hot Springs and the adjacent lakefront communities. Just a few blocks south of the mall, Arkansas 7 crosses Lake Hamilton on a 1930s-style concrete bridge complete with heavy banisters and a narrow road bed.

Lake Hamilton

Lake Hamilton (population 700) is a resort community on the south shore of the lake. Access to marinas, resorts, and residences is provided by Arkansas 290 and 192.

South of Lake Hamilton, Arkansas 7 enters the valley of Fourche a Loupe Creek before ascending Mount Carmel.

Bismarck

Bismarck (population 200) is a crossroads hamlet at the intersection of Ar-

kansas 7 and 84. South of Bismarck, Arkansas 7 parallels the east shore of De Gray Lake. Several marked roads lead to De Gray State Park (see chapter 6) and other recreational areas on the lake shore.

Caddo Valley

Caddo Valley (population 388) is five miles north of Arkadelphia at the junction of Arkansas 7, U.S. 67, and Interstate 30. Many of the village residents are employed in businesses that cater to travelers and visitors to De Gray Lake.

Arkadelphia

Arkadelphia (population 9,770) is a gateway city to the southeastern Ouachita Mountains. Its location on Interstate 30, at the junction of Arkansas 51, 8, and 7, makes it well suited to serve the recreation and tourism demands generated by visitors to nearby De Gray Lake.

Arkadelphia is one of the oldest settlements in central Arkansas. As early as 1811, John Hemphill founded a salt evaporation plant near the Ouachita River after acquiring the rights to a spring by bartering with Indians. The business operated profitably until about 1850. The town, which became the Clark County seat in 1843, was an important Ouachita River port during steamboat days. When the Cairo and Fulton Railroad (now the Missouri Pacific) reached Arkadelphia following the Civil War, commercial activities and plantation agriculture were greatly stimulated. During that time, many blacks immigrated to the area to clear land for cotton cultivation; presently, blacks represent one out of every five Arkadelphia residents.

During the lumber boom that began about 1880, Arkadelphia became an important sawmill town and served as the railroad terminus for a regional network of lumbermill towns. The Arkadelphia

Lumber Company, the largest in the area, built the Ultima Thule, Arkadelphia and Mississippi River Railway and the Antione Valley Railroad.[44] Although industry has declined since these spirited days, it remains important to the Arkadelphian economy.

Arkadelphia's site on upland bluffs allows it to overlook the fertile bottomlands of the Ouachita River. This back country is covered with a thick matting of vegetation including the tangled limbs of water oak, elm, gum, pine, and hanging lianas. The shadier areas are characterized by clumps of rattan and hydrophytic grasses.

Arkadelphia also is known for Ouachita College and Henderson State University. Ouachita College, a coeducational Baptist-supported institution, was founded in 1886 and currently services about 1,500 students. Henderson State University, founded in 1890 as Methodist-supported Henderson-Brown College, was converted to a state teacher's college in 1929; its present enrollment is about 3,000.

Over the past fifty years, Arkadelphia has attracted several manufacturing plants. The larger firms are: Gold Bond Building Products (woodfiber), Levi Strauss and Company (men's slacks), Ouachita Marine and Industrial Corporation (boats), Reynolds Metals Company (aluminum extrusions), and Vassarette, Inc. (lingerie).

TOUR A8: SEARCY TO ARKADELPHIA BY WAY OF U.S. 67 AND INTERSTATE 30

U.S. 67 and Interstate 30 follow the eastern boundary of the Ouachita province. With mountains to the west and the coastal plain to the east the low rolling hills of the area offer a transitional environment. The predominate pine forests are broken by farmland and urban development along this well-populated section of Arkansas.

Searcy

Searcy (population 14,150), first called Sulphur Springs, attained regional recognition as a mid-nineteenth-century health resort when visitors drank the strong smelling, sulphur-laden water from the town's springs.[45] Its location on the military road from Saint Louis to Little Rock and its selection as the seat of sprawling White County helped the town to prosper.

The older business district, mainly two- and three-story brick and stone structures, is clustered around a Romanesque-style, white limestone and red brick courthouse. New string street commercial districts have developed along both U.S. 67 and the portion of Arkansas 16 between the courthouse square and U.S. 67.

The town's older industries—lumbering, cotton ginning, food processing, and retail sales—continue to prosper, but over the past thirty years, several new industries have been added. Searcy's manufacturing plants now produce such diverse products as custom-built truck trailers, industrial rubber, welded tubing, laundry equipment, bronze plaques, automotive tools, aluminum frozen-food containers, stainless-steel sinks, hydraulic valves, hardwood flooring, egg products, and processed beef and pork.

Harding University, at Grand Avenue and East Center Street, is a four-year liberal arts institution affiliated with the Church of Christ.

Searcy is one of the fastest growing cities in Arkansas. Its population increased more than 50 percent during the 1970s, from 9,040 to 13,612. Most of the 544 black residents of Searcy have roots that go back to the pre–Civil War period of agricultural development.

Beebe

Beebe (population 3,860), a mile east of U.S. 67, is an old agricultural community that has shared in the general growth in central Arkansas in recent years. Once an important strawberry shipping point on the Missouri Pacific Railroad, Beebe's population has more than doubled over the past twenty years. Employment opportunities in the town's small manufacturing plants and the ease of commuting to work in Little Rock have contributed to this growth. Among the diverse products manufactured in Beebe are hydraulic cylinders, ladies' coats and suits, mobile homes, and live-stock feeds.

Ward

Ward (population 981), located in north-ern Lonoke County, began as a farm trading center. Today many of its resi-dents are employed in commercial and manufacturing jobs in nearby cities.

Cabot

Cabot (population 6,460) is another of Arkansas' fastest growing cities. Its population has increased more than three-fold over the past twenty years. Although many of Cabot's residents are employed at the Little Rock Air Force Base in Jacksonville and in manufactur-ing and commercial jobs in metropolitan Little Rock, local manufacturers employ many in the production of a variety of items, including mobile homes, bedding and furniture, mobile commercial build-ings, and foundation ventilators.

Cabot's older business district oc-cupies half a dozen blocks about a half mile east of U.S. 67; newer commercial strips, including familiar fast-food res-taurants and motels, have developed along Arkansas 367 and U.S. 67.

Cabot was the boyhood home of Roarke Bradford, author of several books on rural life in Arkansas.[46]

Jacksonville

Jacksonville (population 29,650), Ar-kansas' ninth largest city, has nearly doubled in population since 1960. Once primarily a service center for the sur-rounding fruit and general farms, Jack-sonville's major employer is now the Little Rock Air Force Base. Jacksonville also has nineteen manufacturing plants listed in the *Arkansas Directory of Manufacturers* (1980), which produce such diverse products as prestressed concrete, tunneling lasers, steel door frames, electric motors, truck parts, boats, roof ventilators, exhaust fans, and herbicides.

Little Rock (see chapter 12)

Bryant

Bryant (population 4,490) is an indus-trial town that has been caught up in the suburban growth of metropolitan Little Rock. The bauxite mines and mills located just south of the town have long been an important component of Bryant's economic picture; three manu-facturing plants, producing furniture frames, ground barite and soapstone products, and custom injection mold-ing, are situated inside the city limits. An improved road network and the movement of manufacturing plants and other businesses into the suburban fringes of Little Rock have made Bryant a target for increased growth. Its popula-tion grew from 737 in 1960 to 1,199 in 1970, then climbed sharply to 2,678 by 1980. Unfortunately, layoffs at the nearby bauxite mills during the early 1980s dampened the spirited economic growth.

Bauxite

Bauxite (population 433), a scattered mining settlement, was founded in 1903 as a company town by the Pittsburg Re-duction Company. It passed through sev-ral phases that ranged from a cluster of segregated communities to a unified in-dependent town and finally to extinction in 1969 when the mines shut down.

Its landscape is dominated by open-pit mines, abandoned sheet-metal tool sheds, bauxite processing mills, abandoned streets, and empty lots whose foundations and chimneys have become overgrown with brush. Many of the earlier residents of Bauxite moved away from the town as the mining operations crept closer and closer to their homes and as the yellow dust from the bauxite pits settled over the area.[47] Today, the mining operations of the Aluminum Company of America (Alcoa) occupy most of the area of the town, and only a few buildings remain standing. The sprawling processing plants of the Reynolds Metals Company that converted raw bauxite ore into alumina chemicals and aluminum oxide are being dismantled, but the mining and smelting operations of Alcoa and the American Cyanamid Company continue to provide significant economic support for the area.

The presence of bauxite ore in Arkansas was first reported by John C. Branner, State Geologist, in 1887. It has been mined commercially both in open-pit and underground mines since 1899. Nearly all of the bauxite deposits are centered around large masses of intrusive igneous rock in a 275-square-mile area of Pulaski and Saline counties. For many years, Arkansas produced more than 90 percent of the United States domestic bauxite. The state's output in 1979 totaled over 1.4 million tons with a value in excess of $20.5 million. The primary use of this bauxite is for the making of aluminum metal, but it is also used in the production of chemicals, abrasives, refractories, and alumina cements. The conversion of bauxite ore into alumina takes place in two major plants: the Reynolds' operation at Hurricane Creek and Alcoa's plant in Bauxite. Aluminum metal is produced at two Reynolds Metals Company plants: the

Jones Mill reduction plant on Lake Catherine and the Gum Springs plant in Arkadelphia.

Benton

Benton (population 18,220) is another of the half dozen central Arkansas cities whose recent growth is linked closely with the expansion of the Little Rock metropolitan area. Benton, located on Interstate 30, only thirteen miles from downtown Little Rock, is a prime site for industrial and residential growth.

First subdivided in 1836, Benton was initially supported by a salt works, a racetrack, and after the railroad arrived, the lumber industry. The town's old commercial center, laid out in a grid pattern of wide streets with low brick buildings, surrounds the Saline County Courthouse. A newer string street commercial district, including the familiar franchised fast-food businesses, has evolved along Arkansas 88 where it parallels Interstate 30.

Since World War II, and especially during the 1960s, several manufacturing plants were built in Benton; the jobs thus created attracted many new people to the city. The 1980 *Arkansas Directory of Manufacturers* lists twenty-one plants. Although most of these are small, some employ nearly two hundred workers. These companies produce such diverse products as ceramic grinding material, bauxite clay, wood products, tools and dies, hydraulic equipment, precision springs, steel buildings, furniture, paper products, and recycled aluminum.

Malvern

Malvern (population 10,150), the Hot Springs County seat, is three miles east of Interstate 30. The older business district is built in a network of grid pattern streets surrounding the courthouse; the newer commercial businesses, including the ubiquitous strip of McDonald's,

Burger King, Kentucky Fried Chicken, and other similar establishments, are built along the stretch of U.S. 270 that connects with Interstate 30.

The older residential districts, near the courthouse commercial core, are wood frame, one- and two-story structures built with timber from the surrounding forests; the newer residential areas, built at the edge of town, are a mixture of the well-recognized bungalows, ranch-style, and split-level houses that so typify American suburbia.

Arkadelphia (see tour A7)

East-West Highway Tours

TOUR B1: LITTLE ROCK,
ARKANSAS, TO CHECOTAH,
OKLAHOMA, BY WAY OF
INTERSTATE 40

Little Rock (see chapter 12)

Mayflower

Mayflower (population 1,381) is about a mile south of Reynolds Mountain and Lake Conway in Faulkner County. The town's population nearly tripled during the 1970s.

Conway

Conway (population 23,450) benefits from both its location on the central Arkansas Navigation Channel and the good railroad and highway transportation networks in the corridor between Little Rock and Fort Smith. From its founding in 1871 until 1940, the town grew slowly but steadily. Since 1940, when its population totaled 5,782, Conway has more than quadrupled in size.

The town is named for the Conway family, who moved to the area from Missouri, established an early Red River plantation, and became prominent in Arkansas politics.[1]

Three colleges provide substantial economic support for the town. Arkansas State University, at Bruce Street and Donghey Avenue, is the largest; Central College, at Conway Boulevard and College Avenue, is a Baptist-supported school; and Hendrix College, 1400 Front Street, is affiliated with the Methodist Church.

The older business district is built across the railroad tracks from the yellow brick Faulkner County Courthouse; another commercial district has grown up along the U.S. 64 business route where McDonald's, Wendy's, Kentucky Fried Chicken, and other fast-food establishments are intermixed with motels, restaurants, gasoline stations, and other familiar string-street businesses.

Since World War II, Conway has attracted several important manufacturing plants. The *1980 Arkansas Directory of Manufacturers* list forty-one plants there; among the largest are Aermotor (electric pumps), Baldwin Piano and Organ Company, Barry of Conway (shoes), Castle Industries (mobile homes), and Conway Mill (tampons).

North of Conway, Interstate 40 cuts through Cadron Ridge and then swings west to cross Cadron Creek. Near the mouth of Cadron Creek, where the ridge forms a bluff on the Arkansas River, a trapper named John Standler founded a small settlement in 1778; until 1820, this Cadron settlement rivaled Little Rock for leadership in the Arkansas Valley. After the railroad was built through Conway, seven miles away, however, the town gradually died.

Menifee

Menifee (population 368) is an agricultural hamlet situated alongside the Missouri Pacific Railroad.

Plumerville

Plumerville (population 785) was founded in 1825 when Samuel Plumer established a saddlery there to manufacture harnesses, saddles, and leather goods for sale to the Cherokees. John M. Clayton, a brother of former Governor Powell Clayton, was murdered in Plumerville while investigating a charge of election fraud in 1889.[2] His death was one of the last flare-ups of Reconstruction hatred in the area.

Morrilton

Morrilton (population 7,180) was founded as a shipping point on the Little Rock and Fort Smith Railroad when it was extended up the Arkansas Valley in the 1870s. It is situated on the north bank of the Arkansas River and at the west end of the low, east-west ridge called Burrow Mountain. Petit Jean Mountain (1,100 feet), an Arkansas Valley landmark, rises as a blue-gray massif ten miles to the southwest.

The town is focused around a ten-block downtown commercial district; a newer strip commercial district has grown up along the Arkansas 9 business route leading to and from Interstate 40.

A dozen manufacturing plants provide jobs for residents of Morrilton and the surrounding hinterland. The largest companies are Arrow Automotive Industries, Inc. (auto parts), Arkansas Kraft Corporation (linerboard), Crompton-Arkansas Mills, Inc. (corduroy), Levi Strauss and Company (men's clothing), and Morrilton Plastics Corporation (polyvinyl chloride).

Atkins

Atkins (population 3,170) has more than doubled in population since 1965, partly because of the expansion of coal and natural gas exploration and production in Pope County during the 1970s. The town's largest manufacturing employer is the Atkins Pickle Company, which manufacturers pickled cucumbers, peppers, and other similar products.

South of Atkins, near the mouth of Galla Creek, was the site of the Indian village known as Galla Rock, one of

Five-passenger Climber automobile in the Museum of Automobiles on Petit Jean Mountain. Courtesy of Arkansas Department of Parks and Tourism.

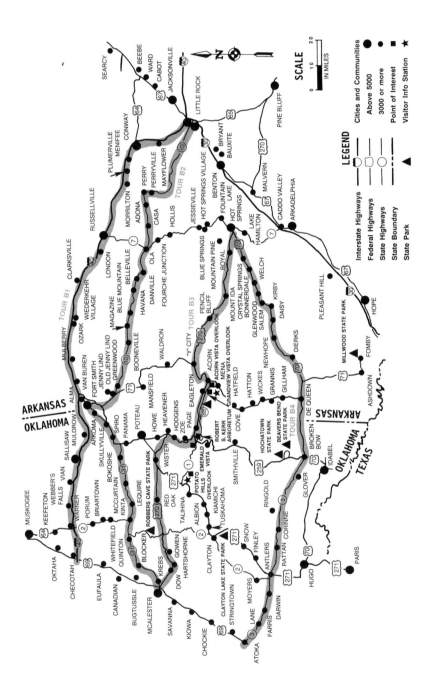

Map 33. East–West Highway Tours. *Adapted from:* Arkansas State Highway and Transportation Department, 1985); Oklahoma State Transportation Map (Oklahoma City: Oklahoma Department of Transportation, 1985).

several established by the Western Cherokee on the upper Arkansas in the early 1800s. John Jolly, who assumed leadership of the Western Cherokee when his brother, Chief Tahlonteskee died, was instrumental in the emergence of Galla Rock as the prosperous village described by Thomas Nuttall during his journey up the Arkansas in 1819.

Ten miles to the south of Atkins and across the Arkansas River, the blue-gray mass of Petit Jean Mountain offers a striking landmark; to the west, Interstate 40 parallels the south flank of Crow Mountain and passes through an agriculturally productive section of the Arkansas Valley. The farms in this area are generally larger than those to the north and south; while some livestock activities exist, crop farming is more important agriculturally. Soybeans have replaced cotton, once dominant in every county in the valley, as the most important crop; cotton still holds that rank in Conway County.

Russellville (see tour A7).

London

London (population 859) is a farm retailing and service center that has tripled in population since 1960. Some of London's residents commute to jobs in Russellville.

Clarksville

Clarksville (population 5,290) is three miles north of the Arkansas River on the tow slope of Stillwell Mountain. Spadra Creek, which bisects the town, carries runoff from the southern slopes of the Ozarks.

Although peach orchards were once abundant on the farms around Clarksville, drought, low prices, and labor shortages during the 1940s and 1950s curtailed production. A few commercial orchards weathered the hard times and, in fact, the production of peaches

has actually grown somewhat in recent years; still, soybeans dominate the riverbottom landscape. Corn, grain sorghum, and wheat are important secondary crops. Poultry farming also has grown steadily since about 1950.

The first coal produced in Arkansas was mined in 1840 at Spadra, about three miles southwest of Clarksville. The following year, when the first boatload of coal reached Little Rock, the *Arkansas Gazette* proclaimed the emergence of a new era in the history of Arkansas. Coal mining did not become important in Arkansas, however, until the 1870s when railroads were built up the valley. The western Arkansas coalfield, which is about thirty-three miles wide and sixty miles long, covers portions of Sebastian, Franklin, Johnson, and Logan counties. More than 2.75 million tons of coal were mined in 1907, but since then production has generally declined.[3] A modest exception to this downward trend has existed since about 1972. The shaft mining techniques used in the past have been replaced gradually by strip mining procedures. Natural gas fields were opened in the same area of western Arkansas in the 1920s.

Clarksville's business district occupies a half dozen blocks near the Johnson County courthouse. Surrounding the business district are blocks of modest one- and two-story frame houses. Several larger homes, classic Victorian and heavily decorated with gingerbread trim, remain from the days when fortunes were made during the coal-mining boom. Subdivisions with contemporary homes have grown up at choice locations on the town's margins.

Fifteen manufacturing companies provide jobs for Clarksville residents. The largest plants are: Greenville Tube Corporation (stainless steel tubing), Herbst Shoe, Eureka Brick and Tile Company, Kim Products Company, Inc. (frozen foods), Clarksville Wood Prod-

Coal mining near Clarksville, Arkansas, *circa* 1925. Courtesy of Arkansas History Commission.

ucts, Inc. (hardwood and pine wood products), Valmac Industries (poultry processing), and Singer Company (electric power tools).

The College of the Ozarks, at the north end of College Avenue, is affiliated with the Presbyterian Church.

Wiederkehr Village

Wiederkehr Village (population 71), three miles north of Altus, is the focal point of the vineyard district of western Arkansas. During the 1880s, Swiss-German Catholics settled in this vicinity. They planted grapes on the soils of the Boston Mountain foothills, overlooking the Arkansas Valley.[4] The wines produced from these grapes became quite popular in central Arkansas, and in recent years, Wiederkehr Wine Cellar has gained a national reputation for its products. Several other wineries in the region also have prospered, and as a re-

sult, the acreage in vineyards has gradually expanded.

These same Swiss-Germans built St. Mary's Catholic Church on Pond Creek Mountain. The church is noted for its paintings of scenes of the life of Christ by local priests using local residents as models.

Ozark

Ozark (population 3,490) is located on a north bend of the Arkansas River where it flows through a narrow channel cut in the mountain. Ozark has been one of the seats of Franklin County since 1838; the other seat, Charleston, is on the other side of the river. Because of the difficulty of crossing the river, several counties that straddle the Arkansas River have adopted this two county seat approach.

The town's main business district is built around the brown brick courthouse; several newer businesses have

Wiederkehr Winery near Altus, Arkansas. Courtesy of Arkansas Department of Parks and Tourism.

Wiederkehr Winery vineyards. Courtesy of Arkansas Department of Parks and Tourism.

been established along the spur leading to Interstate 40. A half dozen manufacturing plants provide employment; the largest of these are Cargill Incorporated (turkey processing) and Garan Manufacturing, Inc. (shirts).

Mulberry

Mulberry (population 1,444), an agricultural trade and service community, is in the Arkansas Valley near the mouth of the Mulberry River. It began as a Methodist campground in the early 1800s. The production of vegetables and fruits (for markets at Fort Smith and canneries at Springdale) was especially important in this area from the 1930s through the 1950s; although a few farmers continue to specialize in vegetables, poultry, beef, and dairy cattle have become the area's chief sources of farm income.

Most of the commercial businesses occupy five or six blocks of one- and two-storied brick, flat-topped buildings near the center of Mulberry. White frame residences surround the business district; a small subdivision of newer houses lies on the outskirts of town. The largest manufacturing employer is the Mulberry Lumber Company, a producer of pallets and crating materials.

Alma

Alma (population 3,040) is located where Little Frog Bayou enters the Arkansas Valley floodplain. The usual assortment of service stations, motels, and restaurants is found at the junction of U.S. 71 and Interstate 40; an older commercial district is strung out along U.S. 64. Many of Alma's residents are employed by Allen Canning Company (canned vegetables) or Bryant Preserving Company (processed melons).

Van Buren

Van Buren (population 12,720), the seat of Crawford County, was once an important frontier outpost and shipping

point on the Arkansas River. Settled in 1818, it was known as Phillips Landing until 1838 when the townsite was purchased by speculators, subdivided, and renamed for President Martin Van Buren. Because of its nearness to Fort Smith, it prospered as an outfitting point for western trading expeditions into Indian Territory.

The Bob Burns House, at 9th and Jefferson, is a local landmark. Burns, who was noted for his down-to-earth humor and his invention of a primitive musical instrument called the "bazooka," lived in the two-story frame structure from childhood until he left high school.

Much of Van Buren's commercial district parallels U.S. 64. Several newer residential subdivisions have been built on the hills to the north of the older part of town. Twenty-seven manufacturing plants contribute to the economy of Van Buren. The largest of these include: Allen Canning Company (vegetables), Bekaert Steel Wire Corporation (wire products), Cement Asbestos Products Company (asbestos cement pipe), Farmer's Coop of Arkansas and Oklahoma (farm supplies), Fort Smith Structural Steel Company, Inc. (steel products), Kay Chair Company (furniture), and the Sigma Manufacturing Company (plastic products).

Fort Smith (See chapter 10)

Westward from Fort Smith and the Arkansas state line, Interstate 40 follows the border area between the Arkansas Valley and the foothills of the Boston Mountains. While the hills are mantled with a scrubby oak-hickory forest, the fertile bottomlands produce bountiful harvests of soybeans and grain sorghum.

Muldrow

Muldrow (population 2,970) is a half mile north of Interstate 40 at the junction of Oklahoma 64B and U.S. 64. The main business district is built along U.S.

64 and the tracks of the Missouri Pacific Railroad. Throughout the Ouachita Mountain province, the vitality of towns seems to be directly related to their accessibility and their proximity to larger urban centers; Muldrow is situated favorably in both respects. Its population has more than doubled in the past twenty years, in part, because many residents are able to commute to work in nearby Fort Smith.

The physical appearance of Muldrow has changed considerably during the past quarter century: many buildings are empty in the old commercial district; new businesses have located along the highway leading to Interstate 40. Three small furniture manufacturing plants employ twenty-nine workers.

Five miles to the west of Muldrow, Interstate 40 crosses Wildhorse Mountain, a mesalike ridge in the Arkansas River Valley. This is the last major ridge on the folded rock strata of the northwestern Ouachita Mountain border.

Sallisaw

Sallisaw (population 7,770), a mile north of Interstate 40 at the junction of U.S. 64 and 59 and Oklahoma 72, is the Sequoyah County seat. It is served by the Kansas City Southern and Missouri Pacific railroads. Once an important trading post, French trappers named the early settlement *Salaison,* meaning salt meat, because of the large salt deposits nearby.[5]

Sallisaw, in the Arkansas Valley, is in a border position between the Ozark Upland to the north and the Ouachita Mountains to the south.

Until about thirty years ago, coal mining was an important part of the economy; now, however, the old mine sites, just southeast of town, are abandoned and overgrown with brush. Sallisaw currently relies on retail trade, tourism, and manufacturing for the bulk of its economic support. Two of the largest em-

ployers are the St. Clair Lime Company, which employs approximately one hundred workers in its quarry and mills to the west of town, and the Holley Special Products Division, which employs approximately five hundred workers in the manufacturing of automobile emission control devices.

Sallisaw's business district parallels the railroad tracks. Highway 59 passes by the old passenger depot that has been converted to an attractive public library. Newer apartment buildings and well-maintained businesses contribute to the town's prosperous appearance.

Vian

Vian (population 1,521) is situated a mile north of Interstate 40 on Oklahoma 82. Its name is a corrupted form of the French word *viande,* meaning meat.[6] Serving as a local retail and service center and as a residence for retired farmers, Vian is also a gateway to the recreation areas around Lake Tenkiller and the Cookson Hills.

Webber's Falls

Webber's Falls (population 461), two miles north of Interstate 40 on U.S. 64, derived its name from Walter Webber, a Cherokee chief, and a nearby waterfall on the Arkansas River; the falls are now submerged under the waters of the Arkansas Navigation Channel.

Warner (see tour A2)

Checotah (see tour A1)

TOUR B2: LITTLE ROCK, ARKANSAS, TO McALESTER, OKLAHOMA, BY WAY OF ARKANSAS 10, U.S. 71, U.S. 271, AND OKLAHOMA 31.

This scenic route traverses the rugged mountain country west of Little Rock, skirting Lake Maumelle and the Maumelle Pinnacles before turning west to follow the Petit Jean River Valley into western Arkansas. West of Fort Smith the tour follows the Poteau River and Sans Bois Creek in a southwesterly direction toward McAlester.

The tour begins at the junction of Interstate 430 and Arkansas 10 in west Little Rock where it proceeds through residential districts that thin out and become five-acre estates in the vicinity of suburban Joe Robinson High School. Highway 10 then winds through a forested ridge and valley landscape, passes to the south and west of Lake Maumelle (see chapter 5), and follows the Maumelle River through Long Mountain to the tiny hamlet of Thornburg.

Thornburg

Thornburg (population 100) is a hamlet consisting of three abandoned stores and about a dozen dwellings. On the south edge of the community is a Work Center of the Winona District of the Ouachita National Forest.

Perryville

Perryville (population 1,058) is in the valley of the Fourche LaFave River at the foot of Toms Mountain. Most of the town's businesses are scattered along Fourche Street (Highway 10). A windshield inventory reveals a discount drugstore, drive-in bank, feedstore, grocery store, farm supply store, café, lodge building, auto parts store, florist, electric cooperative, two car washes, and the Winona Ranger Station of the Ouachita National Forest. The largest structures in town make up the Perryville Senior High and Junior High School complex.

South of Perryville, beyond the Fourche LaFave River bridge and approximately one mile west on a gravel road, is the 1,200-acre ranch of Heifer Project International. This ranch is operated by staff volunteers with the goal of aiding poverty-stricken areas on all continents. The idea of providing breeding stock so small farmers around the world

can achieve a better living was conceived by Dan West. Each year the ranch is involved in a dozen or more domestic and international shipments, involving hundreds of cattle, sheep, goats, swine, and rabbits. While on the ranch, the animals are innoculated and prepared for shipment. The ranch also hosts approximately 3,500 guests each year.[7]

To the north of Perryville, the highway crosses Toms Mountain, an east-west trending hogback ridge that reaches elevations in excess of 1,200 feet. On the north flank of the ridge, at the town of Perry, the ridge turns west and proceeds up the valley of Rocky Cypress Creek.

Perry

Perry (population 254) was founded in 1898 when the Choctaw and Memphis Railroad was extended up Rocky Cypress Creek toward Ola and the Petit Jean River Valley. Like most of the towns on the Chicago, Rock Island, and Pacific Railway (which later purchased the Choctaw and Memphis), Perry served mainly as a shipping point for the lumber products produced by local mills; today, very little is shipped on the railroad. (The Chicago, Rock Island and Pacific right-of-way and rolling stock was purchased by the Little Rock and Western Railroad when the CRI and P declared bankruptcy and sold off its properties during the 1970s.) The poultry and livestock grown in the valley are trucked to market.

Very few services remain in Perry. Along a block-long portion of the street leading off Arkansas 10 are a few old buildings, including the city hall, the post office, a lodge hall, an abandoned hardware store, and an abandoned grocery store. Adjacent to Arkansas 10 are an abandoned school, a muffler shop, and a quick-stop gasoline station. The old railroad depot has been freshly painted and preserved as an office build-

Lumbering in the Ouachita Mountains, *circa* 1940. Courtesy of Arkansas History Commission.

ing for the Little Rock and Western Railroad.

Adona

Adona (population 230), six miles west of Perry on the Little Rock and Western Railroad and Arkansas 10, is another former lumber town that has evolved into a residential hamlet. Since many of the previous residences have been demolished, the remaining houses are widely spaced. Very few of the community's commercial businesses are still open. The few that still exist include a Methodist Church, an automobile and machinery repair shop, and a quick-shop gasoline station. As in many of the towns in the northern and western Ouachitas a cluster of poultry sheds appear on the edge of town.

The landscape in the Rock Cypress Creek Valley is impressive as forested mountains rise abruptly on either side.

The valley floor is more rolling than level; the grassy meadows in this area are bordered by a mottled landscape of dark green pines and yellow-orange oaks during the fall season. Rose Creek Mountain displays an especially bold and persistent outcrop of bedrock on the north side of the valley.

Homewood

Homewood is a community of about a half dozen houses located nearly midway between Adona and Casa. If ever any businesses served this community, they have long since closed and their lumber and foundations have been hauled away for other uses. Homewood's location in a narrow valley between Rose Creek Mountain and Ola Mountain is particularly attractive.

A dozen or so poultry barns in various stages of repair, suggest that the broiler industry has been in the valley for a long time. Most of the residences have neatly trimmed yards, sometimes decorated with old household tools and farm machinery that reflect turn-of-the-century farm life. Neatly stacked ricks of firewood are ubiquitous farmstead features. The houses generally are well-painted and in good repair; but, since the barns that still remain are no longer needed to house draft animals, many have fallen into disrepair though some seem to defy the laws of gravity.

Casa

Casa (population 179) boasts a grocery store, a city water supply, the Casa-Perry Consolidated High School, two churches—Church of Christ and Baptist—and an Exxon station. The residential area, which follows a grid pattern, consists of bungalow-style frame houses on large lots.

Berta

Berta (population 36) consists of a Baptist church, a long-abandoned store building, about a dozen houses strung out along the highway, and a small cluster of poultry sheds.

Ola (see tour A7)

Danville

Nestled in the Petit Jean River Valley, Danville (population 1,698) is the gateway to a large tract of the Ouachita National Forest that stretches west and south across several counties; it is also the southern seat of sprawling Yell County (Dardanelle is the northern county seat). It has a surprising number of retail stores and services for a "backwoods" town far from any major federal highways. Most of the businesses are situated along Arkansas 10 as it passes through the town in an elbow turn. Along Main Street, where a few two-story brick and masonry buildings are mixed with one-story frame structures,

is a Western Auto Store, a Ford agency, the new Yell County courthouse, a convenience store, an Exxon station, an abandoned movie theatre, and an assortment of farm supply and clothing businesses.

The eastern leg of Arkansas 10 passes a Chevrolet dealership, a motel, two or three gasoline stations, a skating rink and bowling alley, the ranger office of the Fourche District of the Ouachita National Forest, and the Save-A-Sum Shopping Center—a small, L-shaped, off-street shopping center that houses about a half dozen businesses.

Danville's two major employers anchor the east and west ends of town. At the west end of the Arkansas 10 business corridor, on the banks of the Petit Jean River, is Petit Jean Poultry, Inc., a processor of broiler chickens. At the east end of town the poultry processing plant, bulk feed plant, and offices of the Wayne Poultry Company and Wayne Farms, a division of Continental Grain, Inc., are located on a ten-acre tract. To the east of the processing plant are several cooling sheds where trucks jammed with broiler chickens park while waiting to discharge their cargo; huge fans in the sheds force cool air through the open-sided trucks, thus keeping the chickens alive during Arkansas' hot and steamy summers.

Belleville

Belleville (population 571) is four miles west of Danville at the junction of Arkansas 10 and Arkansas 7. Mount Magazine, the dominant landmark in western Arkansas and the highest point in the state (2,850 feet above sea level), hovers to the northwest of town.

Belleville's main claim to fame is that it is the birthplace of Mamie Harris, who gained international acclaim as a leading soprano in several European and American opera companies while using the stage name of Mamie McCormic.[8]

Even though Belleville's population increased from 411 in 1940 to 571 in 1980, its commercial functions continued to decline. Many of the buildings in the block-long business district that extends north from the railroad tracks and Highway 10 are empty. As transportation systems have improved, small towns like Belleville have become bedroom communities that can only support convenience stores, gasoline stations, and other small businesses catering to the residents' daily needs. More specialized goods and services are obtained in larger regional centers.

To the west of Belleville, the valley widens. Farmsteads with clusters of low poultry sheds with their characteristic ventilation cupolas provide evidence that the broiler industry is the primary agricultural pursuit. Hay meadows and pasturelands support a modest beef-cattle industry.

Havanna

Havanna (population 352) was founded when the Choctaw and Eastern Railroad was extended up the Petit Jean River Valley in 1898. The original business district was laid out along the north side of the railroad tracks and a one-block street that crossed the tracks. Later a string of one-story businesses was built along the south side of a two-block stretch of Arkansas 10, paralleling the Little Rock and Western tracks; this combination of the railroad right-of-way and the highway created a wide-open area between the two sections of town. Nearly half of the business buildings are now empty; those that continue to operate are mainly those that serve daily needs and conveniences of the population, which has declined by more than 25 percent since 1940.

The commanding view of the Petit Jean Valley, Blue Mountain Lake, and the broad Arkansas Valley from the summit of Mount Magazine is well worth the steep switchback climb north from Havanna through the Ouachita National Forest on Arkansas 309. Thomas Nuttall, in his *Journal of Travels into the Arkansas Territory, 1819,* described Mount Magazine as a "magnificent empurpled mountain whose peculiar form led to the name of Magazine, or Barn, by French hunters." [9] Although some historians have attributed the name to a report that the mountain was the site of a Confederate ammunition magazine during the Civil War, Nuttall's version appears to be more plausible. [10]

West of Havanna the highway traverses an idyllic valley landscape marked by pastures dotted with beef cattle, comfortable homes, and clusters of poultry barns.

Waveland

Waveland (population 85), seven miles west of Havanna, is an old railroad market town that has evolved into a bedroom community. Its location, about a mile north of Blue Mountain Dam and Lake, accounts for its three combination bait shop-gas station-convenience stores. A dozen or so scattered older houses and mobile homes comprise the residential area.

Blue Mountain

Blue Mountain (population 112) is just west of the Logan-Yell county line. A dilapidated railroad depot and a couple of abandoned business buildings are reminders of more properous days when Blue Mountain was a shipping point on the Choctaw and Eastern Railroad. Today, the town consists of a convenience store offering gasoline, bait, and groceries and several older residences scattered along a quarter-mile area just south of the highway.

Magazine

Magazine (population 799) is ten miles southwest of Mount Magazine near the

Cattle graze peacefully upon the hills of the Ouachita Mountains in Arkansas. Courtesy of Arkansas Department of Parks and Tourism.

west end of Blue Mountain Lake. Primarily a residential town, most of the newer houses have been built along Arkansas 10, near the west edge of town. Boasting a water tower and municipal water supply, Magazine also has a high school (whose mascot is the Rattlers) and a branch of the Citizens Bank of Booneville. The main business district is strung out along a two-block stretch of Arkansas 10 and a half-block portion of a northern side street. The buildings, half of which are empty, are predominantly one-story frame structures with false fronts and overhanging sidewalk canopies. The town's high concrete sidewalks and gutters are remnants of an earlier era when cars possessed running boards and greater ground clearance. These, in combination with the un-

tended vacant storefronts, suggest that the town's heydey has long since passed.

Booneville

Booneville (population 3,810), which is the southern seat of Logan County, is built around a turn-of-the-century red brick business district at the intersection of Arkansas 10 and 23. Like many of the larger Ouachita Mountain towns, Booneville is situated in a broad basin of good agricultural land. Whereas vegetables, cotton, grains, and dairy activities once prevailed on this land, beef cattle and poultry activities are now the main agricultural pursuits.

Booneville had a population of 2,324 in 1940 and was supported by "three sawmills, railroad switchery operations on the Rock Island, and two cotton gins . . ."; its principal income, however, was "provided by the Arkansas Tuberculosis Sanitorium." [11] Today, the town's main economic base consists of manufacturing and retail sales and services.

A traverse through Booneville on Arkansas 10 provides an inventory of the commercial and social life of a typical Ouachita Mountain growth center: a new residential subdivision at the west edge of town, a Ford automobile agency, a hospital, a new Jehovah's Witness Kingdom Hall, a used-car dealership, a motel, several blocks of bungalow-style houses, an older business district consisting of two-story brick buildings, several service stations, a supermarket, a post office, realty companies, a police department, a half dozen fast-food restaurants, the ubiquitous Wal-Mart store (a sure sign of a growth town), the Cold Springs ranger station of the Ouachita National Forest, another newer subdivision near the east edge of town, and the sprawling Wolverine Toy Company manufacturing plant.

West of Booneville the highway passes just south of the Fort Chaffee military reservation and enters one of western Arkansas' major coal-mining districts. In 1938, some 1,600 miners worked in the Sebastian County mines gouging tons of bituminous coal from "low" veins twenty-eight to thirty-two inches thick.[12] Although all of the underground mines were closed when the demand for coal sharply declined following World War II, the energy crisis of the 1970s stimulated the expansion of highly mechanized strip mining throughout the county.

Greenwood

Greenwood (population 3,300) is the southern seat of Sebastian County and a bedroom community for metropolitan Fort Smith. The commercial district focuses on the county courthouse. Several new business buildings suggest a relatively strong local economy. Since 1940 when its population was 1,219, Greenwood's population has increased an average of 525 per decade.

West of Greenwood the tour follows U.S. 71 to Fort Smith.

Fort Smith (see chapter 10)

Tour B2 now follows U.S. 271 to its junction with Oklahoma 31 and turns west toward Bokoshe, Oklahoma.

Bokoshe

Bokoshe (population 556) was built along the Fort Smith and Western Railroad around the turn of the century when the coalfields were opened in Haskell and Le Flore counties.[13] The coal mines, whose principal markets were the railroads themselves, attracted domestic coal miners as well as immigrants from the British Isles—Englishmen, Scotchmen, Welshmen, and Irishmen. Later immigrants included Italians, Lithuanians, Slovaks, Poles, Magyars, and Russians. Thus, the ethnic landscape of the region became tremendously varied. The early shatterbelt, comprised of Choctaw and Creek Indians, their black slaves, and white Americans with their Scotch-Irish and English descent, became further "Balkanized" as small, ethnically mixed mining camps emerged.

Because the mines at Bokoshe closed long ago, the countryside is now characterized by a broken maze of water-filled pits and spoil banks overgrown with scrub willows and oaks. The few remaining business buildings along Arkansas 10 include two cafés, a gun and pawn shop, a satellite-dish business, and two convenience store-gasoline stations. Empty two-story brick buildings remain as relics of the earlier, more prosperous days. About a mile east of town is an arena where the Future Farmers of America rodeo is held each year.

Looking south from Bokoshe one can see the Sans Bois Mountains to the southwest and the Winding Stair Range through a purple haze to the southeast.

McCurtain

McCurtain (population 549) is another of Oklahoma's former coal-mining towns that has fallen on hard times. Only a handful of business buildings—a pool hall, a city hall building, and a couple of gasoline stations—still remain along the main street; the remnants of foundations and deserted, roofless buildings with broken windows lend a "bombed out" appearance to a two-block stretch of the old business district.

Lequire

Lequire (population 200), situated at the junction of Oklahoma 31 and 82, consists of a few dozen houses, a post office, a grocery store, and a Baptist Church.

Kinta

Kinta (population 303) is at the west end of a broad basin between Beaver Mountain, Panther Mountain, and Tucker Knob. Because the basin is mainly devoted to hay meadows, the fields are dotted with giant "jellyroll" hay bales during the late summer months: the few cultivated fields of soybeans and corn create a conspicuous contrast.

Kinta's business district occupies two curb-and-guttered blocks along Oklahoma 31. The buildings are primarily rustic one-story, false-fronted frame structures; two or three abandoned brick buildings remain from more prosperous days just after the turn of the century. Among the half dozen remaining businesses are a grocery store, a convenience store-gasoline station, and a car wash.

Quinton

Quinton (population 1,228) is an old farm market that has lost much of its commercial function over the past forty years. Empty and dilapidated business buildings along both the highway and a connecting street attest to more prosperous days when a denser rural population provided a larger market.

Featherstone

Featherstone is a tiny settlement consisting of about a dozen houses and a convenience store-gas station.

Blocker

Blocker (population 225) is a crossroads settlement comprised of widely scattered houses and a convenience store that also caters to visitors to the nearby Jones Creek Arm of Eufaula Lake.

Krebs

Krebs (population 1,754) can trace its existence back to the early coal-mining days in Pittsburg County; the first mine of any significance in the county was opened in 1875 near the present townsite of Krebs by Joshua O. Pusley, a white man who had married into the Choctaw tribe.[14]

Since all early mines were located on land owned by the Choctaw Indians, tribal laws played a very influential role in shaping the nature of these mining operations. The land was leased for exploration and development; royalties were paid on all the coal that was produced. Because the mines were isolated from major population centers, the Choctaws also permitted the "outsiders" to build support facilities such as houses, stores, company offices, and even schools.[15] As additional expansion occurred, the essence of a town frequently evolved.

This transition from a company-owned mining appendage to a legitimate town, with an expanded and more diversified economy, was a natural progression that was repeated time and time again throughout the Ouachita coal-mining areas. With strong mining influences continuing in most of these towns, their development patterns closely reflected fluctuations in the mining industry. Just as towns prospered with boom times in the mines, so did they suffer when mining activities slowed or even ceased. On more than one occasion, the closing of a mine triggered the eventual "closing" of a nearby town.

Some communities, such as Krebs, were able to withstand drastic fluctuations in the mining industry because their economies had become more diversified. The changeover from labor intensive shaft mining to labor extensive (i.e., mechanized) strip mining caused obvious problems for Krebs, yet many of the displaced miners were able to turn to other occupations both in Krebs and nearby McAlester.

A legacy of Krebs' mining experience can be detected in the population composition. Although the first miners came from other parts of the United States, later immigrants came from the British Isles and Southern and Eastern Europe; both Krebs and McAlester attracted a large Italian contingent whose influence is still evident today.[16]

TOUR B3: HOT SPRINGS, ARKANSAS, TO McALESTER, OKLAHOMA, BY WAY OF U.S. 270

This tour is one of the most scenic in the Ouachita region; farms, ranches, towering pines, rugged mountains, and picturesque communities combine to form a tremendously varied landscape. From Hot Springs to Mount Ida is a "rock shop row" where dealers sell spectacular quartz crystals that have been gouged from the nearby mountains. Continuing west, U.S. 270 follows Big Creek Valley into Oklahoma north of Wister Lake. The highway follows the Fourche Maline Valley between the San Bois Mountains and the Winding Stair range and then crosses the Pittsburg County coalfields before reaching McAlester.

Hot Springs (see chapter 11)

Mountain Pine

Mountain Pine (population 1,068) is six miles northwest of Hot Springs on Arkansas 227. The intersection of Arkansas 227 and U.S. 270 is one mile west of Hot Springs.

While Mountain Pine is situated on a fairly level site, hills arise on the northern and eastern sides; farther to the north is Blakely Mountain, one of the ridges within the Zig Zag Range. A mile west of Mountain Pine is Blakely Mountain Dam that formed Ouachita Lake when it was constructed across the Ouachita River in 1952.

Founded in 1928, Mountain Pine is a relatively young town compared to most of the other towns in the region. It was established by the Dierks Brothers Lumber Company in support of a lumber milling operation in the midst of its extensive forest properties. Following the established planning practices for "company towns," the community was laid out in three distinct parts: a mill complex, a black residential district, and a much larger white residential area that included the business district. The houses surrounding the business district were arranged in a grid pattern of "cookie cutter" structures nearly uniform in size and shape.

A number of the current Mountain Pine residents formerly lived in other lumber mill towns owned by the Dierks Company or the Weyerhaeuser Corporation after it purchased the Dierks properties.

West of Mountain Pine, U.S. 270 passes through gently rolling terrain; the land is alternately forested or cleared for hayfields and pasture. Many of the roadside houses are the sprawling bungalows associated with "gentleman" farms or "farmettes." Approximately seven miles west of Hot Springs, U.S 270 crosses the upper arm of Lake Hamilton on a heavily bannistered concrete bridge of a style popular during the 1920s.

Royal

Royal (population 300) is a roadside community situated at the intersection of U.S. 270 and an access road leading to Ouachita Lake and Blakely Mountain Dam. The scattered settlement consists of a post office, a grocery store, a fire station, a ceramic shop, a motel, and several dozen houses.

Crystal Springs

Crystal Springs (population 100), at the junction of U.S. 270 and a lake access road, is a hamlet with a general store that sells gasoline, bait, fishing tackle, camping supplies, and groceries. On the west edge of the community is a shop that produces ornamental windmills.

The pine-forested Crystal Mountains, which rise to the north, derived their name from the many quartz crystal veins found throughout their predominant sandstones. Some of these pointed hexagonal and octagonal crystals form porcupinelike clusters up to five or six feet in diameter. The individual crystals can be two or three feet long. Roadside stands sell the crystals for rock gardens and interior ornaments. Smaller pieces are fashioned into costume jewelry and sold as "Hot Springs Diamonds."

Joplin

Joplin is a scattered collection of houses along a stretch of U.S. 270 where three access roads lead off to the Hickory Nut Mountain and Gap Creek access and camping areas on Ouachita Lake.

Silver

Silver, which consists of a general store and an assemblage of houses spaced randomly along the highway, is also near Ouachita Lake access roads.

Hurricane Grove

Hurricane Grove is another of the ubiquitous hamlets strung out along the many Ouachita Province highways. It consists of a country store, a salvage yard, three rock shops specializing in quartz crystals, a welding shop, and an abandoned drive-in movie. A small subdivision of contemporary homes has recently been built just west of town.

Mount Ida

Mount Ida (population 1,023), the Montgomery County seat, was founded in 1836 when Granville Whittington, a Massachusetts immigrant who, a year earlier, had helped to draft a petition requesting Arkansas statehood, built a general store in the area.[17] Today it is a stable and conservative town that provides shopping and services for the people in the surrounding countryside. Over the past forty years, Mount Ida's population has increased by just 360, an average of nine people a year.

The business district occupies parts of the four square blocks surrounding the sandstone block courthouse. The mix of businesses is typical of those in many Ouachita Mountain towns: a restaurant, a furniture and hardware store, an Oklahoma Tire and Supply store (Otasco), a Sears catalog store, a clothing store, a flower shop, a sawmill maintenance shop, and several garages and service stations. At either end of the town are restaurants, motels, real-estate offices, and rock shops. The post office and "civic center" are important public buildings.

Pencil Bluff

Pencil Bluff (population 120) consists of a small cluster of houses at the junction of U.S. 270 and Arkansas 88, which oc-

Post office at Pine Ridge, Arkansas. Courtesy of Arkansas Department of Parks and Tourism.

cupies an open parklike area in the Ouachita River Valley.

Pine Ridge

Fourteen miles west of Pencil Bluff on Arkansas 88 is the tiny mountain settlement of Pine Ridge. Originally named Waters, it achieved unusual fame since the nationally distributed Lum and Abner radio program was based on the area's backwoods or "hillbilly" life style and humor. Gradually the residents of Waters attempted to adapt the town to the radio-created image of the Arkansas hill country; they even changed the name of the town to match the program's fictitious Pine Ridge.

Many years have passed since the Lum and Abner show was popular; Pine Ridge has been nearly forgotten. The general store has been converted into a

gift and curio shop for the occasional visitor.

To the north of Pencil Bluff, U.S. 270 climbs over Fourche Mountain through a series of curves and switchbacks, then follows Mill Creek Valley to Y City. In the mountains, the highway tunnels through groves of lofty pine trees; in the valleys, there are occasional clearings where hayfields and tree-dotted, parklike pastures are traversed.

Y City (see tour A5)

West of Y City, U.S. 270 follows Johnson Creek for about six miles before turning south as it climbs through a gap in Fourche Mountain, which, in turn, leads to the Acorn Basin.

Acorn

Acorn consists of a few houses and poultry sheds along U.S. 270. It is an old community established by pioneers who recognized the agricultural potential of this headwaters basin on the Ouachita River. Today, very little crop cultivation can be found there; the few farmers left gain their livelihood by raising cattle or poultry, or by off-the-farm activities.

U.S. 270 parallels the tracks of the Kansas City Southern Railway west of Acorn through a canyon cut by Big Creek; the summits of Black Fork Mountain, on the north, and Rich Mountain, on the south, rise over 2,500 feet.

Eagleton

Eagleton is a nearly abandoned hamlet in Big Creek Valley. A few scattered houses and a truck stop are all that remain of the once larger community.

Rich Mountain

Rich Mountain is an abandoned settlement seven miles east of the Oklahoma state line at the junction of U.S. 270 and Arkansas 272. Access to Queen Wilhelmina State Park, which is on the crest of nearby Rich Mountain, can be gained by following Arkansas 272.

Page

Page is a small Oklahoma village in the heart of the Ouachita National Forest. It serves as a convenience stop on U.S. 270 and as an outfitting point for sportsmen and tourists. The village is hemmed in by the narrow Big Creek Valley, Black Fork Mountain, which towers over the settlement to the north, and the steep-walled Rich Mountain, which rises to over 2,500 feet on the south.

Zoe (see tour A4)

Stapp (see tour A4)

Hodgen (see tour A4)

Heavener (see tour A4)

Wister (see tour A3)

Caston (see tour A3)

Fanshawe

Fanshawe (population 416) is an old railroad town founded in the 1890s when the Choctaw Coal and Railway Company was extended westward, through the Choctaw Nation to McAlester.

Hughes

Hughes, a waning coal-mining hamlet about five miles east of Red Oak, was named for Joe Hughes, an early coal mine operator.[18]

Denman

Denman is another nearly abandoned hamlet. Located about two miles east of Red Oak, it was founded as a coal shipping point on the Chicago, Rock Island and Pacific Railway. The community is named for Herbert Denman, another local coal mine operator.[19]

Red Oak

Founded in 1868, Red Oak (population 676) is named after a large red oak tree that stood in the center of town and was used as a whipping post when the community was a court town for the Choctaw Nation. Red Oak was also the site of the last execution under tribal law when Silan Lewis was executed by firing squad on November 5, 1894, for his part in a Nationalist uprising following the 1892 tribal elections.

About two miles northeast from Red Oak on an unnumbered gravel road is the Narrows, a scenic pass that was a part of the Chickasaw immigrant trail of 1838 and the Butterfield Overland stage route between 1858 and 1861. As a low gap in the Red Oak Mountains, it permitted easy travel between Bear Creek Valley and the Fourche Maline Valley. Five miles north of the Narrows is the Thomas Edwards House, a double-pen log structure built in 1858, which is still occupied by Edwards' descendents. Two miles south of Red Oak is Red Oak Ridge, a long narrow hogback that rises in the Fourche Maline Valley; still farther south are Limestone Ridge and the Winding Stair Mountains.

Panola

Panola (population 100) is a hamlet about five miles east of Wilburton in the Fourche Maline Valley. It occupies a picturesque setting between the Sans Bois and Kiamichi Mountains. About three miles northeast is a prominent point called Second Mountain and to the south are Blue Mountain and Limestone Ridge.

Lutie

Lutie (population 150) is a torpid hamlet about two miles east of Wilburton. It was named for Lutie Hailey Walcott, the daughter of Dr. D. M. Hailey, a prominent territorial leader.

Wilburton (see tour A2)

Gowen

Gowen (population 350) is situated alongside U.S. 270 nine miles west of Wilburton. Founded in 1890 and named for a Philadelphia attorney, Frances I. Gowen, this community was the boyhood home of Lincoln Perry, the screen actor who played the popular character, Step'n Fetchit.[20]

Hartshorne and Haileyville

Hartshorne (population 2,380) and Haileyville (population 832), in eastern Pittsburg County, are known locally as the twin cities. Both were established about 1890 and platted in 1902. Hartshorne was named for Dr. Charles Hartshorne, an early settler who was also a railroad official.[21] Haileyville was named for Dr. David Morris Hailey who assisted in sinking the first mine shaft in the McAlester district of the famous Pittsburg County coalfield.[22] The post-World War II decline of large scale coal mining caused economic stagnation and population decline in both these settlements. More recently, several small industrial plants have moved into the area, thus providing employment and increased economic stability. The largest of these manufacturers are Dolese Brothers Company (limestone products) and Oklahoma Aerotronics, Incorporated (electrical equipment).

Dow

Dow (population 100), a now dormant settlement in the Pittsburg County coalfields, is eleven miles southeast of McAlester. It was named for Andrew Dow, an important coal producer.[23] Since the mines have been closed for several years, the ragged rows of spoil banks, where the overlying bedrock and soil were dumped, have developed a green mantle of scrubby trees and bushes.

Alderson

Alderson (population 366), pioneer coal-mining town, is said to have been named for an employee of the Choctaw, Oklahoma, and Gulf Railroad.[24] Alderson was the scene of a unique labor dispute in 1894 when two hundred non-Indian miners and their families were escorted out of the Indian Territory for failure to pay a required tribal tax.[25]

McAlester (see tour A1)

TOUR B4: THE SOUTHERN MARGIN OF THE OUACHITAS BY WAY OF U.S. 70 FROM INTERSTATE 30 IN ARKANSAS TO BROKEN BOW, OKLAHOMA, AND THEN OKLAHOMA 3 AND 7 TO ATOKA, OKLAHOMA

From its junction with Interstate 30 and U.S. 67 east of Hot Springs, U.S. 70 passes through broken piney woods, which are drained by the Saline River, before it follows Ten Mile Creek into the Zig Zag Mountains. Traffic is often heavy but the curves are long and gradual and the grades not terribly steep. On either side of the highway, the view is dominated by mixed pine and hardwood forests. Now and then a tract of forest land has been cleared, sometimes still scorched black from the burning of the slash and litter, and sometimes covered with young Christmas-tree-size pine plantations. Near Hot Springs, U.S. 70 passes down the valley between Grapevine Mountain and Bald Mountain as it passes the Magic Springs theme park.

Hot Springs (see chapter 11)

At the western edge of Hot Springs, U.S. 70 crosses Lake Hamilton (see chapter 5); the highway is lined with gasoline stations, bait shops, quick-shop markets, liquor stores, and lake-related businesses; the lake shore is filled with new apartment buildings and condomin-

Russian Orthodox Church, Hartshorne, Oklahoma. Photo by Fred W. Marvel. Courtesy of Oklahoma Tourism and Recreation Department.

iums; before long, a bucolic landscape re-emerges. Prosperous thoroughbred horse farms with manicured meadows, sprawling ranch-style houses, well-maintained horse barns, and fenced paddocks and pastures are set in a backdrop of dark green pine forests. Interspersed with the horse farms are "farmettes" consisting of contemporary bungalows on three to five acres of cleared land. Most of these neatly landscaped residences are inhabited by those who commute to work in Hot Springs or those who have retired to the Ouachitas. Two-

to four-room mountain cabins are also common features of the cultural landscape; these simple shed-room or cabin-style dwellings, often unpainted and roofed with sheet metal, lend a pleasant turn-of-the-century appearance to the region; the wide porches on these older houses often serve to keep a supply of dry wood close at hand. Backyard gardens produce fresh tomatoes, lettuce, radishes, onions, beans, squash, peppers, potatoes, and other assorted vegetables throughout the summer months. While some homesteads rely upon a few

Grape stomping at Italian festival, McAlester, Oklahoma. Courtesy of Oklahoma Tourism and Recreation Department.

fruit trees for seasonal fruit, mainly apples and peaches, large orchards are not common. The occasional presence of abandoned houses with sagging roofs and widely spreading kudzu and vining roses offers tangible evidence of several generations of rural depopulation.

Pleasant Hill

Pleasant Hill is a rural community without a real nucleus. In addition to a dozen or so houses scattered along the highway, a service station and quick-shop grocery are the only operational businesses.

Pearcy

Pearcy (population 150) is a nearly abandoned hamlet; the post office and an abandoned service station are all that remain of the once larger business district. West of Pearcy, U.S. 70 continues up the valley of Little Mazarn Creek as it passes through tall, heavily scented pine forests and piney meadows.

Bonnerdale

Bonnerdale (population 10), in the northwest corner of Hot Springs County, consists of a country store and two houses.

Welsh

Welsh is an abandoned hamlet ten miles east of Glenwood. The highway between Welsh and Glenwood tunnels through an area of tall pines and pine savanna. Many of the owners of the widely dispersed rural dwellings express their vernacular "artistic" tastes by constructing mailboxes and fences from tools and other household materials from times past. Occasionally, garages and outbuildings have been decorated with automobile license plates or hubcaps; the apparent universal interest in castoffs is most eloquently expressed in the many abandoned stores and service stations that are now serving as "antique shops" and "trading posts."

Glenwood

Glenwood (population 1,402) grew up around a sawmill on the Missouri Pacific Railroad. It does a fairly good business as a shopping and service town; with two lumber mills and a glove factory, Glenwood also serves as a work place for commuters from the surrounding area. The town is situated where the Caddo River cuts through Burnham Mountain. Five miles north of Glenwood on Arkansas 27 is Caddo Gap, a gorge cut by the Caddo River in the

mountain of the same name; both the highway and the Missouri Pacific Railroad follow this gap through the mountains to the town of Caddo Gap.

Salem

Salem (population 150) consists of two country stores and a service station at the junction of U.S. 70 and Arkansas 84. The numerous long, low broiler sheds between Salem and Kirby are indicative of the area's prosperous poultry farms.

Kirby

Kirby (population 250) is a thriving hamlet at the intersection of U.S. 70 and Arkansas 84 and 27. The settlement, which consists of a welding shop, a general store, a gas station, a restaurant, and a cluster of houses, serves as a focal point for visitors to nearby Greeson Lake. To the west of Kirby, U.S. 70 passes close by the lake, which has stimulated the construction of several new houses.

Daisy

Daisy (population 177) is a community whose continued existence can be attributed to the presence of Greeson Lake. It includes two small motels, a grocery store, a trailer park, a lodge and restaurant, two service stations, and a cluster of dwellings.

Newhope

Newhope (population 125) is a scattered and unincorporated settlement near the junction of U.S. 70 and Arkansas 369. The active business—a country store and a gas station—serve both the local residents and visitors to Greeson Lake. The three or four abandoned store buildings give the settlement a somewhat ramshackle appearance.

Dierks

Dierks (population 1,249) has a long history as a focal point for the timber

Ouachita Mountain lumbering, *circa* 1935. Courtesy of Arkansas History Commission.

operations in the surrounding area; it is named after the Dierks family, an early timber producing family who operated in the Ouachitas.

When the Dierks Lumber and Coal Company decided to locate a major milling operation at a siding of the De Queen and Eastern Railroad in 1917, Dierks, which prior to this date was a small settlement built around a gristmill, two blacksmith shops, a cotton gin and two churches, grew both in size and in regional significance.[26] The Dierks Company constructed housing for their many employees; the eastern portion of Dierks became the white residential area; the black residences were concentrated in an area just southwest of the mill. The Dierks company store remained operational until 1970.

Evidence that Dierks was once a company town is still very apparent in rows of nearly identical white, box-like, and hip-roofed houses framed by smoke-stacks of the mill in the background. The black residential area was razed in the 1960s to make room for an expansion of the mill shortly after the sale of all the Dierks Company's holdings in Arkansas and Oklahoma to the Weyerhaeuser Corporation. This development marked the end of legal segregation in Dierks. Though not the predominant force that the Dierks Company once was, Weyerhaeuser is still the single most important employer in town. Among the items produced at its plant are lumber, plywood, logs, and charcoal.

The main business district in Dierks is formed by two blocks of small one-story brick buildings along U.S. 70.

To the west of Dierks, U.S. 70 passes out of the hills and into the bottomlands of the Saline and Cossatot rivers. Here the forests are comprised of even taller pines, in addition to stout oaks and hickories.

Bluegrass music festival in the Ouachita Mountains of Oklahoma. Photo by Fred W. Marvel. Courtesy of Oklahoma Tourism and Recreation Department.

De Queen (see tour A5)

Between De Queen and the Oklahoma boundary, U.S. 70 continues its journey through a rolling landscape covered by a mixed pine-oak-hickory forest. Occasional interruptions in the forest often reveal pasture lands dotted with grazing beef cattle and intermittent service stations and country stores. Many of the stores are now abandoned; others have been converted to new uses such as antique sales; most show clear signs of slowly succumbing to time and the elements.

Eagletown

Eagletown, (population 500), a hamlet just west of the Oklahoma state line on the Texas, Oklahoma and Eastern Railroad, is sixteen miles east of Broken Bow and just south of U.S. 70. Originally settled in 1820, the town was named for the many eagles that nested in

a nearby swamp along the Mountain Fork River. Its Choctaw name, *Apuk-shunubbee,* was derived from that of a chief who died before the tribe's removal from Mississippi.[27]

Eagletown was the first town in Indian Territory on the military road from Little Rock to Fort Towson. The Reverend Cyrus Byington, who authored the *Dictionary of the Choctaw Language,* established the Stockbridge Mission there in 1837; five years later the Choctaw General Council founded the Tyanubbee Seminary for Girls. The buildings of both these institutions have subsequently been destroyed.

Broken Bow (see tour A4)

The portion of this tour between Broken Bow and Atoka follows Oklahoma 7. Along the way are many small, older houses which reflect the rather distinct local styles, bungalows, T-shaped, and

L-shaped houses, many with sheet metal roofs. Some of these homesteads are notable for their unique yard ornaments. Mobile homes, some with wood framed canopies, asphalt-shingled roofs, and attached buildings, are also quite common.

Glover

Glover, a nearly abandoned hamlet a mile south of Oklahoma 7, is a popular put-in and take-out spot for canoe trips on the Glover River.

New Ringold

New Ringold is a bait, gasoline, and sportsman's supply point on the east shore of Pine Creek Lake. The old settlement of Ringold, ten miles northwest, was inundated when the lake was created.

Corinne

Corinne, a hamlet on a south-facing slope overlooking Spencer Creek, consists of an abandoned store and three or four houses scattered along Oklahoma 3. It was named for Corinne LeSeur, a local resident.[28]

Oleta

Oleta, at the junction of Oklahoma 3 and 147, was named for Oleta Ooley, the daughter of an early settler.[29] The general store and half a dozen houses are situated on the slope east of Frazier Creek.

Rattan

Rattan (population 332) is a hamlet near the north end of Hugo Lake in southern Pushmataha County. It was named for Rattan, Texas.[30]

Dela

Dela consists of a few scattered houses along Oklahoma 3, about at mile west of the Kiamichi River. The settlement, which until 1954 boasted its own post office, was named for Dela M. Whitaker, a local schoolteacher.[31]

Antlers (see tour A2)

Darwin

Darwin is a nearly abandoned hamlet nine miles west of Antlers in southwestern Pushmataha County.

Farris

Farris (population 100), which consists of a country store and a dozen scattered houses, is eighteen miles east of Atoka in southeastern Atoka County.

Lane

Lane (population 150) is an old settlement on Oklahoma 3 in southeastern Atoka County. The name is said to stem from the location of the post office, established in 1902, in a store at the end of a lane bounded by rail fencing.[32]

Atoka (see tour A1)

Fort Smith, Hot Springs, and Little Rock are three urban centers in the Arkansas portion of the Ouachitas that, because of their size, their range of services, and the number of their attractions, merit special consideration. For this reason, the major features of each of these centers is discussed separately in this and the next two chapters. All three of these focal points offer the conveniences and services customarily found in larger cities, which include large hotels and convention facilities; a wide variety of dining opportunities ranging from fast-foods and cafeterias to fancy restaurants catering to the dinner set; a selection of movie theaters; supper clubs and other night spots featuring dancing and well-known entertainers; numerous historical and cultural attractions; a complete range of shopping opportunities including large malls and department stores; and a full complement of professional services and excellent medical facilities.

Fort Smith is a prosperous and growing city located in the Arkansas River Valley, very near the Oklahoma boundary. The 1988 version of the U.S. Bureau of the Census's *County and City Data Book* listed the city's 1986 population at 74,320, making it the second largest city in the state. The number of residents in the Fort Smith, Arkansas–Oklahoma Metropolitan Statistical Area (MSA), which consisted of two counties in Arkansas (Crawford and Sebastian) and one county in Oklahoma (Sequoyah), was estimated to be 176,000. The economic importance of this metropolitan area is evidenced by the 1982 retail sales volume of $744.6 million. The number of retail establishments included 42 lumber and hardware stores, 92 food-related businesses, 193 automobile-related businesses, 43 apparel stores, 86 stores selling furniture, and 182 eating and drinking establishments.[1]

Fort Smith has enjoyed prosperity as a major transportation and communications hub. The city is served by Interstate 40, U.S. 71, and Arkansas 59 and 45. Fort Smith is an important port on the Kerr-McClellan Navigation System and is served by three railroads: the Burlington Northern, the Missouri Pacific, and the Kansas City Southern. Scheduled air service is available through the Fort Smith Municipal Air Terminal. A twice-daily newspaper, the *Southwest Times Record,* reaches more than 40,000 businesses and residences in western Arkansas and eastern Oklahoma. Five AM and four FM radio stations and three television stations serve the metropolitan area and other surrounding communities.

Fort Smith's urbanized area, an expression of the geographic or physical city, consists of the city proper (the legal city) and two small incorporated towns —Barling, which is sandwiched between sprawling Fort Chaffee and the easternmost subdivisions of Fort Smith and Arkoma, Oklahoma, which is wedged between the Poteau River and the state line. To the northeast of Fort Smith, just across the Arkansas River in Crawford County, is Van Buren, Arkansas.

HISTORICAL BACKGROUND

The beginnings of Fort Smith can be traced back to the early 1800s when the Cherokee Indians were forced to move west from their Appalachian homelands;

Lighthouse Inn on the Arkansas River at Fort Smith. Courtesy of Arkansas Department of Parks and Tourism.

by 1813 some of these displaced Indians had settled along the St. Francis River in eastern Arkansas. In 1818 the Cherokees were given a large tract in northern Arkansas; this triggered immediate problems since the newly arrived Cherokees, who had incorporated many aspects of the white man's culture, clashed with the more traditional Osage tribe who continued to send hunting parties into their recently vacated homeland and steadfastly clung to their ancient ways through a hundred years of contact with whites. The Osages resented the arrival of the Cherokees[2] and additional hostilities were created when white hunters and squatters began to arrive in increasingly large numbers.[3]

When the overall situation deteriorated to the point where armed battles were commonplace, the Cherokees requested greater protection. The government sent a company of the U.S. Rifle Regiment, under the guidance of Major William Bradford, into the area to establish a military post.

After traveling three months by river from Bellefontaine on the Missouri River north of Saint Louis, Bradford and his men arrived at Belle Point, where the Poteau River joins the Arkansas, on Christmas Day, 1817. Almost immediately, the small contingent began work on a military outpost.[4] With just sixty-four men under Bradford's command, the construction was difficult and slow. Five years later, the new fort, which included two block houses, was named Fort Smith in honor of Bradford's commanding officer, Brigadier General Thomas A. Smith.

That same year (1822), Colonel Matthew Arbuckle arrived with a battalion of the 7th Infantry. He worked closely with James Miller, the Governor of the Arkansas Territory, in an effort to settle the Indian disputes. The Osage reminded Arbuckle and Miller that they were a hunting tribe dependent on wild game for food, clothing, and shelter; they viewed the arrival of both the Cherokees and the white settlers as a serious threat to their survival. In their opinion, the effects of these outsiders were the same as if the Osage had invaded the Cherokee lands, reaping their crops and killing their cattle and hogs. Before a treaty could be negotiated, more eastern Indians, including the Kickapoo, Shawnee, Delaware, Piankasaw, Potawatomi, and Seneca moved into the area. Perhaps the most significant arrival was an advance party of Choctaw, a tribe that boasted it had never shed white blood. The Choctaws passed through Fort Smith on their way to scouting lands further west in Indian Territory;[5] almost immediately thereafter they began fighting with the Osage. After the Osage attacked a group of white hunters who were trespassing on their land in 1824, the original garrison was moved northwestward to Fort Gibson.

Even though the initial fort never fulfilled its primary objective during its brief existence, it did stimulate the establishment of Fort Smith. The first legitimate business was a sutler's store established in 1822 by Captain John Rogers; when the first post office was opened in 1829, Rogers became its first postmaster. In 1834, Rogers further solidified his dominant position when he purchased almost the entire townsite for $450.

In 1838, as a result of considerable political pressure, the U.S. Army began to build a new fort near the site of the original post. The May 23, 1838, *Arkansas Gazette* reported that Captain Rogers sold the government 296 acres of his land for $15,000 for this purpose. The original plans called for a large bastioned, masonry fort; as the costs of construction rose, the plans were modified. The new Fort Smith would become primarily a supply depot for the army's more westerly posts. General Zachary Taylor took command of the still unfinished fort in 1841 and oversaw its completion. Although garrisoned by Arkansas volunteers during the Mexican War, the outpost's primary function was still a supply depot for other frontier forts.

The state assembly granted incorporation to Fort Smith in 1842 when its population totaled nearly five hundred people. News from the West Coast that gold had been discovered in 1848 led to boom times in both Fort Smith and Van Buren since many of those with designs on the Californian gold fields were outfitted there. The arrival of the first Butterfield stagecoach in 1858 was a landmark in the development of Fort Smith; it meant that those traveling the southern route between Saint Louis and California would now pass through Fort Smith along the way.[6]

The Civil War left an imprint on Fort Smith. On April 23, 1861, two weeks before Arkansas seceded from the Union, the U.S. Army troops evacuated the fort and all the other posts within Indian Territory. Confederate soldiers maintained control over the local fort until it was recaptured by the Union in 1863.

The war left a state of chaos and destruction in the area. Many Indian tribes were divided and reduced to poverty. As a part of Reconstruction, the national government organized a Great Council of the Five Civilized Tribes (Cherokee, Choctaw, Creek, Seminole, and Chickasaw) at Fort Smith in 1865 to identify several new rules to be incorporated in the treaties of 1866. Each tribe was informed that slavery was no longer an accepted practice and that many of their former lands were being taken away. In fact, by 1871 the Indian frontier had been pushed so far to the west, the value of Fort Smith as an efficient supply outpost had been greatly reduced; the Army responded by removing its few remaining troops from the fort. A year later the United States Court for the Western District of Arkansas moved in.

Ironically, the end of the Indian raids did not bring peace to Indian Territory, which by now was a conspicuous island in the nation's sea of expansion; the rugged terrain and the legal entanglements caused by the Indians' treaty rights created a near vacuum in law enforcement.

Only the District Court at Fort Smith had jurisdiction over those not subject to the tribal courts; into this vacuum swarmed lawless bands of horse thieves, bandits, and fugitives from justice. A handful of U.S. deputy marshalls fought a sometimes losing battle to maintain law and order.

Under these deplorable conditions, Judge Isaac C. Parker was assigned to the District Court in Western Arkansas in 1875. With a mandate to bring law and order to western Arkansas and the Indian Territory, Judge Parker spent an energetic twenty-one years on the bench (1875–1896). During this tenure, more than 13,000 cases were docketed in his court and over 9,000 defendants were either convicted or pleaded guilty, 344 were tried for capital offenses, and 160 were sentenced to hang. Though only 79 were actually executed, Judge Parker earned a reputation for severity and a nononsense approach. Because as many as 6 prisoners were hanged at one time, Judge Parker became known throughout the area as "the hanging judge." [7]

Sixty-five U.S. deputy marshals, "the men who rode for Parker," were killed in the line of duty, testimony to the difficult task Judge Parker and his supporters faced. Gradually, the efforts of the District Court, the marshals, and concerned citizens led to a greatly improved environment. As new settlers entered the area, they frequently demanded and received a system of local courts; since each new court absorbed a portion of Judge Parker's territory, his court lost its Territorial jurisdiction in September, 1896. Ten weeks later the ailing judge died, a victim, his doctor said, of twenty-one years of overwork. Judge Parker was buried in the Fort Smith National Cemetery.

The arrival of railroads also contributed to the development of Fort Smith. The Little Rock and Fort Smith Railroad (now part of the Missouri Pacific) reached its western destination (Fort Smith) in 1879; three years later the Saint Louis, Arkansas, and Texas Railroad (now part of the Burlington Northern system) was extended through the Boston Mountains from Fayetteville. These railroads stimulated coal mining in the region, provided cheap transportation for agricultural products, and encouraged industries to locate in Fort Smith. This latter development received additional impetus when natural gas was discovered just south of the city in 1901. Over the next two decades, large fields were developed and the availability of inexpensive fuel made Fort Smith an even more attractive industrial site.

The presence of Fort Chaffee, a 72,000 acre military reservation to the southeast of Fort Smith, can be traced back to 1941 when it was originally commissioned as Camp Chaffee in honor of the late General Adna R. Chaffee, chief of staff of the U.S. Army from 1904 until his retirement in 1906 after sixty-four years of military service. This post served as a basic training center for infantry and artillery recruits during World War II and the Korean conflict; it became Fort Chaffee when it was designated a permanent post in 1956. Today the base is used primarily as a summer training site for National Guardsmen and Army Reservists; it is virtually deserted during the winter months. This seasonal trend was temporarily disrupted in 1975 and again in 1980 when, first, Vietnamese and then Cuban refugees were processed and housed on base.

FORT SMITH TODAY

The impact of the original street grid in Fort Smith, which was oriented northeast-southwest and northwest-southeast, is still apparent. Garrison Avenue, the center of the downtown business district and a principal traffic artery, runs southeast from the Arkansas river to the Church of the Immaculate Conception.

Aerial view of downtown Fort Smith. Courtesy of Fort Smith Planning Department.

Originally laid out as a parade ground for soldiers, this exceptionally wide street is the business route of U.S. 64 and Arkansas 22. Running at a right angle to Garrison Avenue, Tenth Street, which becomes Midland Boulevard after a dozen blocks or so, is the route of U.S. 64 and 71 through the city and on to the Arkansas River bridge linking Fort Smith and Van Buren. The Missouri Pacific's tracks run parallel to Midland Boulevard; as might be expected, a number of Fort Smith's industries and warehouses are strung out along this crucial artery, which runs through the Mill Creek and Poteau River floodplains south of the downtown area.

The town is served by a park system that includes eight different sites. A public-use area off the Clayton Expressway (Arkansas 59) provides boat ramps and fishing access to the Arkansas River. There are also three country clubs within

the city limits: Fort Smith Country Club on Midland Boulevard in the northern part of town; the Hardscrabble Country Club on Cliff Drive in the eastern part of town; and the Fianna Hills Country Club alongside the I–540 belt highway in the southern part of town.

Most of the newer housing subdivisions are concentrated in the eastern and southern parts of the city; many of these areas became attractive residential sites with the completion of the I–540 belt highway which runs northeast to southwest along the eastern fringe of the city.

The Fort Smith economic base is fairly diversified. As the major financial, professional, service, and shopping focal point for a large portion of western Arkansas and eastern Oklahoma, the city is within an hour's drive of the 176,000 people in the immediate three-county metropolitan area. Fort Smith is also a major agricultural market that channels livestock, poultry and eggs, fruits, vegetables, and dairy products to local and distant produce shelves. West-ark Community College offers several two-year academic degrees and boasts a technical training school that provides educational opportunities for the city's industrial personnel.

The second most important manufacturing city in the state, Fort Smith is in the center of a rapidly expanding industrial area. More than two hundred manufacturing plants employ over 15,500 workers. No single category dominates the city's diversified industrial base; however, several furniture manufacturing plants employ more than a hundred workers. These include: Ayers Furniture Industries; The Covey Company; De Soto, Inc.; Riverside Furniture, Corp.; Eads Furniture Manufacturing Company; and Flanders Industries, Inc. Other important industrial categories are food and kindred products, clothing, and metal fabrication. The two largest food processors are Gerber Products Company (baby foods) and OK Foods, Inc. (frozen chicken); the most important clothing manufacturers are the Flyer Garment Company, Fort Smith Outerwear, Inc., and the Hill Company, Inc.

Fort Smith is also home to American Can Company (paper containers), Baldor Electric Company (electric motors), Fourco Glass Company (sheet glass), General Electric (air handling equipment), General Tire and Rubber Company (plastics), Gould, Inc. (batteries), Harry G. Barr Company (aluminum doors), Mead Corporation (corrugated boxes), North American Foundry Company, Inc. (iron castings), Plastic Research and Development Company (plastic products), Rheem Manufacturing Company (air conditioning), Southwest Rebuilders, Inc. (automotive parts), and Whirlpool Corporation (freezers) plants.

The cultural opportunities within the Fort Smith metropolitan area also are impressive: while the Fort Smith Little Theatre (3800 North O Street) produces several entertaining shows each year, the Broadway Theatre League sponsors a number of road-show performances annually; the Fort Smith Symphony Association, which is comprised entirely of local musicians, presents numerous concerts each year; the Associated Artists of Fort Smith operate the Fort Smith Art Center at 423 North 6th Street.

Some of the most beautiful scenery in the United States is found in the nearby Ouachita and Ozark Mountains. Each year millions of visitors are drawn to the area by the spectacular fall foliage, the beautiful spring vistas featuring widespread dogwood and wild azalea blooms, and the many outdoor sporting opportunities. Four large lakes within an hour's drive of Fort Smith provide the locale for all kinds of water sports. Swimming, water-skiing, and scuba diving are popular activities for all ages. Fishermen practice their craft in the lakes as well as the many mountain streams; the nearby prairies and woodlands provide hunters with a variety of wild game.

Large numbers of visitors are attracted to the area by annual events such as the Arkansas-Oklahoma Rodeo that is staged in Harper Stadium at the fairgrounds during the last week of May and is one of the world's largest outdoor rodeos. The fairgrounds also hosts the Arkansas-Oklahoma Livestock Exposition and District Fair. The Belle Fort Smith Tour of historic homes is held during the last weekend of April and includes tours of homes not normally open to the public. The Heritage Foundation of Fort Smith provides information about each of the historic houses within a twenty-block area on the north edge of the downtown commercial district that has been designated as the Belle Grove Historic District. Many of these houses

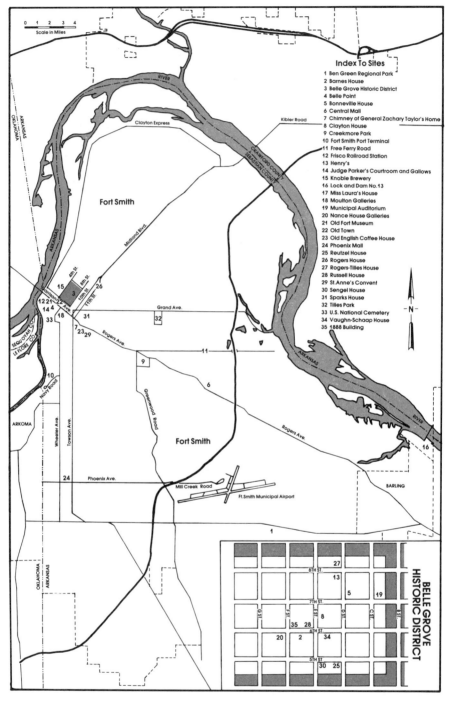

Index To Sites

1 Ben Green Regional Park
2 Barnes House
3 Belle Grove Historic District
4 Belle Point
5 Bonneville House
6 Central Mall
7 Chimney of General Zachary Taylor's Home
8 Clayton House
9 Creekmore Park
10 Fort Smith Port Terminal
11 Free Ferry Road
12 Frisco Railroad Station
13 Henry's
14 Judge Parker's Courtroom and Gallows
15 Knoble Brewery
16 Lock and Dam No.13
17 Miss Laura's House
18 Moulton Galleries
19 Municipal Auditorium
20 Nance House Galleries
21 Old Fort Museum
22 Old Town
23 Old English Coffee House
24 Phoenix Mall
25 Reutzel House
26 Rogers House
27 Rogers-Tilles House
28 Russell House
29 St.Anne's Convent
30 Sengel House
31 Sparks House
32 Tilles Park
33 U.S. National Cemetery
34 Vaughn-Schaap House
35 1888 Building

Map 34. Attractions in Fort Smith. *Adapted from:* Map of Fort Smith (Fort Smith: Fort Smith Chamber of Commerce, 1984).

Historic Bonneville house in Fort Smith. Courtesy of Fort Smith Chamber of Commerce.

are on the National Register of Historic Places, and members of the Heritage Foundation are very active in their efforts to see that more of the city's old homes are restored.

ATTRACTIONS AND POINTS OF
    INTEREST IN FORT SMITH
    (see map 4)

Ben Geren Regional Park is located at Highway 255 and Massard Road. Its facilities include an olympic-size swimming pool, lighted baseball diamonds, tennis courts, hiking trails, bridle paths, picnic pavillions, and an eighteen-hole golf course and club house.

Barnes House (c. 1893), a Richardsonian-Romanesque style residence that occupies 515 North 6th Street, was once the home of James K. Barnes, a prominent attorney and one of the first post-

masters in Fort Smith. It features a rare curved brick projecting bay and the interior includes the original ornate fireplaces and brass hardware.

Belle Grove Historic District, which is listed on the National Register of Historic Places, consists of the area covered by North Fifth, Sixth, Seventh, and Eighth streets from North "C" to North "H" streets.

Belle Point, the site of the original fort built in 1817, is now a National Historic Site at South Third and Rogers.

Bonneville House (c. 1871), an elaborate Victorian Renaissance residence with baroque ornamentation, is located at 318 North Seventh Street. Once the home of Susan Neis Bonneville, widow of General Benjamin Bonneville who was a commandant of Fort Smith's early garrison, the home was restored in

Chimney of General Zachary Taylor's home. Courtesy of Fort Smith Chamber of Commerce.

1962. For a small admission charge, guided tours for small groups can be arranged. For information call (501) 782-7854.

Central Mall is Fort Smith's largest shopping center. On the eastern outskirts at 5111 Rogers Avenue, the mall offers a wide variety of shops.

Clayton House (c. 1882), one of many historic homes in Fort Smith is located at 514 North Sixth Street. It was the home of William H. Clayton, a U.S. District Attorney for the Western District of Arkansas who served fourteen years in Judge Parker's famous court. The elegantly carved double entrance doors, staircase, and ornate fireplaces lend great dignity to this Victorian-Renaissance-Baroque style residence. For a small donation visitors may tour this facility Monday through Saturday.

Creekmore Park is located at the corner of Rogers Avenue and South Thirty-first Street.

Fort Smith Port Terminal (200 Naval Road) services the commercial river traffic that either originates or ends in Fort Smith. The Arkansas River's ice-free channel is nine feet deep at this point.

Free Ferry Road is a street that is lined with many outstanding examples of the "Gilded Age" homes constructed during the early 1900s. The road's name is derived from the fact that it once led to a free ferry that crossed the Arkansas River from the east edge of the city.

Frisco Railroad Station (c. 1904), at First and Garrison, has been remodeled into a steak house.

General Zachary Taylor's Home is now gone, but the chimney can still be seen at the east end of Garrison Avenue on the grounds of the Convent of Mercy.

Henry's is an elegant restaurant situated at 407 North Eighth Street in Fort Smith's Historic District. If offers the tasteful elegance of stained glass, beveled glass, antiques, tiffany-style lamps, brass fixtures, and a copper bar; it is a favorite "watering hole" for locals and a "must see" for visitors. For reservations call (501) 783–7479.

Judge Parker's Courtroom and Gallows is a part of the Belle Point Park National Historic Site situated at Rogers Avenue and South Third Street. From this court-

Judge Parker's courtroom. Courtesy of Arkansas Department of Parks and Tourism.

room, now restored, Judge Isaac C. Parker, the famous "Hanging Judge," administered cases for twenty-one years. The courtroom is open seven days a week at no charge. The deed for this historic site was presented to President John F. Kennedy during his 1961 visit to Fort Smith.[8]

Knobel Brewery (c. 1859) was built by Joseph Knobel, a native of Wittenburg, Germany, shortly after he arrived in Fort Smith in 1857;[9] it includes a fascinating stone-arched underground beer cellar and houses beer-making artifacts and other historic memorabilia. Located at the corner of North Third and "E" streets, tours are available by appointment only. Those interested should call (501) 452-3356.

Lock and Dam No. 13 is situated at Barling, Arkansas, seven miles east of Fort Smith on Highway 22. Part of a $1.2 billion project designed to make the Arkansas River navigable from the Mississippi River to Tulsa, Oklahoma, this huge lock and dam was completed on December 20, 1969, at an estimated cost of $47,600,000.

Miss Laura's House (c. 1899) was constructed when Oklahoma was still a part of Indian Territory; it is the only house remaining of the six that originally comprised "The Row" on Front Street. Victorian Baroque in style, the house is noted for its three oeil-de-boeuf (eye of the ox) cast-iron dormers that are set in a mansard roof.

Moulton Galleries features contempo-

Reconstruction of the standing gallows at Fort Smith. Courtesy of Fort Smith Chamber of Commerce.

Historic Knoble Brewery. Courtesy of Fort Smith Chamber of Commerce.

rary American paintings of the mid-south and southwest, gemstone eggs, and geodes. Located at 501 Garrison Avenue in the Old Town Building, the gallery also offers appraisals and restorations. It is open Monday through Friday.

Municipal Auditorium provides complete convention and theater facilities and is used throughout the year for various forms of entertainment. Located at 55 South Seventh Street, it was constructed at a cost of approximately $2 million.

Nance House Galleria (c. 1880) is an authentic restoration of the Lucas Nance House, built by a wealthy Fort Smith cotton merchant, situated at 601 North Sixth Street.

Old Fort Museum (111 Rogers Avenue) is located in the Commissary Building (1843) of the second Fort Smith; it contains numerous exhibits of early pioneer life. Twice a week (Sundays and Wednesdays) weaving demonstrations are offered using an early hand loom. The building is open daily from 9:00 A.M. to 5:00 P.M. during the tourist

Fort Smith Municipal Auditorium. Courtesy of Fort Smith Chamber of Commerce.

season, but only from 10:00 A.M. to 5:00 P.M. daily for the rest of the year. It is closed on Christmas and New Year's day.

Old Town is a popular tourist attraction at the corner of Garrison and Fifth Street, which consists of several historical (late 1800s) buildings that have been renovated for use as shops, offices, and apartments.

Old English Coffee House, in the City National Bank Building (1222 Rogers Avenue), serves coffee from 9:00 A.M. to 2:00 P.M. The room, decorated with small items from various parts of the world, has an open fireplace and slate floor.

Phoenix Mall is a major shopping center at Phoenix and Towson.

Reutzel House (c. 1850) was built by Casper Reutzel, a co-owner of one of the largest cotton shipping firms on the Arkansas River during the heyday of the steamboat. This plastered structure at 401 North 5th Street has the original half-timber construction with brick nogging; its cut stone cellar walls contain gun ports that are visible beneath the porch.

Rogers Building (222 Garrison) houses displays of antique cars, buggies, harnesses, etc.; the building is open daily from 9:00 A.M. to 5:00 P.M. during the summer tourist season (June–August). During the rest of the year it is open only on weekends and closed for Christmas and New Year's.

Rogers House (c. 1865) holds special historical significance to Fort Smith; it was constructed for William Rogers, son of the founder of the town of Fort Smith, Captain John Rogers. William also played an important role in the development of the city; he was appointed the city's first mayor by the Governor in 1842. The house at 904 North Eleventh Street features Victorian Renaissance style raised cottage brick that is unusual for this part of the country.

Rogers-Tilles House (c. 1840) is believed to have been occupied by the John Rogers family before it was purchased by the Louis Tilles family in 1867. Its architecture and solid brick construction makes it a small scale replica of the barracks building in the second fort; the renovated structure is located at 400 North Eighth Street.

Russell House (c. 1923), at 515 North Seventh, is a restored bungalow typical of the style that prevailed during the early 1900s.

St. Anne's Convent (1906) is a magnificent French Renaissance chateau located on Rogers Avenue just east of the Immaculate Conception Church; it is believed to be the only surviving structure of its type in the state of Arkansas.

Sengel House (c. 1878), a recently restored example of Second Empire Victorian architecture, is located at 421 North Fifth Street.

Sparks House (1887) was built by the prominent son of a pioneer family. With a Victorian Queen Anne style, this structure has an unusual circular front window and an iron flower box. It still possesses the original carved fireplaces and chandeliers with art glass shades. The home at 210 North Fourteenth Street, is now occupied by Taliano's Restaurant.

Tilles Park is at the intersection of Grand Avenue and North Thirty-Seventh Street.

U.S. National Cemetery is located at South Sixth and Garland Streets. Perhaps the most famous person buried there is Judge Isaac C. Parker who was interred on November 17, 1896. The grounds are open to visitors daily.

Vaughn-Schaap House (c. 1879) now houses the Fort Smith Art Center. John

The Vaughn-Schaap house built in 1879 displays Second Empire Victorian styling. Courtesy of Arkansas Department of Parks and Tourism.

Vaughn, the original owner, came to Fort Smith from Tennessee during the 1860s and established a very successful mercantile business that specialized in fine home furnishings. This gracious Victorian Second Empire residence is open Monday through Saturday from 9:00 A.M. to 4:00 P.M. and Sunday from 2:00 P.M. to 4:00 P.M. The address is 423 North Sixth Street.

The 1888 Building (c. 1888), 300–302 North Sixth, was built as the Baer Memorial Temple, Fort Smith's first permanent Masonic Lodge Building. It also housed the Fort Smith Commercial College for several years. When a fire in 1919 totally destroyed the third floor of the structure, the Masons moved to new quarters. The building remained unoccupied and in a state of deterioration until it was renovated to serve as professional offices in 1977.

Hot Springs National Park

Hot Springs' reputation as Arkansas' most cosmopolitan city is a direct consequence of the wide variety of people attracted there by the tourism, recreation, and entertainment oriented economy. From the very beginning, Hot Springs has prospered and grown largely because of the forty-seven hot springs that flow from the base of nearby Hot Springs Mountain. The belief that this water had special healing and therapeutic powers made the city a mecca for people of all ages and all social classes, and even after those claims were discounted by doctors and scientists, Hot Springs maintained its appeal as a recreation and tourist center. The city's estimated population in 1986 was 36,930.

There is little doubt that the growth and development of Hot Springs has been greatly influenced by its location and physical geography. The area to the west is dominated by the Zig-Zag range of the Ouachita Mountains and the pine and oak wilderness of the Ouachita National Forest. To the south and west, a chain of man-made lakes (Lakes Ouachita, Hamilton, and Catherine) prevails along with the Ouachita River as it winds its way across the Mazern Basin and through the area's ridge and valley terrain.

The springs that furnished the initial stimulus for the development of the city are the result of the resurfacing of rainwater that has filtered into the rock layers between West and Sugar Loaf mountains.[1] The water descends until it comes into contact with either a mass of hot rocks or hot gases that are escaping from such rocks. The heated water passes eastward under North Mountain before emerging along a zone of fractured rock (i.e., a fault zone) near the base of Hot Springs Mountain.

The city, originally developed along Gulpha Creek, spread into the adjacent valleys and up the sides of the mountains. The rugged setting has had an obvious impact on the layout and development of the town; the streets thread into narrow valleys as they climb and then descend the ridges; many of the three- and four-story brick buildings downtown appear to have been built into the adjacent mountain walls.

Surrounding the downtown commercial district are older residences that face out on the winding streets. Architectural styles include a mixture of English manor houses, French Provincial homes, rambling Southern mansions, and a great many vernacular houses with no particular pedigree. Because of the city's traditionally large transient population, many of the larger old residences once served as rooming houses; visitors to the many bathhouses would stay in these rooms while in town. The condition of some of these buildings today clearly and sadly reflects their absentee ownership.

Along Hot Springs' most famous street, Central Avenue, which runs through the center of the old downtown core, is the renowned Bathhouse Row and many of the town's older commercial structures. The former consists of eight elaborate stone, brick, and terra cotta buildings, which still comprise Hot Springs' "piece de resistance" of historic elegance. This area was the place where, around the turn of the century, one could view a truly cosmopoli-

Natural thermal springs along Bathhouse Row. Courtesy of Hot Springs Chamber of Commerce.

tan crowd who had made their hegira to the spa. Even as late as the 1930s the bathhouses attracted very large crowds.

The bathing establishments in their central setting of magnolias, young elms, and hedges furnish a back drop for an unceasing procession of vacationing businessmen with expensive clothes and graying temples, fox-furred and lorgnetted dowagers, and sightseers. An Easterner's derby bobbing briskly along the avenue is as common as a shapeless felt hat rocking gently over the loose-jointed gait of a native Arkansas wood-cutter. Canes and monocles pass without a second glance from farmers in jumpers and overalls. The sight of a prominent motion picture star, prize fighter, or major league baseball player "down for the baths" starts only a ripple of comment along a hotel veranda as guests watch sunset shadows climb the wooded slope.[2]

The bathhouses are fed by thermal waters with a constant temperature of 143°F issuing from forty-seven sealed springs; pipes collect the water and carry it to central reservoirs concealed under the west slope of Hot Springs Mountain; from the reservoirs it flows through insulated pipes to the bathhouses, which are now located on property owned by the U.S. National Park Service.

Although only one of the elegant bathhouses remains open, there are a great many permanent residents and visitors who still swear by the therapeutic value of the baths; several of the large hotels are connected to the hot

Downtown Hot Springs. Courtesy of Hot Springs Chamber of Commerce.

World-famous Bathhouse Row. Courtesy of Hot Springs Chamber of Commerce.

Visitor to world-famous Hot Springs National Park in therapeutic hot mineral water. Courtesy of Hot Springs Chamber of Commerce.

springs and still offer hot baths and massages. Many people also believe in the health benefits of drinking the spring water. Those who visit the baths today encounter an environment much as it was in the nineteenth century.

The standard bath encompasses several phases and is initiated with a tub bath. Having first disrobed, the bather, wrapped in a towel or sheet, is ushered into the bathhall or tub room. Here in one of the room's small compartments, the bather spends as much as 20 minutes reclining in a larger tub filled with water of a temperature ranging from 98° to 100°F. The temperature of the water is maintained through the duration of the bath by an occasional addition of hot water. Although this is, by no means, a hot bath. During this phase of the routine the bather is encouraged to drink one or more cups of the thermal water provided by the attendant. . . . Following the tub bath more optional treatments may be elected. Included are douches, the applications of vapors and the sitz bath.[3]

Because of the historic significance and the nostalgic quality of a visit to the town's bathhouses, the National Park Service has initiated a major restoration effort that has included the renovation of the elegant Fordyce Bathhouse as a historic landmark.

HISTORICAL BACKGROUND

While many believe that Hernando De-Soto and his men visited the hot springs as early as 1541, the first reliable report on the springs and their surroundings emerged from an expedition commissioned by President Thomas Jefferson in

1804. That year, William Dunbar and Dr. George Hunter climbed out of the Ouachita River basin, explored the springs, and reported that they had "found an open log cabin and a few huts of split boards, all calculated for summer encampment, and which had been erected by persons resorting to the springs for their health."[4] The huts apparently were built by some of the very early hunters and trappers who had previously entered the Arkansas wilderness.

Jean Emmanuel Prudhomme, a Louisiana farmer, is credited with erecting the first permanent home in the area in 1807.[5] That same year, Isaac Cates and John Perciful built cabins near the springs. The first bathhouses were built in 1830 by Asa Thompson. Two years later, the United States government set aside four sections of land around the springs in an effort to prevent the commercial exploitation of the waters, thus establishing the precedent of governments actively preserving unique environments.[6]

Hot Springs was probably better known to outsiders than to those living in other areas of the state during the first stage of its development. At the outbreak of the Civil War it consisted of little more than a double row of bathhouses, saloons, doctor's offices, and stores. Because the war shut off the flow of visitors from the North and East, it had a devastating impact on the emerging town; as a matter of fact, many of the town's two hundred inhabitants migrated to Texas during the course of the war.

Once the Civil War had ended, Hot Springs was quickly repopulated, and it became the seat of Garland County in 1874. When the Hot Springs Reservation was set apart from the rest of the town in 1875, a presidential commission undertook to lay out the town and survey the reservation for the purpose of beautification. The legality of the government's actions were questioned until 1876 when the U.S. Supreme Court ended a long chain of litigation by voiding the titles of three principal claimants to land near the springs.[7]

In 1875, the completion of the Hot Springs Railroad, a narrow-gage line sometimes referred to as the "Diamond Jo Reynolds Line" after its founder, linked Hot Springs with Malvern to the south and established improved rail connections with points to the north and east by way of the Saint Louis, Iron Mountain and Southern Railroad. Before long, a flood of visitors and immigrants descended on the Hot Springs area. The increased traffic resulted in the construction of several large and decorative bathhouses. By 1882, when the Army and Navy General Hospital was established to make the therapeutic benefits of the waters available to servicemen, the town had ten bathhouses.

The first two decades of the twentieth century were a time of continued growth, prosperity, and rapid change. Because of the increasing incidence of abuse claims, the Federal government established a board to examine and register physicians to prescribe baths in the hot waters. A devastating fire swept through fifty blocks of residences and business buildings in 1913; however, a major rebuilding effort commenced immediately afterward. The Hot Springs Reservation became the Hot Springs National Park in 1921; this change in status was accompanied by a significant increase in government-sponsored improvements.

The value of "taking the waters" and using the hot baths as a treatment for illness began to decline as the twentieth century progressed; improved public education and the growing sophistication and capabilities of the medical profession caused more and more people to question the waters' healing powers. The obvious result, as medical and surgical technology progressed toward the

Hot Springs, Arkansas. Courtesy of Arkansas Department of Parks and Tourism.

alleviation of pain and suffering, was a gradual decline in the attractiveness of the springs. While some visitors continued to return to Hot Springs out of habit, business in the bathhouses consistently declined.

This trend could have been catastrophic, but Hot Springs has benefited from the development of other attractions that have allowed it to emerge as a major resort and recreation center. Several large man-made lakes within easy commuting distance of the city pull in many visitors each year; these lakes are popular sites for condominiums and other residential projects. The Oaklawn Jockey Club is another major force in the local economy[8] when, during the thoroughbred racing season, thousands of people are drawn to the area; the town's many hotels, restaurants, and tourist-related businesses prosper tre-

mendously. A comprehensive listing of Hot Springs' points of interest is presented in a subsequent portion of this chapter.

HOT SPRINGS TODAY

Hot Springs is a city that caters largely to older adults; Census Bureau statistics reveal that nearly 20 percent of the spa's total population of 36,930 is over sixty-five. A casual stroll along Bathhouse Row and the Promenade suggests that this impressive figure may understate the real situation.

The heavy emphasis on recreation and tourism has resulted in an employment base dominated by the provision of personal services. Large numbers of workers are employed by the hotels, motels, and other lodging units as well as numerous restaurants and drinking establishments; the bathing industry requires

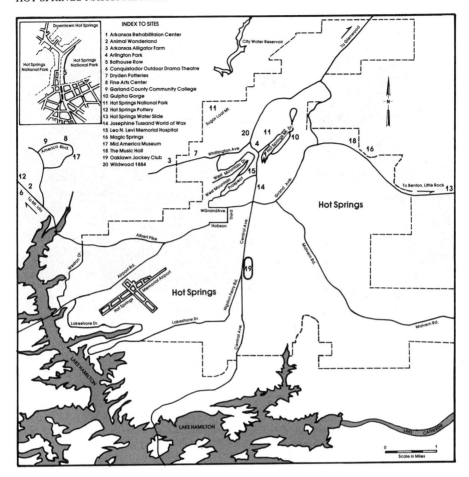

Map 35. Attractions in Hot Springs. *Adapted from:* Map of Hot Springs, (Hot Springs: Hot Springs Chamber of Commerce, 1984).

clerks, massagers, and attendants; and the ubiquitous retail outlets utilize large numbers of sales clerks.

Though Hot Springs' industries are limited, they include: Cordell Tackle Company (fishing rods and lures); Feather Lite Manufacturing Company (aluminum storm windows); General Cable Corporation (aluminum wire); Munro and Company, Inc. (shoes); and Union Carbide Corporation (chemicals).

Three railroads offer freight service —Burlington Northern, Kansas City Southern, and the Missouri Pacific. Since passenger train service was discontinued shortly after World War II, most visitors rely upon Hot Springs' good highways. U.S. 70 and U.S. 270, which connect with Interstate 30 at Malvern, provide excellent east-west connections. Scenic Arkansas 7, the primary north-south highway, cuts across the grain of the Ouachita ridges. Limited air service includes daily flights to Memphis and Dallas-Fort Worth.

Hot Springs is served by several radio stations including: KBHS (590 AM), KXOW (1420 AM), KZNG (1340 AM); KGUS (97.5 FM), KSPA (96.7 FM), and KXOW (106.3 FM); two daily Little Rock newspapers—the *Arkansas Democrat* and the *Arkansas Gazette*— are distributed in Hot Springs and the surrounding area.

Hot Springs is noted for excellent restaurants, clubs, and live entertainment; during the February to April racing season, internationally known entertainers appear at several of the larger nightspots.

ATTRACTIONS AND POINTS OF INTEREST IN HOT SPRINGS
   (see map 35)

Arkansas Rehabilitation Center, which occupies the old Army and Navy General Hospital on the U.S. Reservation, towers over the city from the southwest tip of Hot Springs Mountain. Following the natural contour of the mountain, the complex is laid out in a V-shape. There are two five-story wings and a seven-story center section with a ten-story tower; all the buildings are Spanish style. Although the original hospital was established in 1882, the present structure dates from 1933. The federal government ceased operating the facility after World War II; however, the State of Arkansas has subsequently acquired the complex as a rehabilitation center.

Animal Wonderland, located on U.S. 270 West, features dolphin shows, macaw shows, and a petting zoo where children can touch and feed deer, donkeys, goats, ducks, lambs, and tropical birds. The park is open weekends during May and daily from Memorial Day weekend until Labor Day.

Arkansas Alligator Farm, one of the largest and oldest in the country, has a natural history museum as well as over

Arlington Hotel, Hot Springs, Arkansas. Courtesy of Arkansas Department of Parks and Tourism.

two hundred reptilian specimens ranging from the newly-hatched to some fifteen- and twenty-footers that are over four hundred years old. The farm, on Whittington Avenue, is open throughout the year.

Arlington Resort Hotel and Spa is a charming five-hundred-room structure built into the face of North Mountain adjacent to Bathhouse Row. It features in-house bathing, mountainside hot tubs, and two cascading pools. Recreational facilities include the third floor spas and exercise rooms, eight tennis courts, and two PGA golf courses at the nearby Hot Springs Golf and Country Club. The Arlington's Fountain Room, one of the most famous restaurants in the South, is known for fine tableside service and continental cuisine.

The present hotel opened for business New Year's Eve, 1924; two earlier Ar-

The Promenade, Hot Springs National Park. Courtesy of Arkansas Department of Parks and Tourism.

Bathhouse Row. Courtesy of Arkansas Department of Parks and Tourism.

lington hotels were located on National Park land on the east side of Fountain Street opposite the present hotel. The first hotel, a wood frame structure, was built in 1875; the second Arlington, a brick structure in Spanish motif, was completed in 1893.

Arlington Park is a verdant, landscaped, crescent-shaped area situated north of Bathhouse Row at the base of Hot Springs Mountain. It is built on a base of tufa, a porous rock that has developed as the hot waters from the springs have deposited minerals, especially silica and calcite, in the area.

Bathhouse Row, Hot Springs' most famous landmark, is located along Central Street in the valley of Hot Springs Creek and at the west base of Hot Springs Mountain. A recent advertisement for the last operating bathhouse, the Buckstaff, claimed that "the baths relaxed tension of the young and prolonged active life for the older ages." Renewed

Gulpha Gorge campground and nature area in Hot Springs National Park. Courtesy of Arkansas Department of Parks and Tourism.

Hot Springs National Park Visitor Center. Courtesy of Hot Springs Chamber of Commerce.

interest in historic preservation and the unique architecture of the bathhouses has stimulated rehabilitation efforts. Many of the facilities are now being converted to commercial and profes- sional use. Since the bathhouses are now a part of the Hot Springs National Park, their rehabilitation and use are under the regulation of the U.S. Government. *Conquistador Outdoor Drama Theatre,*

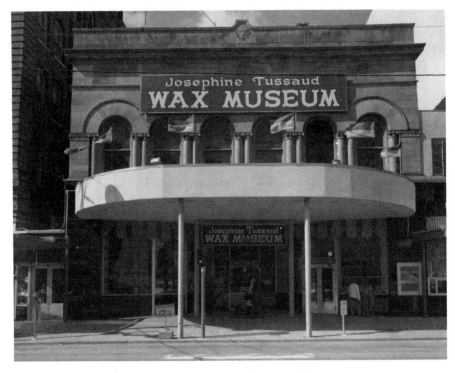

Josephine Tussaud Wax Museum. Courtesy of Hot Springs Chamber of Commerce.

in Mid-America Park on Arkansas 227 West, was built at a cost of $750,000. This outdoor facility features dramatizations of the travels and conquests of Hernando DeSoto, who is generally credited with discovering the hot springs. The play is presented by a professional theater group every night, with the exception of Sundays, from June until Labor Day. Admission is charged.

Dryden Potteries offers free guided tours of the plant and demonstrations of the ancient art of using the potter's wheel. The skilled artists in the facility, located at 341 Whittington, use native Ouachita Mountain clays and quartz crystal glazes to handcraft one-of-a-kind pieces of pottery; many items are for sale to visitors.

The Fine Arts Center of Hot Springs, open to the general public, houses a collection of the works of the local Southern Artists Association. Each exhibit usually consists of the creations of local and visiting artists.

Garland County Community College is located in the Mid-America Park on Arkansas 227 West. With an enrollment of approximately 3,000, the college emphasizes occupational education, continuing education, and a college transfer curriculum. The Arkansas Department of Education has constructed several buildings adjacent to the college to house the Quapaw Vocational School that offers classes designed for industrial technicians.

Gulpha Gorge is the sylvan setting for a National Park Service campground. Situated in a cool, quiet, valley at the foot of the eastern slope of Hot Springs Mountain, it is easy to forget the park is within two miles of the center city. During the summer months activities including outdoor evening programs in the amphitheatre, morning nature walks, craft exhibits on the summit of Hot Springs Mountain, and guided hikes to the novaculite quarries on Indian Mountain are offered.

Hot Springs National Park is a unique downtown National Park established in 1921. Consisting of 1,016 acres, the park extends out to the hills that surround the city and includes Hot Springs Mountain, Sugar Loaf Mountain, Indian Mountain, Government Park, North Mountain, and West Mountain. The latter peak rises to an elevation of 1,320 feet as it towers more than 700 feet above the city.

The park contains a wide variety of plant life; among the wildflowers along many of the hiking trails are violets, wild hyacinth, blue larkspur, coreopsis, partridge peas, purple cones, goldenrod, foxglove, and great blue sage. Signs providing identification assistance are distributed along each of the hiking trails.

In addition to hiking trails, the park offers bike trails, roads, and camping facilities; however, the focal points of the park are Bathhouse Row, the tree-lined Promenade along Central Avenue, and the new observation tower on top of North Mountain. A visitor's center offers a video program and publications pertaining to Hot Springs and the entire Ouachita Mountain province.

Hot Springs Pottery, located on U.S. 270 West, features demonstrations and guided tours of the plant.

Hot Springs Water Slide, on U.S. 70 East at Cedar Creek, just three miles east of Magic Springs theme park, is one of the longest water slides in the nation.

Magic Springs Recreational Park, Hot Springs, Arkansas. Courtesy of Arkansas Department of Parks and Tourism.

Josephine Tussaud World of Wax, the fourteenth museum in this well-known chain, offers over one hundred lifelike representations of real and fictional figures from the past and present. The largest display is the impressive and inspiring depiction of the "Last Supper"; the "Stairway of the Stars" exhibit features famous stars of stage and screen; historical figures seem to live again as U.S. presidents and members of the British and French royalty are presented; "Fantasy Land" includes figures from Cinderella, Alice in Wonderland, Snow White and the Seven Dwarfs, Pinocchio, and Rumplestiltskin. Located at 250 Central Avenue, this attraction requires an admission charge.

Leo N. Levi Memorial Hospital was opened in 1941 to aid charity patients such as the arthritis sufferers who were

Mid-America Museum, Hot Springs, Arkansas. Courtesy of Arkansas Department of Parks and Tourism.

attracted to the springs with hopes for relief of their pain. The hospital, on Prospect Avenue, receives considerable support from the Jewish community.

Magic Springs is a seventy-three-acre theme park approximately 1.5 miles from downtown Hot Springs on U.S. 70 East. Its overriding Victorian theme is presented in three separate areas: a "Turn of the Century" section, a "Frontier" section, and an "Old Fashioned County Fair" section.

Popular rides and attractions include the log flume, the thrilling sky-hook that was once used at Six Flags Over Texas, a one-hundred-foot-high ferris wheel, a roller coaster, boat rides, antique cars, a five-screen mini-theater, puppet shows, arts and crafts displays and demonstrations, and a petting zoo. All the water-related attractions are focused on a small man-made lake. Refreshment concessions and several restaurants make it possible to stay at the park for a full day of fun.

Mid-America Museum, a new $5 million

structure developed by the Arkansas Museum and Cultural Commission, offers visitors a variety of displays that illustrate the flora and fauna of Arkansas as well as the aesthetics of energy and life. This facility is a major component of the Mid-America Park on Arkansas 227 West.

The Music Hall, opened in 1979 on U.S. 70 East near Magic Springs theme park, offers family entertainment ranging from clogging demonstrations to music of all types including country-western, gospel, and old-time favorites. Well-known entertainers appear from time to time.

Oaklawn Jockey Club draws more than a million fans to its fifty-day thoroughbred racing season each year. Since the season begins in February and runs until early April, it occurs between the closing of many tracks in Florida and Louisiana and the opening of the horse racing season in the more northern states. Many well-known stables use Oaklawn as a stopover point as they move from southern to northern tracks. The last week of the Oaklawn meet is hailed as "The Racing Festival of the South." This is an especially exciting period since it includes seven major stake races within seven days, several with six-figure purses including the Fantasy, the Apple Blossom Handicap, and the Arkansas Derby that traditionally is contested on the first Saturday in April.

The original Oaklawn facility was built in 1904, and although the first races

Oaklawn Race Track, Hot Springs, Arkansas. Courtesy of Hot Springs Chamber of Commerce.

Horses leaving the starting gate at Oaklawn, Hot Springs, Arkansas. Courtesy of Arkansas Department of Parks and Tourism.

were conducted the following spring, in 1907 the Arkansas General Assembly passed a law that made betting on horse races illegal. For a number of years the racing operations at Oaklawn were suspended, and the clubhouse, paddock, and tract were used only during the Arkansas State Fair. In 1935 the Arkansas legislature decided to sanction parimutuel betting and established the Arkansas Racing Commission, which allowed Oaklawn to re-emerge as a major spring attraction. Because the current season opens in February, chills are still quite common; a new grandstand has been added to offer the devoted racing fans some protection from the elements. *Wildwood 1884* is a museum housed in a restored home that was originally built during the late-nineteenth century. Situated on Park Avenue, it features a hand-hewn stairway constructed from wild Arkansas cherry, an unusual five window bay, and a fine collection of antiques. Guided tours are available.

Little Rock (1986 estimated population: 181,030), the largest city and the capital of Arkansas, and North Little Rock (63,540), the third largest city in the state, lie on opposite banks of the Arkansas River very near the geographic center of the state. Together, these two cities serve as the focal points of the Little Rock–North Little Rock, Arkansas Metropolitan Statistical Area (MSA), which consists of four counties (Pulaski, Faulkner, Lonoke, and Saline) with a combined population of 505,600. In addition to the two central cities, the MSA encompasses such outlying towns as Conway, Jacksonville, and Benton. Nearly half of the state's total population of 2.4 million reside within sixty miles of the capital city.

As these statistics suggest, Little Rock is truly the predominant city of Arkansas. In addition to being more than twice the size of the next largest city in the state (Fort Smith's 1986 population was 74,320), Little Rock is Arkansas' cultural, political, and economic center. This unchallenged predominance is the result of a number of factors including geographical location and historical development.

HISTORICAL BACKGROUND

Historical accounts indicate that Little Rock's name was derived from a moss-covered rock jutting out from the south bank of the Arkansas River. As early explorers journeyed the 150 miles upriver from Arkansas Post, they noted that this rock marked a transition from the vast, alluvial plain to rough highlands. Benard de la Harpe, while on an expedition from New Orleans in 1722, called this first bedrock outcrop "La Petite Roche" (the "Little Rock") so as to distinguish it from a high bluff further up the river on the north bank;[1] he apparently named this latter feature "French Rock," but it has long been known locally as "Big Rock."

Little Rock was strategically situated where the great Southwestern Trail (also known as the Texas Road or Old Military Road) crossed the Arkansas River, which allowed the emerging city to command the trade from both land and water movements.

Although William Lewis, a hunter, built the first permanent structure, a rough-sawed hut, at the site in 1812, a land speculator from Saint Louis, William Russell, bought the claim for $40 in 1819; he surveyed a townsite the following year. Shortly thereafter, Stephen A. Austin and his brother-in-law James Bryan were moving their bankrupt lead smelting and banking operations from Potosi and Saint Louis, Missouri, to a new settlement in Texas when they laid claim to the site of Little Rock. Austin and Bryan apparently used bogus land claim certificates issued to recompense owners of property destroyed in the New Madrid earthquakes of 1812–13 to stake their claim. A William O'Hara, also from Saint Louis, laid out a second townsite over the one originally surveyed by Russell; he named his town, Acropolis. The dispute over the ownership of the site was resolved in 1821 when Russell's land claim was recognized by the Arkansas Territorial Court. About this same time, Little Rock was designated the second capital of Arkansas Territory.[2]

View of downtown Little Rock. Courtesy of Arkansas Department of Parks and Tourism.

Around 1819, the same year Thomas Nuttall made his famous exploration up the Arkansas River, William E. Woodruff moved his printing press operation upriver from Arkansas Post and established the *Arkansas Gazette*. Although Little Rock remained a boisterous frontier village for many years, newspapers like the *Gazette* were important in frontier life. George W. Featherstonhough, a noted English traveler, described the penchant for newspaper reading in Little Rock in the 1830s in his dry, humorous style:

Americans of certain class, to whatever distant point they go, carry the passion for newspaper reading with them, as if it were a grand end of education. . . . How could a town of 8,000 inhabitants in England support a newspaper printed in the place? Where would its useful and instructive manner come from? Why from those quarters which have already supplied it, to those alone who want it. If such a town has a newspaper, it could not be supported, and therefore it remains without one. But in Little Rock, with a population of 600 people, there are no less than three cheap newspapers, which are not read but devoured by everybody.[3]

Like many other visitors who arrived in Little Rock after weeks of traveling through the sparsely settled forests, Featherstonhough also commented on the town and its inhabitants:

This territory of Arkansas was on the confines of the United States and of Mexico, and, as I had long known, was the occasional residence of many timid and nervous persons, against whom the laws of these respective countries had a grudge. *Gentlemen,* who had taken the liberty to imitate the signatures of other persons; *bankrupts,* who were not disposed to be plundered by their creditors . . . all admired Arkansas on account of the very gentle and tolerant state of public opinion which prevailed there.[4]

Friedrich Gerstäcker, the intrepid German hunter-woodsman, visited Little Rock twice during his trips to the Ouachita Mountains between 1837 and 1843. On his first visit he remarked that the place was a vile place infested with smallpox.[5] After his second visit, he noted that Little Rock was "one of the dullest towns in the United States . . ."[6]

In spite of the sometimes disparaging remarks of visitors, Little Rock shared in the growing prosperity of the region. During the 1830s and 1840s, as great cotton plantations were laid out on the bottomlands up and down the river, Little Rock became the most important cotton-shipping point in Arkansas. Once the *Eagle* inaugurated steamboat traffic on the upper Arkansas River in 1822,[7] the wharfs at the foot of Commerce Street became a beehive of shipping-related activity. Cotton, timber, hides, and grains were loaded for shipment down river; clothing, tools, and molasses were unloaded from boats originating in Saint Louis and New Orleans.

Even though the level of activities were expanding, Little Rock did not experience explosive growth at first. In 1827, when the city consisted of about sixty buildings, only fourteen were frame or brick; all of the others were constructed of logs.[8] When the first steam ferry between Little Rock and the opposite shore went into service in 1838, there were only a handful of cabins on the site of present-day North Little Rock. The 1850 census set Little Rock's population at just 2,167.

As regional hostilities intensified, Arkansas seceded from the Union in 1861. The city remained in Confederate hands until 1863 when General Frederick Steele led a contingent of Federal troops as they advanced upon Little Rock from the east; General Sterling (Old Pap) Price, a former governor of Missouri, commanded the outnumbered Confederate forces. Before retreating to Arkadelphia, Price set fire to eight steamboats to prevent them from falling into the enemy's hands.[9] The capital had previously been moved to Washington, in Hempstead County; upon its capture, Little Rock became the headquarters for both the Northern forces and the military government of Arkansas. Col. Powell Clayton, a Federal commander stationed in Little Rock during the war, remained in Arkansas at the war's conclusion. He took a southern wife, earned a fortune as a planter, became the state's reconstruction governor, and, still later, became a United States senator.

Following the Civil War, Little Rock rapidly became a bustling example of the New South. As railroads expanded during the 1870s and 1880s, Little Rock's position as the dominant transportation center in the state was further solidified; it also emerged as the chief manufacturing city. From a town of 3,727 in 1860, Little Rock grew to a small city of 12,000 in 1870. Continued growth brought with it a sequence of new urban services and facilities: mule-pulled trolleys in 1876, electric trolleys (streetcars) in 1886; telephones in 1879; a waterworks in 1884; and electric street lights in 1888.

It was during Reconstruction that the old wholesaling and light-industry district emerged and developed along the waterfront, much of it along Markham Street, which parallels the river. Between East Markham and the Rock Island Railroad shops, on bottomland once planted in cotton, woodworking plants, furniture factories, flour and feed mills, cottonseed oil plants, a chemical factory, numerous warehouses, and small industries were built. Between many of the larger plants, blocks of small, white frame bungalows were built to house the workers.

Reconstruction, from about 1870 to 1920, also initiated the expansion of the central business district (CBD) from a few stores along Markham, Main, and Broadway to what was to become a nearly four-square-mile area of two- to twelve-story buildings extending from the river southward to Roosevelt Road and from Battery Street eastward to Commerce Street. Initially, many of the areas immediately surrounding the CBD were occupied by a mixture of stately, pillared mansions and Victorian-style frame houses heavily decorated with gingerbread and steamboat-style trim. Following the Civil War, several new architectural styles were introduced in this part of the United States. All of these followed the picturesque line that had started before the war with the Gothic Revival and the Italianato styles. In Little Rock, Queen Anne architecture prevailed over all others into the late nineteenth century. The English medieval elements found in this style—half timbering, prominent paneled chimneys, and small-paned windows—were common in many of Little Rock's older upperclass neighborhoods.[10] Many of these impressive old family homes have since been converted to rooming houses, apartment buildings, mortuaries, and other commercial uses as the central business district expanded.

Between 1899 and 1916 the new state capitol complex was built on the upland west of the CBD, the highest and coolest part of the city. Soon afterward, residences were built in the same general area by suburbanites who liked the atmosphere of the piney hillsides and the intermittent ravines. The West End Land and Improvement Company and the City Electric Street Railway Company were organized primarily to "aid in the development of 'Choice Residential Property' west of Little Rock."[11] About the same time, South Broadway emerged as an "automobile row" with blocks of showrooms and garages.

Beyond the downtown commercial district and the surrounding transitional zone of apartments and parking lots, the pre-World War II belt of bungalows extends southward to the breaks along Fourche Creek, eastward beyond the Missouri Pacific Railroad tracks, and westward into neighborhoods around Fair Park and Allsop Park. Most of the residential growth of the 1950s through the 1970s was on the periphery of the city, particularly to the west and south. The most rapid growth of subdivisions in the 1970s and 1980s was in the vicinity of Interstate 430. Like the major-

ity of American cities, the population of the central neighborhoods of Little Rock (and North Little Rock) has declined for the past twenty years or more.

North Little Rock, which originally was a collection of towns including Lavey, Rose City, and Argenta, experienced a different pattern of growth. The bottomlands that North Little Rock occupies were well-suited for the development of railroad switching yards and industries; delays in bridging the Arkansas River stimulated the town's growth as a railroad terminal and manufacturing center. North Little Rock benefited from transportation linkages and from a cheap and abundant supply of water derived from the river and the sandy aquifers that lie below the floodplain. During the latter decades of the nineteenth century as repair shops of the Missouri Pacific Railroad were built and expanded and stockyards, cottonseed-oil mills, packinghouses, and warehouses were added, North Little Rock became a predominantly blue-collar city. The better residences developed on Park Hill, a site overlooking the city from the north. In recent years a number of large motels have sprung up on the south slope of Park Hill, close to Interstate 40, where visitors are provided a commanding view of both North Little Rock and downtown Little Rock.

LITTLE ROCK TODAY

The widespread availability of automobiles since World War II and improvements in the regional system of highways have permitted, and even encouraged, Greater Little Rock to expand considerably in all directions. From the Arkansas River on the east, the physical city now extends several miles west of the Interstate 30 Bypass (I–430). Newer neighborhoods in the western suburbs include Cammack Village, Leawood Heights, Brookfield, Ellis Acres, Twin

Aerial view of Little Rock and North Little Rock. Courtesy of Little Rock Planning Department.

Lakes, Douglasville, Rosedale, Birchwood, and Pleasant Valley; the southern subdivisions and suburbs now extend well beyond Base Line Road (Arkansas 338) and include Westwood, Geyer Springs, Meadowcliff, Wadefield Village, and Mabelvale.[12] The continuation of Interstate 30 south from Little Rock, through Saline County, and ultimately on to the Texas border (Texarkana) and beyond, has enabled several large commuter subdivisions to develop as far south as Benton. The built-up area in North Little Rock extends north to Camp Robinson and beyond, along John F. Kennedy Boulevard.

Little Rock is well-situated to capitalize on the economic trends of the 1970s and 1980s; its location near the geographic center of the state affords tremendous accessibility. In addition to the Arkansas River, transportation is augmented by Interstates 30 and 40, U.S. 65, U.S. 70, and U.S. 67/167, which are just a few of the major highways leading to and from Little Rock; the city also has regular airline service to many of the country's main hub centers. These factors have helped to make Little Rock the state's center of finance, education, transportation, industry, medicine, and government. In this capital city, local, state, and federal government employees account for over 20 percent of the total civilian labor force in the metropolitan area.[13]

The Little Rock Air Force Base, on land donated to the federal government in 1951, is located in Jacksonville, seventeen miles northeast of the city. Currently a part of the Military Airlift Command, the base is a center for nearly 7,000 military and 1,000 civilian personnel. Recent statistics show expen-

The Henry Moore sculpture in Little Rock's Metrocentre Mall. Courtesy of Arkansas Department of Parks and Tourism.

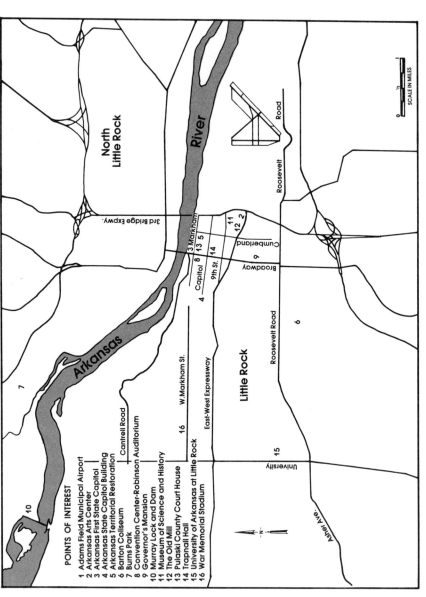

POINTS OF INTEREST

1 Adams Field Municipal Airport
2 Arkansas Arts Center
3 Arkansas First State Capitol
4 Arkansas State Capitol Building
5 Arkansas Territorial Restoration
6 Barton Coliseum
7 Burns Park
8 Convention Center-Robinson Auditorium
9 Governor's Mansion
10 Murray Lock and Dam
11 Museum of Science and History
12 The Old Mill
13 Pulaski County Court House
14 Trapnall Hall
15 University of Arkansas at Little Rock
16 War Memorial Stadium

Map 36. Attractions in Little Rock. *Adapted from:* Map of Little Rock (Little Rock: Little Rock Chamber of Com-

ditures by base staff and their families approaches $150 million for goods and services in Arkansas.

Little Rock is Arkansas' pre-eminent regional trade center with approximately 650 wholesalers in the Little Rock–North Little Rock MSA with sales over $5 billion a year; retail outlets in the same area totaled over $2.3 billion in sales in 1982.

A complete and diversified retail structure exists; free-standing commercial developments are found in the vicinity of the larger shopping centers, and strung out along the most heavily traveled roads; "strip commercial" areas characterize many of the major arterial streets including Markham Street, Shackelford Road, Rodney Parham Road, University Avenue, Asher Road, and Baseline-Geyer Springs Road.

The Little Rock metropolitan area also offers shopping centers ranging from small, unplanned "strip centers" to massive super-regional malls anchored by several major department stores. The state's largest shopping center, McCain Mall, is located in North Little Rock (McCain Boulevard and I–40); other notable centers in North Little Rock include North Park Mall (J.F.K. Boulevard and I-40), and Indian Hills Shopping Center (6929 J.F.K. Boulevard). The major retail centers in Little Rock include MetroCenter (downtown Little Rock), Park Plaza (W. Markham and University), Breckenridge (Rodney Parham at I–430), Galleria (9700 Rodney Parham), Village Shopping Center (Asher and University), Broadmoore Shopping Center (3300 University), Town and Country (Asher and University), Trellis Square (10720 Rodney Parham), Southwest City Mall (Geyer Springs and I–30), and Market Place (11121 Rodney Parham).

Office development in the Little Rock area has expanded greatly over the past fifteen years; there are now approximately eighty buildings with at least 10,000 square feet of office space: the total supply of office space in the metropolitan area exceeds 5 million square feet.[14]

Little Rock is Arkansas' chief manufacturing city. Over the years many new industries, particularly metal fabrication, electrical apparatus, paper products, and chemicals, have been added to the older, and once dominant, agriculturally oriented manufacturers. A recent directory listed 208 manufacturing operations in Little Rock and 82 in North Little Rock. A majority of the plants are small; 204 of the 290 industries (70 percent) in these two cities employ fewer than fifty workers; many of these plants are locally owned. The largest employers are A. O. Smith-Inland, Inc. (vinyl pipe), Coca Cola Bottling Company of Arkansas, Jacuzzi Brothers, Inc. (swimming pool equipment), Little Rock Furniture Manufacturing Company, Munsey Products, Inc. (electrical appliances), Teletype Corporation (data communication equipment), Timex Corporation (watches), Windsor Door Company (garage doors), Chicopee Manufacturing Company (textiles), and Maybelline Company (cosmetics).[15]

ATTRACTIONS AND POINTS OF INTEREST IN LITTLE ROCK
(see map 36)

Adams Field Municipal Airport is on the Arkansas River bottoms at the northeast edge of Little Rock at Fourteenth Street and Harrington Avenue. Conveniently located for downtown Little Rock traffic, it is readily accessible to the rest of the metropolitan area by way of nearby Interstate 30 and Roosevelt Road.

In addition to serving the air transportation needs of the half million people in the Little Rock-North Little Rock MSA, Adams Airport draws passengers from

The Arkansas Arts Center in McArthur Park. Courtesy of Arkansas Department of Parks and Tourism.

the entire central part of the state, which includes six cities with populations in excess of 10,000. With such a sizeable potential market, the airport is able to support a regular schedule of domestic and transcontinental flights.

The original field of 40.5 acres served as a supply depot for the Army Air Corps in 1917; after being expanded, it was turned into a National Guard airport in 1926. After the city took control of the field, an era of continued expansion and modernization began; more hangars were built; new and extended runways were established; and in 1972, a new terminal building was added that is unusually large among cities of a similar size. *Arkansas Arts Center,* in McArthur Park, is one of Mid-America's finest art centers; it features a combination of permanent and changing exhibits.

Arkansas' First State Capitol is recognized as one of the most beautiful examples of antebellum architecture in the South. The elegant Greek Revival building was easily the most ambitious and fashionable structure in Arkansas when it was built at a cost of $125,000 between 1833 and 1842.[16] Although still under construction, the building was used in 1836 as the meeting place for the first state legislature and as the site of the inauguration of Arkansas' first governor.

Once called the War Memorial Building, the name was officially changed to the Old State House by the 1951 legislature, and it was later redesignated Arkansas' First State Capitol. Located at

The first State Capitol. Courtesy of Arkansas Department of Parks and Tourism.

Arkansas State Capitol. Courtesy of Arkansas Department of Parks and Tourism.

Arkansas Territorial Restoration in downtown Little Rock. Courtesy of Arkansas Department of Parks and Tourism.

300 West Markham Avenue, the facility, still owned and maintained by the state, now houses the Arkansas Museum of History and Architecture.

Arkansas State Capitol Building is located at Woodlawn and Capitol Streets on an elevated site west of the central business district. From this site the capitol building commands an impressive view of downtown Little Rock and the waterfront. The building's position guaranteed its prominence on the Little Rock horizon; even today it is still an impressive sight, especially at night when the structure is illuminated by floodlights.

Built between 1899 and 1915, the Neoclassical Revival building was designed by George Mann. Long wings extend north and south from a classic portico; the tall dome, encircled by Ionic columns, rises from the center of the complex.

Arkansas Territorial Restoration, at Third and Cumberland, is a small area of restored buildings that includes the two-story log home and print shop of William E. Woodruff, the founder of the *Arkansas Gazette.* A garden area includes a boxwood grown from original two-hundred-year-old plants taken from President George Washington's home at Mt. Vernon.

Barton Coliseum is one of the nation's finest indoor arenas; it has 7,112 permanent seats and can be easily expanded to a capacity of 10,012. Surrounded by twenty acres of open space for outdoor attractions and parking, the Coliseum complex, on West Roosevelt Road, is the site of the Arkansas State Fair and Livestock Show each fall.

Burns Park, in North Little Rock, is one of the largest and most complete city parks in the United States. Its 1,575

Museum of Natural History and Antiquities in McArthur Park. Courtesy of Arkansas Department of Parks and Tourism.

acres include ten miles of roads that wind past many recreational facilities; the park even has an authentically designed New England-style covered bridge.

The Governor's Mansion is a two-story brick Georgian Colonial structure constructed in 1950 at Eighteenth and Center streets on a beautifully landscaped six-acre tract.

Little Rock Convention Center (Robinson Auditorium), at Markham and Broadway streets, was completed in 1940 and named in honor of Joseph Taylor (Joe T.) Robinson (1872–1937), a former governor and U.S. senator. The complex features eleven meeting rooms, dining facilities for 1,000 people, and an underground garage.[17]

McArthur Park is located on land at Ninth and Commerce that was acquired by the U.S. government in 1836 for use as a military post. Two years after its purchase, an arsenal was built on the site. Both the post and the arsenal were seized by Confederate forces at the outset of the Civil War; when forced to evacuate the capital in 1863, the Rebels vainly tried to burn the site. Largely undamaged, the facility remained a United States Army post until 1893 when it was traded to the City of Little Rock for 1,000 acres atop Big Rock across the river.

Now developed as a city park, the facility houses the Museum of Natural History and Antiquities in the Tower Building, one of the original buildings in the Arsenal. This museum features a collection that traces the history of Arkansas' development. McArthur Park is named for General Douglas McArthur who was born at the post.

Murray Lock and Dam located in western Little Rock, is one of seventeen locks in the $1.2 billion McClellan-Kerr Arkansas River Navigation System.

The Old Mill is a replica of an old grist mill that is located in Lakewood. It was photographed for one of the opening scenes in the epic picture, "Gone With the Wind."

Pulaski County Court House, at the corner of Markham and Spring, is a four-story Italian Renaissance structure with an elaborate pillared rotunda. The appearance of this structure, which still serves as the main headquarters of Pulaski County operations, was modified somewhat in 1961 when the upper portion of its tower was removed.[18] The county and therefore the courthouse are named after Count Casimir Pulaski, a Polish soldier who fought the British during the U.S. Revolutionary War.

Quapaw Quarter, one of Arkansas' oldest and most architectually significant districts, is bounded by the Arkansas River on the north, Fourche Creek on the south, Little Rock Regional Airport on the east, and the State Capitol on the west. Nineteenth-century homes once occupied by former governor and U.S. Senator Augustus Hill Garland, prominent lawyer Albert Pike, Pulitzer Prize-winning poet John Gould Fletcher, and founder and editor of the *Arkansas Gazette* William Woodruff, are among about three hundred restored private residences, businesses, public museums, and other historic sites in the nine-square mile Quarter. Many of the historic homes are concentrated near McArthur Park and the governor's mansion, and both areas are listed on the National Register of Historic Places. A third area, Marshall Square, is also included on the National Register. The district's name commemorates the Quapaw Indians—the earliest residents of the area; a treaty of August 24, 1818, bound the Indians to the east of the Quapaw Line, which ran north to south from the "little rock" landmark on the Arkansas River to a point on the Saline River.

Trapnall Hall is listed on the National Register of Historic Places; originally built in 1843, it was restored by the Little Rock Junior League as a pilot project for the Quapaw Quarter. Acquired by the state in 1976, Trapnall Hall was designated as the Governor's Official Receiving Hall and is available for rent to the public.

The Villa Marre is a nineteenth-century restored house and museum at 1321 Scott Street; it is open daily Wednesday through Friday and for special tours on weekends.

University of Arkansas at Little Rock is located on a 150 acre, tree-studded campus at University and Thirty-Third Street. Although the main campus of the University of Arkansas is in Fayetteville, this branch facility, opened in response to the large population concentration in central Arkansas, has a current enrollment of nearly 10,000.

War Memorial Stadium seats 53,000 when the University of Arkansas Razorbacks play their scheduled football games in Little Rock; the professional baseball field seats 8,000. The stadium is located at West Markham and Van Buren streets.

Major Events in the Ouachita Mountains

Entertainment in the Ouachita Mountains has changed considerably over the years. As technology has developed and social changes have occurred, entertainment forms have been modified. The old forms still persist to some extent, mainly in the sections where roads and rails were slow to penetrate, but for the most part, the established entertainment in the Ouachitas today is not unlike that of other sparsely populated, rural sections of the United States.

A renewed interest in preserving or reviving some of the traditional forms of entertainment, as well as old-time crafts and skills, has emerged in recent years. This trend has been accomplished in large part through fairs, festivals, and other special events where traditional crafts, music, and art forms are displayed and demonstrated.

Most of the festivals—old-fiddler contests, bluegrass music get-togethers, bass fishing derbies, rodeos, and arts and crafts shows—are held during the spring, summer, and fall when the weather is more cooperative and the visitors more numerous.

For convenience, the following list of the major events within the Ouachita Mountains is organized first by state—Arkansas and Oklahoma—and then by season—spring, summer, or fall. The information was supplied by the tourism departments of Arkansas and Oklahoma; cancellations of events are to be expected and are not the responsibility of these agencies; other "new" events may have evolved after the list was prepared. Only major annual events are included. For additional information and more specific dates, contact Arkansas Department

of Parks and Tourism, One Capitol Mall, Little Rock, Arkansas 72201, telephone (501) 682-7777, or Oklahoma Tourism and Recreation Department, State Parks Division, 500 Will Rogers Building, Oklahoma City, Oklahoma 73110, telephone (405) 521-3411 or 521-2409 (see map 37).

MAJOR EVENTS IN ARKANSAS

Continuing Events

Dardanelle

Lake Dardanelle Sail Day (Lake Dardanelle)   This monthly event consists of sailboat races and sailing demonstrations. Contact: Dardanelle Chamber of Commerce, P.O. Box 208, Dardanelle, Arkansas 71834, telephone (501) 229-3328.

Hot Springs

Magic Springs Family Fun Theme Park Entertainment for the entire family is provided in the form of amusement rides, shows, arts and crafts demonstrations, restaurants, gift shops, and an ice-cream parlor. Open only weekends from early spring until Memorial Day; daily from Memorial Day to Labor Day; and weekends in the fall. Contact: General Manager, Magic Springs Family Fun Theme Park, 2001 U.S. 70 East, Hot Springs, Arkansas 71901, telephone (501) 624-5411.

T.A.G. Outdoor Art Show (Arlington Park)   Virtually every month the Traditional Art Guild sponsors an art show in which their members display their works. Most of the artworks are for sale. No admission. Saturday and Sunday afternoons. Contact: Greater Hot Springs

Chamber of Commerce, P.O. Box 1500, Hot Springs, Arkansas 71902, telephone (501) 321-1700.

Little Rock

Arkansas Artists Gallery Opening (Arkansas Territorial Restoration) Each month a different Arkansas artist's works are displayed in this gallery. The materials are usually available for purchase. The first Sunday of each month is "Free Sunday," when no admission to the Restoration is charged. Contact: Arkansas Territorial Restoration, Third and Scott Streets, Little Rock, Arkansas 72201, telephone (501) 371-2348.

Arkansas Symphony Orchestra (Convention Center Music Hall) The Arkansas Symphony Orchestra offers a regular concert series throughout the year. Contact: Arkansas Symphony Orchestra, 2500 North Tyler, Little Rock, Arkansas 72207, telephone (501) 666-1761.

Crafts as Art Exhibition (Arkansas Arts Center) This exhibition in the teaching gallery explores the relationship between crafts and fine art. Contact: Director of Education, Arkansas Arts Center, McArthur Park, P.O. Box 2137, Little Rock, Arkansas 72203, telephone (501) 372-4000.

Artist-In-Action (Arkansas Arts Center) This free program of lectures and demonstrations is held every Sunday afternoon. Contact: Director of Education, Arkansas Arts Center, McArthur Park, P.O. Box 2137, Little Rock, Arkansas 72203, telephone (501) 372-4000.

Make-A-Thing (Arkansas Arts Center) A free, supervised "media experience" for children offered every Sunday afternoon in the "Yellow Space Place" (Children's Gallery). Contact: Director of Education, Arkansas Arts Center, McArthur Park, P.O. Box 2137, Little Rock, Arkansas 72203, telephone (501) 372-4000.

Film Series (Arkansas Arts Center) A different film is shown every Sunday evening. A small admission fee is charged. Contact: Assistant to the Director, Arkansas Arts Center, McArthur Park, P.O. Box 2137, Little Rock, Arkansas 72203, telephone (501) 372-4000.

Exhibit for the Blind (Arkansas Arts Center) Surfaces, environments, and objects perceived in a non-visual manner are on exhibit in the "Yellow Space Place" (Children's Gallery). Contact: Director of Education, Arkansas Arts Center, McArthur Park, P.O. Box 2137, Little Rock, Arkansas 72203, telephone (501) 372-4000.

Russellville

Weekly Bass Tournament (Lake Dardanelle State Park) Each week the boat docks at the Russellville and Dardanelle units of this state park sponsor a bass tournament. Contact: Superintendent, Lake Dardanelle State Park, Route 5, Box 527, Russellville, Arkansas 72801, telephone (501) 967-5516.

January Events

North Little Rock

Regional Silver Gloves Boxing Tournament This event, sponsored by the Golden Gloves Association, is held at the North Heights Community Center. The winners of these three-round boxing matches go on to compete in the national tournament. Contact: North Heights Community Center, 4801 Allen Street, North Little Rock, Arkansas 72114, telephone (501) 758-1908.

February Events

Hot Springs

Beaux Arts Ball (Fine Arts Center) Proceeds from this annual extravaganza are used to finance improvements at the Fine Arts Center. The fancy dress costume ball is usually keyed to a chosen

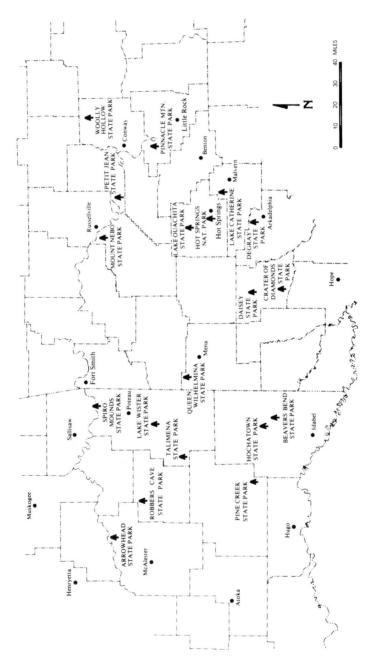

Map 37. State Parks. *Adapted from:* Arkansas State Highway Map (Little Rock: Arkansas State Highway and Transportation Department, 1985); Oklahoma Official Transportation Map (Oklahoma City: Oklahoma Department of Transportation, 1985).

theme. Contact: Fine Arts Council, First National Bank of Hot Springs, P.O. Box 1000, Hot Springs, Arkansas 71901, telephone (501) 321-8000.

Thoroughbred Racing (Oaklawn Jockey Club) The fifty-day thoroughbred racing season extends daily (except Sundays) from late February through early April. Some of the nation's top horses and jockeys participate. Post time is 1:30 P.M. (1:00 P.M. on the last two Saturdays). Several $50,000 handicaps, $75,000 handicaps, and $125,000 feature races are staged. The season is climaxed by the running of the annual Arkansas Derby. Contact: Oaklawn Jockey Club, P.O. Box 699, Hot Springs, Arkansas 71901, telephone (501) 623-4411.

Annual Valentine Ball (Arlington Hotel Crystal Ballroom) Sponsored by the Beta Sigma Phi Council, this festive event is open to the public. Contact: Greater Hot Springs Chamber of Commerce, P.O. Box 1500, Hot Springs, Arkansas 71902, telephone (501) 321-1700.

Annual Boat Show A showing of all types of the latest water crafts. There is no spectator fee; participants travel to Lake Hamilton marinas and in-town sporting goods stores on their own. Sponsored by the Hot Springs Marine Association, Arkansas Bank & Trust Co., and First National Bank of Hot Springs. Contact: Elizabeth King & Assoc., P.O. Box 54, Hot Springs, Arkansas 71901, telephone (501) 624-6753.

Little Rock

Annual Black History Series (Arkansas Arts Center) A tradition in Little Rock, this event brings black celebrities to the AAC to discuss the contributions which black Americans have made to both Arkansas and the United States. Contact: Neighborhood Arts Program Coordinator, Arkansas Arts Center, McArthur Park, P.O. Box 2137, Little Rock, Arkansas 72203, telephone (501) 372-4000.

March Events

Booneville

Annual Arkansas Marathon This race is an official AAU-sanctioned 26-mile, 385-yard competition. Groupings are by age, and the race is limited to the first 500 entrants. Trophies and/or certificates are awarded to all finishers. Contact: Booneville Chamber of Commerce, Second and Bennett Streets, Booneville, Arkansas 72927, telephone (501) 675-2666.

Fort Smith

Spring Arts and Crafts Show (Phoenix Village Mall) All types of handcrafted goods are displayed for sale. No resale items are permitted in the show. Contact: Phoenix Village Mall, Fort Smith, Arkansas 72901, telephone (501) 646-7889.

Little Rock

Mid-Southern Watercolorists Exhibition (Arkansas Arts Center) This annual exhibition, organized by the AAC, is a juried showing of watercolors submitted by Mid-Southern members. Contact: Museum Registrar, McArthur Park, P.O. Box 2137, Little Rock, Arkansas 72203, telephone (501) 372-4000.

North Little Rock

State Golden Gloves Boxing Tournament Amateur boxers from all over Arkansas compete in three-round matches for a chance at the national title in this Golden Gloves Association sponsored tournament. Contact: North Heights Community Center, 4801 Allen Street, North Little Rock, Arkansas 72114, telephone (501) 758-1908.

Roland

Pinnacle Mountain Wildflower Weekend (Pinnacle Mountain State Park) Guided walks are conducted by park naturalists who help identify and discuss the area's wildflowers. Hikes are scheduled daily at 9 A.M., 1 P.M., and 3 P.M. Contact: Superintendent, Pinnacle Mountain State Park, Route 1, P.O. Box 34, Roland, Arkansas 72135, telephone (501) 868-5806.

Russellville

Annual Evinrude Bass Tournament (Lake Dardanelle State Park) This major event is sponsored by Evinrude, Inc. and the Dardanelle Marine Service. Contact: Superintendent, Lake Dardanelle State Park, Route 5, Box 527, Russellville, Arkansas 72801, telephone (501) 967-5516.

April Events

Arkadelphia

Tiger Traks (Ouachita Baptist University) Billed as "Arkansas' Most Exciting College Weekend", this event is open to the public. The scheduled activities include bicycle and tricycle races, gymnastics, a celebrity tennis match, and a concert. There is fun for the whole family. Contact: Information Office, Ouachita Baptist University, Box 754, Arkadelphia, Arkansas 71923, telephone (501) 246-4531, ext. 173.

Booneville

Booneville Riding Club Trail Ride A one-day horseback ride through the Ouachita National Forest. A campfire supper is held at the end of the ride. Participants must supply their own horse. Contact: Booneville Chamber of Commerce, Second and Bennett Streets, Booneville, Arkansas 72927, telephone (501) 675-2666.

Annual Burl Lynch Trail Ride A four- to five-day trail ride through the beautiful Ouachita National Forest. Participants must supply their own horse, feed, supplies, and bedroll. It is possible to ride one day only, or for the entire time.

The membership fee is $5. Contact: Booneville Chamber of Commerce, Second and Bennett Streets, Booneville, Arkansas 72927, telephone (501) 675-2666.

Fort Smith

Annual Miss Westark Pageant (Westark Community College, Breedlove Auditorium) A beauty contest and pageant. Contact: Student Activities Director, Westark Community College, P.O. Box 3649, Fort Smith, Arkansas 72913, telephone (501) 785-7199.

Annual Spring Concert (Westark Community College, Breedlove Auditorium) The Westark choir and ensemble present a variety of selections during this annual spring concert. Contact: Chairman, Music Department, Westark Community College, P.O. Box 3649, Fort Smith, Arkansas 72913, telephone (501) 785-7000.

Belle Fort Smith Tour A tour of selected historic sites not normally open to the public. Contact: Architectural Historian, City of Fort Smith, P.O. Box 1908, Fort Smith, Arkansas 72902, telephone (501) 785-2801.

Hot Springs

S.A.A. Spring Outdoor Art Show (Arlington Park) Members of the Southern Artists Association exhibit their artwork. Most items are available for purchase. Contact: Greater Hot Springs Chamber of Commerce, P.O. Box 1500, Hot Springs, Arkansas 71902, telephone (501) 321-1700.

Racing Festival of the South (Oaklawn Jockey Club) This week of feature races concludes the fifty-day Oaklawn race meet. The renown Arkansas Derby is run on the final day. Contact: Oaklawn Jockey Club, P.O. Box 699, Hot Springs, Arkansas 71901, telephone (501) 623-4411.

Tour of Iris Gardens This annual event

is open to the public. Participants, who travel in their own cars, meet at the Garland County Courthouse. A Dutch-treat lunch is served at noon. Contact: Greater Hot Springs Chamber of Commerce, P.O. Box 1500, Hot Springs, Arkansas 71902, telephone (501) 321-1700.

Lions Club Annual Pancake Breakfast (Convention Auditorium) Members of the South Hot Springs Lions Club prepare a delicious breakfast of pancakes, bacon, sausage, and coffee. The event is open to the public; proceeds go to Lions' Project for the Blind. Contact: South Hot Springs Lions Club, 2007 Main Street, Hot Springs, Arkansas 71901, telephone (501) 623-5304.

Annual Easter Sunrise Service (Summit of Hot Springs Mountain) The story of the Resurrection is told in song by the Garland County Community College Choir; there are also readings and messages offered by Hot Springs ministers. The beautiful outdoor setting creates an impressive atmosphere for this event which originated in 1935. The service is sponsored by the Greater Hot Springs Chamber of Commerce, Hot Springs Ministerial Alliance, and Garland County in cooperation with the National Park Service. Contact: Special Events Director, Greater Hot Springs Chamber of Commerce, P.O. Box 1500, Hot Springs, Arkansas 71902, telephone (501) 321-1700.

Little Rock

Annual Governor's Conference on Tourism (Camelot Inn) A conference of tourism professionals and businesspersons designed to promote tourism in Arkansas. Contact: Director of Tourism, Arkansas Department of Parks and Tourism, 1 Capitol Mall, Little Rock, Arkansas 72201, telephone (501) 682-7777.

Quapaw Quarter Spring Tour (Quapaw Quarter Historic District) A candlelight tour of some of Little Rock's restored historic homes. Contact: Quapaw Quarter Association, P.O. Box 1104, Little Rock, Arkansas 72203, telephone (501) 371-0005.

Arkansas Orchestra Society (Convention Center Music Hall) A series of special concerts featuring local and guest musicians. Contact: Arkansas Symphony Orchestra, 2500 North Tyler, Little Rock, Arkansas 72207, telephone (501) 666-1761.

Mena

Arkansas Health and Fitness Run This 13.1 mile run starts at Janssen Park in Mena and ends at Queen Wilhelmina State Park. It is sponsored by the Mena Ridge Runners. Contact: Mena Area Chamber of Commerce, 524 Sherwood, Mena, Arkansas 71953, telephone (501) 394-2912.

Morrilton

Petit Jean Day (Petit Jean State Park) Brief presentations are given by park staff at selected points throughout the park and on the mountaintop. Among the topics discussed are park facilities, park programs, work done by the Civilian Conservation Corp (CCC), a living history of the area, and points of interest outside the park. Safety, wildlife and natural area preservation, and environmental education are stressed. Booths and displays are set up by interested groups. An evening barbecue is held in the park picnic area. Contact: Superintendent, Petit Jean State Park, Route 3, Box 340, Morrilton, Arkansas 72110, telephone (800) 628-7936.

Mount Ida

Ouachita River Canoe Races These canoe and kayak races are held in cooperation with the Arkansas Canoe and Kayak Association. Contact: Mount Ida

Area Chamber of Commerce, P.O. Box 6, Mount Ida, Arkansas 71957, telephone (501) 867-2723.

May Events

Arkadelphia

Festival of Two Rivers The activities at this celebration include a "Miss Two Rivers" Pageant, a tennis tournament, a five-kilometer run, a bicycle race, a checkers challenge, a frog-jumping contest, a turtle race, an historical costume contest, and a variety of games. Contact: Arkadelphia Chamber of Commerce, P.O. Box 38, Arkadelphia, Arkansas 71923, telephone (501) 246-5542.

Booneville

Booneville Riding Club Spring Rodeo (Fairgrounds) Rodeo events and livestock highlight this spring happening that draws participants from many surrounding and western states. Contact: Booneville Chamber of Commerce, Second and Bennett Streets, Booneville, Arkansas 72927, telephone (501) 675-2666.

Dardanelle

Annual Mount Nebo Chicken Fry (Mount Nebo State Park) A large old-fashioned picnic with horseshoe pitching, sack and turtle races, wood chopping and sawing contests, musical entertainment, political speeches, and door prizes. Fried chicken is available for dinner and supper. Two dances are held in the evening, one for adults and one for young people. Contact: Dardanelle Chamber of Commerce, P.O. Box 208, Dardanelle, Arkansas 72834, telephone (501) 229-3328.

Fort Smith

Arkansas-Oklahoma Rodeo and Old Fort Days (Rodeo Grounds) A parade, the world's "richest barrel race," Old Fort Days festivities, and one of the nation's top Professional Rodeo Cowboys Association (PRCA)-approved rodeos make up this early summer event. Contact: Fort Smith Chamber of Commerce, 613 Garrison Avenue, P.O. Box 1668, Fort Smith, Arkansas 72902, telephone (501) 783-6118.

Hot Springs

Gem and Mineral Show (Convention Auditorium) The exhibitors in this show come from all parts of the country. There are polished stones, crystals, geodes, turquoise, garnets, and other semi-precious specimens. Some have been crafted into rings, necklaces, and other jewelry. Varicolored sands, worked into intricate designs, are also displayed. Contact: Greater Hot Springs Chamber of Commerce, P.O. Box 1500, Hot Springs, Arkansas 71902, telephone (501) 321-1700.

Hot Springs Country Club Four-Ball Golf Tournament (Hot Springs Country Club) This open tournament is played on the Arlington course, a championship course that was used in the late 1950s and early 1960s for PGA Tournaments. Contact: Golf Pro, Hot Springs Golf and Country Club, 3400 Malvern Avenue, Hot Springs, Arkansas 71901, telephone (501) 624-2661.

Memorial Day Weekend Golf Tournament (Lakeside Country Club) Contact: Lakeside Golf Club, U.S. 270 East, Hot Springs, Arkansas 71901, telephone (501) 262-4346.

Little Rock

Annual Prints, Drawings and Crafts Exhibition (Arkansas Arts Center) Organized by the AAC, this is a competitive, juried exhibition of prints, drawings, photographs, and crafts in all media. The competition is open to all artists either born or residing in the seven-state delta area (Arkansas, Texas, Missis-

sippi, Oklahoma, Missouri, Louisiana, Tennessee). Contact: Museum Registrar, Arkansas Arts Center, McArthur Park, P.O. Box 2137, Little Rock, Arkansas 72203, telephone (501) 372-4000.
Arkansas Territorial Restoration Crafts Show (Arkansas Territorial Restoration) Craftsmen exhibit pottery, leathercraft, woodworking, weaving, and other crafts on the grounds of the Restoration while musicians perform. Contact: Arkansas Territorial Restoration, Third and Scott Streets, Little Rock, Arkansas 72201, telephone (501) 371-2348.
Children's Theater Week (Arkansas Arts Center) Groups of students from around the state participate in this drama competition. The plays must be written by the students. Awards are given at the end of the week, and all the presentations are open to the public. Numbers from current Broadway hits are performed during the Awards Night ceremonies. Contact: Children's Theater Coordinator, Arkansas Arts Center, McArthur Park, P.O. Box 2137, Little Rock, Arkansas 72203, telephone (501) 372-4000.

Russellville

Annual Memorial Day Bass Tournament (Lake Dardanelle State Park) This event is sponsored by the Dardanelle Bass Club and Dennis Marine Service. Contact: Superintendent, Lake Dardanelle State Park, Route 5, Box 527, Russellville, Arkansas 72801, telephone (501) 967-5516.

June Events

Clarksville

Annual Johnson County Peach Festival The activities in this festival include a soapbox derby, a terrapin race, horseshoe pitching, and a street dance. Three beauty pageants are held: Princess Elberta (5–6 years), Queen Elberta (17–

26 years), and Miss Arkansas Valley (17–26 years). While the Queen Elberta contestants must be from Johnson County, the Miss Arkansas Valley contestants may be from anywhere in Arkansas. Both pageants are preliminaries for the Miss Arkansas Contest. Contact: Clarksville Chamber of Commerce, P.O. Box 396, Clarksville, Arkansas 72830, telephone (501) 754-2340.

Conway

Annual Hendrix College Summer Institute (Hendrix College Mills Center) A series of lectures and seminars on various topics, with one overriding theme. This is the only "vacation" college in Arkansas. The speakers include Hendrix College faculty members and selected well-known speakers. Contact: Director of College Relations, Hendrix College, Conway, Arkansas 73032, telephone (501) 329-6811.

Hot Springs

Annual Arkansas Fun Festival Arts and crafts, golf and tennis tournaments, bowling, the Miss Hot Springs pageant, a Community Players production, and evening entertainment features comprise the major activities in this festival. There are also multiple games of skill and a parade of boats. The Fun Festival, which features special events for every member of the family, takes place at various locations, indoors and out, in the city and on the big lakes in the area. Contact: Special Events Director, Greater Hot Springs Chamber of Commerce, P.O. Box 1500, Hot Springs, Arkansas 71902, telephone (501) 321-1700.
Open Trophy Horse Show (New Arena) A summer horse show sponsored annually by the South Central Arkansas Horse Show Association and the Hot Springs Saddle Club. All classes are welcome. There is a small entry fee, but no admission is charged for spectators.

Contact: Bud Palmer, Weyerhaeuser Corporation, 810 Whittington Avenue, Hot Springs, Arkansas 71901, telephone (501) 624-5631.

Morrilton

Swap Meet and Auto Fair   This annual swap and display of antique automobiles is held at Petit Jean Mountain. Contact: Morrilton Chamber of Commerce, 120 North Division Street, P.O. Box 589, Morrilton, Arkansas 72110, telephone (501) 354-2393.

Roland

Annual Big Maumelle Canoe Race (Pinnacle Mountain State Park) Two-person teams race a distance of approximately four miles. There are two divisions of competition: Division A (16 years and older) and Division B (15 years and younger). Contact: Superintendent, Pinnacle Mountain State Park, Route 1, Box 34, Roland, Arkansas 72135, telephone (501) 868-5806.

July Events

Benton

Libertyfest   This annual 4th of July festival is sponsored by the Tourism Committee of the Saline County Chamber of Commerce. The usual activities include a fireworks display, food stands, arts and crafts, carnival rides, and musical entertainment. Contact: Saline County Chamber of Commerce, 607 North Market Street, Benton, Arkansas 72015, telephone (501) 778-8272.

Bismarck

Annual DeGray State Park Four-Ball Tournament (DeGray State Park) Open to all, this popular golfing event involves a field of two-person teams. A trophy and gift certificate are awarded to the winners in each flight. A new automobile is offered for a hole-in-one on a

designated hole. Contact: Golf Course Manager, DeGray State Park, Route 1, Box 144, Bismarck, Arkansas 71929, telephone (501) 865-3700.

Malvern

Malvern Brickfest (Hot Springs County Courthouse) Arts and crafts booths, games, concessions, entertainment, and a kiddie carnival are staged on the Hot Springs County Courthouse lawn during this weekend event. Contact: Malvern Chamber of Commerce, 213 West Third Street, P.O. Box 266, Malvern, Arkansas 72104, telephone (501) 332-2721.

Morrilton

Libertyfest (Petit Jean State Park)   This 4th of July celebration at Petit Jean State Park includes a fireworks display and an arts and crafts fair. Contact: Morrilton Chamber of Commerce, 120 North Division Street, P.O. Box 589, Morrilton, Arkansas 72110, telephone (501) 354-2393.

North Little Rock

Fourth of July Celebration (Burns Park) This patriotic event features a concert and fireworks display. Contact: North Little Rock Advertising and Promotion Commission, North Little Rock Chamber of Commerce, 301 North Broadway, P.O. Box 634, North Little Rock, Arkansas 72115, telephone (501) 374-3601.

Russellville

River Valley Jubilee (Lake Dardanelle State Park) This annual celebration, sponsored by the Russellville Jaycees, features exhibits, concession stands, and a fireworks display. Contact: Superintendent, Lake Dardanelle State Park, Route 5, Box 527, Russellville, Arkansas 72801, telephone (501) 967-5516.

August Events

Booneville

Booneville Riding Club Fall Trail Ride
A one-day horseback ride through the Ouachita National Forest with a camp-fire supper at the day's end. Participants must supply their own horse. Contact: Booneville Chamber of Commerce, Second and Bennett Streets, Booneville, Arkansas 72927, telephone (501) 675-2666.

Dierks

Pine Tree Festival   Country music concerts, a parade, pie baking and sewing contests, egg throwing, women's arm wrestling, bait casting, and skillet throwing contests are among the activities scheduled to honor Dierks' main industry. Contact: Dierks Jaycees, P.O. Box 2, Dierks, Arkansas 71833, telephone (501) 286-2990.

Hot Springs

Belvedere Open Junior and Adult Tennis Tournaments (Belvedere Country Club) Contact: Tennis Pro, Belvedere Country Club, Highway 7 North, Hot Springs, Arkansas 71901, telephone (501) 623-2305.
Garland County Seniors Golf Association Four-Ball Tournament (Hot Springs Country Club)   Contact: Golf Pro, Hot Springs Golf and Country Club, 3400 Malvern Avenue, Hot Springs, Arkansas 71901, telephone (501) 624-2661.

Maumelle

Annual Weekend with the Arts   Over fifty artists and craftsmen exhibit and sell their work at this free festival. Usually a wide variety of works are included: oils, acrylics, watercolors, prints, jewelry, pottery, quilts, caricatures, photography, stained glass, cottage crafts, wood carvings, sculpture, and china painting. Special entertainment is offered throughout the afternoon. Contact: Artist-in-Residence, Odom Enterprises, Inc., 550 Edgewood Drive, Maumelle, Arkansas 72118, telephone (501) 851-1110.

Morrilton

Wooten Bluegrass Festival (Roger Wooten Memorial Park) Contact: Morrilton Chamber of Commerce, 120 North Division Street, P.O. Box 589, Morrilton, Arkansas 72110, telephone (501) 354-2393.

Mena

Lum and Abner Days (Janssen Park) These festivities include a Miss Lum and Abner contest, a parade, and nightly music in the park. Contact: Mena Area Chamber of Commerce, 524 Sherwood, Mena, Arkansas 71953, telephone (501) 394-2912.
Southwest Artists Sidewalk Show   Contact: Mena Area Chamber of Commerce, 524 Sherwood, Mena, Arkansas 71953, telephone (501) 394-2912.
Old Settlers Reunion (Janssen Park) This celebration features a picnic, a fiddler's contest, singing, and games. Contact: Mena Area Chamber of Commerce, 524 Sherwood, Mena, Arkansas 71953, telephone (501) 394-2912.
Classic Car Show (Queen Wilhelmina State Park)   This display of street and performance classic cars is held on Rich Mountain. The event also features games and contests. Contact: Mena Area Chamber of Commerce, 524 Sherwood, Mena, Arkansas 71953, telephone (501) 394-2912.

Nashville

Annual Hell's Valley Bluegrass Festival
Bands from all over Arkansas and neighboring states gather together for this event. Camping spaces and hookups are available. Contact: Bill Hailey, P.O. Box 104, Nashville, Arkansas 71852.

North Little Rock

Summerset (Burns Park) This three-day festival features arts and crafts, a five-kilometer run, hot-air balloon races, exotic foods, and musical entertainment. Contact: North Little Rock Advertising and Promotion Commission, North Little Rock Chamber of Commerce, P.O. Box 634, North Little Rock, Arkansas 72115, telephone (501) 374-3601.

September Events

Arkadelphia

Clark County Fair (Fairgrounds) Arts and crafts exhibits, judging of county livestock, carnival rides, and the selection of the Clark County Fair Queen and Little Miss comprise this event. Contact: Arkadelphia Chamber of Commerce, P.O. Box 38, Arkadelphia, Arkansas 71923, telephone (501) 246-5542.

Fiddler's Contest (Pine Plaza Shopping Center) Fiddlers come from several states to join in the fun of this contest. Prizes are awarded to first, second, and third place winners. The competition begins at 6:00 P.M. on Saturday and continues until all have had a chance to perform. Contact: Hap Robertson, Golf Village, I-30 South, Arkadelphia, Arkansas 71923, telephone (501) 246-2040.

Annual Festival of Two Rivers Two fun-filled days of tennis and golf tournaments, the Two Rivers Run (four-mile run), sidewalk sales, skateboarding, nail driving, tobacco spitting, watermelon eating, and horseshoe pitching contests. Contact: Arkadelphia Chamber of Commerce, P.O. Box 38, Arkadelphia, Arkansas 71923, telephone (501) 246-5542.

Bryant

Saline County Fair (Benton Fairgrounds) This fair features carnival rides, night rodeos, animals, domestic arts and crafts,

and a parade. Contact: Chairman, Saline County Fair Board, Bryant, Arkansas 72022, telephone (501) 847-3649.

Fort Smith

United Way Raft Race (Arkansas River) The proceeds from this annual raft race on the Arkansas River go to the Fort Smith United Way. Contact: United Way, 320 South Eighteenth Street, Fort Smith, Arkansas 72901, telephone (501) 782-1311.

Arkansas-Oklahoma Livestock Exposition and District Fair (Exposition Park) A large midway, grandstand entertainment, and many exhibits are high points of this major fair. Contact: Fort Smith Chamber of Commerce, 613 Garrison Avenue, P.O. Box 1668, Fort Smith, Arkansas 72902, telephone (501) 783-6118.

Hot Springs

Labor Day Weekend Four-Ball Golf Tournament (Lakeside Country Club) This four-ball golf tournament is open to the public. Contact: Lakeside Country Club, U.S. Hwy. 270 East, Hot Springs, Arkansas 71901, telephone (501) 262-4346.

Annual Parade of Harmony (Convention Auditorium) Guest stars frequently appear at this barbershop quartet singing event. Contact: Wayne Steward, Jordan Oldsmobile-Buick, 4901 Central Avenue, Hot Springs, Arkansas 71913, telephone (501) 525-4291.

Southwest Seniors Golf Tournament (Hot Springs Country Club) A tournament open to senior golfers in the Southwest Association area. Contact: Club Pro, Hot Springs Golf and Country Club, 3400 Malvern Avenue, Hot Springs, Arkansas 71901, telephone (501) 624-2661.

Garland County Fair and Livestock Show (Fairgrounds) A county fair complete with carnival rides, concessions, rodeo, demolition derby, livestock show, and parade. Contact: President, Fair Association, Farm Bureau of Garland County, 701 Hobson, Hot Springs, Arkansas 71913, telephone (501) 624-5691.

Senior Women's Arkansas Golf Association (SWAGS) Tournament (Hot Springs Country Club) This tournament is for members of the SWAGS. Contact: Club Pro, Hot Springs Golf and Country Club, 3400 Malvern Avenue, Hot Springs, Arkansas 71901, telephone (501) 624-2661.

Fall Outdoor Art Show (Arlington Park) Contact: Greater Hot Springs Chamber of Commerce, P.O. Box 1500, Hot Springs, Arkansas 71902, telephone (501) 321-1700.

Little Rock

Arkansas State Fair and Livestock Show (Fairgrounds) The annual Arkansas State Fair and Livestock Show features champion livestock exhibits from all over Arkansas and the surrounding states, top entertainment, a rodeo, a youth talent competition, and several beauty contests. It is Arkansas' largest annual event with an attendance of over 300,000. Contact: Arkansas State Fair, P.O. Box 907, Little Rock, Arkansas 72203, telephone (501) 372-8341.

Mena

Polk County Fair (Fairgrounds) Contact: Mena Area Chamber of Commerce, 524 Sherwood, Mena, Arkansas 71953, telephone (501) 394-2912.

Mulberry

Crawford County Free Fair (Fairgrounds) Livestock, poultry, swine, rabbit, and other exhibits, carnival rides and concessions, and Queen and Little Princess contests are the main activities in this fair. Contact: Mayor, P.O. Box 448, Mulberry, Arkansas 72947, telephone (501) 997-1321.

North Little Rock

Burns Park Arts and Crafts Fair (Burns Park) Late each September, over two hundred exhibitors show and sell their work under the trees in this picturesque setting. Contact: North Little Rock Parks and Recreation Department, 2700 Willow Street, North Little Rock, Arkansas 72114, telephone (501) 758-2445.

Roland

Hawk Watch (Pinnacle Mountain State Park) Participants should bring their binoculars to this one-day-a-year special activity held in the morning at Arkansas' wilderness park on the edge of Little Rock. Contact: Superintendent, Pinnacle Mountain State Park, Route 1, Box 34, Roland, Arkansas 72135, telephone (501) 868-5806.

Russellville

Bluegrass Festival Bluegrass music performed by local musicians and invited guests highlights this festival. Contact: Russellville Chamber of Commerce, P.O. Box 822, 1019 West Main, Russellville, Arkansas 72801, telephone (501) 968-2530.

Pope County Fair (Fairgrounds) Exhibits, livestock judging, foods, crafts, flowers, and a carnival midway are the main features of these festivities that are held during the second week in September. Contact: Russellville Chamber of Commerce, 1019 West Main Street, P.O. Box 822, Russellville, Arkansas 72801, telephone (501) 968-2530.

October Events

Benton

Old Fashioned Day These festivities are held on the courthouse lawn and in the First Methodist Church on the second Saturday in October. The main attractions include arts and crafts displays, horseshoe pitching, a dunking booth, and musical entertainment. Contact: Senior Adult Center, 210 Jefferson, Benton, Arkansas 72015, telephone (501) 776-0255.

Fort Smith

Garrison Avenue Gala (Garrison Avenue) A gala celebration held in the historic district. Contact: Fort Smith Chamber of Commerce, 613 Garrison Avenue, P.O. Box 1668, Fort Smith, Arkansas 72902, telephone (501) 783-6118.

Hot Springs

S.A.A. Outdoor Art Show (Arlington Park) This free outdoor exhibition of paintings, sculpture, and pottery features the work of Southern Artists Association members. Most of the items are available for purchase. Contact: Greater Hot Springs Chamber of Commerce, P.O. Box 1500, Hot Springs, Arkansas 71902, telephone (501) 321-1700.

Annual Arkansas Oktoberfest (Convention Auditorium) This fall celebration includes German food, band music, polka and waltz dancing, costume contests, nightly door prizes, arts and crafts exhibitions, road races, a German dog show, and a soccer game. Contact: Greater Hot Springs Chamber of Commerce, P.O. Box 1500, Hot Springs, Arkansas 71902, telephone (501) 321-1700.

Mena

Annual Queen Wilhemina Fall Photo Contest (Queen Wilhelmina State Park) Color and black-and-white photography taken in the park during the autumn leaf change must be submitted by early November for judging by park officials. Winners are entitled to free lodging or camping in a state park of their choice. Contact: Superintendent, Queen Wilhelmina State Park, P.O. Box 470, Mena, Arkansas 71953, telephone (501) 394-2864.

Mount Ida

Quartz Crystal and Native Arts and Crafts Festival (Montgomery County Fairgrounds) Quartz crystal mine owners and local crafts people display their materials for sale at this event. Contact: Mount Ida Area Chamber of Commerce, P.O. Box 6, Mount Ida, Arkansas 71957, telephone (501) 867-2723.

North Little Rock

Annual Rock Swap (Burns Park) The Central Arkansas Gem, Mineral, and Geology Society sponsors this mid-October swap meet for rockhounds and the general public. Contact: North Little Rock Advertising and Promotion Commission, North Little Rock Chamber of Commerce, P.O. Box 634, North Little Rock, Arkansas 72115, telephone (501) 374-3601.

YMCA Arts and Crafts Sale Colorful arts and crafts are displayed and sold with the proceeds going to the local Young Men's Christian Association. Contact: Northside YMCA, 6101 John F. Kennedy Boulevard, North Little Rock, Arkansas 72116, telephone (501) 758-3170.

Arkansas Open Golf Championship (Burns Park Golf Course) This mid-October, week-long golf tournament features large cash prizes for professional golfers. Contact: Burns Park Golf Course, P.O. Box 973, North Little Rock, Arkansas 72114, telephone (501) 758-5800.

Annual Minutemen 10K Race The Arkansas National Guard sponsors this certified ten-kilometer race over a rolling course. Contact: Arkansas National Guard, Camp Robinson, North Little Rock, Arkansas 72116, telephone (501) 771-5200.

Paris

Mount Magazine Frontier Days Celebration (Mount Magazine) This annual heritage celebration features events such as nail driving, turtle races, horseshoe pitching, craft displays, and food concessions. Contact: North Logan County Chamber of Commerce, 404 West Walnut, P.O. Box 88, Paris, Arkansas 72855, telephone (501) 963-2244.

Roland

Fall Rambles (Pinnacle Mountain State Park) Naturalist guides lead hikes on park trails during the height of the autumn leaf change. Hours: morning by reservation only. Contact: Superintendent, Pinnacle Mountain State Park, Route 1, Box 34, Roland, Arkansas 72135, telephone (501) 868-5806.

November Events

Fort Smith

Fall Arts and Crafts Show (Phoenix Village Mall) All types of handcrafted items are displayed for sale. No resale items are permitted. Contact: Phoenix Village Mall, Fort Smith, Arkansas 72901, telephone (501) 646-7889.

Little Rock

Arkansas Arts, Crafts and Design Fair (Convention Center Exhibit Hall) This annual juried exhibition and sale of art work features approximately two hundred invited artists from Arkansas and the surrounding states. Contact: Greater Little Rock Chamber of Commerce, 1 Spring Street, P.O. Box 1, Little Rock, Arkansas 72201, telephone (501) 374-4871.

Ozark-Michelob Rugby Tournament (Burns Park) This two-day action-packed event in early November is sponsored by the Central Arkansas Rugby Club. Competitors from five states compete for a chance to attend the national championship. Contact: Greater Little Rock Chamber of Commerce, 1 Spring Street, P.O. Box 1, Little Rock, Arkansas 72201, telephone (501) 374-4871.

Paris

Annual Chili Supper Contact: North Logan County Chamber of Commerce, 404 West Walnut, P.O. Box 88, Paris, Arkansas 72855, telephone (501) 963-2244.

Russellville

Arkansas Valley Arts and Crafts Fair (Arkansas Polytechnical University, Tucker Coliseum) This event features handcrafted and/or hand-decorated articles for exhibit and sale. Contact: Russellville Chamber of Commerce, 1019 West Main, P.O. Box 822, Russellville, Arkansas 72801, telephone (501) 968-2530.

December Events

Hot Springs

Christmas Concert (Mackey Theater, Hot Springs High School) A holiday concert featuring various vocal groups from Hot Springs High School. Contact: Vocal Music Director, Hot Springs High School, 701 Emory, Hot Springs, Arkansas 71913, telephone (501) 624-5286.

Christmas Parade (Central Avenue) This annual parade includes decorated floats, bands, drill teams, and clowns. The holly trees along Bathouse Row are lighted and the Rehabilitation Center is decorated for the occasion. Contact: Hot Springs Jaycees, % Kallman Studio, 5926 Central Avenue, Hot Springs, Arkansas 71901, telephone (501) 525-3170.

Annual Christmas Concert (Convention Auditorium) This holiday concert features the Arkansas Symphony Chamber Orchestra and the Garland County Community College Chorus. Contact: Greater Hot Springs Chamber of Commerce, P.O. Box 1500, Hot Springs, Arkansas 71902, telephone (501) 321-1700.

"A Christmas to Share" (Convention Auditorium) A complimentary holiday event for all senior citizens of Hot Springs and the surrounding area. There is group singing of Christmas carols, refreshments, Bible reading of the Nativity, and music for dancing. Contact: Greater Hot Springs Chamber of Commerce, P.O. Box 1500, Hot Springs, Arkansas 71902, telephone (501) 321-1700.

Little Rock

Christmas Open House (Arkansas Arts Center) Contact: Museum Registrar, Arkansas Arts Center, P.O. Box 2137, Little Rock, Arkansas 72203, telephone (501) 372-4000.

Arkansas Territorial Restoration Open House (Arkansas Territorial Restoration) Traditional decorations of the territorial period, musicians, and refreshments mark the holidays at this impressive Restoration. Contact: Arkansas Territorial Restoration, Third and Scott Streets, Little Rock, Arkansas 72201, telephone (501) 371-2348.

Christmas Parade (Main Street) The North Little Rock Sertoma Club sponsors this colorful Christmas parade in early December. The parade passes down Main Street and ends at the beautifully decorated City Hall. Contact: North Little Rock Sertoma Club, 2800 Willow Street, North Little Rock, Arkansas 72114, telephone (501) 758-1540.

Mena

Annual Christmas on the Mountain (Queen Wilhelmina State Park) A variety of events both during the day and at night for guests of the Queen Wilhelmina Inn and visitors. Santa Claus makes an appearance on Christmas Eve and gifts are exchanged. Contact: Superintendent, Queen Wilhelmina State

Park, P.O. Box 470, Mena, Arkansas 71953, telephone (501) 394-2864.

Van Buren

Christmas Parade (Downtown) Prizes are awarded for the best floats and bands in this parade. Contact: Manager, Van Buren Chamber of Commerce, P.O. Box 652, Van Buren, Arkansas 72956, telephone (501) 474-2761.

MAJOR EVENTS IN OKLAHOMA

May Events

McAlester

Italian Festival (Shilley Field) The residents of Pittsburg County say "Veniti tutti" or "Come one, come all" to help celebrate this festival. This coal-rich area experienced an influx of Italian miners in the 1880s, and their descendants now perpetuate their heritage with folk music, dances, native costumes, an arts and crafts show, and a variety of ethnic culinary delights. Contact: McAlester Chamber of Commerce, P.O. Box 759, McAlester, Oklahoma 74502, telephone (918) 423-2550.

June Events

Broken Bow

Kiamichi Owa Chito (Beaver's Bend State Park) These festivities commemorate the Choctaw heritage in Oklahoma. Among the featured activities are big-name entertainment, a forestry skills contest, a talent show, a kiddie contest, canoe races, a golf tournament, dances, and Choctaw food. Contact: Broken Bow Chamber of Commerce, 214 Craig Road, P.O. Box 249, Broken Bow, Oklahoma 74728, telephone (405) 584-3393.

McAlester

Sanders Family Bluegrass Festival One of the largest bluegrass festivals in the United States, the four-day event is held

Prison rodeo, McAlester, Oklahoma. Courtesy of Oklahoma Tourism and Recreation Department.

five miles west of McAlester on U.S. 270. Camper spaces with electrical hookups are available. Contact: Freddie Sanders, Route 6, Box 15, McAlester, Oklahoma 74501, telephone (918) 423-4891.

Porum

Belle Starr Day This one-day festival, which is sponsored by the Lady Outlaws, features mock gunfights, games, and a street dance. Contact: Jessie Meeks, P.O. Box 133, Porum, Oklahoma 74455, telephone (918) 484-5246.

Wilburton

Belle Starr Festival During the 1880s, the deeds of this famous female outlaw were hardly a cause for celebration; but the festival that remembers her legend is pure, law-abiding fun. Belle and her gang ride into town each day at noon to perform. There are also rodeos, parades, an art show, contests, melo-

drama, and a medicine show. Contact: Wilburton Chamber of Commerce, 302 West Main, P.O. Box 555, Wilburton, Oklahoma 74578, telephone (918) 465-5330.

July Events

Porum

Belle Starr Stampede Rodeo This rodeo is sponsored by the Porum Roundup Club. Contact: A. B. Fleming, P.O. Box 324, Porum, Oklahoma 74455, telephone (918) 484-5292.

Poteau

Poteau Pioneer Days The featured events include an International Professional Rodeo Association-sponsored rodeo, a pioneer reunion, the Miss Poteau Frontier Rodeo pageant, a fiddlers' contest, gospel singing, an arts and crafts show, and dancing. Contact: Poteau Chamber of Commerce, 201 South

Front Street, Poteau, Oklahoma 74953, telephone (918) 647-9179.

August Events

Heavener

I.P.R.A. Rodeo (Oklahoma Rodeo Grounds) This rodeo, which is sanctioned by the International Professional Rodeo Association, is held during the first weekend in August. The usual events include a parade and a grand entry procession. Contact: Heavener Chamber of Commerce, 600 West First, P.O. Box 27, Heavener, Oklahoma 74937, telephone (918) 653-4303.

Arts, Crafts, and Antique Fair (Old West Side Grade School) This three-day display and sale is held on the first weekend in November. Other activities include music by local western bands and the Green Country Cloggers. Contact: Heavener Chamber of Commerce, 600 West First, P.O. Box 27, Heavener, Oklahoma 74937, telephone (918) 653-4303.

Eufaula

National Championship Super Stock Outboard Motor Race (Lake Eufaula) Top racers compete in the elimination heats beginning at 10 A.M. and the main events starting at 1:30 P.M. Contact: Lake Eufaula Association, Route 4, Box 168, Eufaula, Oklahoma 74432, telephone (918) 689-7751.

September Events

McAlester

Oklahoma State Prison Rodeo (State Prison Rodeo Arena) In addition to steer wrestling and roping competitions by professional cowboys, the prison inmates try their luck at such unusual contests as wild-cow milking, a "mad scramble" mule, bull and horse races, and "Money the Hard Way," which involves retrieving a purse full of cash from the horns of a cranky bull. Performances begin at 8 P.M. each day. Contact: McAlester Chamber of Commerce, 17 East Carl Albert Parkway, P.O. Box 759, McAlester, Oklahoma 74502, telephone (918) 423-2550.

Italian Festival This annual Memorial Day weekend event features authentic Italian dinners, souvenirs, concessions, a fine-arts show, and a crafts show. Contact: McAlester Chamber of Commerce, 17 East Carl Albert Parkway, P.O. Box 759, McAlester, Oklahoma 74502, telephone (918) 423-2550.

14

Vacation Information

There are numerous public and private sources of tourist information. Those interested in the history and geography of the Ouachita Mountains can find additional information in the many references that follow the final chapter of this book. Included in this list of references is a fairly comprehensive collection of tourist brochures that deal with nearly all facets of the Ouachitas' tourism-recreation industry.

The national bicentennial and numerous centennial commemorations of Ouachita towns founded during the railroad building and timber exploitation era have generated considerable interest in local history, geography, and culture. This, in turn, has stimulated the preparation of numerous useful accounts of local town and county events.

Although the Ouachita Province has only recently attracted the attention of many professional scholars, there are several worthwhile articles published in a number of professional journals. As an example, the *Arkansas Historical Quarterly* and *The Chronicles of Oklahoma* contain articles focusing on the settlement, economy, and culture of the Ouachita Mountains.

Those electing to "experience" the Ouachitas by traveling through the area would be wise to carry several of the following books for reference: *The Trees of Arkansas,* which can be obtained from the Arkansas Forestry Commission (3821 East Roosevelt Road, Little Rock, Arkansas, 72204) is a useful guide for identifying the major commercial and decorative trees found throughout the Ouachita Mountain region; *Game Fish of Arkansas* is a helpful brochure published by the Arkansas Fish and Game Commission (State Capitol Mall, Little Rock, Arkansas 72201); a similar brochure, *Fishing in Oklahoma,* is available from the Oklahoma Department of Wildlife Conservation (1801 North Lincoln, Oklahoma City, Oklahoma 73105).

The best references pertaining to the geology and landforms of the Ouachita Mountains include: William D. Thornbury, *Regional Geomorphology of the United States* (New York: John Wiley and Sons, Inc., 1965); *Field Guide to Structure and Stratigraphy of the Ouachita Mountains and the Arkoma Basin* (Oklahoma City: Association of American Petroleum Geologists, 1978); Charles G. Stone, et al., *A Guidebook to the Geology of the Ouachita Mountains, Arkansas* (Little Rock: Arkansas Geological Commission, 1973); and Norman Williams, *A Guidebook to the Geology of the Arkansas Paleozoic Area* (Little Rock: Arkansas Geological Commission, 1977). The readers of these books should be familiar with geological terms.

A free index map showing the topographic maps available for the Ouachita Mountains of Arkansas and Oklahoma is available from: The Distribution Section, U.S. Geological Survey, Federal Center, Denver, Colorado 80225. The 1:250,000 scale topographic maps are especially useful in understanding the geography and landforms of the region. Four sheets, *Fort Smith, Hot Springs, McAlester,* and *Russellville,* provide full coverage of the Ouachita Mountains.

Information pertaining to the area's attractions, accommodations, schedules, and services may be obtained by directly contacting any of a number of tourist and recreation information offices. As an example, both Oklahoma and Arkansas maintain tourism bureaus. There are also regional tourist associations in the vicinity of some of the major lakes, and the chambers of commerce of larger towns often collect and distribute information to travelers and visitors.

The state tourism departments, the U.S. Army Corps of Engineers district offices, and the headquarters offices of the national forests provide a great variety of very useful information including color maps at various scales, factual bulletins, rules for use of facilities, and fee structures. These agencies have excellent materials on hand and can usually provide the desired information if needs are stated clearly. Specific reference materials and sources of information are noted in the earlier chapters on hunting, fishing, and camping.

The following list of addresses and telephone numbers should prove useful to those who wish to request more information about a particular area of the Ouachitas.

STATE TOURISM AND RELATED OFFICES

Arkansas Department of Parks
and Tourism
One Capitol Mall
Little Rock, Arkansas 72201
Telephone (501) 682-7777

Arkansas Game and Fish
Commission
2 Natural Resources Drive
Little Rock, Arkansas 72205
Telephone (501) 223-6300

Oklahoma Department of Wildlife
Conservation
1801 Lincoln Boulevard
Oklahoma City, Oklahoma 73105
Telephone (405) 521-3851

Oklahoma State Board of Tourism
505 Will Rogers Building

P.O. Box 60000
Oklahoma City, Oklahoma 73146
Telephone (405) 521-2406 or
(800) 652-6552

NATIONAL FORESTS AND PARKS

Hot Springs National Park
P.O. Box 1500
Hot Springs, Arkansas 71901
Telephone (501) 624-3383

Ouachita National Forest
P.O. Box 1270
Hot Springs, Arkansas 71901
Telephone (501) 321-5202

Ozark National Forest
P.O. Box 1008
Russellville, Arkansas 72801
Telephone (501) 968-2354

U.S. ARMY CORPS OF ENGINEERS

District Engineer
U.S. Army Corps of Engineers
224 South Boulder
Tulsa, Oklahoma 74103
Telephone (918) 581-7307

District Engineer
U.S. Army Corps of Engineers
668 Clifford David Federal Building
Memphis, Tennessee 38103
Telephone (901) 544-3221

District Engineer
U.S. Army Corps of Engineers
P.O. Box 867
Little Rock, Arkansas 72203
Telephone (501) 378-5551

District Engineer
U.S. Army Corps of Engineers
P.O. Box 60
Vicksburg, Mississippi 39181
Telephone (601) 631-5012

STATE PARKS

Arkansas

Daisy State Park
Daisy Route Box 66

Kirby, Arkansas 71950
Telephone (501) 398-4487

De Gray State Park Lodge
Box 375
Arkadelphia, Arkansas 71923
Telephone (501) 865-4591

Lake Catherine State Park
Route 19, Box 360
Hot Springs, Arkansas 71901
Telephone (501) 844-4176

Lake Dardanelle State Park
Route 5, Box 527
Russellville, Arkansas 72801
Telephone (501) 967-5516

Lake Ouachita State Park
Star Route 1, Box 160A
Mountain Pine, Arkansas 71956
Telephone (501) 767-9366

Mount Nebo State Park
Dardanelle, Arkansas 72834
Telephone (501) 229-3655

Petit Jean State Park
Route 3, Box 340
Morrilton, Arkansas 72110
Telephone (800) 628-7936

Pinnacle Mountain State Park
Route 1, Box 34
Roland, Arkansas 72135
Telephone (501) 868-5806

Queen Wilhelmina State Park
P.O. Box 470
Mena, Arkansas 71953
Telephone (501) 394-2864

Oklahoma

Arrowhead State Park and Resort
HC67, Box 57
Canadian, Oklahoma 74425
Telephone (918) 339-2204

Beavers Bend State Park
Box 10
Broken Bow, Oklahoma 74728
Telephone (405) 494-6538

Fountainhead State Park
P.O. Box HC60-1340
Checotah, Oklahoma 74426
Telephone (918) 689-5311

Heavener Runestone State Park
Heavener, Oklahoma 74937
Telephone (918) 653-2241

Hochatown State Park
Box 10
Broken Bow, Oklahoma 74728
Telephone (405) 494-6452

Robbers Cave State Park
P.O. Box 9
Wilburton, Oklahoma 74578
Telephone (918) 465-2562

Talimena State Park
P.O. Box 318
Talihina, Oklahoma 74571
Telephone (918) 567-2052

Wister Lake State Park
Route 2, Box 6B
Wister, Oklahoma 74966
Telephone (918) 655-7756

TOURIST ASSOCIATIONS AND CHAMBERS OF COMMERCE

Arkansas

Alma Area Chamber of Commerce
825 Fayetteville Avenue
P.O. Box 2467
Alma, Arkansas 72921
Telephone (501) 632-4127

Arkadelphia Chamber of Commerce
107 North 6th Street
P.O. Box 38
Arkadelphia, Arkansas 71923
Telephone (501) 246-5542

Arkansas State Chamber of
 Commerce
100 Main Street
P.O. Box 3645
Little Rock, Arkansas 72203
Telephone (501) 374-9225

Booneville Chamber of Commerce
Second and Bennett Streets
Booneville, Arkansas 72927
Telephone (501) 675-2666

Bryant Chamber of Commerce
P.O. Box 261
Bryant, Arkansas 72022
Telephone (501) 847-4702

Cabot Chamber of Commerce
Second and Main
P.O. Box 631
Cabot, Arkansas 72023
Telephone (501) 843-2136

Clarksville Chamber of Commerce
P.O. Box 396
Clarksville, Arkansas 72830
Telephone (501) 754-2340

Conway Chamber of Commerce
1234 Main
P.O. Box 1492
Conway, Arkansas 72032
Telephone (501) 327-7789

Dardanelle Chamber of Commerce
Union Street or Highway 7 S
P.O. Box 208
Dardanelle, Arkansas 72834
Telephone (501) 229-3328

De Queen/Sevier County Chamber
   of Commerce
306 De Queen Avenue
P.O. Box 67
De Queen, Arkansas 71832
Telephone (501) 584-3225

Dierks Chamber of Commerce
P.O. Box 292
Dierks, Arkansas 71833
Telephone (501) 286-2643

El Dorado Chamber of Commerce
201 North Jackson
P.O. Box 1271
El Dorado, Arkansas 71730
Telephone (501) 863-6113

Fort Smith Chamber of Commerce
613 Garrison Avenue

P.O. Box 1668
Fort Smith, Arkansas 72902
Telephone (501) 783-6118

Greater Hot Springs Chamber
   of Commerce
P.O. Box 1500
Hot Springs, Arkansas 71902
Telephone (501) 321-1700

Greater Little Rock Chamber
   of Commerce
One Spring Street
P.O. Box 1
Little Rock, Arkansas 72201
Telephone (501) 374-4871, 4872
   or 4873

Greenwood Chamber of Commerce
P.O. Box 511
Greenwood, Arkansas 72936
Telephone (501) 996-2019

Hot Springs Convention and Visitors
   Bureau
134 Convention Boulevard
P.O. Box K
Hot Springs, Arkansas 71902
Telephone (501) 321-2835 or
   (800) 543-BATH

Jacksonville Chamber of Commerce
1400 Main Street
Jacksonville, Arkansas 72076
Telephone (501) 982-1512

Little River Chamber of Commerce
Courthouse Annex Building
Ashdown, Arkansas 71822-2753
Telephone (501) 898-2758

Little Rock Convention and Visitors
   Bureau
P.O. Box 3232
Little Rock, Arkansas 72203
Telephone (501) 376-4781

Lonoke Area Chamber of Commerce
118 South Center
P.O. Box 294
Lonoke, Arkansas 72086
Telephone (501) 676-6218

Magic Springs Family Fun
Theme Park
General Manager
2001 U.S. 70 East
Hot Springs, Arkansas 71901
Telephone (501) 624-5411

Malvern Chamber of Commerce
213 West Third
P.O. Box 266
Malvern, Arkansas 72104
Telephone (501) 332-2721

Mena/Polk County Chamber
of Commerce
524 Sherwood Street
Mena, Arkansas 71953
Telephone (501) 394-2912

Morrilton Chamber of Commerce
120 North Division Street
P.O. Box 589
Morrilton, Arkansas 72110
Telephone (501) 354-2393

Mount Ida Area Chamber
of Commerce
P.O. Box 6
Mount Ida, Arkansas 71957-0006
Telephone (501) 867-2723

North Little Rock Advertising and
Promotion Commission
North Little Rock Chamber
of Commerce
301 North Broadway
P.O. Box 634
North Little Rock, Arkansas 72115
Telephone (501) 374-3601

North Logan County Chamber
of Commerce
404 West Walnut
P.O. Box 88
Paris, Arkansas 72855
Telephone (501) 963-2244

Ozark Area Chamber of Commerce
P.O. Box 283
Ozark, Arkansas 72949
Telephone (501) 667-2525

Russellville Chamber of Commerce
1019 West Main
P.O. Box 822
Russellville, Arkansas 72801
Telephone (501) 968-2530

Saline County Chamber
of Commerce
607 North Market Street
Benton, Arkansas 72015
Telephone (501) 778-8272

Searcy Chamber of Commerce
200 South Spring Street
Searcy, Arkansas 72143
Telephone (501) 268-2458

Van Buren Chamber of Commerce
813 Main Street
P.O. Box 652
Van Buren, Arkansas 72956
Telephone (501) 474-2761

Waldron Area Chamber
of Commerce
310 Washington Street
P.O. Box 36
Waldron, Arkansas 72958
Telephone (501) 637-2775

Oklahoma

Atoka County Chamber
of Commerce
P.O. Box 709
Atoka, Oklahoma 74525
Telephone (405) 889-2410

Broken Bow Chamber of Commerce
214 Craig Road
P.O. Box 249
Broken Bow, Oklahoma 74728
Telephone (405) 584-3393

Checotah Chamber of Commerce
114 North Broadway
P.O. Box 505
Checotah, Oklahoma 74426
Telephone (918) 473-2070

Clayton Chamber of Commerce
P.O. Box 8

Clayton, Oklahoma 74536
Telephone (918) 569-4776

Greater Eufaula Area Chamber
of Commerce
402 North Main
Eufaula, Oklahoma 74432
Telephone (918) 689-2791

Greater Muskogee Chamber
of Commerce
425 Boston
P.O. Box 797
Muskogee, Oklahoma 74401
Telephone (918) 682-2401

Hartshorne Chamber of Commerce
P.O. Box 257
Hartshorne, Oklahoma 74547

Heavener Chamber of Commerce
600 West First, Highway 59 South
P.O. Box 27
Heavener, Oklahoma 74937
Telephone (918) 653-4303

Hugo Chamber of Commerce
200 South Broadway
Hugo, Oklahoma 74743
Telephone (405) 326-7511

Idabel Chamber of Commerce
13 North Central
Idabel, Oklahoma 74745
(405) 286-3305

Lake Eufaula Association
Route 4 Box 168
Eufaula, Oklahoma 74432
Telephone (918) 689-7751

McAlester Chamber of Commerce
17 East Carl Albert Parkway
P.O. Box 759
McAlester, Oklahoma 74502
Telephone (918) 423-2550

Poteau Chamber of Commerce
201 South Front Street
Poteau, Oklahoma 74953
Telephone (918) 647-9179

Pushmataha County Chamber
of Commerce
100 S.E. Second Street
Antlers, Oklahoma 74523
Telephone (405) 298-2488

Sallisaw Chamber of Commerce
P.O. Box 251
Sallisaw, Oklahoma 74955
Telephone (918) 775-2558

Stigler Chamber of Commerce
204 East Main
P.O. Box 482
Stigler, Oklahoma 74462
Telephone (918) 967-8681

Warner Chamber of Commerce
P.O. Box 9
Warner, Oklahoma 74469
Telephone (918) 463-2921

Wilburton Chamber of Commerce
302 West Main
P.O. Box 555
Wilburton, Oklahoma 74578
Telephone (918) 465-5330

Notes

CHAPTER 1

1. Nevin M. Fenneman, *Physiography of Eastern United States* (New York: McGraw-Hill, 1938), 665–68.
2. Glenn T. Trewartha, *An Introduction to Climate* (New York: McGraw-Hill, 1954), 302–12.
3. John E. Oliver, *Climate and Man's Environment: An Introduction to Applied Climatology* (New York: John Wiley and Sons, 1973), 200–202.
4. Ibid., 200.
5. Hubert B. Stroud and Gerald T. Hanson, *Arkansas Geography: The Physical Landscape and the Historical Cultural Setting* (Little Rock: Rose, 1981), 13.

CHAPTER 2

1. Dallas T. Herndon, ed., *Centennial History of Arkansas* (Chicago: S.J. Clarke, 1922), 73–90.
2. Ibid., 505.
3. Milton D. Rafferty, *The Ozarks: Land and Life* (Norman: University of Oklahoma Press, 1980), 50; John W. Morris, Charles R. Goins, and Edwin C. McReynolds, *Historical Atlas of Oklahoma* (Norman: University of Oklahoma Press, 1976), 24.
4. Ibid., 24.
5. Ibid., 27.
6. Ibid., 24.
7. Herndon, *Centennial History of Arkansas,* 507–508.
8. Ibid., 513.
9. Carl N. Tyson, *The Red River in Southwestern History* (Norman: University of Oklahoma Press, 1981), 88–102.
10. Angie Debo, *The Rise and Fall of the Choctaw Republic* (Norman: University of Oklahoma Press, 1961), 114.
11. Jesse O. McKee and Jon A. Schlenker, *The Choctaws: Cultural Evolution of a Native American Tribe* (Jackson: University Press of Mississippi, 1980), 76.
12. Ibid., 84.
13. Ibid., 121.

14. Paul Bonnifield, "Choctaw Nation on the Eve of the Civil War," *Journal of the West* 12 (July 1973): 386–402.
15. N. A. Graebner, "Pioneer Agriculture in Oklahoma," *Chronicles of Oklahoma* 23 (Autumn 1945): 232–48.
16. Frederick Lynne Ryan, *The Rehabilitation of Oklahoma Coal Mining Communities* (Norman: University of Oklahoma Press, 1935), 25.
17. Ibid., 26.
18. Clifton E. Hull, *Shortline Railroads of Arkansas* (Norman: University of Oklahoma Press, 1969), 113–305.
19. Ibid., 26.
20. Ryan, *The Rehabilitation of Oklahoma Coal Mining Communities,* 27–28.
21. Herndon, *Centennial History of Arkansas,* 470.
22. Ibid.
23. Ryan, *Rehabilitation of Oklahoma Coal Mining Communities,* 25–49.
24. Herndon, *Centennial History of Arkansas,* 275–76.
25. Ibid., 272.
26. John Hickman and Alan Smith, "Behind the Sunbelt's Growth," *Economic Review,* Federal Reserve Bank of Atlanta (March 1982), 4–13.
27. U.S. Travel Data Center, *1984 Economic Impact of Travel on Arkansas Counties* (Washington, D.C.: U.S. Travel Data Center, 1985), 1–12.

CHAPTER 3

1. Angie Debo, *The Rise and Fall of the Choctaw Republic* (Norman: University of Oklahoma Press, 1961), 228–29.
2. Friedrich Gerstäker, *Wild Sports in the Far West* (Durham, N.C.: Duke University Press, 1968), 239–59. See also G. W. Featherstonhaugh, *Excursion through the Slave States* (New York: Negro Universities Press, 1968), 82–125.
3. Joseph D. Clark, *1984 Black Bear Harvest Report.* Wildlife Management Divi-

sion, Arkansas Game and Fish Commission, Little Rock, Ark., April 1959, 1–17.

4. *The Arkansas Game and Fish Commission,* (unpublished history). Arkansas Game and Fish Commission, Little Rock, Ark., 1985, 1–2.

5. Juanita Mahaffey, "Past and Future of Wildlife Conservation in Oklahoma," *Oklahoma Game and Fish News* 13. 4 (April 1957): 3.

6. Ibid.

7. *The Arkansas Game and Fish Commission* (unpublished history), 2.

8. Mahaffey, "Past and Future of Wildlife Conservation in Oklahoma," 7.

9. *Fishing and Hunting in Arkansas.* Arkansas Game and Fish Commission and the Arkansas Parks, Recreation and Travel Commission, Little Rock, Ark., n.d., 7.

10. J. Michael Aledger, *1984–1985 Turkey Harvest.* Arkansas Game and Fish Commission, Little Rock, Ark., 1985, 1–9.

11. Byron Dalrymple, *Complete Guide to Hunting Across North America* (New York: Popular Science, 1970), 363–67.

12. *Fishing and Hunting in Arkansas,* 7.

13. *Oklahoma Mammals.* Oklahoma Department of Wildlife Conservation, Oklahoma City, Okla., 1985, 9.

14. James Spencer, "National State Deer Profile: The Ouachita Mountains," *Arkansas Sportsman,* October 1985, 13.

15. *Oklahoma Mammals,* 3.

16. Ibid., 1.

17. Tom R. Johnson, "Missouri's Venomous Snakes," *The Missouri Conservationist,* June 1979, 5.

CHAPTER 4

1. *Sport Fish of Oklahoma.* Oklahoma Department of Conservation, Oklahoma City, Okla., 1980.

2. *Trout Fishing in Arkansas.* Arkansas Game and Fish Commission, Little Rock, Ark., n.d.

3. *The Float Streams of Arkansas.* Arkansas Game and Fish Commission and the Arkansas Department of Parks and Tourism, Little Rock, Ark., 1979.

4. *Ouachita Geo-Float Trail.* U.S. Army Corps of Engineers, Vicksburg District, Vicksburg, Miss., 1978.

CHAPTER 5

1. Dan Saults et al., eds., *Sport Fishing U.S.A.* (Washington, D.C.: U.S. Department of Interior, Bureau of Sport Fisheries and Wildlife, Fish and Wildlife Service, 1971), 234.

2. Data compiled from U.S. Army Corps of Engineers lake maps and *A Guide to Lakes Hamilton and Catherine,* Arkansas Power and Light Company, Public Affairs Department, Little Rock, Arkansas, n.d.

3. Saults, *Sport Fishing U.S.A.,* 235.

4. Jim Murphy, "Summer Fishing is Hot," *Outdoor Oklahoma* 39 (July/August 1983): 29.

5. David Warren, "Swamp Fishing," *Outdoor Oklahoma* 39, (May/June 1983): 2–7.

6. Bruce Stromp, "Fish the Riprap," *Outdoor Oklahoma* 39 (May/June 1983): 28–33.

7. *Blue Mountain Lake Map,* Department of the Army, Corps of Engineers, Little Rock District, Little Rock, Ark., 1974.

8. *Broken Bow Lake Map,* Department of the Army, Corps of Engineers, Tulsa District, Tulsa, Okla., n.d.

9. *A Guide to Lakes Hamilton and Catherine,* Arkansas Power and Light Company, Public Affairs Department, Little Rock, Arkansas, n.d.

10. *Lake Conway Map,* Arkansas Game and Fish Commission, Little Rock, Arkansas, n.d.

11. *Dardanelle Lake Map,* Department of the Army, Corps of Engineers, Little Rock District, Little Rock, Ark., 1979.

12. *De Gray Lake Map,* Department of the Army, Corps of Engineers, Vicksburg District, Vicksburg, Miss., 1980.

13. *De Queen Lake Map,* Department of the Army, Corps of Engineers, Tulsa District, Tulsa, Okla., 1978.

14. *Dierks Lake Map,* Department of the Army, Corps of Engineers, Tulsa District, Tulsa, Okla., 1980.

15. *Eufaula Lake Map,* Department of the Army, Corps of Engineers, Tulsa District, Tulsa, Okla., 1977.

16. *Gillham Lake Map,* Department of the Army, Corps of Engineers, Tulsa District, Tulsa, Okla., 1980.

17. *Greeson Lake Map,* Department of the Army, Corps of Engineers, Vicksburg District, Vicksburg, Miss., 1977.

18. *A Guide to Lakes Hamilton and Catherine,* Arkansas Power and Light Company, Public Affairs Department, Little Rock, Ark., n.d.

19. *Hugo Lake Map,* Department of the Army, Corps of Engineers, Tulsa District, Tulsa, Okla., 1978.

20. *Robert S. Kerr Lake and Dam Map,* Department of the Army, Corps of Engineers, Tulsa District, Tulsa, Okla., 1978.

21. *Lake Maumelle Map,* Little Rock Municipal Water Works, Little Rock, Ark., 1959.

22. *Nimrod Lake Map,* Department of the Army, Corps of Engineers, Little Rock District, Little Rock, Ark., 1973.

23. *Ouachita Lake Map,* Department of the Army, Corps of Engineers, Vicksburg District, Vicksburg, Miss., 1980.

24. *Ozark Lake Map,* Department of the Army, Corps of Engineers, Little Rock District, Little Rock, Ark., 1976.

25. *Pine Creek Lake Map,* Department of the Army, Corps of Engineers, Tulsa District, Tulsa, Okla., 1976.

26. *Clayton Lake Map* (now Sardis Lake), Department of the Army, Corps of Engineers, Tulsa District, Tulsa, Okla., 1981.

27. *Lake Winona Map,* Little Rock Municipal Water Works, Little Rock, Ark., 1959.

28. *Wister Dam and Reservoir Map,* Department of the Army, Corps of Engineers, Tulsa District, Tulsa, Okla., 1969.

CHAPTER 6 (no notes)

CHAPTER 7

1. Nevin M. Fenneman, *Physiography of Eastern United States* (New York: McGraw-Hill, 1938), 671–74.

2. John Wickham, "Ouachita Foldbelt: A Paleozoic Continental Margin," a paper published in Glenn Visher, Charles Stone, and Boyd Haley, *Field Guide to the Structure and Stratigraphy of the Ouachita Mountains and the Arkoma Basin* (Oklahoma City: American Association of Petroleum Geologists, 1978), 51–52.

3. William D. Thornbury, *Regional Geomorphology of the United States* (New York: John Wiley and Sons, 1965), 284.

4. Dallas T. Herndon, *Centennial History of Arkansas* (Chicago: S. J. Clarke, 1922), 473–74.

5. Ibid., 463.

6. Norman Williams, *Mineral Resources of Arkansas,* Bulletin 6, Arkansas Geological and Conservation Commission, Little Rock, Ark., 1959, 71.

7. Charles G. Stone, Boyd R. Haley, and George W. Viele, *A Guidebook to the Geology of the Ouachita Mountains, Arkansas,* Arkansas Geological Commission, Little Rock, Ark., 1977, 38.

8. G. W. Featherstonhaugh, *Excursion Through the Slave States.* Originally published in 1844 by Harper and Brothers. (New York: Negro Universities Press, 1968), 167.

9. *Geology of Magnet Cove* (mimeographed information leaflet). (Little Rock: Arkansas Geological Commission, n.d.), 3–4. See also Norman Williams, *Field Trip Guidebook Central Arkansas Economic Geology and Petrology* (Little Rock: Arkansas Geological Commission, 1967), 10–17.

10. Stone, *A Guidebook to the Ouachita Mountains, Arkansas,* 84–86.

CHAPTER 8

1. Population figures over 2,500 are from the U.S. Census Bureau's *County and City Data Book, 1988.* They are the U.S. Census Bureau's estimates for 1986, which are available only for places with populations of 2,500 or more. Population figures of less than 2,500 are from the 1980 U.S. Census.

2. George H. Shirk, *Oklahoma Place Names,* 2d ed. (Norman: University of Oklahoma Press, 1974), 167.

3. Odie Faulk, *Muskogee: City and County* (Muskogee, Okla: The Five Civilized Tribes Museum, 1982), 24.

4. Thomas Nuttall, *A Journal of Travels into the Arkansas Territory during the Year 1819* (Norman: University of Oklahoma Press, 1980), 192. First published in 1821 by T. H. Palmer in Philadelphia under the title, *A Journal of Travels into the Arkansas Territory During the Year 1819.*

5. Washington Irving, *A Tour on the Prairies* (Norman: University of Oklahoma Press, 1956).

6. Faulk, *Muskogee: City and County*, 75–76.

7. Kent Ruth, ed., *Oklahoma: A Guide to the Sooner State*, Rev. ed. (Norman: University of Oklahoma Press, 1957), 167.

8. Shirk, *Oklahoma Place Names*, 177.

9. Ibid., 48.

10. Ibid., 85.

11. Ruth, *Oklahoma: A Guide to the Sooner State*, 400.

12. Shirk, *Oklahoma Place Names*, 33–34.

13. Ruth, *Oklahoma: A Guide to the Sooner State*, 353.

14. Ibid., 402.

15. Shirk, *Oklahoma Place Names*, 134.

16. Ibid., 50.

17. Ibid., 228.

18. Ibid., 13.

19. Ruth, *Oklahoma: A Guide to the Sooner State*, 403.

20. Ibid., 265–66.

21. Shirk, *Oklahoma Place Names*, 255.

22. Ibid., 261.

23. Ibid., 165–66.

24. Kent Ruth, *Oklahoma Travel Handbook* (Norman: University of Oklahoma Press, 1977), 36.

25. John W. Morris, *Ghost Towns of Oklahoma* (Norman: University of Oklahoma Press, 1978), 177.

26. Shirk, *Oklahoma Place Names*, 19.

27. Ibid., 196.

28. Ruth, *Oklahoma Travel Handbook*, 247.

29. Shirk, *Oklahoma Place Names*, 232.

30. Ibid., 132.

31. Ruth, *Oklahoma Travel Handbook*, 232.

32. Shirk, *Oklahoma Place Names*, 240.

33. Ruth, *Oklahoma Travel Handbook*, 121–22.

34. Ibid., 122.

35. Morris, *Ghost Towns of Oklahoma*, 28.

36. Hubert B. Stroud and Gerald T. Hanson, *Arkansas Geography: The Physical Landscapes and the Historical-Cultural Setting* (Little Rock: Rose, 1981), 73–74.

37. Arkansas State Planning Board and the Writers' Project of the Works Progress Administration, *Arkansas: A Guide to the State*, American Guide Series (New York: Hastings House, 1941), 318.

38. Ibid., 236.

39. Clifton E. Hull, *Shortline Railroads of Arkansas* (Norman: University of Oklahoma Press, 1969), 390–91.

40. *Arkansas: A Guide to the State*, 248.

41. Nuttall, *A Journal of Travels Into the Arkansas Territory*, 127.

42. *Arkansas: A Guide to the State*, 285.

43. Hull, *Shortline Railroads of Arkansas*, 140.

44. Ibid., 281–82.

45. *Arkansas: A Guide to the State*, 209.

46. Ibid., 210.

47. Ibid., 231.

CHAPTER 9

1. Arkansas State Planning Board and the Writers' Project of the Works Progress Administration, *Arkansas: A Guide to the State*, American Guide Series (New York: Hastings House, 1941), 243.

2. Ibid., 245.

3. Hubert B. Stroud and Gerald T. Hanson, *Arkansas Geography*, 73.

4. *Arkansas: A Guide to the State*, 253.

5. George H. Shirk, *Oklahoma Place Names*, 2nd ed. (Norman: University of Oklahoma Press, 1974), 212.

6. Ibid., 243.

7. *The Sun Never Sets*, (Perryville, Ark.: The Heifer Project International, n.d.).

8. *Arkansas: A Guide to the State*, 364.

9. Thomas Nuttall, *Journal of Travels into Arkansas Territory During the Year 1819* (Norman: University of Oklahoma Press, 1980).

10. *Arkansas: A Guide to the State*, 364.

11. Ibid.

12. Frederick Lynne Ryan, *The Rehabilitation of Oklahoma Coal Mining Communities*, University of Oklahoma Economic Studies (Norman: University of Oklahoma Press, 1935), 317.

13. Ibid., 26.

14. Ibid., 34.

15. Ibid., 35.

16. Ibid., 27.

17. *Arkansas: A Guide to the State*, 338.

18. Shirk, *Oklahoma Place Names*, 121.

19. Ibid., 68.

20. Kent Ruth, ed., *Oklahoma: A Guide to the Sooner State* (Norman: University of Oklahoma Press, 1957), 351.

21. Shirk, *Oklahoma Place Names*, 110.

22. Ibid., 107.
23. Ibid., 72.
24. Ibid., 6.
25. Ruth, *Oklahoma: A Guide to the Sooner State*, 352.
26. Clifton E. Hull, *Shortline Railroads of Arkansas* (Norman: University of Oklahoma Press, 1969), 390.
27. Ruth, *Oklahoma: A Guide to the Sooner State*, 371.
28. Shirk, *Oklahoma Place Names*, 57.
29. Ibid., 177.
30. Ibid., 202.
31. Ibid., 67.
32. Ibid., 137.

CHAPTER 10

1. *Fort Smith Economic Profile* (unbound leaflets). Fort Smith Chamber of Commerce, Fort Smith, Ark., 1981.
2. Grace Steele Woodward, *The Cherokees* (Norman: University of Oklahoma Press, 1963), 239.
3. Ed Bearss and Arrell M. Gibson, *Fort Smith: Little Gibralter on the Arkansas* (Norman: University of Oklahoma Press, 1969), 9.
4. Ibid., 19.
5. Jesse O. McKee and Jon A. Schlenker, *The Choctaws: Cultural Evolution of a Native American Tribe* (Jackson: University of Mississippi Press, 1980), 81.
6. Bearss, *Fort Smith: Little Gibralter on the Arkansas*, 217.
7. Glenn Shirley, *Law West of Fort Smith* (Lincoln: University of Nebraska Press, 1968), 9–40.
8. Ruth B. Mapes, *Old Fort Smith: Cultural Center on the Southwestern Frontier* (Little Rock: Pioneer, 1965), 2.
9. Arkansas State Planning Board and the Writers' Project of the Works Progress Administration, *Arkansas: A Guide to the State*, American Guide Series (New York: Hastings House, 1941), 151.

CHAPTER 11

1. Arkansas State Planning Board and the Writers' Project of the Works Progress Administration, *Arkansas: A Guide to the State*, American Guide Series (New York: Hastings House, 1941), 154–55.
2. Kirk Bryan, "The Hot Water Supply of the Hot Springs, Arkansas," *Journal of Geology* 30 (1922): 425–49.
3. Stanley F. Norsworthy, "Hot Springs, Arkansas: A Geographic Analysis of the Spa's Resort Service Area," (Ph.D. diss., University of California, Los Angeles, 1970), 92–93.
4. John McDermott, ed., "The Western Journals of Dr. George Hunter, 1796–1805" *Transactions of the American Philosophical Society* 53. 3 (1963): 94.
5. *Arkansas: A Guide to the State*, 156.
6. U.S. Congress. *Register of Debates in Congress VIII*, Part 2, 2311, 4 stat. 5050., 1833.
7. Norsworthy, "Hot Springs, Arkansas," 33.
8. Francis J. Scully, *Hot Springs, Arkansas and Hot Springs National Park: The Story of a City and the Nation's Health Resort* (Little Rock, Ark.: Hanson, 1966), 116–20.

CHAPTER 12

1. Arkansas State Planning Board and the Writers' Project of the Works Projects Administration, *Arkansas: A Guide to the State*, American Guide Series (New York: Hastings House, 1941), 171–72.
2. Hampton F. Roy, Sr., Charles Whitsell, Jr. and Cheryl G. Nichols, *How We Lived: Little Rock as an American City* (Little Rock: August House, 1984), 17–18.
3. G. W. Featherstonhaugh, *Excursion Through the Slave States* (Originally published in 1844 by Harper and Brothers, N.Y.). (New York: Negro Universities Press, 1968), 96.
4. Ibid., 95.
5. Friedrich Gerstäcker, *Wild Sports in the Far West* (Durham, N.C.: Duke University Press, 1968), 95.
6. Ibid., 355.
7. *Arkansas Gazette*, Little Rock, 19 March 1822, 1.
8. Roy, Hampton F., Sr., Charles Whitsell, Jr., and Cheryl G. Nichols. *How We Lived*, 25.
9. Thomas Belser, Jr., "Military Operations in Missouri and Arkansas, 1861–1865 (2 vols)." (Ph.D. diss., Vanderbilt University, 1958), 584.
10. Roy, Hampton F., Sr., Charles Whit-

sell, Jr. and Cheryl G. Nichols. *How We Lived,* 110.

11. Ibid., 127.

12. Team Four, Inc., *Development Capacity Analysis: Phase I, Extraterritorial Plan.* Office of Comprehensive Planning, City of Little Rock, Ark., 1981, 1–15.

13. *The Metropolitan Economy: Greater Little Rock.* Office of Comprehensive Planning, City of Little Rock, Ark., 1981, 15.

14. Ibid., 13.

15. *Metropolitan Manufacturer's Guide.* Research Department of the Greater Little Rock Chamber of Commerce, Little Rock, Ark., 1981, 1–66.

16. Roy, Hampton F., Sr., Charles Whitsell, Jr., and Cheryl G. Nichols. *How We Lived,* 48.

17. Ibid., 205.

18. Ibid., 168.

Selected References

HISTORY AND GEOGRAPHY

Allsopp, Fred W. *Folklore of Romanic Arkansas*. Kansas City: The Grober Society, 1931.

Arkansas Gazette. Little Rock: 19 March 1922.

Arkansas Industrial Development Foundation. *Directory of Arkansas Manufacturers. 1976*. Little Rock, 1976.

Arkansas Power and Light Company. *A Guide to Lakes Hamilton and Catherine*. Little Rock: Arkansas Power and Light Company, Public Affairs Department, n.d.

Arkansas State Planning Board and the Writers' Project of the Works Progress Administration. *Arkansas: A Guide to the State*. American Guide Series. New York: Hastings House, 1941.

Bearss, Ed and Arrell M. Gibson. *Fort Smith: Little Gibralter on the Arkansas*. Norman: University of Oklahoma Press, 1969.

Belser, Thomas A. "Military Operations in Missouri and Arkansas, 1861–1865." Vols. 1 and 2. Ph.D. dissertation, Vanderbilt University, 1958.

Bonnifield, Paul. "Choctaw Nation on the Eve of the Civil War." *Journal of the West* 12 (July 1973): 386–402.

Bryan, Kirk. "The Hot Water Supply of the Hot Springs, Arkansas." *Journal of Geology* 30 (1922): 425–29.

Dale, Edward Everett. *Cherokee Cavaliers*. Norman: University of Oklahoma Press, 1939.

Debo, Angie. *The Rise and Fall of the Choctaw Republic*. Norman: University of Oklahoma Press, 1961.

Faulk, Odie. *Muskogee: City and County*. Muskogee, Okla.: The Five Civilized Tribes Museum, 1982.

Fenneman, Nevin M. *Physiography of Eastern United States*. New York: McGraw-Hill, 1938.

Featherstonhaugh, G. W. *Excursion through the Slave States* (Originally published in 1844 by Harper and Brothers). New York: Negro Universities Press, 1968.

Fletcher, John Gould. *Arkansas*. 1947. Reprint. Fayetteville, Ark.: The University of Arkansas Press, 1989.

Foreman, Grant. *Advancing the Frontier*. Norman: University of Oklahoma Press, 1933.

———. *The Five Civilized Tribes*. Norman: University of Oklahoma Press, 1934.

———. *A History of Oklahoma*. Norman: University of Oklahoma Press, 1942.

Fort Smith Economic Profile (unbound leaflets). Fort Smith Chamber of Commerce, Fort Smith, Ark., 1981.

Geology of Magnet Cave (mimeographed information leaflet). Little Rock: Arkansas Geological Commission, n.d.

Gerstäker, Friedrich. *Wild Sports in the Far West*. Durham, N.C.: Duke University Press, 1968.

Goodspeed, Weston Arthur. *Arkansas*. Madison: The Western Historical Association, 1904.

Gould, Charles N. *Oklahoma Place Names*. Norman: University of Oklahoma Press, 1933.

Graebner, N. A. "Pioneer Agriculture in Oklahoma." *Chronicles of Oklahoma* 23 (Autumn 1945): 232–48.

Hart, J. F. "The Changing American Countryside." In *Problems and Trends in American Geography*, edited by Saul B. Cohen. New York: Basic Books, Inc. 1967.

Herndon, Dallas, T., ed. *Centennial History of Arkansas*. Chicago: S. J. Clarke, 1922.

Hickman, John and Alan Smith. "Behind the Sunbelt's Growth." *Economic Review*, 4–13 Federal Reserve Bank of Atlanta, March 1982.

Hoover, Herbert and Bernal L. Green. "Human Resources in the Ozarks Region . . . With Emphasis on the Poor." *Agricultural Economic Report No. 182*. Economic Research Service. Washington, D.C.: U.S. Department of Agriculture cooperating with the Agricultural Experiment Stations, University of Missouri and University of Arkansas, May 1970.

Hull, Clifton E. *Shortline Railroads of Arkansas*. Norman: University of Oklahoma Press, 1969.

Irving, Washington. *A Tour on the Prairies*. (Originally published in 1835 by Carey, Lea, and Blanchard, Philadelphia.) John Francis McDermott, ed. Norman: University of Oklahoma Press, 1956.

Jordan, Max F. and Lloyd Bender. "An Economic Survey of the Ozark Region." *Agricultural Economic Report No. 19*. Economic Research Service. Washington, D.C.: U.S. Department of Agriculture cooperating with the Agricultural Experiment Station, University of Arkansas, July 1966.

Long, E. B. *The Civil War Day By Day: An Almanac, 1861–1865*. New York: Doubleday, 1971.

McClellan, John L. Chairman, Committee on Government Operations. *The Economic and Social Condition of Rural America in the 1970s. The Distribution of Federal Outlays Among U.S. Counties*. Economic Development Division, Economic Research Service. Washington, D.C.: U.S. Department of Agriculture for the Committee on Government Operations, U.S. Senate, 92nd Congress, First Session, December, 1971.

McDermott, John F., ed. "The Western Journals of Dr. George Hunter, 1796–1805." *Transactions of the American Philosophical Society* 53. 3 (1963), 5–127.

McKee, Jesse O. and Jon A. Schlenker. *The Choctaws: Cultural Evolution of a Native American Tribe*. Jackson: University of Mississippi Press, 1980.

McReynolds, Edwin C. *Oklahoma: A History of the Sooner State*. Norman: University of Oklahoma Press, 1964.

Mahaffey, Juanita. "Past and Future of Wildlife Conservation in Oklahoma." *Oklahoma Game and Fish News* 13. 4 (April 1957): 3–8.

Mapes, Ruth B. *Old Fort Smith: Cultural Center on the Southwestern Frontier*. Little Rock: Pioneer, 1965.

The Metropolitan Economy: Greater Little Rock. Office of Comprehensive Planning, City of Little Rock, Ark., 1981.

Metropolitan Manufacturer's Guide. Research Department of the Greater Little Rock Chamber of Commerce, Little Rock, Ark., 1981.

Morris, John W. *Ghost Towns of Oklahoma*. Norman: University of Oklahoma Press, 1978.

Morris, John W., Charles R. Goins, and Edwin C. McReynolds. *Historical Atlas of Oklahoma*. Norman: University of Oklahoma Press, 1976.

Norsworthy, Stanley F. "Hot Springs, Arkansas: A Geographic Analysis of the Spa's Resort Service Area," Ph.D. dissertation, University of California, Los Angeles, 1970.

Nuttall, Thomas. *A Journal of Travels Into the Arkansas Territory during the Year 1819*. (Originally published in 1821 by T. H. Palmer, Philadelphia.) Norman: University of Oklahoma Press, 1980.

Oklahoma Historical Society. *Chronicles of Oklahoma*. Oklahoma City: Oklahoma Historical Society, 1921.

Oliver, John E. *Climate and Man's Environment: An Introduction to Applied Climatology*. New York: John Wiley and Sons, 1973.

Paullin, Charles O. *Atlas of the Historical Geography of the United States*. Washington, D.C.: Carnegie Institute of Washington, 1932.

Rafferty, Milton D. *The Ozarks: Land and Life*. Norman: University of Oklahoma Press, 1980.

Reid, John P. *A Law of Blood: The Primitive Law of the Cherokee Nation*. New York: New York University Press, 1970.

Roark, Michael O. "Nineteenth Century Population Distributions of the Five Civilized

Tribes in Indian Territory, Oklahoma." Discussion Paper Series. Department of Geography. Syracuse, N.Y.: Syracuse University, 1976.

Roy, Hampton, F., Sr., Charles Whitsell, Jr., and Cheryl G. Nichols. *How We Lived: Little Rock as an American City.* Little Rock: August House, 1984.

Ruth, Kent, ed. *Oklahoma: A Guide to the Sooner State.* Rev. ed. Norman: University of Oklahoma Press, 1957.

Ruth, Kent. *Oklahoma Travel Handbook.* Norman: University of Oklahoma Press, 1977.

Ryan, Frederick Lynne. *The Rehabilitation of Oklahoma Coal Mining Communities.* University of Oklahoma Economic Studies. Norman: University of Oklahoma Press, 1935.

Shirk, George H. *Oklahoma Place Names.* 2nd ed. Norman: University of Oklahoma Press, 1974.

Shinn, Josiah H. *Pioneers and Makers of Arkansas.* Baltimore: Genealogical Publishing Co., 1967.

Shirley, Glenn. *Law West of Fort Smith.* Lincoln: University of Nebraska Press, 1968.

Scully, Francis J. *Hot Springs, Arkansas and Hot Springs National Park: The Story of a City and the Nation's Health Resort.* Little Rock: Hanson, 1966.

Snider, Luther Crocker. *Geography of Oklahoma.* Norman: Oklahoma Geological Survey, 1917.

Spurlock, Hughes H. "Rural Housing Conditions in the Arkansas, Missouri, and Oklahoma Ozarks," *Bulletin 736.* Economic Research Service. Washington, D.C.: U.S. Department of Agriculture cooperating with the Agricultural Experiment Station, University of Arkansas, December 1968.

Stone, Charles G., Boyd R. Haley, and George W. Viele. *A Guidebook to the Geology of the Ouachita Mountains, Arkansas.* Little Rock: Arkansas Geological Commission, 1977.

Stroud, Hubert B. and Gerald T. Hanson. *Arkansas Geography: The Physical Landscape and the Historical Cultural Setting.* Little Rock: Rose, 1981.

The Sun Never Sets (brochure). Perryville, Ark.: The Heifer Project International, n.d.

Team Four, Inc. *Development Capacity Analysis: Phase I, Extraterritorial Plan.* Office of Comprehensive Planning, City of Little Rock, Ark., 1981.

Thoburn, Joseph B., and Muriel H. Wright. *Oklahoma, a History of the State and Its People,* Vols. I–IV. New York: Lewis Historical Publishing Co., 1929.

Thornbury, William D. *Regional Geomorphology of the United States.* New York: John Wiley and Sons, 1965.

Trewartha, Glenn T. *An Introduction to Climate.* New York: McGraw-Hill, 1954.

Tyson, Carl N. *The Red River in Southwestern History.* Norman: University of Oklahoma Press, 1981.

U.S. Congress. *Register of Debates in Congress VIII,* Part 2, 2311, 4 stat. 5050, 1833.

U.S. Bureau of the Census. *County and City Data Book, 1988.* Washington, D.C.: Government Printing Office, 1988.

U.S. Travel Data Center, *1984 Economic Impact of Travel on Arkansas Counties,* 1–12. Washington, D.C.: U.S. Travel Data Center, 1985.

War of the Rebellion: A Compilation of the Official Records of the Union and Confederate Armies. 70 volumes in 128 parts, atlas. Washington, D.C.: Government Printing Office, 1880–1901.

Wickham, John. "Ouachita Foldbelt: A Paleozoic Continental Margin." A paper published in Glenn Visher, Charles Stone, and Boyd Haley. *Field Guide to the Structure and Stratigraphy of the Ouachita Mountains and Arkoma Basin.* Oklahoma City: American Association of Petroleum Geologists, 1978.

Williams, Norman. *Mineral Resources of Arkansas,* Bulletin 6. Little Rock: Arkansas Geological and Conservation Commission, 1959.

Williams, Norman. *Field Trip Guidebook Central Arkansas Economic Geology and Petrology.* Little Rock: Arkansas Geological Commission, 1967.

Woodward, Grace Steele. *The Cherokees.* Norman: University of Oklahoma Press, 1963.

FISH AND WILDLIFE

Aledger, J. Michael, *1984–1985 Turkey Harvest*. Little Rock: Arkansas Game and Fish Commission, 1985.

The Arkansas Game and Fish Commission (unpublished history). Little Rock: Arkansas Game and Fish Commission, 1985.

Brooks, Joe. *Complete Guide to Fishing across North America*. New York: Harper and Row, 1966.

Clark, Joseph D. *1984 Black Bear Harvest Report*. Wildlife Management Division, 1–17. Little Rock: Arkansas Game and Fish Commission, April 1959.

Dalrymple, Byron. *Complete Guide to Hunting Across North America*. New York: Popular Science, 1970.

Fishing and Hunting in Arkansas. Little Rock: Arkansas Game and Fish Commission and the Arkansas Parks, Recreation and Travel Commission, n.d.

Fishing Edition, 1980. Little Rock: Arkansas Game and Fish Commission, 1980.

Fishing in Oklahoma. Oklahoma City: Oklahoma Department of Wildlife Conservation, 1980.

The Float Streams of Arkansas. Little Rock: Arkansas Game and Fish Commission and the Arkansas Department of Parks and Tourism, 1979.

Game Fish of Arkansas. Little Rock: Arkansas Game and Fish Commission, 1979.

Hunting Edition, 1979–80. Little Rock: Arkansas Game and Fish Commission, 1980.

Hunting in Oklahoma. Oklahoma City: Oklahoma Department of Wildlife Conservation, 1980.

Johnson, Tom R. "Missouri's Venomous Snakes," *The Missouri Conservationist*, June, 1979, 5.

Mahaffey, Juanita. "Past and Future of Wildlife Conservation in Oklahoma." *Oklahoma Game and Fish News* 13. 4 (April 1957): 3–6.

Major Smallmouth Streams of Arkansas. Little Rock: Arkansas Game and Fish Commission, n.d.

Murphy, Jim. "Summer Fishing is Hot." *Outdoor Oklahoma* 39 (July/August 1983): 2–31.

Oklahoma Mammals. Oklahoma City: Oklahoma Department of Wildlife Conservation, 1985.

Public Owned Fishing Lakes. Little Rock: Arkansas Game and Fish Commission, n.d.

Saults, Dan, Michael Walker, Bob Hines, Rex G. Schmidt, eds. *Sport Fishing U.S.A.* Washington, D.C.: The U.S. Department of Interior, Bureau of Sport Fisheries and Wildlife, Fish and Wildlife Service, 1971.

Spencer, James. "National State Deer Profile: The Ouachita Mountains." *Arkansas Sportsman*, October, 1985.

Sport Fish of Oklahoma. Oklahoma City: Department of Wildlife Conservation, 1980.

Stomp, Bruce. "Fish the Riprap." *Outdoor Oklahoma* 39 (May/June 1983): 28–33.

Trails of Arkansas. Little Rock: Arkansas Game and Fish Commission, n.d.

Trout Fishing in Arkansas. Little Rock: Arkansas Game and Fish Commission, n.d.

Trout Streams in Oklahoma. Oklahoma City: Department of Wildlife Conservation, 1980.

Warren, David. "Swamp Fishing." *Outdoor Oklahoma* 39 (May/June 1983): 2–7.

GAME LAWS

Arkansas

Arkansas Game and Fish Commission 1979–80 Hunting Regulations. (booklet). Little Rock: Arkansas Game and Fish Commission, 1980.

Arkansas Game and Fish Commission 1980 Fishing Edition Regulations. Little Rock: Arkansas Game and Fish Commission, 1980.

Game Fish of Arkansas. Little Rock: Arkansas Game and Fish Commission, 1980.

Trails of Arkansas. Little Rock: Arkansas Department of Parks and Tourism, 1980.

Oklahoma

1980 Oklahoma Fishing Regulation. Oklahoma City: Oklahoma Department of Wildlife Conservation, 1980.
1979–80 Oklahoma Hunting Regulations. Oklahoma City: Oklahoma Department of Wildlife Conservation, 1980.

TOURISM AND RECREATION—GENERAL

Arkansas State Planning Board and the Writers' Project of the Works Progress Administration. *Arkansas: A Guide to the State.* American Guide Series. New York: Hastings House, 1941.
Carra, Andrew J., ed. *The Complete Guide to Hiking and Backpacking.* New York, Winchester Press, 1977.
Dulles, Foster Rhea. *A History of Recreation: America Learns to Play.* New York: Meredith, 1965.
Gertäker, Friedrich. *Wild Sports in the Far West.* Durham, N.C.: Duke University Press, 1968.
Hull, Clifton E. *Shortline Railroads of Arkansas.* Norman: University of Oklahoma Press, 1969.

TOURIST ATTRACTIONS

Arkansas

An Invitation to Discover the Heart of Arkansas. Little Rock: Heart of Arkansas Travel Association, 1976.
Arkansas Calendar of Events. Little Rock: Arkansas Department of Parks and Tourism, 1980.
Arkansas 1980 State Highway Map. Little Rock: Arkansas State Highway Department, 1980.
Arkansas Tour Guide 1980. Little Rock: The Woods Brothers Agency, 1980.
Arkansas Camper's Guide. Little Rock: Travel Division, Department of Parks and Tourism, 1980.
Arkansas Destinations. Little Rock: Arkansas Department of Parks and Tourism, 1980.
Arkansas is a Natural. Little Rock: Arkansas Department of Parks and Tourism, n.d.
Bonanza Land. Fort Smith, Ark.: Bonanza Land, Inc., 1979.
DeGray State Park. Little Rock: Department of Parks and Tourism, 1979.
Follow Your Senses to the Natural State: Arkansas. Little Rock: Tourism Division Arkansas Department of Parks and Tourism, 1978.
Fort Smith Today. Fort Smith: Fort Smith Chamber of Commerce.
Golf Courses in the Natural State: Arkansas. Little Rock Tourism Division. Little Rock: Arkansas Department of Parks and Tourism, 1978.
Little Rock's Guide to Pulaski County. Little Rock: Little Rock Bureau for Conventions and Visitors, 1980.
Little Rock, North Little Rock, Pulaski County. Little Rock: Little Rock Bureau for Conventions and Visitors, n.d.
Little Rock Today. Little Rock: Little Rock Today.
McWilliam, Ailen, Lloyd Dane, and Homer L. Johnston. *Talimena Scenic Drive Guide.*
Ouachita National Forest. Little Rock: Talimena Scenic Drive Interpretive Association in cooperation with the Oklahoma Tourism and Recreation Department, Arkansas Department of Parks and Tourism, and the Forest Service, U.S. Department of Agriculture, 1978.
Ouachita Geo-Float Trail. Vicksburg, Miss.: U.S. Army Corps of Engineers, 1978.
Popular Trails of Arkansas. Little Rock: Arkansas Department of Parks and Tourism, 1978.
Tour Guide: Arkansas, 1979. Little Rock: Woods Brothers Agency, 1979.
Twenty Exciting Destinations in the Natural State of Arkansas. Little Rock: Arkansas Department of Parks and Tourism, n.d.
Western Arkansas is Bonanza Land. Little Rock: Woods Brothers Agency, 1978.

Oklahoma

Lake Eufaula: Oklahoma's Gentle Giant. Eufaula, Okla.: Lake Eufaula Association, 1979.

Oklahoma 1975 Calendar of Events, 1979. Oklahoma City: Oklahoma Department of Tourism and Recreation, 1979.

Oklahoma Campers Guide. Oklahoma City: Oklahoma Department of Tourism and Recreation Division of Tourism Promotion, 1979.

Oklahoma's Canoeing: River Floating. Oklahoma City: Oklahoma Department of Tourism and Recreation, 1979.

Oklahoma's Kiamichi County. Idabel, Okla.: Idabel Chamber of Commerce, n.d.

Oklahoma Lakes (map). Oklahoma City: State of Oklahoma and Oklahoma Department of Tourism and Recreation, n.d.

Oklahoma 1980 map. Oklahoma City: Oklahoma Department of Transportation, n.d.

Oklahoma Oklahoma Oklahoma: State of Many Countries. Oklahoma City: Oklahoma Department of Tourism and Recreation, n.d.

Oklahoma Resorts. Oklahoma City: Oklahoma Department of Tourism and Recreation, n.d.

Oklahoma State Lodges. Oklahoma City: Oklahoma Department of Tourism and Recreation, n.d.

Oklahoma State Parks Oklahoma City: Oklahoma Department of Tourism and Recreation, n.d.

Oklahoma Tourism 1972 (economic report). Oklahoma City: Oklahoma Department of Tourism and Recreation, Publicity and Information Division, 1972.

Oklahoma Trails Guide. Oklahoma City: Oklahoma Department of Tourism and Recreation, n.d.

Oklahoma Turnpikes (map). San Jose, Calif.: H. H. Gousha Company, 1979.

Oklahoma USA. Oklahoma City: Tourism Promotion Division Oklahoma Department of Tourism and Recreation, n.d.

Index

Access areas: *see* lake geography
Acorn, Ark.: 213
Acorn Scenic Overlook: 184
Acropolis: 254
Addresses: national forests and parks, 37, 72; state wildlife and game commissions, 51, 72; for maps, 57, 285–86; lake managers, 72–75; geological surveys, 123–24; state tourism and recreation departments, 286; U.S. Army Corps of Engineers district offices, 286; state parks, 286–87; tourist associations and chambers of commerce, 287–90
Adona, Ark.: 205
Agriculture: 23; cotton, 23; corn, 27; soybeans, 29; broiler chickens, 35; turkeys, 35; grain sorghum, 199
Albert, Carl (U.S. congressman): 164
Albion, Okla.: 174
Alderson, Okla.: 215
Alma, Ark.: 202
Alum Fork: 117
Aluminum Company of America: 194
Antlers, Okla.: 170
Antoine River: 58
Appalachian Mountains: 7
Arbuckle, Col. Matthew: 23, 223
Arkadelphia, Ark.: 5, 191–92; major events, 272, 274, 278
Arkadelphia Lumber Company: 192
Arkansas Diamond Company: 154–56
Arkansas Game and Fish Department: 37
Arkansas Gazette (newspaper): 199, 224, 225
Arkansas Geological Commission: 124
Arkansas-Oklahoma Rodeo: 227

Arkansas Power and Light Company: 79, 99
Arkansas River: 3, 5, 21
"Arkansas Stone": 156
Arkoma, Okla.: 222
Arts and crafts: 269, 271, 272, 274, 276–78, 280, 281, 283
Athens Piedmont Plateau: 7
Atkins, Ark.: 197
Atoka, Okla.: 5, 19, 165
Atoka Baptist Academy: 165
Austin, Stephen A.: 254
Automobile shows: 276

Backpacking: 122–23
Bacone College: 166–67
Baits: 57–58
"Balkanization": 209
Barkman, Jacob: 20
Barling, Ark.: 222
Barnes House: 229
Batesville: 19
Bauxite, Ark.: 33, 193
Bauxite (mineral): 30
Bazooka: 202
Bean, Robert: 19, 23
Bears: 36
Beavers: 48
Beaver's Bend State Park: 77, 179
Beebe, Ark.: 192–93
Belle Fort Smith tour: 227
Belle Grove Historic District: 227
Belle Point: 223
Belleville, Ark.: 206–207
Ben Geren Regional Park: 229
Benton, Ark.: 19, 194; major events, 276, 279
Berta, Ark.: 206
Big Cedar, Okla.: 178
Big Goat Island: 99
Bismarck, Ark.: 191; major events, 276
Bison: 36
Blakely Mountain Dam: 111
Blocker, Okla.: 210
Bluegrass music: *see* music festivals
Blue Mountain, Ark.: 207
Blue Mountain Lake: 75–77

Blue Springs: 189
Boating and canoeing: 52–63; canoe rentals, 55; rules of safety, 56–57; maps, 57; *see also* individual streams and lakes; boat shows; boat races
Boat races: 268, 273, 278, 282, 284
Boat shows: 271
Bob Burns House: 202
Bobcats: 49
Bobwhite quail: 40–41
Boggy Depot: 19
Bokoshe, Okla.: 209
Bonnerdale, Ark.: 218
Booneville, Ark.: 208; major events, 271, 272, 274, 277
Boston Mountains: 3
Boundaries, Ouachita Mountain region: 3–5
Boxing tournaments: 269
Bradford, Roarke: 193
Bradford, Maj. William: 223
Branner, Dr. John C.: 33, 194
Briartown, Okla.: 166
Britton's Ferry: 19
Broiler chickens: 35
Broken Bow, Okla.: 179, 220–21; major events, 282
Brown-Henderson Improvement and Timber Company: 27
Bryan, James: 254
Bryant, Ark.: 193; major events, 278
Bugtussle, Okla.: 164
Butterfield Stage Line: 19, 224
Byington, Rev. Cyrus: 220

Cabot, Ark.: 193
Caddo Gap: 159
Caddo Indians: 17
Caddo Mountains: 7
Caddo River: 59
Caddo Valley, Ark.: 191
Cairo and Fulton Railroad: 23, 191
California Trail: 164; *see also* trails

Camping and hiking rules: 122–23
Camping areas: 125–50; in Ozark National Forest, 125–29; in Arkansas state parks, 129–33; in Oklahoma state parks, 133–35; in U.S. Army Corps of Engineers projects, 135–50
Camping equipment: 122
Camping hazards: 122–23
Canadian, Okla.: 163–64
Canadian River: 93
Canoe rentals: see boating and canoeing
Cape Girardeau: 19
Carl Albert Junior College: 173
Casa, Ark.: 206
Caston, Okla.: 173
Catholics: 200
Catlin, George (artist): 161
Centerville, Ark.: 188
Central Arkansas State University: 196
Chaffee, Gen. Adna R.: 225
Checotah, Okla.: 161–63
Cheote, Samuel: 163
Cherokee Indians: 222–23
Chickasaw Indians: 21
Chief Black Fox: 187
Chisholm, Jesse: 19, 23
Chockie, Okla.: 165
Choctaw and Gulf Railroad: 25
Choctaw and Memphis Railroad: 204
Choctaw Indians: 2, 21, 36, 210; see also Indians
Chouteau, Auguste P.: 161
Civilian Conservation Corps (CCC): 27
Civil War: 224
Clarksville, Ark.: 199; major events, 275
Clayton, John M.: 196
Clayton, Okla.: 168
Climate: 7–15
Clothing: 15–16
Coal: 25, 30; mining, 172, 209
Colbert's Ferry: 19
Coleman's Rock Shop: 189
College of the Ozarks: 200
Commercial areas: in Fort Smith, 225–26; in Hot Springs, 243–44; in Little Rock, 261; see also individual towns
Company towns: 211
Confederates: 20

Continental influences (on climate): 7
Conway, Col. George S.: 158
Conway, Ark.: 196; major events, 275
Cookson Hills: 203
Cooper Communities, Inc.: 189
Corinne, Okla.: 221
Corps of Engineers: see U.S. Army Corps of Engineers
Cossatot Mountains: 7
Cossatot River: 59–60
Costume balls: 269
Cotton: see agriculture
Cottontail rabbits: 43–44
Cove, Ark.: 181
Coyotes: 45
Crafts: see arts and crafts
Crater of Diamonds State Park: 159
Crittenden, Robert: 187
Cross Mountains: 7
Cruce, Lee (governor): 165
Crystal Mountains: 7, 212
Crystal Springs, Ark.: 212
Cubans: 225

Daisy, Ark.: 218
Damon, Okla.: 168
Danville, Ark.: 206
Dardanelle, Ark.: 186–87; major events, 268, 274
Dardanelle, Ola, and Southern Railroad: 25
Dardanelle and Russellville Railway: 187
Dardanelle Lock and Dam: 81–87
Dardanelle Rock: 187
Dardenne, Jean Baptiste: 187
Darwin, Okla.: 221
Davis, J. Porum (Dave Porum): 166
Davis, Jeff (senator and governor): 186
Deer: 43
Dela, Okla.: 221
Delaware Indians: 224
Denman, Herbert: 214
Denman, Okla.: 214
De la Harpe, Bernard: 254
De Queen, Ark.: 182–83, 220
DeQueen and Eastern Railroad: 27
De Soto, Hernando: 19
Diamond Jo Quarry: 158
Diamonds: mining, 151; see also minerals, quartz crystals

Dierks, Ark.: 218–19; major events, 277
Dierks Lumber and Coal Company: 179, 183, 211, 219
Dingell-Johnson Act: 37
Doves: see mourning doves
Dow, Andrew: 215
Dow, Okla.: 215
Dwarf forests: 185

Eagle, The (steamboat): 256
Eagleton, Ark.: 213, 220
Eastern Oklahoma State University: 168
Economy: agriculture, 29; mining, 31–33; manufacturing, 33–35; see also individual towns and cities
Encore a Fabri: 21
English: 209
Ethnic groups: 5, 209
Eufaula, Okla.: 163; major events, 284
European immigrants: 27

Fanshawe, Okla.: 214
Farmettes: 212
Farris, Okla.: 221
Featherstone, Okla.: 210
Featherstonhaugh, George: 158, 255
Finley, Okla.: 176
Fish: river game fish, 52–54; largemouth black bass, 52–53; smallmouth black bass, 53; spotted black bass, 53; crappie, 53, 69; green sunfish, 53; channel catfish, 53, 71; trout, 53–54; white bass, 68; walleye, 69; black bass, 70; see also fish habits and habitat
Fish habits and habitat: 68–72; crappie, 69; walleye, 69; white bass, 69–70; black bass, 70–71; catfish, 71–72; trout, 72
Fishing: on headwaters, 52; on river floats, 55–56; water temperature, 64; reasons for fish not biting, 64–65; guidelines, 65; baits and lures, 65–66; contests, 269, 271, 272, 274
Fishing rules: 65
Five Civilized Tribes: 21, 224
"Flagged" trees: 185
Float fishing: 54–55

Floating: *see* boating and canoeing
Forest Festival: 179
Fort Chaffee: 222, 225
Fort Gibson: 19, 224
Fort Smith (military post): 223–24
Fort Smith, Ark.: 222–36; settlement and history, 222–25; present landscape, 225–29; economy, 225–29; manufacturing, 227; attractions, 229–36; major events, 271, 272, 274, 278, 280, 281 ff.
Fort Towson: 23
Fort Washita: 19
Fountain Lake, Ark.: 190–91
Fourche Junction: 188
Fourche LaFave River: 5, 7, 59, 105
Foxes: 48–49
Fuller, John T.: 154–55
Fur-bearing animals: 39

Galla Rock: 197–99
Game and Fish Protective Association: 37
Game laws: 36–37
Gem and mineral shows: 274, 280
Geology: 3–7; folding and faulting, 153–54; information sources, 285
Germans: *see* Swiss-Germans
Gerstäker, Friedrich: 255
Gillham, Ark.: 182
Glenwood, Ark.: 218
Glover, Okla.: 221
Glover River: 59
Goff, Norris: 181
Golf tournaments: 278–80
Gowen, Okla.: 215
Grandview Overlook: 184
Grannis, Ark.: 182
Great Raft: 20–21, 23
Greene, Peter: 190
Greenwood, Ark.: 180, 209
Greeson Lake Public Hunting Area: 99
Gulf Coastal Plain: 3

Hailey, Dr. David Morris: 215
Haileyville, Okla.: 215
Hand-pulled glass: 171
The Hanging Judge: *see* Parker, Judge Isaac C.
Harding University: 192
Harjo, Oktahasars (Sands): 161

Harris, Mamie (opera star Mamie McCormick): 206
Hartsville, Okla.: 215
Hatfield, Ark.: 181
Hatobi: 179
Hatton, Ark.: 181
Havanna, Ark.: 207
Health spas: 237–42
Heavener, Joseph: 177
Heavener, Okla.: 177; major events, 284
Heavener Runestone State Park: 178
Heifer Project International: 204
Hemphill, John: 191
Henderson State University: 192
Hendrix College: 196
Hillbilly: 27
Hochatown State Park: 179
Hodgen, Okla.: 178
Holla Bend National Wildlife Area: 188
Hollis, Ark.: 188
Homewood, Ark.: 205
Horse racing: 271
"Hot Springs diamonds": *see* minerals, quartz crystals
Hot Springs National Park, Ark.: 191, 237–53; bathhouses, 237–40; settlement and history, 237–42; manufacturing, 243–44; present landscape, 243–44; attractions, 244–53; major events, 268, 269, 273–75, 277, 279, 280, 281 ff.
Hot Springs Railroad (Diamond Jo Line): 27
Hot Springs Village, Ark.: 189
"Hot Western": *see* Little Rock and Hot Springs Western Railroad
Howe, Dr. Herbert M.: 177
Howe, Okla.: 177
Huddleston, John W.: 154–56
Hughes, Okla.: 214
Hunting regulations: 51; *see also* game laws
Hurricane Creek, Ark.: 194
Hurricane Grove, Ark.: 212

Indian mounds: 171
Indians: 21–22; Caddo, 17; Quapaw, 17; Choctaw, 20–23; Chickasaw, 21; Osage, 223; Kickapoo, 224; Piankashaw, 224; Seneca,

224 n.; Shawnee, 224
Indian Territory: 224
International Paper Company: 30
Irish: 209
Irving, Washington: 161
Italian Festival: 282
Italians: 5

Jackfork Creek: 117
Jackfork sandstones: 5
Jacksonville, Ark.: 193
Jessieville, Ark.: 189
Johnboat: 55
Johnson, W. W.: 155
Jones, R. N.: 23
Joplin, Ark.: 212

Kansas City, Pittsburg, and Gulf Railway: 177
Kansas City Southern Railroad: 171–72, 177, 178, 181, 182, 203
Keefe, J. H.: 166
Keefeton, Okla.: 166
Kerr, Sen. Robert S.: 172
Kerr-McClellan Arkansas Navigation System: 81–87, 113, 222
Kerr Museum: 172
Kiamichi, Okla.: 175
Kiamichi Mountains: 174
Kiamichi River: 19, 59–60, 174, 175
Kickapoo Indians: 224
Kimberlite Diamond Company: 156
Kimsey Calcite Quarry: 158
Kinta, Okla.: 167, 210
Kiowa, Okla.: 165
Kirby, Ark.: 218
Krebs, Okla.: 210

Lake fishing productivity: 65–66
Lake geography: 75–121; Blue Mountain Lake, 75–77; Broken Bow Lake, 77–79; Lake Catherine, 79; Lake Conway, 81; Dardanelle Lake, 81–87; DeGray Lake, 87–88; De Queen Lake, 88–91; Dierks Lake, 91–92; Eufaula Lake, 92–95; Gillham Lake, 95; Greeson Lake, 95–99; Hamilton Lake, 99–100; Hugo Lake, 100; Robert S. Kerr Lake, 103–105; Lake Moumelle,

105; McGee Creek Reservoir, 105; Nimrod Lake, 105–108; Ouachita Lake, 108–11; Ozark Lake, 111–15; Pine Creek Lake, 115–17; Sardis Lake, 117; Lake Winona, 117–19; Wister Lake, 119–21
Lake Hamilton, Ark.: 191
Lakes: see lake geography
Landforms: 5–7
Lane, Okla.: 221
Lane Processing, Inc.: 182
La Petite Roche: 254
Lauck, Chester: 181
Law enforcement: see Parker, Judge Isaac L.
LeFlore, Capt. Charles: 165
LeFlore, Chickiechockie: 165
Lequire, Okla.: 210
Lewis, William: 254
Lewisville, Okla.: 167
Lithuanians: 209
Little Goat Island: 99
Little Missouri River: 7, 60
Little River: 7, 91, 115–17
Little Rock, Ark.: early appearance, 256; manufacturing, 256–57, 261; economy, 256–61; streetcars, 257; impact of automobiles, 257–58; modern urban morphology, 257–61; attractions, 261–67; major events, 268–69, 271, 273, 274, 279, 281, 282
Little Rock, Maumelle, and Western Railroad: 25
Little Rock Air Force Base: 193, 258
Little Rock and Fort Smith Railroad: 225
Little Rock and Hot Springs Western Railroad: 27
Little Rock Municipal Waterworks: 105
Little Rock-North Little Rock Standard Metropolitan Area (SMA): 254
Locke, Victor M.: 170
"Locke War": see Locke, Victor M.
London, Ark.: 199
Long Island: 99
Lum and Abner: 181, 213, 277
Lum and Abner Days: 277
Lumbering: 23–30 ff.
Lutie, Okla.: 214

McAlester, James J.: 164
McAlester, Okla.: 5, 164–65; major events, 282–84
McCurtain, Okla.: 210
McGee Creek Dam: 105
Magazine, Ark.: 207–208
Magazine Mountain: 5
Magnet Cove: 157
Magnet Cove Titanium Corporation: 158
Magyars: 209
Malvern, Ark.: 19, 194; major events, 276
Mansfield, Ark.: 180
Manufacturing: 33–34; in Fort Smith, 227; in Little Rock, 256–57; in Hot Springs, 343–44
Map sources: for river floating and fishing, 57; for hiking, 123–24; topographic maps, 285–86; index maps, 285; see also individual rivers and lakes
Marshals: see U.S. deputy marshals
Massard Prairie: 31
Maumelle, Ark., major events: 277
Mayflower, Ark.: 196
Memorial Indian Museum: 179
Memphis, Paris, and Gulf Railroad: 27
Mena, Ark.: 181; major events, 273, 277, 279, 280, 282
Menifee, Ark.: 196
Military Road: see trails
Miller, Gov. James: 223
Minerals: peridotite, 151; quartz crystals (Hot Springs diamonds), 154, 156, 158; noveculite, 156; calcite, 157; titanium, 158; garnet crystals, 159; diamonds, 159
Mining: 151–56; coal, 164, 168, 172, 199, 210–11, 214, 225; bauxite, 194; natural gas, 197, 225
Minks: 48
Mississippi River: 17
Missouri-Kansas-Texas Railroad: 25, 161, 163–65
Missouri Pacific Railroad: 188
Morrilton, Ark.: 197; major events, 273, 276, 277
Mountain Fork River: 60–61, 77–78

Mountain Pine, Ark.: 211
Mountain Valley, Ark.: 190
Mountain Valley Hotel: 190
Mountain Valley Spring: 190
Mount Cavanal: 172
Mount Ida, Ark.: 212; major events, 273, 280
Mount Magazine: 75, 207
Mourning doves: 40
Moyers, Okla.: 170
Mulberry, Ark.: 202; major events, 279
Muldrow, Okla.: 202–203
Murfreesboro: 97, 151
Murrow, Rev. J. S.: 165
Murrow Indian Orphan's Home: 165–66
Music festivals: 277–79, 281–83
Muskogee, Okla.: 5, 19, 160–61

Nashville, major events: 277
Natchitoches, La.: 20
National Road: see trails
Natural gas: 31
Negroes: 27; see also slaves
New Hope, Ark.: 218
New Madrid earthquake: 254
New Ringold, Okla.: 221
Night fishing: 69–70
Norris Goff House: 181
North Little Rock, Ark.: 254–67; major events, 269, 276, 278–80
Novaculite anticlinorium: 151
Nunih Wayah: 176
Nutfall, Thomas: 186, 207, 255

O'Hara, William: 254
Oklahoma Department of Wildlife: 37
Oklahoma Department of Wildlife Conservation: 78, 103, 120
Oklahoma Geological Survey: 124
Oklahoma Historical Museum: 171
Oktaha: 161
Ola, Ark.: 188
Oleta, Okla.: 221
Opossums: 45
Osage Indians: 223
Ouachita College: 192
Ouachita Council of the Boy Scouts of America: 99

Ouachita Geo-Float Trail: 62
Ouachita Mountains: as a region, 1–7; history, 2–35; boundaries, 3–5; landforms, 5–7
Ouachita National Forest: 39, 105, 178
Ouachita River: 7, 20, 62
"Ouachita stone": 156
Ozark, Ark.: 200
Ozark-Jeta Taylor Lock and Dam: 84, 111–13
Ozark region: 3

Page, Okla.: 214
Paleozoic rocks: 3
Panama, Okla.: 171–72
Panola, Okla.: 214
Paris, Ark., major events: 281
Parker, Isaac C. (judge): 225
Peaches: 199
Pearcy, Ark.: 218
Pencil Bluff, Ark.: 212–13
Perry, Ark.: 204
Perryville, Ark.: 204
Petit Jean Mountain: 197
Petit Jean River: 5, 7, 61, 75–76
Petit Jean State Park: 188
Photography contests: 280
Piankashaw Indians: 224
Pine Ridge, Ark.: 213
Pittman-Robertson Act: 37
Pittsburg Reduction Company: 193
Pleasant Hill, Ark.: 217
Plumerville, Ark.: 196
Poles: 209
Porum, Okla.: 166; major events, 283
Potato Hills: 174
Potato Hills Overlook: 186
Poteau, Okla.: 172, 177; major events, 283–84
Poteau River: 5, 7, 21, 61, 119
Potawatomi Indians: 224
Prairie of the Tall Grass: 177
Precipitation: 7–15; table, 10
Prescott and Northwestern Railroad: 27
Price, Gen. Sterling: 20
Progressive Works Administration: 117
Public access areas: 87, 91

Quapaw Indians: 17
Queen Wilhelmina State Park: 185
Quinton, Okla.: 210

Raccoons: 45
Rattan, Okla.: 221
Red Oak, Okla.: 214
Red River: 7, 20, 100
Remmel Dam: 79
Reynolds, "Diamond Jo": 27
Reynolds Aluminum Company: 194
Rich Mountain: 59
Rich Mountain, Ark.: 213
Ridge Road: see trails
Ridge and Valley Province: 7
Rivers: see individual rivers by name
Robbers Cave State Park: 167–68
Robert S. Kerr Arboretum: 185–86
Rock City: 168, 169
Rock Island Railroad: 164
Rocks: sedimentary, 151, 154; igneous, 151; shale, 151; quartz crystals, 154, 156; novaculite, 156; ijolite, 157, 158; carbonatite, 158; phonolite, 158; garnet pseudoleucite syenite, 158; nepheline syenite, 158; jacupirangite, 158; graywacke, 159
Rock shops: 156–57
Rodeos: 274, 283, 284
Rogers, Capt. John: 224
Roland, Ark., major events: 271, 276, 279, 281
Rolling Fork River: 88, 91
Royal, Ark.: 212
Russell, Dr. T. J.: 186
Russell, William: 254
Russellville, Ark.: 186; major events, 172, 269, 275, 276, 279, 281
Russians: 209

Saint Louis: 19
Saint Louis, Arkansas, and Texas Railroad: 225
Saint Louis, Iron Mountain, and Southern Railroad: 23
Salem, Ark.: 218
Saline River: 63–64, 91
Sallisaw, Okla.: 103, 203
Salt making: 191
Sardis Lake Recreation Area: 176

Savanna, Okla.: 165
Scotch-Irish: 21, 209
Scots: 209
Scullyville, Okla.: 170–71
Searcy, Ark.: 5, 192
Seneca Indians: 224
Settlement: 17–29; frontier phase, 19–23; new south phase, 23–27; modern phase, 27–29; ethnic groups, 164–65, 200, 211
Shawnee Indians: 224
Shoals: 63
Silver, Ark.: 212
Skunks: 48
Slaves: 23
Slovaks: 209
Smith, Brig. Gen. Thomas A.: 223
Smithville, Okla.: 179
Snakes: venomous, 49–51; precautionary rules, 49; identification, 49–51; diagram, 50; copperhead, 50; western pigmy rattlesnake, 50–51; timber rattlesnake, 51
Snow, Okla.: 176
Snowbelt: 33
Snowfall: 11–13
Songbirds: 37
Southern Anthracite Coal Company: 188
Southwestern Trail: 254; see also trails
Southwest Times Record: 222
Soybeans: 210
Spadra, Ark.: 31
Spiro, Okla.: 171
Spiro Indian mounds: 171, 173
Stapp, Okla.: 178
Starr, Tom: 166
Steamboats: 20; Robert Thompson, 20; The Dime, 20, 161, 187
Stevens, Robert: 165
Stringtown, Okla.: 165
Sugarloaf Mining Company: 30–31
Sugar Loaf Mountain: 172
Sulphur Springs: see Stringtown
Summer: 11–13
Sunbelt: 33
Swap meet: 276
Swiss-Germans: 200

Talihina, Okla.: 174

Talimena Skyline Drive: 59,
  183–84
Taylor, Gen. Zachary: 224
Theme parks: 268
Thomas Edwards House: 214
Thornburg, Ark.: 204
Three Forks settlement: *see*
  Muskogee, Okla.
Timber industry: 29
Topographic maps: 123–24
Tourism: 29, 33–35; in Hot
  Springs, 237–53; informa-
  tion sources, 285–90
Trail ride: 272, 277
Trails: 19; Ridge Road, 19;
  Southwest Trail, 19, 23;
  Texas Trail, 19, 161, 164;
  California Trail, 164; Fort
  Smith-Fort Towson Military
  Road, 185
Trap Mountains: 7
Treaty of Dancing Rabbit
  Creek: 21, 175
Tri-state mining district: 19
Tuskahoma, Okla.: 175

U.S. Army Corps of Engi-
  neers: 29, 88, 94, 95, 105,
  110–11, 117, 119
U.S. Court for the Western

District of Arkansas: 224
U.S. deputy marshals: 225

Van Buren, Ark.: 202, 222;
  major events, 282
Vian, Okla.: 203
Vicksburg, Miss.: 21
Vietnamese: 225
Vineyards: 200

Waldron, Ark.: 181
Ward, Ark.: 193
Warner, Sen. William: 166
Warner, Okla.: 166
Washington, Ark.: 20
Waterfowl: 41
Waveland, Ark.: 207
Weather: 7–16; tornadoes, 11;
  winter conditions, 11; wind
  chill, 11; temperature, 11;
  summer conditions, 11;
  wind, 11; temperature-
  humidity index, 11–13; In-
  dian summer, 13; fog, 13;
  thunderstorms, 14; floods,
  15; clothing, 15–16
Webber's Falls, Okla.: 203
Welsh: 209
Welsh, Ark.: 218
Westark Community College:
  227

Weyerhaeuser Corporation: 30,
  179, 182, 211
Whitefield, George (Methodist
  bishop): 167
Whitefield, Okla.: 167
Wickes, Ark.: 182
Wiederkehr Village: 200
Wilburton, Okla.: 168; major
  events, 283
Wildlife: depletion, 36; man-
  agement, 36–37; songbirds,
  37; waterfowl, 41–43; game
  species, 43–49
Wind: 11–12
Wind chill: 11; table, 12
Winding Stair Mountains: 174,
  178
Wine: 200
Winters: 11–13
Wister: 173
Woodruff, William: 255
Works Progress Administration
  (WPA): 27
World War I: 17

Yanush, Okla.: 168
Y City, Ark.: 181

Zig Zag Mountains: 7
Zinc smelting: 33
Zoe, Okla.: 178